SPIRITS OF THE COLD WAR

RHETORIC AND PUBLIC AFFAIRS SERIES

- *Eisenhower's War of Words: Rhetoric and Leadership*, Martin J. Medhurst, editor
- *The Nuclear Freeze Campaign: Rhetoric and Foreign Policy in the Telepolitical Age*, J. Michael Hogan
- *Mansfield and Vietnam: A Study in Rhetorical Adaptation*, Gregory A. Olson
- *Truman and the Hiroshima Cult*, Robert P. Newman
- *Post-Realism: The Rhetorical Turn in International Relations*, Francis A. Beer and Robert Hariman, editors
- *Rhetoric and Political Culture in Nineteenth-Century America*, Thomas W. Benson, editor
- *Frederick Douglass: Freedom's Voice, 1818–1845*, Gregory P. Lampe
- *Angelina Grimké: Rhetoric, Identity, and the Radical Imagination*, Stephen Howard Browne
- *Strategic Deception: Rhetoric, Science, and Politics in Missile Defense Advocacy*, Gordon R. Mitchell
- *Rostow, Kennedy, and the Rhetoric of Foreign Aid*, Kimber Charles Pearce
- *Visions of Poverty: Welfare Policy and Political Imagination*, Robert Asen
- *General Eisenhower: Ideology and Discourse*, Ira Chernus
- *The Reconstruction Desegregation Debate: The Politics of Equality and the Rhetoric of Place, 1870–1875*, Kirt H. Wilson
- *Shared Land/Conflicting Identity: Trajectories of Israeli and Palestinian Symbol Use*, Robert C. Rowland and David A. Frank
- *Darwinism, Design, and Public Education*, John Angus Campbell and Stephen C. Meyer, editors
- *Religious Expression and the American Constitution*, Franklyn S. Haiman
- *Christianity and the Mass Media in America: Toward a Democratic Accommodation*, Quentin J. Schultze
- *Bending Spines: The Propagandas of Nazi Germany and the German Democratic Republic*, Randall L. Bytwerk
- *Malcolm X: Inventing Radical Judgment*, Robert E. Terrill
- *Metaphorical World Politics*, Francis A. Beer and Christ'l De Landtsheer, editors
- *The Lyceum and Public Culture in the Nineteenth-Century United States*, Angela G. Ray
- *The Political Style of Conspiracy: Chase, Sumner, and Lincoln*, Michael William Pfau
- *The Character of Justice: Rhetoric, Law, and Politics in the Supreme Court Confirmation Process*, Trevor Parry-Giles
- *Rhetorical Vectors of Memory in National and International Holocaust Trials*, Marouf A. Hasian Jr.
- *Judging the Supreme Court: Constructions of Motives in Bush v. Gore*, Clarke Rountree
- *Everyday Subversion: From Joking to Revolting in the German Democratic Republic*, Kerry Kathleen Riley
- *In the Wake of Violence: Image and Social Reform*, Cheryl R. Jorgensen-Earp
- *Rhetoric and Democracy: Pedagogical and Political Practices*, Todd F. McDorman and David M. Timmerman, editors
- *Invoking the Invisible Hand: Social Security and the Privatization Debates*, Robert Asen
- *With Faith in the Works of Words: The Beginnings of Reconciliation in South Africa, 1985–1995*, Erik Doxtader
- *Public Address and Moral Judgment: Critical Studies in Ethical Tensions*, Shawn J. Parry-Giles and Trevor Parry-Giles, editors
- *Executing Democracy: Capital Punishment and the Making of America, 1683–1807*, Stephen John Hartnett
- *Enemyship: Democracy and Counter-Revolution in the Early Republic*, Jeremy Engels

SPIRITS OF THE COLD WAR

CONTESTING WORLDVIEWS IN THE CLASSICAL AGE OF AMERICAN SECURITY STRATEGY

Ned O'Gorman

MICHIGAN STATE UNIVERSITY PRESS • *East Lansing*

Copyright © 2012 by Ned O'Gorman

∞ The paper used in this publication meets the minimum requirements of ANSI/NISO Z39.48-1992 (R 1997) (Permanence of Paper).

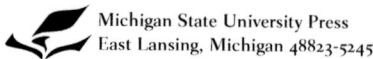
Michigan State University Press
East Lansing, Michigan 48823-5245

Printed and bound in the United States of America.

20 19 18 17 16 15 14 13   1 2 3 4 5 6 7 8 9 10

SERIES EDITOR
Martin J. Medhurst, *Baylor University*

EDITORIAL BOARD
Denise M. Bostdorff, *College of Wooster*
G. Thomas Goodnight, *University of Southern California*
Robert Hariman, *Northwestern University*
David Henry, *University of Nevada, Las Vegas*
J. Michael Hogan, *Penn State University*
Robert L. Ivie, *Indiana University*
Mark Lawrence McPhail, *Southern Methodist University*
John M. Murphy, *University of Illinois*
Shawn J. Parry-Giles, *University of Maryland*
Angela G. Ray, *Northwestern University*
Kirt H. Wilson, *University of Minnesota*
David Zarefsky, *Northwestern University*

LIBRARY OF CONGRESS CATALOGING-IN-PUBLICATION DATA
O'Gorman, Ned.
Spirits of the Cold War : contesting worldviews in the classical age of American security strategy / Ned O'Gorman.
   p. cm. — (Rhetoric and public affairs series)
Includes bibliographical references and index.
ISBN 978-1-61186-020-7 (cloth : alk. paper) 1. United States—Foreign relations—1945–1989—Philosophy. 2. National security—United States—Philosophy. 3. Kennan, George F. (George Frost), 1904–2005—Political and social views. 4. Dulles, John Foster, 1888–1959—Political and social views. 5. Jackson, C. D. (Charles Douglas), 1902–1964—Political and social views. 6. United States—Foreign relations—Soviet Union. 7. Soviet Union—Foreign relations—United States. 8. Cold War. I. Title.
E840.O36 2012
355'.033073—dc22
2011006508

Cover and book design by Charlie Sharp, Sharp Des!gns, Lansing, MI

g **green** Michigan State University Press is a member of the Green Press Initiative and is committed
press to developing and encouraging ecologically responsible publishing practices. For more
INITIATIVE
information about the Green Press Initiative and the use of recycled paper in book publishing, please visit www.greenpressinitiative.org.

Visit Michigan State University Press on the World Wide Web at *www.msupress.msu.edu*

For my father,
and in memory of my mother.

What *spirit* [*Geist*] is, my friend, cannot be described, drawn, painted—but it can be felt, it expresses itself through thoughts, movements, through striving, force, and effect.
> Johann Gottfried Herder, "Letters Concerning the Progress of Humanity"

From the start the "spirit" is afflicted with the curse of being "burdened" with matter, which here makes its appearance in the form of agitated layers of air, sounds, in short of language.
> Marx and Engels, *The German Ideology*

... test the spirits ...
> 1 John 4:1

Contents

PREFACE ·xi

ACKNOWLEDGMENTS · xix

INTRODUCTION · I

CHAPTER 1. The Care of the Self: Kennan, Containment, and Stoicism · 21

CHAPTER 2. Protest and Power: Dulles, Massive Retaliation, and Evangelicalism · 75

CHAPTER 3. Deeds Undone: C. D. Jackson, Liberation, and Adventurism · 123

CHAPTER 4. The American Sublime: Eisenhower, Deterrence, and Romanticism · 167

CONCLUSION · 233

NOTES · 251

BIBLIOGRAPHY · 299

INDEX · 315

Preface

> In all these undertakings the decisive fact will be the spirit, the resolve, the determination with which we bend to the task.
> —Dwight D. Eisenhower, foreign policy speech in San Francisco, October 8, 1952

This book examines the worldviews inherent within four major strategic statements in the early Cold War: containment, massive retaliation, deterrence, and liberation. The early Cold War (the period lasting, in my view, from 1946 through the pivotal year of *Sputnik*, 1957) represents the rise of American world supremacy, the crucible of powerful American ideologies, and the context in which the United States assumed the power to destroy the world with nuclear weapons. It also constitutes the "classical age" of American security strategy, returned to repeatedly in contemporary debates about foreign policy as a source of ideas, inspiration, and historical precedent. For all these reasons and more, the period has epochal significance in American and world histories. This book combines the theoretical and conceptual resources of rhetorical studies with those of philosophy, intellectual history, and sociology to show how major strategic ideas in early Cold War expressed divergent worldviews.

"Worldview" has become a cliché in some circles, and thus risks vapidity. Worse, it has become an ideological cudgel used by the so-called Religious Right to divide peoples of the world categorically into an "us" versus "them." Finally, it can connote a false human and cultural anthropology, suggesting that humans and their cultures are essentially ideational. I am aware of all these problems with the term *worldview*, but have decided to use the concept anyway. When I invoke *worldview* I do so in its fullest, and perhaps oldest, sense. *Weltanschauung* is a way of apprehending the world, entailing not only a way of seeing the world, but a way of *being* in it, and ultimately a distinct way of *talking* about it. Johann Gottfried Herder (1744–1803), who is credited with developing the concept, took "worldview" to represent a full array of ideas, sentiments, and habits *rooted in language.* "Each language, each culture, in this view, expresses a particular way of seeing and feeling, a distinct perception of the world, together with a certain manner of responding to its challenges. The word *Weltanschauung*, in its most literal sense, captures perhaps best the compass of divergent ways of encountering the outside from the inside."[1] Indeed, Herder held that to know the world from the "inside" is to know it from within a *Lebensform*, a form of life inextricable from language.[2] Worldviews thus denote far more than ideational rubrics; they are not mere psychological states. Rather, they are embedded in ways of speaking and being. Indeed, once solidified in speech, worldviews can become *objects* exterior to the self: objects of commitment, discipline, devotion, and aspiration.[3] In this way they can become "ethics," or at least proto-ethics, which motivate action. My argument is that major strategic statements in the early Cold War were motivated at least as much by worldviews (having the character of "objects") as they were by external exigencies, and that for key political actors these worldviews approached the status of "ethics" for the nation.

Thus the worldviews I am concerned with here—stoicism, evangelicalism, adventurism, and romanticism—have distinct ethical aspects. But more than ethics, they are rhetorics. I approach each as a worldview embedded within discrete rhetorical traditions, that is, distinct ways public actors have historically addressed the nation. Each of these worldviews represents a robust way of talking about America in the world. I argue that stoicism, evangelicalism, adventurism, and romanticism, seen as rhetorics, help explain the logical and ethical coherence of security strategies, namely containment, massive retaliation, liberation, and nuclear deterrence respectively. By "coherence" I mean the most basic sense of *cohere*, "hold together," not that which is strictly logical, thoroughly rational, or even entirely sane. In approaching strategic discourse this way, I am interested in the ways instrumental rationality (*Zweckrationalität*) can be subsumed within value rationality (*Wertrationalität*), as well as in the implications of multiple value rationalities (*Wertrationalitäten*) at play in strategic discourse. At the very least, I assume that "strategy" entails more than a mere form of instrumental rationality, but is also a means of expression, of "spirit."[4] Moreover, by approaching strategy through worldview, I probe the "motive forces" of strategy beyond strict security, survival, or power.

The motive for this book, as I address directly in the conclusion, is to enrich the theory and terminology by which we understand different historic approaches to American foreign policy. Neither historical inquiry nor political theory has produced a rhetorically based conceptual apparatus by which to account for the different ways in which Americans have talked about, and thus made judgments about, the place and role of the nation in the world. Whether the terminology is *realism* versus *idealism*, *protectionism* versus *internationalism*, or *Jacksonians* versus *Wilsonians*, *Hamiltonians*, and *Jeffersonians*, approaches to the guiding spirits of American foreign policy have always been one step removed from the ways in which actual political actors persuade publics about American intentions and actions in the world.[5]

For example, Wilsonianism represents a major school, ideology, or impulse—depending on your perspective—among foreign policy specialists. Yet invoking Wilsonianism or even the school's main tenets has about as much effect in persuading publics or political actors that a course of action should be pursued as does invoking Kant's categorical imperative to urge a particular ethical course of action. Schools of foreign policy as such have little motive force, even if they do help delimit a field of intellectual inquiry. Motive force instead depends on rich national languages that appear to many coherent, compelling, and consistent with "America." When it comes to foreign policy debate, scholars sometimes presume that the contest is among such competing schools, and jump quickly to a discussion of relatively abstract philosophies with little or no attention paid to the language of the debates themselves.[6] On the other hand, by attending to the rhetorical nuances of foreign policy debates, we may find that language itself is a ground not only for motivation but for political judgment and, in turn, develop a more grounded analytic for understanding America's various actions in the world of nations. Alas, the typology I form in this book does not represent a fully grounded approach to political rhetoric, which is too diffuse and complex to typify. It does represent an attempt to attend to the discourse of the debates themselves and glean from them a set of "ideal types" through which we can better understand divergent approaches to American foreign policy, at least with respect to security strategy.

In constructing this typology, I work with particular historical texts and with broader traditions of American political culture in a mode of inquiry distinct from deduction and induction, sometimes called "abduction." The philosopher Charles Sanders Peirce, drawing on Aristotle, found in abduction a form of logical inference concerned with the new, whether newly discovered problems, new phenomena, or new insights, that resulted in conclusions that are inescapably "problematic or conjectural" but theoretically rich.[7] In rhetorical criticism abduction has been presented as a method as well as a mode of logic. As James Jasinski writes, abduction in criticism works in "a back and forth tacking movement between text and the concept or concepts that are being investigated simultaneously," and entails "the constant interaction of careful reading and rigorous conceptual reflection."[8] Accordingly, this book introduces a new problem to the corpus of rhetorical scholarship on American foreign policy, which, as I discuss further in the introduction, has worked with great skill from views of language as strategic, metaphorical, or ideological, but has largely left unattended the thick "world-making" capacity of language. Like the rhetorical scholarship to which this book is indebted, my arguments depend on careful readings of primary sources from the early Cold War; but to address the world-making capacity of language I attend as well to the broader activist and intellectual histories of the worldviews I discern in primary texts. I tack back and forth. My aim has been to write a historically grounded study of strategic discourse in the early Cold War that is also a partial account of the career of worldviews, and thus to shed light on both the strategic discourse of a crucial era in American security strategy and the power of intellectually tinged cultural languages to shape, from the inside out, America's interactions with the world.

The first chapter of the book is devoted to George F. Kennan's strategic concept of "containment." Looking at a wide range of archival material, but especially at Kennan's famous 1946 "long telegram," his subsequent 1947 "X" article in *Foreign Affairs*, and his 1951 *American Diplomacy*, I argue that Kennan's somewhat elusive notion of containment, and indeed his overall historical and philosophical outlook, was stoic in worldview. Chapter 1 discusses the influences of stoicism upon political thought in Europe and America in order to identify a set of family characteristics that in turn illuminate central ideas and arguments in Kennan's thought, above all his notion of containment. At its core, I argue, was an ideal of the state as devoted to the rational care of the self before irrational and violent forces, and thus to an ideal of the state in the abstract as independent, strong, and reasonable. Kennan's concepts and judgments, of which containment was a part, habitually relied on this fundamentally stoic ideal.

The second chapter looks at John Foster Dulles's "massive retaliation." Kennan's *American Diplomacy* was deeply critical of what he called "legalism" and "moralism," and no doubt Dulles was one of his chief contemporaneous targets. As Eisenhower's secretary of state, Dulles's most famous public strategic statement came before the Council on Foreign Relations in 1954, his "massive retaliation" speech. I argue in chapter 2 that indeed the speech was an instance of moralism, and it was tied to Dulles's legalism. However, I argue that it was an expression of a form of moralism and legalism with a profound history in America, one that neither can nor should be so readily dismissed as Kennan wished. The spirit of massive retaliation was evangelical in nature, in that its worldview entailed a stalwart sense of America's role in the world as a kind of "city upon a hill," a strong sense of responsibility for activism in the world, and an implicit but powerful notion of covenant—covenant within America and covenant among nations. Through readings of his speeches in the 1940s and early 1950s, I show that by the time Dulles reached the State Department he had come to position the Soviets as covenant-breakers, and that for him the significance of massive retaliation had less to do with nuclear deterrence per se than with moral protest. I argue that the spirit of massive retaliation, however misunderstood, entailed a relatively coherent, albeit ultimately equivocal, form of evangelical moralism.

Chapter 3 examines Charles Douglas (C. D.) Jackson's approach to "liberation." A prototypical "quiet American," Jackson was Eisenhower's chief psychological warfare advisor during the first year of the presidency, a major speechwriter for the president, a founder of Radio Free Europe, and an employee and close ally of Henry Luce. Throughout the 1950s, when a strategy of liberation was largely unpopular, Jackson remained committed to the ideal and worked vigorously within and without the administration to forward it. Jackson's most ambitious effort in this respect in the 1950s was the World Economic Plan, first proposed to the Eisenhower administration by Jackson, Walt Rostow, and Max Millikan in 1954 as an American-led international economic development plan by which to push back the power and influence of the Soviets.[9] To be sure, the World Economic Plan was a product of many factors: the apparent success of the Marshall Plan, Rostow's new theory of modernization, anxieties about apparent increases in Soviet economic growth, a new-found nationalistic zeal among so-called underdeveloped nations, and an open-door ideology tied to a capitalistic desire for more markets.[10] However, behind the World Economic Plan, I argue, was an ideological and aesthetic ideal of American "adventurism" abroad. Adventurism explains the plan's explicit connection to a policy of liberation and its ties to Henry Luce's "American Century." As Luce's essay had argued just before World War II, America's economic, political, and spiritual vitality was tied to its capacity to perform great deeds on the world stage. I argue that behind Jackson's World Economic Plan and his commitment to a policy of liberation was this ideal.

Finally, chapter 4 considers Eisenhower's approach to nuclear deterrence. While for understandable reasons contemporary observers and subsequent scholars approached Dulles's and Eisenhower's strategic outlook as coterminous, or see Jackson as Ike's strategic kin, I argue that Eisenhower's approach to nuclear deterrence, and indeed strategy in general, was distinct from Dulles's and Jackson's with regard to worldview. Massive retaliation was in an important respect merely the extension of an ethic of community policing via moral spectacle, its declaration a reiteration of covenantal moral protest. Deterrence as "punishment" was presented within a strongly moral structure, as a moral *right*. The result was both a pronounced moral vigor vis-à-vis deterrence and an ultimate moral equivocation. "Liberation," though on the surface amoral, entailed in fact a thick idealism with respect to national action. Eisenhower, however, articulated deterrence within a strongly instrumental structure. Deterrence was a means of utilitarian calculation, instrumental control, and of furthering a material order only loosely tied to moral order. Nuclear bombs and missiles were thus functionally analogous to Jeremy Bentham's central tower in his *Panopticon*. Nevertheless, this militant instrumentalism jeopardized America's status as the "free world" leader. Eisenhower's articulation of deterrence therefore relied on a sharp division between "spirit" and "matter" vis-à-vis the nation. In his speeches and writings, Eisenhower repeatedly addressed the problems of legitimation by disassociating the intent of deterrence from the manifest danger of its material means. Eisenhower's nuclear deterrence, I argue, depended for its hoped-for success on a romantic rhetorical and hermeneutical approach. It stressed the role of interpretation vis-à-vis forwarding in its rhetoric the spiritual purposes and essences of material signs.

Historically and practically, romanticism represents an attempt at synthesis, borrowing themes of self-control from stoicism, spiritual and moral purposes from evangelicalism, and heroism from adventurism. In the conclusion, I suggest that the classical age of American security strategy may have become a romantic age, and so directed the course of American strategic discourse in the remainder of the Cold War toward the hyper-instrumental and hyper-symbolic. Eisenhower forwarded an "umbrella language" that seemingly could reconcile contesting worldviews. In this regard, he may be thought of as the defining rhetorical president of the American Cold War, and indeed beyond.

I would like to think that this book could function as a kind of preface to a modern-day critical "Rhetoric" of American security strategy discourse, one that provides the basis for more robust descriptions of American self-understanding and understanding of the world by beginning with a discrete set of texts and working abductively to typify the texts. Aristotle's *Rhetoric* has been identified with a strategic view of language, as it was concerned with "the available means of persuasion." But the *Rhetoric* was also the product of cultural diagnostics, containing a kind of catalogue of common cultural ideas, sayings, attitudes, and arguments, as well as formal classifications of types of speech. In the twentieth century, Kenneth Burke's *A Rhetoric of Motives* expanded this tradition by probing the "intermediate area of expression that is not wholly deliberate, yet not wholly unconscious," and providing a conceptual catalogue for such probing. Burke's work suggests that a "Rhetoric" might not only present material that can be used by political actors, but delves into cultural languages that themselves "use," so to speak, political actors.[11] This book could serve as a preface to such an enterprise with respect to American security strategy discourse, as it addresses not only that intermediate area of expression between the conscious and unconscious use of language, but also attempts in its method to work a middle ground between historical description and abstract conceptual analysis. Indeed, the great virtue of rhetorical studies throughout its long and varied history from antiquity on has been its consistent attempts to work between theory and practice with regard to the uses and abuses of language. Political philosophy has too often kept its distance from political actors. Meanwhile, historical writing has often neglected theoretical and philosophical inquiry. Rhetorical studies have frequently tried to find a middle way. Such is the spirit of this book.

Acknowledgments

There are far more who have been integral to the composition of this book than I can acknowledge here. First, there are all the authors and their books—those works and words, sacred and profane—without which I could not have conceived of this project, let alone pursued it to some sort of end. Then there are all my teachers, so many. And friends and family, colleagues and classmates, etc. Nevertheless, some of the people that deserve more than acknowledgement are Scott Althaus, Jim Aune, Tim Bossenbroek, John Carlson, Cliff Christians, Nathan Crick, Todd Daley, Danny Day, Jeff Dryden, Jon Ebel, Jean Bethke Elshtain, Mike Farley, Sheila Felton-O'Gorman, Cara Finnegan, Pat Gill, Kevin Hamilton, John Haralson, Ken Harris, Stephen Hartnett, Debbie Hawhee, Giorgio Hiatt, Clay Holland, Ewan Kennedy, Ed Killeen, Nick and Peggy Korn, Irene Koshik, John Lucaites, Sam McCormick, Paul McNamara, Bart Moseman, John Murphy, Eileen O'Gorman, Fran O'Gorman, Kyle Painter, John Durham Peters, Chris Roberts, Nick Rudd,

David Suryk, Michael Svoboda, Dave Tell, Greg Thompson, David Timmerman, Henry Tom, Josh Yates, and Wes Zell.

The idea for this book began about a year after I arrived at the University of Illinois, and the work was finished there as well. I have not only my colleagues in Illinois's Department of Communication to thank for helping me see it through (some listed above), but the university itself, particularly the Illinois Program for Research in the Humanities, the Campus Research Board, and the Department of Communication—each of which gave me release time to work on this project. I also want to thank the department heads I worked with successively in Illinois's Department of Communication as I wrote this book. Barbara Wilson and the late and sorely missed Dale Brashers were excellent mentors. Dave Tewksbury provided cheerful support as this book went to press, and I am quite grateful to him for so ably picking up where Barb and Dale left off.

While this book is not an outgrowth of my dissertation, and is in some ways a significant departure from anything I studied in graduate school, I owe my graduate teachers and mentors at the Pennsylvania State University a great deal of gratitude. Each shaped my work in significant ways: Tom Benson, Rosa Eberly, Cheryl Glenn, Christopher Johnstone, Michael Hogan, Jack Selzer, and Jorge Reina Schement. And then there was my dissertation advisor, Stephen Howard Browne, who taught me above all that it is okay not to be a literalist. I also have had other graduate teachers and mentors that made more than a mark on me: Janet Atwill, Linda Bensel-Meyers, Jack Collins, Donald Guthrie, Russel Hirst, Esther Meek, and Mike Williams.

Thanks are also due to the Center for Writing Studies at the University of Illinois, the Department of Communication at the University of Kansas, and the Center for the Study of Religion and Conflict at Arizona State University for opportunities to present portions of this work, as well as to the anonymous reviewers who have engaged portions of it in journal article form.

The graduate students of the Department of Communication at the University of Illinois have been both an inspiration and an aid to this work. I want to thank, in particular, Marissa Bambrey Wolfe, Sabrina Marsh, and Ian Hill for their valuable work as research assistants. And my colleagues in the American Society for the History of Rhetoric represent a significant inspiration for the work that follows.

Marty Medhurst, the general editor of this series, has been like a patient bull: strong enough to get things done, gentle enough to ensure that I survive the process. I also want to thank Ira Chernus for his review, as well as the two other reviewers of the manuscript who remained anonymous. Many thanks to the professionals at Michigan State University Press, who have been outstanding. I want to thank as well the archivists and staff at the Dwight D. Eisenhower Library, the Harry S. Truman Library, and the Seely G. Mudd Manuscript Library at Princeton University.

My children—Graham, Will, and Mariclare—are for me continual sources of motivation as well as diversion. Finally, there's my wife, Linda, who has never been overly impressed with my work, but only because she has no need for such impressions. For this I am ever grateful.

Introduction

> A motive is not some fixed thing, like a table, which one can go and look at. It is a term of interpretation, and being such it will naturally take its place within the framework of our *Weltanschauung* as a whole.
> —Kenneth Burke, *Permanence and Change*

When in the summer of 1945 the United States brought a world-historical culmination to World War II by dropping atomic bombs on Japan's Hiroshima and Nagasaki (immediately killing well over 100,000 Japanese and leaving tens of thousands more to die slowly of radiation sickness), many in America believed that the United States' overwhelming technological, economic, and now bomb power would ensure, at last, a just and durable peace for the world. It is therefore one of those great ironies of American history, to use a Niebuhrian phrase, that America's rise to overwhelming power at the close of World

War II corresponded with the deterioration of relations with a most important wartime ally, the Soviet Union, inaugurating what would soon come to be called the Cold War.[1] In the wake of an überdisplay of power, the United States was left scrambling, improvising, and debating what to do with the Reds. A climate of contestation rather than concord came to characterize American foreign policy in the years subsequent to America's victory in World War II.

So much so that in the fall of 1952, for the first time since Herbert Hoover in 1929, a Republican was elected to the presidency. A war hero and a major participant in the U.S. reconstruction of Europe under Truman, Dwight D. Eisenhower ran for the presidency on a platform that promised to end the ugly war in Korea and begin a new, more vigorous, Cold War initiative, especially in the area of "psychological warfare." Upon entering the White House, however, Eisenhower kept the contest over American security strategy alive for bit longer. On May 8, 1953, a few months into his presidency, he held an off-the-record meeting in the White House solarium with some of his closest advisors. Eisenhower set out to discuss, in broad terms, the state of America's foreign affairs. The president sounded a somber note. "In the world chess game, the Reds today have the better position. . . . Practically everywhere one looks, there is no strong holding point and danger everywhere of Communist penetration."[2] John Foster Dulles, Eisenhower's peripatetic secretary of state, concurred and urged that the administration take a firmer, more resolute stance toward the Soviets. He claimed a new policy was needed, and a new attitude.

The discussion gave Eisenhower an idea. Why not assemble "teams of bright young fellows" and have them go to work, each team promoting a distinct policy program for confronting the Soviet challenge? And so he launched Project Solarium, "an exercise unique in the history of national security policy making."[3] Project Solarium formed three task-force teams. Each task force was given a discrete strategic framework and asked to research its strengths and weaknesses, culminating in a report to the National Security Council (NSC) that would make the best possible case for the given strategy. Task Force A would argue for a basic continuation of the Truman administration's policies. Appropriately, George F. Kennan, known as the architect of Truman's "containment" policy, chaired Task

Force A. Task Force B, chaired by Army Major General James McCormack Jr., would argue for a clearer and firmer policy of deterrence. And Task Force C, led by Vice Admiral R. L. Conolly of the navy, was charged with arguing for an aggressive psychological, diplomatic, economic, and even limited military, campaign to dissolve Soviet strength and "to produce a climate of victory encouraging to the free world."[4]

On July 16 the task forces made their presentations before the NSC. While each report addressed a wide variety of secondary strategic issues, about which the task forces shared some common ground, the general thrust of each presentation was sharply divergent. Task Force A argued that a balance of power had temporarily existed in the postwar world between the United States and the USSR, and that initial U.S. Cold War policy had therefore worked. The only decisive victory the Communists had won was in China.[5] Yet Kennan's group worried about more recent trends. "The last couple of years have witnessed a marked decline in the confidence with which the U.S. is viewed in a great many parts of the non-Communist world," they claimed (10). Simultaneously, Stalin's death had undermined Soviet strength in the world. The result was a general imbalance in world power, seen vividly in "the rise to new vigor and self-assertion of numerous forces between the American and Soviet centers of power" (11). Consequently, Task Force A urged,

> It is evident that this is a time for the greatest of prudence and penetration in the selection of the lines of conduct which this Government pursues, and for a clear identification and strict observance of the basic realities of the situation. Whether these qualities are or are not achieved in the formulation of American policy, represents in our opinion a large part of the answer to the question as to whether time is on our side. (11–12)

Dismissing the imminent threat of Soviet military offensives as highly unlikely, Task Force A instead emphasized the importance of America's reputation before the world. "The members of Task Force A are struck with the fact that there is one single factor which is essential to the successful pursuit of *all* our objectives with regard to Soviet power: that is the political climate of the non-Communist world, and particularly its response to American policies and initiatives." Hence, the "quality of American leadership and the wisdom of American policies" would be crucial for the fate of the world (12). "Constancy and determination in our policy," Task Force A insisted, would be vital to U.S. success in the Cold War. Conversely, "every indication of abruptness or erratic behavior" by the United States would undermine world confidence and put the nation's leadership in jeopardy (14). Therefore, what Task Force A emphasized, above all, was the *manner* in which the United States pursued its policies. Prudence, wisdom, constancy, focus—upon such qualities, they argued, depended the success of U.S. policy.

Task Force B followed A in emphasizing the importance of world confidence in the United States, but stressed making absolutely clear America's military and moral *strength*. Task Force B stressed clarity over constancy of purpose, advocating a vigorous policy of deterrence.[6] Addressing squarely the problem of "atomic plenty," Major General McCormack's group urged a "military offensive capability so invulnerable to Soviet attack that regardless of the damage that might be done on this continent, the USSR could not expect to escape an unacceptable counterblow" (4–5). A clear policy of deterrence, Task Force B suggested, could serve two vital purposes. First, it could bring greater stability and certainty to world affairs vis-à-vis the prevention of war: "A clear indication that further military aggression by the Soviet Bloc would result immediately in general war will reduce the likelihood that such a war will occur" (11). But it could also make clear to the world America's moral leadership. "The moral foundation for the policy seems to us to be of critical importance," they argued, "and we think it would be inadequate unless the policy were put forth in terms of an unassailable statement of principle" (8). In this way, Task Force B advocated a policy that stressed America's material and moral force.

While Task Force C concurred with B that "Our task is to command respect, not necessarily love and devotion," they minimized the importance of principled moral leadership (6, Report).[7] Instead, Admiral Conolly's group argued for a policy that would "Prosecute relentlessly a forward and aggressive political strategy in all fields and by all means: military, economic, diplomatic, covert and propaganda" (25, summary outline). This effort would even include "covertly using a national program of deception and concealment from public disclosure and Soviet discernment as to the depth and extent of our challenge" (26, summary outline). Indeed, their argument was relentless: "The most feasible method of attaining U.S. security, and of avoiding general war, is to end the cold war. The only to end the cold war is to win it" (24, summary outline). Therefore, the United States should pursue, as a first step, an "All-out political offensive to overthrow Satellite governments and bring them into the family of free nations" (6, Report). The task force argued that the pursuit of containment, deterrence, or otherwise "static" policies would result in greater problems for the United States (13–14 Report). In response to Task Force A's talk of a balance of power and Task Force B's advocacy of greater certainty and stability through deterrence, Task Force C retorted, "In this conflict one is either winning or losing. There can be no continuing balance, no state of real world stability in the face of this implacable conspiracy" (10, Report). The United States had to *wage* "cold war," which the task force defined as "the condition of international struggle in which we are now engaged. This encompasses every form of military and political conflict *short of* a general war of global scope" (11, Report). Consequently, Task Force C advocated incessant aggressive *action*.

Project Solarium's purpose was to give the NSC a wide range of arguments and ideas with which to work in formulating a new Cold War policy. However, Project Solarium's significance goes further. It left a visible trace, now sitting in the U.S. government archives, of an extraordinarily wide range of ways of talking about America. Policymakers—many of them cut from the same social cloth, and many who would work together under Eisenhower to fight the Cold War—had at their disposal divergent ways of envisioning the character and identity of America vis-à-vis its role in the world. To be sure, all the participants in Project Solarium agreed that the Soviets were an aggressive and implacable enemy, that the United States represented the USSR's only formidable foe, that nuclear weapons made the conflict between the two nations potentially dire, and that general war should be avoided if possible, but beyond this we witness in Project Solarium a significant range of ideas about how America was to *be* in the world.

To typify their distinct approaches: Task Force A approached America as the wise leader of the free world, instilling resiliency and confidence in allies through its constancy, purposefulness, caution, and prudence. Task Force B, on the other hand, imagined America as a strongly militant force in the world, using the might of U.S. armed forces to deter Soviet aggression and stand up for moral principle. Task Force C's outlook saw the nation as an assertive and surreptitious activist on the world stage, using a wide range of military and nonmilitary means and observing neither principle nor strict caution to aggressively pursue victory. These disparate visions of potential American geopolitical identities corresponded with sharply divergent visions of the world of nations. One group saw that world in terms of a balance of powers, while another aspired to U.S hegemony, and a third almost mocked both notions, seeing the world only as a battlefield for victory and the Cold War as a zero-sum game.

Nevertheless, all three policies were vigorously and plausibly argued before Eisenhower's NSC. Indeed, the members of both Task Force A and Task Force C declared in their reports that the views they expressed were not mere hypothetical conclusions, but genuine beliefs about the general course U.S. Cold War policy needed follow. Only Task Force B (the course, as it so happened, that Eisenhower's New Look most nearly approximated) inserted a clear disclaimer in its report.[8] Thus, Project Solarium stands as a testament to the pliability of understandings of America and the world by people running in the same circles at a crucial moment in American foreign affairs. The three task forces bespoke, consciously or otherwise, profoundly different visions of the nation and the world of nations. And they did so with such skill, force, and readily available language that we cannot now dismiss their respective visions as mere ad hoc inventions for the sake of an exercise in strategic planning. Indeed, the persuasive power of their respective visions suggests that when they addressed the character of America and the nature of the world of nations, they voiced their ideas in thick historical American languages congealed in worldviews.

Language-views as Worldviews

"A language-view is a worldview."[9] This book entails an effort to come to terms with different American languages and worldviews, and thus the pliability of visions of America in the context of national security strategy discourse. In the pages that follow, I embark on a rather extensive effort to bring some order to the apparent indeterminacy of American self- and world-understanding as exemplified in Project Solarium. Indeed, that such divergent and yet plausible pictures of America and the world could be simultaneously circulated might be, for a citizen, quite disturbing. It suggests that American policymakers can simply make the nation, and indeed the world, into their own desired image in order to satisfy their policy goals. Eisenhower gave each task force a different and distinct policy agenda; in turn, each task force drew up corresponding images of America and the world order to render the preset policy plausible. The identity of America, this exercise suggests, is sufficiently indeterminate to justify and render publicly meaningful a wide variety of political, military, or economic agendas. One might therefore conclude that image management, recasting America, and revising the nation's story are merely part of will-to-power politics within and among states.

Yes and no. Or so concludes this book. I suggest that indeed American self-understanding and understanding of the world of nations is pliable, and policymakers can usually find some way of constructing American identity and the identity of the world that can render plausible, at least to some, their policies and actions—no matter how un-American, undemocratic, unconstitutional, or just plain foolish those policies and actions may seem to others. However, I want to argue that the options for American self-understanding are nevertheless limited. "America" is not a thoroughly indeterminate entity (inasmuch as it can be thought of as an entity at all). Rather, because it is a *historical* being, it is determined, in a soft sense, by its histories, traditions, memories, and typical discourses. And because it is a *social* entity, its ideas about itself and the world cannot be invented *ex nihilo* and still be plausible to others. Social meaning requires two or more entities and some prior language through which the two or more are constituted. In order for a political actor to put forward a plausible picture of the nation and the world, some recognition, some assent, some sanction, some "amen" must come from some group or groups of others, and this can only be if the picture draws upon some already shared set of sentiments, ideas, images, and languages.

These shared sentiments, ideas, images, and languages are sometimes called traditions, and I will sometimes refer to them in this way. However tradition (*trâditiô*, "handing over or down"—a distinctly selective process) does not quite do justice to the less-than-fully-conscious ways collective meanings and social identities are inherited. Indeed, *ideology* captures better this less-than-fully-conscious aspect, but ideology is most often a term of politics, concerned with a set of basic convictions, or a consciousness, that corresponds to a political structure, and the tensions and contradictions therein. I am concerned instead with a subset, even substratum, of politics: shared sentiments, ideas, images, and languages, but ones that cannot be readily correlated with particular historical structures of power. The most satisfactory way of conceiving them, therefore, may be as "worldviews." A worldview is a term of sociology and ethics. It can be conceived of as a relatively coherent way of seeing self, or society, and world that is embedded in language and that comprises a motive force in social action. In this framework, divergent ways of addressing self and world in language express contending motives. Collected together they form a set of available means of describing and accounting for action in the world, and this set would in turn inform a larger culture. In political culture, political actors have to speak within a worldview or some hybrid of worldviews in order to render a program of political action meaningful. To typify the worldviews of a political culture is to bring some order to the apparent muddle of such meaning-making discourses. This book represents just such an attempt with respect to American security strategy in the early Cold War, a period that since the end of the Cold War has come to function as the "classical period" in American security strategy, and thus is a pivotal period for the study of American strategic languages.

Language as Strategy, Strategy as Language

Strategy and language are distinct concepts, but overlapping phenomena. Strategy is often approached as a matter of what Max Weber referred to as *Zweckrational* action, or action predicated on a means-end logic. One dictionary defines it as "a plan, method, or series of maneuvers or stratagems for obtaining a specific goal or result."[10] In this way, strategy represents a mode of human action. Therefore, while the etymology of *strategy* is martial—from the Greek *stratêgos*, general—its semantic reach has been extended into domains as seemingly diverse as business philosophy, game theory, and rhetorical theory.[11]

Indeed, one of the more influential frameworks for approaching the rhetoric of foreign policy has been as "strategic discourse." "Under this view," writes Martin Medhurst, one of the chief exponents of the approach, "rhetoric is an art whose central focus is learning how to find and construct the arguments that are most likely to be persuasive in the case at hand. It is a strategic art in the sense that the speaker must analyze the situation, develop a persuasive goal, invent the lines of argument, that seem most capable of moving the target audience toward acceptance of that goal, organize the discourse for maximum effectiveness, and select the time, place, occasion, and audience that is most conducive to achievement of the goal."[12] In this way Medhurst draws a distinct parallel between the art of war and the art of speech. Both are conceived as modes of social action in which the most effective means to achieve predetermined ends is sought. Thus, Medhurst identifies a strategic view of rhetorical action with a "realist" outlook on international relations, arguing that it is predicated on "not the world as it ought to be or as we might wish it to be, but the world as it currently exists."[13] Such an approach, he argues, entails a view of rhetoric as "an amoral tool," normatively bounded, if it is to be so bound, only by "the values of the speaker."[14]

Yet others have argued that strategies, whether martial or rhetorical, are shaped profoundly by values, entailing what Weber called *Wertrational* action.[15] Indeed, debates about and differences over strategy, while certainly taking into account capabilities, resources, and other apparently more objective factors, cannot be shown to be exclusively based on such considerations. As ideological critics, "postrealists," and poststructural international relations theorists have variously argued, strategies are conceived and contested *in language,* and thus an account of "discursive power" is needed alongside one of "power politics."[16] As Francis Beer and Robert Hariman write, "The discourses of international relations . . . are productive and generative. A productive discourse builds something, in this case, a self-sufficient political order. A generative discourse creates resources for innovative problem solving and for articulating new experiences and modes of action."[17] Two implications relevant to the overlapping phenomena of strategy and language follow.

First, as language is inescapably value-laden, so must be the language of strategy. Discursive accounts of strategy therefore in one way or another address questions of values, norms, ideas, and ideologies. For example, Robert L. Ivie has argued that language has the capacity to "narrow the range of choices for managing international relations realistically," as in language, especially in its metaphorical aspect, political motives take shape through "the extension of a master image into a perspective or general framework of interpretation."[18] In a different vein, Philip Wander has argued that the ideological power of language can "camouflage the facts of international politics under the colors of domestic politics."[19] Here language is inescapably value-laden, but politically problematic because it obscures the facts. These approaches to foreign policy discourse call for sensitivity to what might be called the nonstrategic uses of language, uses where "the most effective means to achieve predetermined ends," to quote Medhurst, may not be the overriding issue.

Second, attention to discursive power does not preclude attention to the strategic use of language. Indeed, the strategic and nonstrategic approaches to language that have characterized the preponderance of scholarship on the rhetoric of foreign policy can and often do complement one another. As Shawn Parry-Giles writes, one can forward a rhetorical perspective that "emphasizes the ideological as well as the strategic."[20] And in his introductory essay to a volume that collects Medhurst's, Ivie's, and Wander's essays, Robert L. Scott argues that the essays collected together evince a "pluralistic" approach to Cold War criticism.[21] To be sure, while divergent critical approaches draw attention to different aspects of language, they share a common concern with what language *does* over and against some dimension of reality or possible reality. Therefore, these approaches to rhetorical criticism each attend to some instrumental aspect of language, where language is seen in terms of how it functions vis-à-vis the interests of some personal (strategic view), impersonal structural-historical (ideological view), or semipersonal collective linguistic "agent" (metaphorical approach).

Still, there is an aspect of language that rhetorical scholars of foreign policy have little addressed, one implicit in Weber's notion of *Wertrational* action, indebted to "counter-Enlightenment" thinkers like Giambattista Vico, Herder, and even Marx: the "world-making" capacity of language.

Here we approach a dimension of language that transcends instrumentality as it stretches toward the transcendent, aspirational, or "ideal." Thus while language must be critiqued in terms of what it does adversely or positively over and against a standard of judgment, Weber's interest in "subjective meaning" meant an understanding of language that could not be limited to the instrumental.[22] While forces, ranging from the individual intentions of political actors to political-economic structures to political culture, *drive* the rhetoric of foreign policy, and more specifically the rhetoric of strategy, such rhetoric is also *drawn toward* aspirations, ideals, and the fulfillment of desires. Language contains an aspirational aspect. Thus, the rhetoric of foreign policy is pulled as well as pushed. Or, to use terms familiar to students of foreign policy, the "ideal," as well as the "real," motivates foreign policy discourse, but not as well-intended supplement or misguided distortion, but rather as an intrinsic aspect of language itself. Thus the "ideal" appears not only as an object of critique, but necessarily as a basis from which to critique, inasmuch as critique is enacted in language.

That such *Wertrational* action, mediated by and constituted in language, conditions and can strongly influence, even trump, *Zweckrational* action in military and security strategy debates and deliberations is not a new insight. Carl von Clausewitz in *On War* not only lists the "moral" among "strategic elements" but leads us, in his conception of "strategy," to place the moral at its heart.[23] "Strategy is the use of engagement for the purpose of the war. The strategist must therefore define an aim for the entire operational side of the war *that will be in accordance with its purpose.*"[24] Strategy is thus subordinated by Clausewitz to "purpose." Of course, the purpose of strategy cannot be to destroy the object it seeks to defend. This would be either maniacal or treasonous. And in the modern world, nation-states are the object of national defense. Therefore, the purpose of strategy cannot legitimately include undermining the integrity of the nation-state. And the integrity of nation-states includes identity, values, and ideologies that have both instrumental and aspirational modes. Consequently, the "purpose" of strategy has inextricable value dimensions, and strategy itself will have inextricable aspirational dimensions.

Yet the aspirational, value dimensions of strategy—with the exception of just war theory and its equivalents—is largely underdeveloped in scholarship. Clausewitz's work itself suggests one major reason why. His approach to what he calls the "moral elements" of strategy is largely romantic.

> The moral elements are among the most important in war. They constitute the spirit that permeates war as a whole, and at an early stage they establish close affinity with the will that moves and leads the whole mass of force, practically merging with it, since the will is itself a moral quantity. Unfortunately, they will not yield to academic wisdom. They cannot be classified or counted. They have to be seen or felt.[25]

Thus he suggests that intuition and experience, rather than reason and analysis, are best suited to understanding and evaluating the "moral elements" of strategy. Here Clausewitz is referring to something like "morale," but his assumptions carry over into a great deal of work on the value dimensions of national strategies. They are assumed to lie beyond a rational domain of critical inquiry, and thus be impenetrable by "academic wisdom."

The ineffable genius of the nation, the inscrutability of the collective will, the sublime power of organic social forces—such romantic themes have done far more to justify the excesses of collective action than they have done to encourage understanding among students of war, strategy, and foreign policy. Moreover, these themes stand against the Herdian insight that motive forces are *objectified in language,* and thus *can* yield to a degree of "academic wisdom." From this hermeneutical perspective, to address the "spirit" (*Geist*) of a people is not to address an ineffable and impenetrable subjective realm, but an empirical if inexact realm of outward human conduct. The subjective is objective.

This means, among other things, that language is context as well as text. Thus while one may argue, as Parry-Giles does, that critics must attend to the distinction between the private motives of the speaker and his or her public articulations, it is also the case that whether in private or public, as Marx confessed, we always work with "borrowed language."

> Man makes his own history, but he does not make it out of the whole cloth; he does not make it out of conditions chosen by himself, but out

of such as he finds close at hand. The tradition of all past generations weighs like an alp upon the brain of the living. At the very time when men appear engaged in revolutionizing things and themselves, in bringing about what never was before, at such very epochs of revolutionary crises do they anxiously conjure up into their service the spirits of the past, assume their names, their battle cries, their costumes to enact a new historic scene in such time-honored disguises and with such borrowed language.[26]

Borrowed language, which is always borrowed through the media of sociality and publicity, means that while political actors assume a distinction between their private thoughts and their public performances, and while there is good reason for historians and critics to ground their analyses in such a distinction, it is the case as well that public performances of the past are the context for present private thoughts, and moreover that the public performances of an individual actor will inevitably have a kind of "feedback" effect on his or her subsequent private thoughts.

Thus while strategy and language are distinct concepts, strategy is deliberated, articulated, and debated in and through "given" public languages. Inasmuch as these languages contain an aspirational as well as an instrumental aspect, they reach toward some purpose, end, value, or ideal that is rational in the sense of being *contestable*.[27]

Contesting Strategy

This contestability has to do with world making, as language, Hannah Arendt writes, offers a "very articulate and obstinate testimony" about the sort of world humans have made. Indeed, Arendt argues that language can teach us as much about our world as can our theories.[28] Sensitive readings of the texts people have left us represent a means of understanding the sort of world they imagined themselves to be a part of. In articulation we can discern a set of attitudes, ideas, and communicative habits that constitutes a way of seeing and being in the world, and an aspirational horizon.

To articulate—the act of putting ideas and feelings into words—once principally meant, and sometimes still does mean, "to joint." With respect to speech, articulation therefore suggests the ways in which in speaking we imagine ourselves jointing ideas and attitudes to words. When we struggle to articulate something, it is precisely this act of jointing that we are seeking. Often we struggle to articulate properly because we feel that what we have said has been misunderstood, taken to mean something we did not intend. These experiences tell us less about the act of speaking than they do about the nature of speech and agency. In speaking, we join subjective experience to objective language, and the process often feels imperfect or incomplete. This is because speech can disclose both less and more than we intend. Speech defies and transcends our intentions. What we say falls into the nebulous zone that Kenneth Burke described as an "intermediate area of expression that is not wholly deliberate, yet not wholly unconscious. It lies midway between aimless utterance and speech directly purposive."[29] The historical and encoded nature of language gives it the capacity, at any given moment, to reflect what we meant, reflect more than we meant, or fail to reflect our meaning. Very much like the tools a woodworker uses to joint, language opens up, limits, and sometimes altogether frustrates our action in the world.

Thus the agency of rhetorical actors is constrained. As Karlyn Kohrs Campbell writes, "Because they are linked to cultures and collectivities, [rhetorical actors] must negotiate among institutional powers and are best described as 'points of articulation' rather than originators."[30] Indeed, one of the striking things we learn from the biographies of architects of strategy is that they frequently end up feeling as though what they intended by way of policy was either misunderstood or misappropriated. Moreover, we often see them struggling to articulate their ideas. There is indeed something tragic about these failures and struggles. Perhaps the most famous Cold War expression of the tragedy of strategy can be found in Eisenhower's "Farewell Speech," where the president warned against that which he himself had helped create, the "military industrial complex." Eisenhower's warning was, in part, a warning against misunderstanding the tenor of his policies. He wanted to make explicit the place of *Wertrational* action in his approach. And this was neither pure self-justification nor sentimentality. Eisenhower's "Farewell Speech" reflects the brutal realities of political leadership and policymaking as many have experienced them. And it is such experiences that drive most leaders to seek, either consciously or semiconsciously, some sort of moral structure by which to justify—and sometimes condemn—their actions. Therefore, contrary to what abstract power politics might suggest or desire, political leaders, especially in societies based on popular sovereignty, necessarily develop a moral language in which their policies are framed. Leadership—or *power*—calls for it.

Together the chapters of this book consider various articulations of strategy to present a coherent account of contending worldviews within the early Cold War—by which I mean, in view of the aspirational aspect of language, different historical outlooks and dispositions with respect to the way America should *be* in the context of the Cold War. However, because these dispositions were contending does not mean that in practice they were mutually exclusive. Indeed, the first decade of the Cold War saw degrees of compromise among them. But there is a sense in which the spirit of each excluded or at least opposed that of the others. And while this book is not directly about debates over strategy, I do argue that such debates had to do with conflicting worldviews. *Wertrational* action, and not just *Zweckrational* action, drove debates about strategy in the early Cold War.

Each chapter begins with a touchstone strategic statement from the period, and then proceeds to examine at length its author, its context, and its ethical and rhetorical history. In each chapter I take up four questions: (1) What was the core vision of the strategy with respect to a conception of a national way of being in the world? (2) Wherein resided the intellectual roots and cultural power of that core vision? (3) What were the characteristic attributes of its articulation? (4) What is commendable or problematic about the spirit of the strategy? With respect to the first question, I assume that for the political leaders of the period, the terms of strategy were constrained by the terms of nationhood. No strategic vision could be broadly implemented without it appearing to a significant group of people to be "fitting" for the nation given the crisis with the Soviets. Therefore, we can ask, what sort of nation did this strategy appear to fit? To answer this question is to describe the core of the strategy's worldview.

With respect to the second question, I suggest that—given access to political power, itself no small thing—what made a strategy compelling was not strictly a utilitarian metric of cost-benefit analysis, but also a vision of the way things were or could or should be with respect to the nation and the world. With regard to persuading others, the success or failure of a strategy within the halls of government depended in part on aligning the worldview of the strategy with the norms of those who needed to be persuaded, whether they were bureaucrats or officeholders or, more broadly, the public. In essence, question number 2 presupposes that strategies are never pushed through unilaterally but always require the cooperation of others who function as rhetorical audiences, capable of affirming or frustrating a strategic plan, and that it is only by tapping into shared cultural values and ideas that a strategy can be widely influential.

Therefore, a great portion of the following chapters is devoted to question number 3. I seek to explain what it was about the discourse of a political actor that made him (in a world still dominated by *him*) a participant in a distinct worldview. I presume that if I can show that the rhetoric of a given political actor had attributes that can be strongly linked with broad but powerful traditional ways of addressing the world, then that political actor can be placed within that broad tradition. Herein too we can find, I suggest, a basic "logic" of a strategy. Of course, answering question 3 entails addressing the prior two questions. All in all, therefore, questions 1 to 3 amount to one overarching question: What was the spirit of the strategy?

Question number 4 is distinct, and calls most obviously for my own particular judgments. While this book is not a work in ethics as such, and therefore will not be dominated by my own arguments concerning the ethics of national security, it is a work that is critical in nature. I ask that readers judge the soundness of my criticisms on a case-by-case basis, for that is how I have approached the critical task before me. Within the confines of the narrative of this book, which represent, I believe, the confines of the limited languages of American foreign policy, I find myself caught between stoicism and evangelicalism (worldviews that I describe in chapters 2 and 3 respectively) and looking for, but simply incapable of inventing *ex nihilo*, a third way. I make no claim to possess a metalanguage by which to neatly critique the languages of my subjects. As a critic I try to affirm with reason that which seems to be good with regard to the relative well-being of the nation among other nations and critique with reason that which seems destructive or problematic. I have designed my arguments to be sufficient for thought, rather than conclusive.

A Typology of American Worldviews

As I have said, my aim throughout these chapters is not to provide a proper history of the first decade of American Cold War strategy—others have done that already, and better than I could—but rather to demonstrate the differences among central political actors and their notions of strategy by showing divergences with regard to worldviews. In this way, this book is an inventive iteration of Weber's "ideal type" mode of understanding. Its main claims, while intimately tied to specific political actors and particular strategic statements, are general in aim.[31] I want to introduce, in one work, a set of ethical ideal types that can be used to understand particular historical actors and actions, as well as—as I take up in my conclusion—to help supplement regnant typologies like realism versus idealism and further account for the general tensions and tendencies of American foreign policy with respect to American cultural ideals. I hope that my overall argument will serve as a useful heuristic and a "a peculiarly plausible hypothesis"—for this, Weber argued, was the best one could achieve when seeking to generalize from particulars.[32]

In light of this, before proceeding into my studies themselves I want to forward here the key features of the four worldviews I consider, which I have here laid out in a table. I will not replicate this severely schematic presentation again in the book. My approach will be far more descriptive. However, this table does provide a quick abstract view of the family characteristics, relative to one another, of the worldviews I address. Importantly, I have derived this schema through rhetorical criticism. The schema has arisen *through* my readings of a wide swath of historical texts—it has no other direct source, albeit it is deeply indebted to that "school" of humanistic thought, if it may be described as such, which sees linguistic modes as "givens" that can be subject to relatively systemic accounting.[33]

While the columns present an overview of these traditions, the rows provide a sense of the sorts of issues I will address when discussing them.

A Typology of American Foreign Policy Worldviews

STOICISM	EVANGELICALISM	ADVENTURISM	ROMANTICISM
Typical image of political society and world			
Society as a *self* in an *inhospitable* world of appearances	Society as a *moral community* in a ultimately *moral* world	Society as a *dramatic actor* bringing meaning to an otherwise *meaningless* world	Society as a *mystical self* in a *dualistic* world
Typical tropological mode			
Metaphor	Metonymy	Irony	Synecdoche
Typical epistemological mode			
Skeptical	Fiduciary	Skeptical	Fiduciary
Typical prescription			
Care of the self	Moral reform, protest, and proclamation	Dramatic action	Technological instrumentalism and symbolic celebration
Typical means of addressing the tensions of foreign policy			
Vigilant self-critique	Equivocation	Irony	Dualism

Crucial is the image of "political society" to which the different worldviews are drawn as well as their corresponding visions of the world.[34] These images are closely related both to basic epistemological modes and to typical prescriptions vis-à-vis world crises. Moreover, they are funneled through, so to speak, a characteristic tropological mode. Crucial also is the manner by which these worldviews typically address the inevitable tensions, even contradictions, of American foreign policy: we see in this chart that each worldview entails tactics for addressing such tensions, ranging from stoicism's tactic of self-critique to adventurism's almost playful appeal to irony.

The meaning of a "typical tropological mode" may be foreign to some readers, as it entails a complex technical language derived from rhetorical theory. The word *trope* is often used derisively, as a term of dismissal—a *mere* trope. My use of the term in contrast is technical and philosophical, referring to what can be thought of as the "deep form" of traditional ways of addressing the world in thought and speech (the presumption being that speech and thought cannot be neatly separated). Since the Renaissance, metaphor, metonymy, synecdoche, and irony have been considered the four major tropes (or "master tropes," as Kenneth Burke calls them). They have been described as "modes of consciousness" providing "the basis for a distinctive linguistic protocol," or a coherent way of speaking about the world around, historical events, and intellectual ideas.[35] Claude Lévi-Strauss, for example, argued metaphor and metonymy were central to the form of myth, and Hayden White used all four major tropes in his metahistorical analysis of nineteenth-century historiography and philosophy of history.[36] An understanding of tropological modes helps critics comprehend the characteristic form of a given discourse; such is the aim of my use of the technical language of tropology in this book. However, I have tried to keep the book from being bogged down with tropology. Indeed, I do not enter into any extensive discussion of tropes until I address Eisenhower in chapter 4. At that point, tropology becomes more or less necessary to my argument, and by that time I will have established for readers some of the broader analytical and methodological concepts and approaches of the book.

Finally, the table suggests correctly that my interest is in more or less coherent worldviews, and moreover, that I will interpret the subjects and strategic concepts addressed in this book as part of these relatively coherent worldviews. Some of the more devastating critiques of "rational actor" theories of international relations began in the 1970s via social psychology, which argued that government actors and governments do not always proceed rationally in their relations with other governments.[37] Simultaneously, the rise of "deconstruction" and Foucauldian analyses in the humanities tended to focus on exposing the inherent contradictions and undoings of purportedly coherent concepts, metanarratives, and traditions. Consequently, it became not only legitimate but somewhat fashionable to focus studies on the inherent contradictions of a thinker, thought-system, or discursive tradition. This has become for some an ethical mission, one that I sympathize with. Yet, for all the undoings and exposures of contradictions, people nevertheless tend to evince patterns of thought, habits of behavior, and rhythms of reaction. Moreover, while history is always far messier than any story reflects, public meaning tends to be considerably more coherent than unnarrated historical events. Strategy and strategic thinkers act as much upon the field of public meaning as they do within "history." Hence, to consider their place within relatively coherent "types" is to consider the ultimately public dimension of strategy without embracing the presuppositions of rational-actor theories.

Eisenhower's call for a strategic summit in Project Solarium in which divergent approaches to the Cold War would be articulated reflected not only the vibrant arguments and debates in Cold War policy in the early 1950s, but substantive differences in more basic understandings that the nation. It suggested that in choosing strategy, a nation's leadership chooses not just what it will do, but who it will aspire to *be* in the world of nations. In this respect, as in more instrumental approaches to strategy, the options were not limitless. In fact, they were relatively restricted. Nevertheless, there were real options and real choices to be made.

CHAPTER 1

The Care of the Self: Kennan, Containment, and Stoicism

> Among so many dangers therefore, as the natural lusts of men do daily threaten each other withal, to have a care of one's self is not a matter so scornfully to be looked upon, as if so be there had not been a power and will left in one to have done otherwise.
> —Thomas Hobbes, *De Cive*

The eminent Cold War historian and Kennan biographer John Lewis Gaddis describes strategy as "quite simply the process by which ends are related to means, intentions to capabilities, objectives to resources."[1] However, this conception of strategy is deceptively simple. As Paul Kennedy has shown, approaches to strategy in the twentieth century grew increasingly broad. The two world wars and the long Cold War pushed strategic thinkers to consider more and more "the longer-term and *political* purposes of the belligerent state as a whole."[2] The failure to win a long-term peace after World War I forced strategists to ask again what is meant by "victory," and what is meant by "defeat." Similarly, the conflict between the United States and the USSR caused many to ask what is meant by "war," and what is meant by "peace." As the scope and nature of such key terms in strategic thinking were broadened, so was the scope of strategy itself, reaching its apogee in an understanding of "grand strategy." This understanding, Kennedy notes, concerns peace as much as war, reflects on the long-term economic and psychological factors of war and peace, recognizes the crucial place of diplomacy, and addresses issues of political culture. "The crux of grand strategy," Kennedy concludes, "lies therefore in *policy*, that is, in the capacity of the nation's leaders to bring together all of the elements, both military and nonmilitary, for the preservation and enhancement of the nation's long-term (that is, wartime *and* peacetime) best interests."[3] In this way, there is far more to strategy than Gaddis's definition might suggest. Strategy entails reckoning with a nation's "best interests." It seeks to organize a nation for successful being in the world, however, and by whomever, that is envisioned.

George F. Kennan's "containment" is widely considered the preeminent strategic concept of the Cold War, gaining the distinction as a model "grand strategy." In its most straightforward formulation, containment is presented as a strategy that aimed at restraining Soviet expansionism through the projection of U.S. power and the building of resilient alliances with non-Communist states. Kennan's own oft-cited words from his enormously influential "X" article in *Foreign Affairs* in 1947 (reprinted soon after in publications like *Reader's Digest* and *Life*) underlie this understanding of containment.

> In these circumstances it is clear that the main element of any United States policy toward the Soviet Union must be that of a long-term, patient but firm and vigilant containment of Russian expansive tendencies.

And,

> Soviet society may well contain deficiencies which will eventually weaken its own total potential. This would of itself warrant the United

States entering with reasonable confidence upon a firm containment, designed to confront the Russians with unalterable counterforce at every point where they show signs of encroaching upon the interests of a peaceful and stable world.[4]

Yet, as numerous commentators since have shown, these summary statements, pithy though they were, were also deceptively simple. Kennan's "X" article (hereafter simply X), as well as its famous antecedent, the "long telegram" (LT), left unanswered vital questions about the means of containment, the limits of the strategy, and even one of its central foci, the precise nature of Soviet motivations. The result was a legacy of confusion that rivaled containment's legacy of influence.[5]

Since the publication of Kennan's *Memoirs* in 1967, in which Kennan himself tried to clarify his thinking, numerous critics and scholars have tried to sort out the meaning of containment.[6] Unsatisfied with Kennan's own explanation, these writers have presented a critical puzzle with a consistent form: *how is it that the obviously flawed or incomplete articulations of containment in LT and X still had such tremendous influence?* Thus, in 1972 Charles Gati speculated that the powerful but troubled legacy of X may be due to "a subtle yet important difference between *what* Kennan said and *how* he said it." Kennan's "relatively simple explanation of the Soviet challenge in world affairs" made X tremendously influential, to the point, according to Gati, that it became "ingrained in the American political conscience," but it nevertheless belied Kennan's more complex understanding of the Cold War.[7] So too, in one of the most important studies of the 1970s of Kennan's containment, C. Ben Wright suggested that Kennan's words in the LT ran ahead of him as he felt he had to "exaggerate" the problem in order to "alert" policymakers. Meanwhile, "Some of Kennan's proposals were vague at best, suggesting different things to different people."[8] Wright argues that Kennan's early articulations of containment were rigid, militaristic, and globalizing, despite Kennan's efforts in his *Memoirs* to say otherwise. Furthermore, Wright intimates that it was precisely this rigidity that made Kennan's containment so influential, and so problematic.

More recently, Frank Costigliola has argued that the rhetorical power of LT, X, and other early Cold War writings by Kennan lay in "metaphors of gender and pathology" that provoked sharp emotional responses in readers. Costigliola argues the emotive source of this language was Kennan's "quasi-mystical [and eroticized] hope of becoming . . . a link enabling Russian society and American society to help each other."[9] His hopes and desires unfulfilled, Kennan blamed the Soviets and invoked "a basic polarity between masculine and feminine" in his language to "emotionalize and polarize issues."[10] While this gendered polarity strengthened Kennan's rhetoric, Costigliola argues it compromised the analyses of LT and X. Indeed, pathos (and pathology) has appeared paradoxically in critical analyses of Kennan's work as both a principal source of its persuasive power and as central to its analytical confusion. More than paradox, Robert Ivie suggests, the place of pathos in Kennan's thought was "self-defeating," as Kennan ended up trying "to manage unacknowledged affect instead of understanding its influence on the deliberative process."[11] The realist thus pursued an unrealistic ideal of the American democratic polity.[12]

These important studies, although distinct in their particular concerns and conclusions, together point to several key characteristics of Kennan's rhetoric. First is *simplicity*, whether understood as his simple presentation of Soviet motives, the rigidity and firmness of his viewpoint, rigid binaries like feminine versus masculine, or a failure to reckon with the polity as it is. Second, each critic rightly notes that in fact the global situation was more complex than Kennan's simplicities allowed. Third, each study turns to the complex role of pathos in Kennan's thought. Their consensus, therefore, is that through simplicity Kennan's containment gained in rhetorical power what it lost in analytical weight, and that pathos played a central role in this trade-off. Not coincidentally, all four writers present Kennan as ultimately confused, conflicted, or, at the very least, inconsistent.

Yet there is a consistency in this inconsistency, or so I will argue, one that makes Kennan's rhetoric more than a powerful peculiarity in the annals of American foreign policy, or even an important example of a conflicted Cold War realism, but the expression of a historic worldview. In articulating containment, I argue, Kennan was in a certain sense possessed by an ideal not his own, the historic stoic ideal of, in one word, *constancy*. Constancy, I argue, helps account for the apparent vacillations in his strategic thought, the curious admixture in his prose of appeals to "simplicity" and appeals to "complexity," and the vexed place of pathos. At the core of the stoic ideal is the notion of the complexity of simplicity. Constancy represents the emotive dimension of that notion. I want to argue that constancy is at the core of Kennan's containment, and that Kennan imagined America, in its ideal posture, metaphorically as a stoic state. Stoicism, broadly conceived, comprised the worldview of containment. Thus, in response to the question, *How is it that a flawed "containment" still had such tremendous influence?* I would add an answer as yet unaccounted for: stoicism as a worldview. Because worldviews are language views, they have rhetorical power, as they offer an aspirational horizon and a common, historic, and relatively consistent means of emplacement in the world.

Stoicism as Worldview

Historically speaking, my turn to stoicism is in no way a leap, despite the fact that students and scholars of Kennan have neglected this aspect of his approach to the Cold War. As Richard Tuck has argued, neostoicism of the seventeenth century, a new philosophy of the state, had a profound influence on the development of political realism, as much if not more so than Machiavelli.[13] A century later, at the time of the founding of the United States, stoicism enjoyed tremendous cultural capital as both an ethical and a political concept. It was, along with civic republicanism, part of a culture-wide neoclassical preoccupation, and it is, in the end, impossible to disentangle it fully from other classical concepts and concerns in the early American republic. Nevertheless, the distinct influence of stoicism can be seen in George Washington's "Farewell Address" (composed, over the course of a number of years, in consultation with James Madison and Alexander Hamilton), where the importance of a self-care based on a disinterested appraisal of "interest," according to the "natural course of things," is explicitly set against the confusions, complications, and passions of the world of appearances at large (as distinct from, although not at all opposed to, civic republican emphases on the importance of virtue, the public good, public participation, and the corruptive influences of luxury and sloth).[14] "Excessive partiality," Washington warned of international relations, "for one foreign nation and excessive dislike of another, cause those whom they actuate to see danger only on one side, and serve to veil and even second the arts of influence on the other."[15] Here and elsewhere, as I will discuss, neostoicism entailed a political philosophy, indeed a political ethic, that urged rational self-care and outward action limited to, as Washington wrote, "interests" and "the natural course of things" within a world of real or potential upheaval, suffering, fanaticism, and general irrationality. A similar ethic would find new life in the Cold War, as American infantrymen, generals, pilots, scientists, workers, politicians, and citizens were summoned to a singular national character type, one that looked coolly upon the crises of the world, rationally calculated effective responses according to the logic of necessity, and acted accordingly. In sum, in turning to stoicism I am turning not merely to an ancient ethical ideal, but to a profound influence upon both European and American modern cultures.[16]

Moreover, features of Kennan's language so often highlighted by historians and critics—language like *firmness*, *manliness*, *strength*, and *objectivity*—represent an ethical vocabulary whose history is impossible to tell without some reference to stoicism. To read Kennan at any point in his career is to be confronted with recurring commonplaces that are part of the ethic of stoicism: the need for a sober outlook on world affairs; the imperative of a long-term perspective on history; the problems of America's "legalism" and "moralism"; the trouble with public opinion, popular leadership, and mass media; the importance of a "balance of powers" in the world; a concern with the "mind-set" of other peoples and nations; and, above all, the primacy of America taking care of itself and living rationally within given limits. As these ideas were woven into Kennan's discourse, containment was more than merely a principle of counterforce vis-à-vis the Soviets. It was a way of seeing and being in the world, and thus came with normative as well as strictly instrumental imperatives. It entailed, as the conclusion to X insisted, Americans "pulling themselves together and accepting the responsibilities of moral and political leadership that history plainly intended them to bear."[17] Or, as LT stated, "Finally, we must have [the] courage and self-confidence to cling to our own methods and conceptions of human society."[18] To be sure, containment had military and other traditional strategic components, but it was something more than this. It was, at a minimum, very much like the sort of "grand strategy" that Kennedy describes, bringing together "all of the elements . . . for the preservation and enhancement of the nation's long-term . . . best interests."

Indeed, early in 1949 the Commission on the Organization of the Executive Branch of Government, known as the Hoover Commission after its chair, former president Herbert Hoover, submitted its findings to Congress, arguing that Truman's Policy Planning Staff, of which Kennan was director, needed to turn from day-to-day operational concerns to long-range planning. As Wilson D. Miscamble shows, Kennan embraced the recommendations—turning to issues of European integration, Britain's future, and the long-range issues of nuclear weapons—even as he would become frustrated with their implementation.[19] Thus, in the winter of 1949 he developed further a distinction he had made in "The Sources of Soviet Conduct" between "the momentary whims of democratic opinion" and "intelligent long-range policies," arguing that the nation should move beyond a focus on the means-ends "objectives" of foreign policy toward a "guiding element."[20] "It lies really," he argued in a public lecture at Dartmouth College, faintly echoing Washington, "in our concept of ourselves in relation to our world environment. It lies in the way we picture to ourselves our own personality as a nation, and the nature of the world around us, and our function as a member of the international community. It lies, if you will, in the way we cast ourselves, as one of the actors, in the drama of world history." Thus "containment" was forwarded as a kind of ethical script for America, embedded in a worldview. Indeed, he went on at Dartmouth to urge that his conclusions about state of world affairs entailed certain duties for America.

> Above all, they obligate us to greater modesty and greater humility in our estimate of ourselves. They obligate to fight over-confidence like the plague. They obligate us to watch out for comfortable and grand catchwords like "world leadership" and "selling democracy" and "raising living standards everywhere." They obligate us not to let the term "world peace" become an abstract thing, but rather to insist upon looking at it in the context of political realities. And finally, they obligate us to bear in mind that foreign policy is not a glamorous form of escape from the

unpleasantness of domestic problems, but that foreign policy begins at home. It begins with keeping the top-soil from sliding off these hills outside of Hanover here; it begins with clearing out the blight that is fastening on the big cities; it begins with finding democratic ways in which to channel the new leisure and the cash surpluses which are finding their way into the hands of people in this country into something more satisfying and more constructive than slot machines and the television sets.[21]

"We have got to save ourselves first," Kennan concluded, echoing the stoic "care of the self."

Almost forty years later, Kennan argued publicly again, this time in the pages of *Foreign Affairs,* that the spirit of his "containment" was much broader than a narrow strategy of resisting Soviet expansion. The language he used to describe this broader notion of containment strongly echoed that which he had used at Dartmouth.

There is much in our own life, here in this country, that needs early containment. It could, in fact, be said that the first thing we Americans need to learn to contain is, in some ways, ourselves: our own environmental destructiveness, our tendency to live beyond our means and to borrow ourselves into disaster, our apparent inability to reduce a devastating budgetary deficit, our comparable inability to control the immigration into our midst of great masses of people of wholly different cultural and political traditions.[22]

So containment was a political ethic. What John Lukacs has written of a Kennan foreign policy speech in 1953 can be said of Kennan's containment: "There was much more at stake here than foreign policy. Kennan's concerns were with nothing less than the mind and character of his native people."[23] The question before this chapter is what gave containment as a political ethic its motive force? In what sort of worldview did containment gain purchase upon the social imaginary of the nation? My turn to stoicism ventures an answer that not only helps make further sense of the motive force of containment, but helps account for the increasing scope of strategy in the modern age.

To be sure, if we are to take Kennan's (and Kennedy's) idea that strategy always entails thinking in excess of means-ends rationality, then we must pursue "containment" as more than a *mere* metaphor. Indeed, it was a metaphor, but one with historic, normative force that cannot be fully separated from modern developments in state sovereignty, democratic self-rule, and the rise of the welfare state. Thus, we should be cautious about concluding that Kennan's frequent criticisms of American culture were mere instances of a predilection for antidemocratic authoritarianism or, as several have suggested, residual romanticism.[24] Kennan's containment pushed a powerful worldview, inflected through realism and grand strategy, both toward its logical conclusions and its inevitable aporias. With respect to the former, if grand strategy includes the management of the national economy, concern with national morale and political culture, diplomatic effort, and the fostering of a national image abroad, then how could it not also entail, at its heart, the care of the national self, a notion born in modernity largely through neostoicism? But, with respect to the latter, how could this sort of self-care, to have national reach, be anything but historically and morally informed, and thus profoundly cultural and a "mere" metaphor? Kennan's "realism" was not betrayed by a strongly normative vision and tropological character; it was formed by it. Built into his realist framework of international anarchy and national sovereignty was not only the imperative of national self-care, but a historic image of the strong state, which stoicism, in particular, helps us better understand.

Stoicism, the State, and History

Stoicism's place in European and Anglo-American culture is diffuse but consequential. Its influences can be traced back to some of the most captivating concepts offered to us by ancient Greek thinkers, concepts like the rule of reason, the authority of nature (*physis*), and the Socratic call to "know thyself." In this regard, the prototype of the theory of "containment" derives not from philosophies of interstate relations per se, but from ancient Greek emphases on forms of self-containment. Plato's dialogues, composed against the backdrop of Athenian imperial crises, repeatedly return to themes of restraint before arbitrary forces via self-knowledge and the rule of reason. And for Plato such containment, though it began with an ethic, had unmistakable political implications. In *Gorgias,* for example, the political tyrant is portrayed as morally reproachable because he, more than any other type of personality, lacks true freedom and power over his own person, and therefore over the state. The egotistic tyrant, represented therein by Callicles, imagines that he knows what is good for him, but his notion of the good, which makes natural strength equivalent to justice, is delusional and therefore (self-) destructive. Discordance with the self is his original problem.[25] False belief rather than a true and realistic appraisal of things is the basis of his crimes.[26] His fault, at its core, is self-deception about the true nature of self-interest, and therefore the interest of the polis. The tyrant, claiming only to be doing that which is in his own interest, actually acts against his own interest because he knows neither the world as it is nor himself. Political disaster is the consequence.

Plato's famed philosopher-king in the *Republic* thus stands as a countertype to the tyrant. Indeed, the philosopher-king anticipates political realism inasmuch as he makes a disinterested appraisal of "reality" the arch-measure of his rule. Socrates claims, "And thus our State . . . will be administered in a spirit unlike that of other States, in which men fight with one another about shadows only and are distracted in the struggle for power, which in their eyes is a great good. Whereas the truth is that the State in which rulers are most reluctant to govern is always the best and most quietly governed, and the State in which they are most eager, the worst."[27] The argument of the *Republic* is for a polis wherein the political judgments of rulers are made in accord with a definitive reality, rather than a provisional situation, such that the outcomes of political judgment and action can finally be guaranteed. To be sure, while the *Republic* is an argument for an elitist politics, it is important to note, the argument of Karl Popper notwithstanding, that nothing in its basic premises would preclude a perfectly "free" society, as long as all shared the true knowledge of reality (which, of course, for Plato they do not).[28] Indeed, the philosopher-king has retained a degree of credibility even in the nonutopian, egalitarian-oriented societies of the modern West for reasons partly consistent with those that have made realism so compelling: both posit a normative connection between political rule and a decisive reality. Thus it is plausible to read Plato along with the ancient figurehead of modern-day realists, Thucydides, as intimating a political critique of imperial Athens in which its unnatural expansionism and illusory self-aggrandizement is blamed—the ethical, and indeed political, principle being that wherever a people seek to stretch beyond its nature, it produces evil consequences.

"Containment" in this sense has its provenance within a Socratic vision of ethical and political life, but it was stoicism, not Platonism, neo-Platonism, or Academic Skepticism, that came to represent the principal carrier of this tradition. In the thought of the ancient stoic philosopher Epictetus, Socrates' model of dispassionate strength, self-control, and commitment to reason amidst turmoil and trial stood as a preeminent exemplar.[29] "If you always remember what is yours and concerns someone else, you will never be disturbed," Epictetus advised, urging his own form of self-containment.[30] As Martha Nussbaum writes of stoic and other Hellenistic philosophical schools, "These philosophers claim that the pursuit of logical validity, intellectual coherence, and truth delivers freedom from the tyranny of custom and convention, creating a community of beings who can take charge of their own life story and their own thought."[31] Indeed, at the heart of the stoic ethic was a commitment to self-sufficiency that was also a commitment to freedom that was also a commitment to self-preservation. Because the ancient stoics presumed that ultimately there was a profound order (*logos*) to the world (behind the world of appearances, or *phantasmata*), they could advocate a life devoted to living according to nature that was also understood as a life of liberty. Indeed, to be virtuous was to be free, for it was to be controlled or constrained by no external force. The ethical person acts as she wishes not because she has managed to transcend contingencies and circumstances, but because through understanding and self-discipline she has learned to perfectly align subjective desires with objective actions and constraints. The stoic was never "carried away" by excessive emotion or unrealistic desire.[32] This, in turn, led to a form of self-preservation, understood as preserving the integrity of the highest faculty of the soul, the rational faculty. Through a life of freedom predicated on fidelity to reason, one could "show respect for what is most worthy in oneself, for what is most truly oneself," without asserting the subjective over the objective.[33] Be true to yourself, the stoics insisted, and you would be true to the world.

It is in this regard that stoicism has always entailed a critique of "moralism," seen as the assertion of a subjectively derived moral framework *over and against* nature. Stoics thus guarded against the overassertion of the self. "What we *should* take to be good or evil according to Stoicism . . . is only our own moral condition, our own virtue and vice, respectively."[34] The stoic moral life is in this sense profoundly oriented toward the care and criticism of the self. Moreover, morality meant restraining that faculty most characteristically effusive, the affections. Stoic vice entailed a pathetically driven excess of rational bounds (which, again, are the boundaries of reality); virtue entailed the rational containment of pathos. Morality and moral criticism was thus not simply a matter of conformity to a moral law. Rather, the moral life was a life of self-improvement, akin to exercise. Indeed, the self-improvement vocabulary developed by the stoics was allied to notions of masculine strength, fortitude, and constancy. As Nussbaum writes, in stoic thought we see philosophy associated with "*toning up* the soul—developing its muscles, assisting it to use its own capabilities more effectively."[35] Through reason, self-control, and *apatheia* "disorderly and disturbing motions of the soul" could be displaced by "calm and orderly" ones.[36] Not surprisingly, therefore, stoic thought was wedded to metaphors of medicine and therapy more than judicial metaphors of obedience to law. It, as Nussbaum has emphasized, "saw the philosopher as a compassionate physician whose arts could heal many types of human suffering."[37] Indeed, Nussbaum argues that the medical analogy was "more pervasive and more highly developed in Stoic texts than it is in those of any other Hellenistic school."[38] This developed vocabulary of pathology and therapy made stoicism the first full-fledged psychotherapy, or therapy of the soul.[39]

Yet, this therapeutic outlook produced a curious relationship to social critique, leading to a noticeable aporia within stoic thought: for society as well as the self constituted a source of pathologies. The human-made world, stoics assumed, was riddled with false conventions, irrational actors, and turbulent circumstances. Thus stoicism could never quite stop at the borders of the self. Its ideal of self-mastery was set in relation to the world without, and therefore often included a critique of society as well as practical strategies for coping with the indeterminacies and upheavals social life offered. "Say to yourself in the early morning," Marcus

Aurelius advised, "I shall meet today inquisitive, ungrateful, violent, treacherous, envious, uncharitable men. All these things have come upon them through ignorance of real good and ill."[40] Indeed, one major practical problem with stoicism was that it could not quite suffer its own call to self-sufficiency: it could be a thoroughly reactive ethic, motivated not simply by an aspiration to realize a true self, but equally, if not more so, by a desire to become subjectively invulnerable to the chaos and incertitude of the social world around. In practice, the line between coping with the human world and caring for the self was often unclear.

But whether the world or the self was in view, reason was seen as the preeminent disciplining power. This meant, importantly, that the philosopher's ethos could come to resemble that of the warrior, as with Marcus Aurelius. Indeed, some sixteen hundred years after the death of Aurelius, Immanuel Kant admired in the warrior what he no doubt saw the Enlightenment philosopher doing: he "shrinks from nothing . . . fears nothing, and therefore does not yield to danger, but rather goes to face it vigorously with the most complete deliberation."[41] Stoicism thus offered a flexible ideal of rational strength predicated on the mastery of emotions and, importantly, on a corresponding capacity to envision, in the midst of turbulent circumstances, some distant good and to act on that vision. Thus Justus Lipsius (1547–1606), the most important early-modern interpreter of stoic thought and a self-styled advisor to princes, urged that *constantia,* constancy, must accompany *prudentia,* prudence.[42] As Thomas Hobbes, under Lipsius's influence, argued in his *De Homine,*

> Emotions or *perturbations* of the mind are species of appetite or aversion, their differences having been taken from the diversity and circumstances of the objects we desire or shun. They are called *perturbations* because they frequently obstruct right reasoning. The obstruct right reasoning in this, that they militate against the real good and in favor of the apparent and most immediate good, which turns out frequently to be evil when everything associated with it hath been considered. . . . Therefore although the real good must be sought in the long term, which is the job of reason, appetite seizeth upon a present good without foreseeing the greater evils that necessarily attach to it. Therefore

appetite perturbs and impedes the operation of reason; whence it is rightly called a *perturbation*.[43]

Here we see in this early-modern text as clearly as in any ancient stoic work the rudiments of the stoic self: the capacity to reason rightly in light of "necessity" before perturbations within and apparent and immediately pressing evils, masking as goods, without. Stoic rational strength is thus principally a *deliberative* strength.[44]

This brings us to a closely related modern legacy of stoicism, a vital one for approaching Kennan, the conception of political society as a self. To be sure, the notion of the state as a singular body, a kind of self, precedes the neostoicism of the sixteenth and seventeenth centuries, for example, in the medieval writer John of Salisbury.[45] However, such medieval metaphors were less about a unified political society and more about the unity of a complex and diverse hierarchy, the right order of a great chain of being.[46] Amidst the political and religious upheaval of the early-modern period neostoics gave the metaphor new meaning and urgency as they presented the body politic as a unified soul, or self. For example, Lipsius argued for the preeminence of a monarchical form of government by quoting Tacitus, the Roman historian: "It seems that one body politic should be governed by one soul." "And the government by many," he added, "what do you think that brings? Chaos." Thus, he concluded (again citing Tacitus), "It serves the interest of peace if all power is concentrated in one person."[47] Here the neostoics advanced the argument for the "body politic" a step further than their medieval predecessors by justifying it in terms of political stability. Their argument, precisely speaking, was not one for social hierarchy per se (in the way that John of Salisbury argued), and it was certainly not one for managerial efficiency; rather it was one for the stability of union.

To be sure, neostoicism's linking of social stability to the unity of the body stretched back to the ancient stoics. For example, Aurelius argued that even before the treachery of others he must maintain an attitude of peace: "I [cannot] be angry with my kinsman or hate him; for we have come into the world to work together, like feet, like hands, like eyelids, like the rows of upper and lower teeth."[48] Such bodily metaphors reinforced stoic notions of the cosmopolis and enabled others under the influence of stoic thought, like St. Paul, to conceive of social bodies as selves in arguments for social harmony: "The body is a unit, though it is made up of many parts; and though all its parts are many, they form one body," St. Paul wrote to the quarrelsome ecclesial social body in Corinth.[49] Thus, when early-moderns like Lipsius and Hobbes envisioned the strong state as a stalwart self, they had biblical as well as classical proof texts. Hobbes recognized the artificiality of this metaphorical transference without scruple. The commonwealth (*civitas*), he wrote, is "an artificial man" and sovereignty "an artificial *soul*."[50] At its head and embodying its person was the sovereign, who would in Hobbes's vision of the social compact possess the exclusive right and complete liberty to "be judge both of the means of peace and defence, and of the hinderances, and disturbances of the same; and to do whatsover he shall think necessary to be done, both beforehand, for the preserving of peace and security, by prevention of discord at home, and hostility from abroad."[51] In this way, the sovereign enfolded society into a kind of national-security self composed of political strength, free power, self-sufficiency, and self-determination.

As John M. Cooper argues, here was prefigured the modern ideals of state autonomy and power as a means by which to eliminate "the external causes of the widespread mental pain and distress" of a commonwealth.[52] But it also prefigured a basic tenet of Niebuhrian realism, one that Kennan described as a "wholly sound observation," namely that "morality is not the same thing for an individual, responsible only to himself, as it is for a government."[53] The "self" that is the state is a transformed self, one that acts in the world according to different laws, even moral laws, than individual selves. If at the core of the neostoic project was the translation of the stoic psychological ideal into a *political* ideal, then this translation also entailed a transformation that helped form the norms of modern geopolitics. A strong, well-disciplined, and resilient state with complete freedom and confidence in matters of national security was conceived not only as the solution to national social and political ills, but Europe's ills more broadly. In this way, the neostoic ideal has reinforced realism's notion that states survive in the anarchic international arena through prudent rational action, predicated on relative freedom and sovereignty, and that a stable international order will consist of a balance of powers, where a strong state or federation of states functions to restrain the misuse of power by another strong state or alliance of states.

Lest, however, one quickly conclude that this neostoic concept of the state as a self could reinforce only a conservative order, John Locke's famous revolutionary chapter, "Of the Dissolution of Government," in his second treatise on government, seems to draw from the same well.

> That which makes the Community, and brings Men out of the loose state of Nature into *one Politick Society,* is the Agreement which every one has with the rest to incorporate and act as one Body and so be one distinct Commonwealth. The usual, and almost only way whereby *this Union is dissolved,* is the Inroad of Foreign Force making a Conquest upon them. For in that Case (not being able to maintain and support themselves, as *one intire* and *independent Body*) the Union belonging to that body, which consisted therein, must necessarily cease, and so every one return to the state he was in before, with a liberty to shift for himself and provide for his own Safety, as he thinks fit in some other Society.[54]

Locke goes onto argue as well that domestic kings, nobility, and even parliaments can de facto dissolve their own social body through the misuse of their power.[55] Yet, whether discussing externally or internally wrought dissolution, Locke's theory draws the same crucial connection as is seen in Hobbes: that between a unified political body and political stability. It is excess, whether in the form of a foreign force or an internal tyrannical one, that destroys the peace by not respecting the constituent unity of a body politic.

Coupled to the vision of a strong unified state was the detached, and often ironic, perspective on history bestowed by stoicism. In this way, Tacitus, who for seventeenth-century neostoics displaced Cicero as the chief exemplar, avowed in *The Annals of Imperial Rome* that his account of the dissembling, ruthless, and often outrageous political life of the Roman Empire would be carried out "without either bitterness or partiality, from any motives to which I am far removed."[56] Over a millennium and a half later, this statement reverberated in the pages of a work that Kennan considered to be one of his most important influences,

Edward Gibbon's *The Decline and Fall of the Roman Empire*.[57] Gibbon's work, which echoed Lipsius and other neostoics in its concern with "the triumph of barbarism and religion," professed to be a "candid and rational" account of the empire's decline. As J. B. Bury writes of Gibbon, "He hated excess, and the immoderation of the multitude. . . . In the spirit of Cicero or Tacitus he despised the superstitions of the vulgar, and regarded the unmeasured enthusiasm of the early Christians as many sober Churchmen regard the fanaticism of Islam" (xiii). With a critical style ironic and skeptical, Gibbon described in *The Decline* the gradual fall of "a polite and powerful empire" through "a slow and secret poison"—an apt stoic medical analogy (1:34, 44). The argument for "decline" hinged on a rather ideal portrait of the Empire at its supposed height. "If a man were called to fix the period in the history of the world during which the condition of the human race was most happy and prosperous, he would, without hesitation, name that which elapsed from the death of Domitian to the accession of Commodus" (1:61). This happiness, Gibbon argues, was due to a wise disciplining of the citizenry and the exercise of imperial restraint. The empire embraced a "moderate system" and fidelity to "those limits which nature seemed to have placed" as its boundaries (1:2). In military affairs, "it became the duty, as well as interest, of every Roman general, to guard the frontiers intrusted to his care without aspiring to conquests which might have proved no less fatal to himself than to the vanquished barbarians" (1:2). Through unified rule and careful affective balance, the empire achieved international tranquility: "The terror of the Roman arms added weight and dignity to the moderation of the emperors. They preserved peace by a constant preparation for war; and while justice regulated their conduct, they announced to the nations on their confines that they were as little disposed to endure as to offer injury" (1:6–7). Propelling Gibbon's narrative, therefore, was the image of the strong, well-disciplined state existing within its natural boundaries. If Lipsius began the transformation of stoicism into neostoicism, a philosophy of the state, and Hobbes dramatically furthered it, Gibbon, through his remarkable narrative, completed it.

Yet neostoicism near the end of eighteenth century was not restricted to bookish political philosophy and historiography. It represented a broader sentiment, a language within a political culture, and a mode of addressing the new world of nation-states. Indeed, the language of neostoicism can be found in the discourse of early American federalism, especially with regard to foreign relations. "Among the numerous advantages promised by a well constructed Union, none deserves to be more accurately developed than its tendency to break and control the violence of faction," James Madison began Federalist 10, still haunted by the terrors of religious and nationalist violence in Europe over a century before.[58] Alexander Hamilton's Federalist 11 explained the relationship of a strong Union to security: "A nation, despicable by its weakness, forfeits even the privilege of being neutral," he wrote. "Under a vigorous national government the natural strength and resources of the country, directed to a common interest, would baffle all the combinations of European jealousy to restrain our growth."[59] (Indeed, one can see here that "psychological warfare" has a much older lineage than most present-day studies permit.) So too, about a half-century later, was the attitude of Lincoln toward the slavery question, famously declaring, "'A house divided against itself cannot stand.' I believe this government cannot endure permanently half slave and half free. I do not expect the Union to be dissolved—I do not expect the house to fall—but I do expect it will cease to be divided. It will become all one thing, or all the other." In a neostoic manner, "House Divided" associated union with strength and peace, and division with weakness and violence. "If we stand firm, we *shall not fail*," Lincoln concluded.[60] Such language, which was used frequently in Lincoln's discourse, is indebted to the same notion of state-as-a-self found in Lipsius, Hobbes, Locke, and Gibbon.[61] Though stoicism was certainly not the exclusive source for such language, it was the most significant one, and it would eventually inform Kennan's conclusion to X: "Thus the decision will really fall in large measure in this country itself. The issue of Soviet-American relations is in essence a test of the over-all worth of the United States as a nation among nations. To avoid destruction the United States need only measure up to its own best traditions and prove itself worthy of preservation as a great nation" (582). Indeed, Kennan was but here rearticulating stoicism as a kind of "best tradition." "Only see to it," wrote Aurelius, "that you make a choice that will not betray you."[62] Kennan's cautious confidence at the conclusion of X reflected a self-assurance in the power of self-care.

Still, by the twentieth century the stoic spirit had undergone an important modification relative to its forerunners. In 1964, nearly two hundred years after Gibbon's *The Decline* was penned, Edmund Stillman and William Pfaff wrote in *The Politics of Hysteria,*

> Skepticism and stoicism (qualities largely lost in the political life of the modern West) are essential to arm men to endure the waste and perplexity of history; only they can save us from despair, or from the self-destroying recourse to a magical totalitarianism. They are not everything; they are not sovereign virtues. To recommend them is to leave much—perhaps nearly everything—about the nature and destiny of Western man unsaid, for belief, idealism, impatience, vision, are, for Western man at least, indispensable to politics. We could not practice politics without our determination to dominate the endless change and development of history. We of the West are a coercive culture—and will be so until the end. Our real hope lies not with exorcising ambition, but in moderating it and bending it in politics to finite ends. It is when our West loses grip on a prudent discrimination between real ambition and fantasy that we lose our grip on politics. Without prudence, we turn to political crime or error. We have seen this in the West time and again.[63]

Stillman and Pfaff's Cold War critique of political culture bore all the marks of neostoicism: a characterization of history as littered with disarray and delusion; a strong critique of the fanatical (or "hysterical") thrust of popular politics; a call for living within limits; an appeal to moderation, restraint, and realism; and an abiding sense of the perennial nature of political problems. Their critique, however, departed from older neostoic accounts of political life in one critical way: its assertion that "We of the West are a coercive culture—and will be so until the end." Seventeenth-century neostoic thought argued that humans would seek self-preservation above all. Stillman and Pfaff presume more than this; they argue that with respect to "the West," at least, peoples are driven by an ambition to dominate, coerce, and control.

This modification is crucial because it represents a shift from a political vision based at least nominally on "natural right" (the right to self-preservation) to one based on the abnormalities of a will to power. It is attributable to the influence of he whom I take to be the last great heir to the neostoic legacy, Sigmund Freud, whose *Civilization and Its Discontents* portrayed civilization itself as riddled with destructive tendencies, dangerous desires, and abnormal behaviors. His "pleasure principle" was set antagonistically over and against "the regulations of the universe," or the way things actually are in the world.[64] He argued that the "reality principle" mediated this conflict by accepting forms of suffering and deferring types of pleasure in order to achieve a more moderate state of satisfaction. In a passage with striking allusions Hobbes's primeval scene of the "war, as is of every man, against every man," Freud wrote in *Civilization and Its Discontents,*

> Against the suffering which may come upon one from human relationships the readiest safeguard is voluntary isolation, keeping oneself aloof from other people. The happiness which can be achieved along this path is, as we see, the happiness of quietness. Against the dreaded external world one can only defend oneself by some kind of turning away from it, if one intends to solve the task by oneself. There is, indeed, another and better path: that of becoming a member of the human community, and, with the help of a technique guided by science, going over to the attack against nature and subjecting her to the human will. Then one is working with all for the good of all.[65]

Indeed, a basic tension of stoicism is that between individual well-being and the possibility that community offers a "better path" toward its realization. Freud differed from the ancient stoics principally in his assertion that the universe is not ultimately in harmony with human flourishing. The *logos* of the cosmos is out of step with the *logos* of the human psyche. The latter, Freud asserted, is compelled by pleasure and necessity; the former resists satisfying the pleasure drive and makes necessities hard to get. Thus, as Firmin DeBrabander writes, "Whereas Stoic therapy is fatally optimistic, trumpeting the wise man's victory over fortune, . . . Freudian models of therapy call for resignation regarding our existential condition."[66] At the axis of the Freudian approach was therefore a form of care of the self that regulated subjectivity in order to moderate the inherent disharmonies of existence, especially social existence. As Howard L. Kaye has written, the "moral aim" of Freud "was not to satisfy our craving for order but to enhance our individual autonomy through greater intellectual clarity and self-consciousness, not as ends in themselves, but ultimately as a means of achieving the highest form of human life—a life of rational self-command and rational devotion to a transcendent cultural cause."[67]

Thus, Freud not only reinterpreted traditional neostoic notions of "interest" through a more perverse lens, he reinvigorated an old stoic style of looking at the world. "Freud," John Durham Peters writes, "could look at anything without losing heart and took great pride in this."[68] In this respect Freud followed closely in the footsteps of the ancient stoics that Gibbon and other neostoics so strongly admired. "And so," Aurelius mused, "if a man has a feeling for, and a deeper insight into the process of the Universe, there is hardly one but will somehow appear to present itself pleasantly to him. . . . Such a man also will feel no less pleasure in looking at the actual jaws of wild beasts than at the imitations which painters and sculptors exhibit."[69] Seneca wrote in similar vein, "The soul that is elevated and well regulated, that passes through any experience as if it counted for comparatively little, that smiles at all the things we fear or pray for, is impelled by a force that comes from heaven."[70] Indeed, stoicism's legacy in the twentieth century has been channeled largely through the Freud-like habit of experts to observe even the most malign and catastrophic events with clinical acuity.

Freud's influence on twentieth-century worries about crowd psychology, mass politics, and fanaticism is well known. The "managerial" class of the early and middle century owed its authority in great part to the idea that irrational forces needed to be rationally contained according to the best interest of society. Kennan disliked the social-scientific managerial approach; he thus sharply differed from many of his technocratic contemporaries.[71] However, he shared with them a concern with mass subjectivity. Indeed, at the heart of his political and analytical project in the postwar period was the problem of mass subjectivity. His "containment" derived from this problem, as did his approach to the whole question of America's role in the world.

Kennan and the Problem of Subjectivity

Sometime in the mid-1960s, around the same time Stillman and Pfaff published *The Politics of Hysteria,* Kennan scribbled down some observations regarding his "public philosophy." The notes, written in the truncated style of telegraphy he had used so often in his official diplomatic correspondence, were on the one hand deeply pessimistic. Referring directly to Freud, Kennan wrote of a "conflict between discipline of civilized life and certain inborn traits and instincts." "Two anarchical instincts," he claimed, dominated the human condition: the desire for sex and the lust for power. "For these reason, life can never be other than tragic." "Utopianism" he continued, was "almost criminally unforgivable. Life [is] hard enough, even though one looks at it realistically." Nevertheless, he described life as "eminently worth living." It is "a profoundly positive experience even to live tragically—so much so that I sometimes wonder if it could ever be so positive if it were not tragic." "Out of these components," he concluded, "I build my own public philosophy. I put at the center of it: need for preservation of human experience as such."[72]

Neostoics of the seventeenth century had put at the center of their philosophy the preservation of human life as such. Theirs was a philosophy of material safety and security. Kennan put the preservation of human *experience* at the heart of his public philosophy. His was a public philosophy of subjectivity. Indeed, the problem of subjectivity, especially what could be called national subjectivity, pervaded Kennan's work in the first two decades of the Cold War and drove his critiques of his contemporaries. Walter Hixson writes of Kennan in the mid-1950s, "Kennan still sought to contain communism across the globe but he doubted whether America possessed the maturity that was required to spearhead the struggle."[73] There was a profound pessimism in this doubt, one that found a hoped-for antidote in civility, maturity, integrity, reason, and respect. As Robert Ivie writes, "Kennan's response to the savagery of the human condition has been to advance the ideal of civility in the orderly and rational pursuit of national self-interests."[74] Yet the antidote was not merely a cure. It represented an end, an ideal, an aspirational horizon that gave worth to human life as such. As Kennan wrote in a draft lecture from 1964,

> Surely genuine dignity of behavior always has its deepest origins in the needs of the person who practices it and not in external compulsions. The main reasons for such things as integrity and courtesy in the approach to others is not that we should be able to live with others (although for this, too, they are important) but that we should be able to live with ourselves. We have an image of ourselves to nourish and preserve. On it depends our self-respect, and something even deeper which is hard to define but which might be called the ultimate affirmation of our right to live.[75]

Here we see national "behavior" cast out of the context of geopolitical struggles, national interests, and survival into the realm of an internal freedom oriented toward preservation of an ideal of the self and the affirmation of human life.

Indeed, the freedom of humans to pursue rightful, self-determined, and self-respecting ends drove Kennan's public philosophy and philosophy of international relations. "No outside power," he argued in a 1967 letter to Arthur Schlesinger concerning the United State's role in Vietnam, "can hope to do more than the government of that country can do for itself. It is impossible, in other words, for outsiders to help such a regime in a degree greater than it is willing and able to help itself."[76] More than a concession to the limits of international intervention and activism, such sentiments stretched into the realm of historical hope, for good and ill. "I am none the less convinced," Kennan wrote of the Russians but one year after his fateful telegram from Moscow, "that the capacity for free development is latent somewhere in the Russian soul and that only if it can be touched and brought into action will the Russians fulfill the tremendous role which I—for one—am sure history is reserving for them."[77] And this historical hope was not limited to the Americans, Europeans, and Soviets; nor was it limited to the agency of history. It extended to the manifestly oppressed on the continent of Africa, and to armchair policy thinking.

> You mention the color problem, and what you said came close to my thoughts. Again, with my proclivity for thinking the wrong things, I am bound to say I have a soft spot in my mind for *apartheid*—not as practiced in South Africa but as a concept. I would rather see the negroes

advance to self-respect and self-realization as a racial community than to witness the agonizing and unsuccessful efforts now being made in this country to find a proper place for them in our society by pretending to ignore the fact of their color.[78]

Thus a particular form of self-respecting, self-realizing "human experience" constituted a universal ideal for Kennan. It is in terms of this ideal, as much as in terms of his pessimistic assumptions about human nature, that we can approach Kennan's politics and policies. Indeed, in Kennan's work we see as clearly as in any figure of the Cold War the interdependency of pessimism and expectation, realism and idealism, a tempered pragmatism and an audacious hope. Was it through the tragic that Kennan proceeded toward a positive vision of human life, or was it the positive vision of human life that repeatedly disappointed, driving him back into despair?

In one of the preeminent studies of Kennan's thought, Anders Stephanson argues that Kennan was an "organic conservative." "Organic conservatism," he writes, "was part of a larger contradictory reaction to the coming of capitalist society which may be classed as romantic." Kennan's thought, according to Stephanson, represented the "right-wing form of the romantic current."[79] Indeed, passages like those above lead one to presume a sort of conservative, even reactionary, romanticism is at work. The problems with this view, however, were evident even to Stephanson himself, who explains the various ways in which Kennan ignored, minimized, or betrayed his apparent organic conservatism by arguing that Kennan was "consistently inconsistent."[80] Thus, while an organic approach would seem to prohibit a strong emphasis on external intervention in world affairs, Kennan advocated such interventions: for example, he was a principal architect of the Marshall Plan, heavily contributed to CIA designs in Eastern Europe, and supported U.S. propaganda efforts within the Soviet Union. Furthermore, Kennan was sharply critical of what he called "romantic nationalism," blaming it for the disintegration of Europe.[81] Finally, organic conservatism, as Stephanson explores, was quite at odds with the social and political structure of the United States that Kennan certainly questioned, but still dutifully worked within.[82]

These inconsistencies, however, gain a certain consistency if we assume that Kennan's principal commitment was to an ideal of an international system of strong states, not to the right to autonomy of any people that could claim "nationhood."[83] To be sure, the language of romantic conservatism is to be found in Kennan's corpus, but I want to argue that it operated beneath an overarching metaphor, formed in stoic traditions, of society as a self. My position discloses a broader consistency in Kennan's approach, without assuming that Kennan was a fully coherent thinker, including the consistency of the organic metaphors with Kennan's policy objectives. "Beware of the evils of speculation," Kennan wrote a young diplomat, "and remember that what you are studying is the personality of a living organism, in which every trait is the product and concomitant of every other trait. Let each of you, therefore, regard himself as a philosopher attempting to grasp the essence of the Soviet phenomenon."[84] For Kennan, organicism represented less an ideology than an attitude—the attitude that political units are finite and coherent, but complex. Like the stoic image of the soul, which could be harmoniously ruled by the rational faculty, and like the neostoic conception of the state, which could be peaceably governed by a prudent sovereign, more often than not Kennan's comparisons of state and society to organism and nature—which I take to be metaphorical rather than literal, the latter being the case in certain forms of romantic "bio-politics"—functioned to orient modes of practical thought and action rather than shape ideological reactions to the world.[85]

Indeed, Kennan's historical ideal for European society, the age of the Austro-Hungarian empire, represented a condition much nearer to the Hobbsian neostoic ideal than any romantic conservative organicism. In fact, Kennan argued that a form of romanticism had brought about the ruin of Europe. It engendered, in his words, "a new sort of nationalism, based no longer on the power and glamour of the ruling princely family, but rather on the group instincts and loyalties of the individual, particularly as they are related to the common bond of language." Imagining himself looking forward from the heyday of the Austro-Hungarian empire, Kennan described at the National War College in 1949 the ominous rise of romantic nationalism.

> This new emotional force is destined to sweep over Europe with a truly revolutionary effect. It is destined, in the course of time, to disintegrate

the multi-lingual empire of Austria and Hungary, to unite the thirty-three German-speaking principalities into a single dynamic state, and to leave France and the other seaboard countries of the European continent militarily outclassed, defensive-minded, clinging precariously and nervously to a bridgehead on the shores of the Atlantic, looking for their security to the powers of the Atlantic world which are at least conscious of having a stake in their survival.[86]

Kennan thus argued that romantic nationalism produced only a facade of the strong state, for while it could engender terrifying totalitarian regimes, its utopianism kept it from confronting the tragic nature of human existence and experiencing it positively. To be sure, Kennan could be a proponent of "racial community," ethnic solidarity, and forms of national pride. But these troubling aspects of his thought make some sense in light of the stoic virtues of self-respect, self-realization, self-sufficiency, and self-help—the core of his concept of maturity. Kennan seems to have held that a common collective identity was pragmatically helpful for groups of people to achieve together these virtues. He suggested, however, that romanticism's utopianism and organic literalism undermined rather than served this project.

If for Kennan self-respect, self-realization, and self-help represented arch virtues, romanticism was part of a triad of archvices. The two other vices were legalism and moralism. All three orientations, he believed, undermined a mature experience of the world. Romanticism, as I said, represented the chief problem Europe faced. In America, however, the main vices were legalism and moralism. Kennan held that Americans, less unified socially and politically, wrongly turned to legalism and moralism in order to generate group identity, national loyalty, and a meaningful existence in the modern world.

Kennan's best-known critique of legalism and moralism in America came in his 1951 *American Diplomacy*. The product of a series of lectures at the University of Chicago, *American Diplomacy*, in the words of Christopher Lasch, "set the tone of cold war historiography."[87] Although Lasch does not recognize it as such—he places the book within a "liberal" and "realist" tradition—that tone was thoroughly Gibbonian. In stoic fashion, Gibbon had described the decline of the Roman Empire in psychic and pathological terms: "This long peace, and the uniform government of the Romans, introduced a slow and secret poison into the vitals of the empire. The minds of men were gradually reduced to the same level, the fire of genius was extinguished, and even the military spirit evaporated."[88] So too Kennan's *American Diplomacy* began with a narrative arc of decline in American "consciousness," overlaying American history on top of Rome's:

> A half-century ago people in this country had a sense of security vis-à-vis their world environment such as I suppose no people had ever had since the days of the Roman Empire. Today that pattern is almost reversed—our national consciousness is dominated at present by a sense of insecurity greater than that of many of the peoples of western Europe who stand closer to, and in a position far more vulnerable to, those things that are the main source of our concern.[89]

The central aim of *American Diplomacy*, therefore, was to determine the causes behind this decline, and it is legalism and moralism that are portrayed as the principal pathologies. The book was framed as a history of significant moments in American diplomacy in the first half of the twentieth century; it read, however, as a set of morality tales for the Cold War.

The first chapter, "The War with Spain," warned against the dangers of an American "smugness" that produced both an expansionist appetite and legalistic discourse vis-à-vis world affairs (12). Kennan argued that the security America had enjoyed in the nineteenth century rested on a delicate combination of friendly relations with Canada and Britain together with a balance of power on the European continent (10). This situation meant that no European power could be both a dominant land and sea power, and thus engage in "an overseas expansion hostile to ourselves and supported by the immense resources of the interior of Europe and Asia" (10). Yet, he argued, nineteenth-century Americans did not recognize that their own security "had any foundations at all outside our continent" (11). They were "oblivious" (11). A "general torpor and smugness" typified America's attitude toward the world (12). Those who did have some inkling of understanding, he suggested, still did not recognize the power of "psychological and political reactions—of such things as fear, ambition, insecurity, jealousy, and perhaps even boredom—as prime movers of events" (11). And it was within this general oblivion and ignorance that the United States went to war with Spain in 1898. Indeed, he argued, it was above all American *public opinion* that brought about the war with Spain. Despite the lack of evidence that Spain was responsible for the sinking of the battleship *Maine,* Americans were "shocked and outraged." This, together with a leaked letter from Spain criticizing President McKinley, drove the United States into war. The decision to go to war, he concluded, was

> attributable to the state of American opinion, to the fact that it was a year of congressional elections, to the unabashed and really fantastic warmongering of a section of the American press, and to the political pressures which were freely and bluntly exerted on the President from various political quarters. (It is an interesting fact, incidentally, that financial and business circles, allegedly the instigators of war, had no part in this and generally frowned on the idea of our involvement in the hostilities.) (15–16)

All along, Kennan argued, "measures short of war" had not yet been exhausted (16). Furthermore, he lamented, this action represented "a turning point . . . in the whole concept of the American political system," as "1898 represented the first extensions of United States sovereignty to important territories beyond the continental limits of North America." The war with Spain represented the beginning of American colonialism abroad, and a new kind of American expansionism (18).

Yet Kennan went further, arguing that the war with Spain was the product of something more than a politics of hysteria. Behind all of this was "something deeper," a spirit of adventurism:

> American people of that day, or at least many of their more influential spokesmen, simply liked the smell of empire and felt an urge to range themselves among the colonial powers of the time, to see our flag flying on distant tropical isles, to feel the thrill of foreign adventure and authority, to bask in the sunshine of recognition as one of the great imperial powers of the world. (20–21)

Therefore the American public failed to heed the wisdom of those "anti-imperialists" of the time, who had argued that "the concept of the social compact has no business taking responsibility for people who have no place in that concept and who are supposed to appear on the scene in the role of subjects and not of citizens. Kings can have subjects; it is a question whether a republic can" (21). In this way, it was in republican terms that Kennan objected to America's bold entrance into imperialism at the turn of the century.

Republicanism, Kennan argued, "can extend only to people of our own kind—people who have grown up in the same peculiar spirit of independence and self-reliance, people who can accept, and enjoy, and content themselves with our institutions. In this case, the ruling of distant people is not our dish" (22). The argument is indeed a classic republican one, found, for example, in Kant's essay "To Perpetual Peace." "A nation," Kant argued, "is not (like the ground on which it is located) a possession. It is a society of men whom no one other than the nation itself can command or dispose of. Since, like a tree, each nation has its own roots, to incorporate it into another nation as a graft, denies its existence as a moral person. . . . Everyone is aware of the danger that this purported right of acquisition by the marriage of nations to one another . . . has brought to Europe."[90] Kant's objection to the legal binding of nations one to another through marriage, beneath the metaphor of a nation as a "moral person," anticipated Kennan's objection to "legalism." "One is moved to wonder," Kennan concluded his chapter on the war with Spain, "whether our most signal political failures as a nation have not lain in our attempts to establish a political bond of obligation between the main body of our people and other peoples or groups to whom, whether because we wished it so or because there was no other practical solution, we were not in a position to concede the full status of citizenship" (22). Legalism, Kennan suggested, was the ultimate American pathology with regard to the war with Spain, legitimating the nation's imperial appetite.

If chapter 1 of *American Diplomacy* can be read in this way as a morality tale about the dangers of legalism, chapter 2, "Mr. Hippisley and the Open Door," can be read as about the dangers of moralism. The chapter told the story of Secretary of State John Hay's announcement of an "Open Door" policy in China, a policy that frowned upon other powers making exclusive deals with the foreign power. Hay, Kennan argued, had been manipulated into pursuing the Open Door policy by Alfred Hippisley, a British customs official who Kennan claimed acted against the will of the official government of Great Britain (30). However, more troubling for Kennan than the manipulative nature of Hippisley's feat was that the Open Door policy gave Americans a sense of "resounding diplomatic triumph" and moral superiority in the world (33). In essence, Kennan asserted, the Open Door policy was a backward one, inconsistent with the changing circumstances of international affairs and at odds with America's own realistic responsibilities (36). Nevertheless, it went forward, ultimately because it fed America's strong sense of moral superiority. The core problem, Kennan's declared "central point," was "that the American public found no difficulty in accepting this action as a major diplomatic achievement. Its imagination was fired, its admiration won" (36).

In this way, Kennan concluded that both legalism and moralism were problems rooted in the American national consciousness. America's decline into a state of insecurity, fear, and uncertainty was the result of a turn-of-the-century pride and ignorance that comes before the fall. Indeed, it was the problem of American subjectivity that dominated the middle chapters of *American Diplomacy*. Chapter 3, "America and the Orient," chapter 4, "World War I," and chapter 5, "World War II," each returned to this issue. Of America's relations with China, Kennan wrote, "Looking backward, over a half-century of American diplomacy in the Far East, we see curious [and problematic] phenomena which undoubtedly have their origin in our own emotional complexes" (49). From World War I, Kennan held, we learn that "The counsels of impatience and hatred can always be supported by the crudest and cheapest symbols; for the counsels of moderation, the reasons are often intricate, rather than emotional, and difficult to explain" (56). And reflecting in *American Diplomacy* on his assessment of the postwar international situation in X, he wrote, "We were right about the nature of Soviet power; but we were wrong about the ability of American democracy at this stage in its history to bear for long a situation full of instability, inconvenience, and military danger" (76).

It is crucial at this juncture to note just how stoic Kennan's argument was in *American Diplomacy*. He did not argue that the world was in disarray because the relations of nations were irrational. Rather, he said at once that the nations were not fundamentally different from each other vis-à-vis their interests, and that they nevertheless could be dramatically different from each other subjectively, that is, with regard to culture, sentiment, language, and style. The book suggested that diplomacy should therefore seek as much as possible to communicate with others in terms of interests—interests constituted for him a kind of universal transcultural "language" that corresponded to his universal ideal of the strong, self-respecting state. Nations, especially nations very different from each other culturally, he suggested, should not rely in their relations on moral and legal language because such language was so unstable and culturally specific. However, as interests constituted a universal basis for state-to-state communications and negotiations, *self-interested action* was more or less identical and was universally recognizable. There was therefore in Kennan's argument an implicit ethics, so to speak, of interests, and one that was universal. In making this argument, Kennan, of course, articulated a "realist" perspective.[91] But in doing so he managed only to reframe the stoic idea that reason constitutes the universal faculty of the soul, that it dictates self-preservation, and that communities may achieve equilibrium inasmuch as they are guided by the rational pursuit of self-preservation, which culminates in self-respect.

Therefore *American Diplomacy* concluded with a call for "professionalism" in foreign affairs over and against the "legalistic-moralistic approach" (81–82). The former meant the institutional cultivation of "privacy, deliberateness, or the long-term approach" (82). The latter, he argued, was fraught with problems that prevented professionalism: it held "that it should be possible to suppress the chaotic and dangerous aspirations of governments in the international field by the acceptance of some system of legal rules and restraints" (83). It assumed that all states are alike (and like the United States) and reinforced romantic nationalism: "The very principle of 'one government, one vote,' regardless of physical or political differences between states, glorifies the concept of national sovereignty and makes it the exclusive form of participation in international life" (84). And it culminated in a static view of international life when in fact the "world environment is constantly changing," and so should organizational forms (85). However, Kennan concluded that the greatest problem with the legalistic-moralistic framework was "the inevitable association of legalistic ideas with moralistic ones: the carrying-over into the affairs of states of the concepts of right and wrong, the assumption that state behavior is a fit subject for moral judgment" (86–87). Indeed, it was Kennan's critique of moral judgment that stirred the strongest responses to *American Diplomacy,* and it was the question of morality that he repeatedly tried to clearly address in the subsequent years, always feeling that he had been misunderstood.

Arnold Toynbee, for example, celebrated *American Diplomacy* as "a sermon . . . against self-righteousness," but complained that Kennan's critique of moralism was at odds with the overall spirit of the book. In one of his most revealing statements about the issue, Kennan wrote Toynbee in reply,

> You are right in what you say about morality. I have wished many times that I had been more explicit about this. What I had in mind was our tendency to read moral values, positive or negative, into the national aspirations of other peoples and the behavior of other governments, and to do so on the basis of criteria highly subjective and inadequate. I have never meant to say that we Americans should not shape *our* behavior in a manner that conforms to our own sense of decency and dignity and generosity—that we should not comport ourselves, in other words, in such a manner that we live easily with ourselves and be satisfied in our national conscience. I believe that "right" consists in our being faithful to our best and simplest and most genuine American tradition, which most of us understand quite well. But I do not think that we can expect to know what is right and wrong in the behavior of other peoples. I feel rather that we must take that behavior as a natural phenomenon; to be understood rather than taken under the microscope of moral judgment; and that we should do our best to adjust to it without being disrespectful or spendthrift of our own interests. The best humanity can hope for, it seems to me, is an even and undramatic muddling along on its mysterious and unknowable paths, avoiding all that is abrupt, avoiding the great orgies of violence and acquire their own momentum and get out of hand.[92]

The sort of ethical vision that possessed Kennan was therefore one that was deeply skeptical of the "moral" because it was deeply suspicious of the motives, aptitudes, and judgments of the self. Kennan never quite claimed that there was no moral law; rather he insisted over and over that humans could not trust themselves to know it. The impulse was skeptical. The logic, however, was stoic. For rather than urge a life of contemplation so as to come to know the truth, Kennan argued for a practical ethic of detachment, disinterestedness, and "muddling along" in politics. As with the neostoics of the seventeenth century, a stoic subjectivity represented for Kennan the key not merely to personal tranquility, but to a more stable and constant social order, "avoiding all that is abrupt, avoiding the great orgies of violence."

But this was, as I suggested earlier, a stoicism inflected through Freud. Kennan's skepticism of legalism and moralism was supplemented by a skepticism of ideology. In a letter to Isaiah Berlin a year prior to the lectures of *American Diplomacy,* Kennan reflected on the causes of totalitarianism, and coupled them to the causes of American mass consumerism. Both, he mused, have to do with the "effects on people over a long period of time of a continued unscrupulous exploitation of the irrational sides of their nature." "Is skepticism rising?" he asked Berlin. Might skepticism represent the limit of hysterical mass politics? Russia, he argued, represented a case in point: there the secret police and terror had to assume the place of ideological manipulation, for the people of Russia had come to distrust the ideological claims of the Party. "Nature," however, persisted in exerting its power.

> Nature, it seems to me, has prescribed our objectives for us out of its own good judgment, and has decreed that we shall desire to remain alive, generally speaking as long as possible and to multiply our kind—simple and clear objectives, if not very inspiring. About all that we can do nothing, nor about the infinite ramifications of all that in the workings of the human ego. What we can do is to make sure that the pursuit of those objectives, in whatever sublimated forms they may appear, is conducted with methods characterized by a due humility in the sense of a recognition of our mortal weaknesses and susceptibility to error,

and by a consideration for all that in human personality which we recognized to be clear and more dignified and more hopeful.

Thus Kennan told Berlin that "the only vital and important distinctions in human behavior are distinctions of method, not objective."[93] The most basic objectives, whether for individuals or nations, were predetermined and intransigent. Methods, on the other hand, represented the attitudinal framework.

Kennan therefore held that the substance of the life of nations was given, but that style was contingent and indeed normative. "The conduct of foreign policy," he wrote Adlai Stevenson, "first of all, is like tennis: primarily a matter of style rather than of purpose. It is more a question of the 'how' than the 'what.'"[94] For Kennan the *how* made all the difference, in both an existential and an ethical sense. Existentially, he held that the "how" would determine whether humanity would find relative peace and freedom or ruin itself in disaster. Ethically, and in neostoic fashion, he held that a principled and prudent care of the self was paramount. Writing George Kateb in 1967, Kennan confessed, "I fear I have never yet properly stated my own view on the connection between morality and foreign policy. I don't object to our *acting* decently. I object only to our admiring ourselves publicly as we do, and I think it imprudent to try to hold other people up to our standards and concepts of morality." Admitting his place within what is essentially a neostoic tradition, Kennan wrote Kateb, "I think your observation that I am intellectually a conservative European shows much penetration."[95] "Conservative" here should not be confused with ideas of free-market libertarianism. In fact, in his letter to Berlin, Kennan expressed a degree of indifference about such matters: "Provided method accepts and clings to these restraints [of "due humility"]," he wrote, "I see no reason to fear the objective, whether it be a planned economy or the chaotic freedoms of American life."[96] Kennan's "conservatism" concerned attitude and style.

Kennan's allegiances, in sum, were to a *type*—a stoic type. In a 1944 letter to his friend Cyrus Vollmer, Kennan reported on a return trip he had made to a childhood stomping ground just before he was to leave the country again.

You would hardly know the place as it is now. . . . I have been out this morning to see the trees. With our evergreens—with most of them, at least—it is hard to tell the conditions of health. The littles [sic] stoics are slow in showing their reaction to anything; and if they stand up straight, you never know whether it's because they are feeling their oats or because they were propped up that way. I think most of them are doing very well; although those that you and I planted were almost all bent over by the strong north wind that blew on the day after they were set in.

As for walnuts, planted in the long grass across the little stream, their development varies. Some are putting forth leaflets and thrusting themselves up with the most uninhibited abandon. Those I call the extroverts. They accept the strange soil and the strange environment as a matter of course. They ask no questions and entertain no anxieties. If not dragged down by some catastrophe, they will get more sunshine, and eventually crowd many of the others out. But they, the children of fortune, will be relatively easy meat for the pests. And their fruit will be, like California fruits—human and otherwise, big and lush and relatively tasteless.

Others of the walnuts are still meek and troubled little creatures, hiding away in the deep grass, putting out only two or three modest shoots to essay the fortunes—and reap the blessings—of this world. Many of these will suffer, and many will not last at all. But to them that last shall be given gifts that no extrovert can boast of: inner strength, and fortitude born out of suffering, and great persistence. And their fruit, fine-flavored and delicate, will be the prize of the epicures.

That my dear Cyrus, ends my little Sunday morning sermon; and I hope it gives you greater consolation than I myself derive from it. I am apparently going abroad again soon: very far, and for a long time; and I am sad to think how little I am leaving behind in this country, besides these neglected acres, which could draw me back again.[97]

Only two years later Kennan would compose another typological analysis, his "long telegram" to the secretary of state. Written on the heels of Stalin's election speech and in response to the USSR's refusal to join the

World Bank and International Monetary Fund, Kennan's "long telegram," too, hinged on an allegiance to the stoic type.

Containment and Constancy

John Lewis Gaddis has written of the LT, "Rarely in the course of diplomacy does an individual manage to express, within a single document, ideas of such force and persuasiveness that they immediately change a nation's foreign policy. That was the effect, though, of the 8,000-word telegram dispatched from Moscow by Kennan on February 22, 1946."[98] To this remark one could add that it is rare for a single diplomatic document to receive the scope of scholarly treatment the LT has. Together with Winston Churchill's "Iron Curtain" speech, it has been approached as having almost constitutional status in the Cold War.[99] This said, its influence, meaning, and reputation is impossible to measure apart from X, the subsequent public elaboration of the ideas of the LT. Indeed, the LT and X are as near to each other in their rhetorical legacy as are the Declaration of Independence and the U.S. Constitution. To read one is to be possessed by the words of the other.

But there was a third possession, so to speak, that of stoicism, which constitutes the spirit of Kennan's LT, X, and the notion of "containment" these document conspired to produce. The background vision, the grounds of judgment, the ideational and rhetorical landscape upon which Kennan built his argument was the sort of neostoic ethic I have described. In the winter of 1946 and the summer of 1947 Kennan offered first the U.S. government, and then the U.S. public, respectively, a study in "political personality," ostensibly that of the Soviet leaders.[100] But the scope of the argument reached well beyond the Soviets. Kennan's allegiances, I have argued, were to a stoic type; in this vein, the aspiration of his pivotal policy statements was to advocate a reformation of American, and thus the balance of international, subjectivity. But even as the LT and X addressed the problem of subjectivity, advocating a stoic attitude, just as importantly they *performed* for readers a stoic subjectivity. Whatever criticisms the LT and X deserve, they do not warrant criticism of inconsistency vis-à-vis form and function.

X was presented in the pages of *Foreign Affairs* as the international bipolarity that would characterize the next forty-plus years was coming into clear relief: in 1947 Poland rejected participation in the Marshall Plan and the rule there of a Communist-Socialist coalition was solidified, the Soviet bloc strengthened its political and ideological ties vis-à-vis Cominform, the Truman Doctrine was announced, and Walter Lippmann popularized the phrase *the Cold War* in the United States with a book of the same name.[101] As the lines of the Cold War were hardened in these contentious ways, X presented a cool study in "political personality." Indeed, the original title of "The Sources of Soviet Conduct" was "Psychological Background of Soviet Foreign Policy."[102] Similarly, the LT presented itself as a study of "Soviet outlook" (344). Kennan's reports, however, were more specific in aim than these broad declarations suggest. They were studies of *pathological* political personality, and not simply a Soviet one. Indeed, Kennan drew heavily upon the commonplaces of psychotherapy, and his conspicuous clinical posture signaled a concern about American pathology. "Our first step must be to apprehend, and recognize for what it is, the nature of the movement with which we are dealing. We must study it with same courage, detachment, objectivity, and same determination not to be emotionally provoked or unseated by it, with which doctor studies unruly, and unreasonable individual" (LT 708). Kennan's clinical posture was in some respects merely the expression of his habitual analytical attitude—he regularly stressed the importance of distance, cool reason, and keen intelligence in foreign affairs thinking, and habitually used categories, types, and generalizations in his analyses. However, by 1946 this clinical stance carried with it as well a concern that the United States would be fatally duped by the Soviets. In a 1945 telegram to Secretary of State Edward Stettinius about relations with China, Kennan urged an attitude of clinical objectivity with regard to the Soviets as a bulwark against America's international anxieties. He warned against "undue reliance on Russian aid" with regard to China, and described the "tragic" potential of the combination of "our natural anxiety for Russian support" and "Stalin's cautious affability and his use of words which mean all things to all people." "I think it is our obligation," he wrote, anticipating the LT and X, "to study with clinical objectivity the real character and the ultimate implications for ourselves of these Russian views and aims concerning the Far East."[103]

Kennan's clinical posture, therefore, was not simply an aspect of his own character as an analyst; it was a means of registering a worry about, and offering a subtle warning against, pathological American behavior in the world of nations. In this way, the LT and X culminated in challenges to the United States to address the Soviet problem with "courage and self-confidence," with Americans "pulling themselves together and accepting the responsibilities of moral and political leadership" (LT 709, X 582). The essence of his argument, as Kennan later wrote, was that "what has to be done lies not with relation to Russia but within ourselves—within our own national societies and within the pattern of relations among the free nations. Let us find health and vigor and hope, and the diseased portion of the earth will fall behind of its own doing."[104] Herein lies the ethical logic of containment: care for the self and the rest of the world will "fall behind."

As Robert Ivie has shown, this argument rested on a metaphorical association between the health of persons and those of states.[105] But the success of this association depended on the prior strength of an analogy between selves and societies, the same analogy Hobbes relied upon. The LT's and X's strongest argument for the validity of this analogy came not explicitly, but implicitly through the analysis of the Soviet pathological personality itself. To address a society as if it were a personality is to presume the validity of the analogy; to do so poignantly and persuasively is to, in turn, validate the analogy before readers. Kennan's arguments, at their ethical core, rested upon the strength of this analogy, and not on his analysis of Soviet "political personality" or "outlook" itself. For if the analogy could stand, Kennan could then call upon his U.S. audiences to consider most important their own self-care.

It was an analysis of the Soviet pathological personality that quantitatively dominated the LT and X. The Soviet personality, X began, is "the product of ideology and circumstances" that belies reduction to either one or the other (566). Thus, as Lynn Hinds and Theodore Windt have argued, Kennan provided an "ideological analysis" in LT of Soviet motives when others like Charles Bohlen were focusing on Soviet self-interest and self-protection.[106] Nevertheless, what is surprising about X and the LT given the ideological legacy Hinds and Windt stress is the extent to which Kennan claimed that the sources of Soviet behavior lay deeper than either ideology or circumstance. Communist "ideology" was presented in psychological terms as "a highly convenient rationalization for . . . instinctive desires" (X 567), and "circumstances" were made fundamentally topographical: "At bottom of Kremlin's neurotic view of world affairs," Kennan wrote in the LT, "is traditional and instinctive Russian sense of insecurity. Originally, this was insecurity of a peaceful agricultural people trying to live on vast exposed plain in neighborhood of fierce nomadic peoples" (699). The suspicion and antipathy of Russia's encounters with the West, Kennan argued in the LT, were fueled by this basic nomadic pathology.

> To this [nomadic experience] was added, as Russia came into contact with economically advanced West, fear of more competent, more powerful, more highly organized societies in that area. But this latter type of insecurity was one which afflicted rather Russian rulers than Russian people; for Russian rulers have invariably sensed that their rule was relatively archaic in form fragile and artificial in its psychological foundation, unable to stand comparison or contact with political systems of Western countries. For this reason they have always feared foreign penetration, feared direct contact between Western world and their own, feared what would happen if Russians learned truth about world without or if foreigners learned truth about world within. And they have learned to seek security only in patient but deadly struggle for total destruction of rival power, never in compacts and compromises with it. (699)

In this way, Kennan argued that beneath ideology and circumstance stood power and fear, or "insecurity."[107] Importantly, insecurity emerged in this way, as it did elsewhere in Kennan's analyses, as neurosis, a sickness of the soul. In Kennan's logic, there is no such thing as "healthy insecurity." Rather, there are "interests." Interests are rational; insecurities, on the contrary, emotive and instinctual. The key to a healthy national life was for him the rational management of emotion and instinct, or the rule of interests.

In this way, as has often been noted, the LT and X presented the Soviets as fundamentally irrational. They were, however, not merely diseased, neurotic, and degenerate. They were, in Kennan's argument, the latest, and perhaps greatest, instantiation of the archenemy of seventeenth- and eighteenth-century neostoics, fanaticism and barbarism. The Russian revolutionaries, Kennan argued, found in Marxism only a "pseudo-scientific justification" for the instinctual pursuit of revenge and power (567). "This is a phenomenon as old as human nature itself," Kennan explained in X.

> It has never been more aptly described than by Edward Gibbon, who wrote in "The Decline and Fall of the Roman Empire": "From enthusiasm to imposture the step is perilous and slippery; the demon of Socrates affords a memorable instance how a wise man may deceive himself, how a good man may deceive others, how the conscience may slumber in a mixed and middle state between self-illusion and voluntary fraud." (567)

Thus, he argued the most basic problem with the postwar Soviet outlook was a perennial human one of self-illusion. As Kennan stated in the LT, "Premises on which this party line is based are for most part simply not true" (698).

Kennan thus argued that the Soviets would not see the world as it is. It was not precisely, he suggested, that they could not see the reality of power politics or understand the logic of interest; it was that they could not be psychologically at ease amidst the brute fact of plurality, difference, or otherness. They had, Kennan wrote, adopted a "particular brand of fanaticism, unmodified by any of the Anglo-Saxon traditions of compromise" (X 568). "They carried with them," he continued, "a skepticism as to the possibilities of permanent and peaceful coexistence of rival forces" (568). Kennan held that for the Soviets both domestic and international power was seen as viable only in monolithic form, producing dictatorship at home and aggressive antagonism abroad (see 570). And this mentality, he argued, included a strong epistemological dimension, underlying the Kremlin's claims to infallibility and its pursuit of "iron discipline" (573). "The Soviet concept of power, which permits no focal points of organization outside the Party itself, requires that the Party leadership remain in theory the sole repository of truth. For if truth were to be found elsewhere, there would be justification for its expression in organized activity" (573). This "fanaticism," he argued, paradoxically produced behaviorism:

> The accumulative effect of these factors is to give to the whole subordinate apparatus of Soviet power an unshakeable stubbornness and steadfastness in its orientation. This orientation can be changed at will by the Kremlin but by no other power. . . . The individuals who are the components of this machine are unamenable to argument or reason which comes to them from outside sources. Their whole training has taught them to mistrust and discount the glib persuasiveness of the outside world. Like the white dog before the phonograph, they hear only the "master's voice." (574)

Indeed, this reference to behaviorism was consistent with Kennan's ethical argument, for the social-scientific experiments and philosophical doctrines of behaviorism were premised on precisely the opposite of those premises he valued. Behaviorism systematically excluded from the domain of inquiry internal psychological processes, subjective attitudes, or states of mind. It thus denied outright the vision of ethical freedom upon which Kennan constructed his approach to the Cold War. Behaviorism, Kennan suggested, was the paradoxical progeny of fanaticism, for both deny the essential integrity and core importance—envisioned in terms of self or society—of subjective freedom and its rational management.

Kennan's appeal to "containment" in X was not merely set against this ethical backdrop; it was explicitly situated within it. The now legendary line from X stated, "In these circumstances it is clear that the main element of any United States policy toward the Soviet Union must be that of a long-term, patient but firm and vigilant containment of Russian expansive tendencies" (575). Logically, Kennan's call for containment as a grand strategy depended upon the existence of a set of "circumstances" that made the imperative of containment "clear." Grammatically, the antecedent of "these circumstances" was placed, *in nuce,* in the paragraph immediately prior. Of Soviet diplomacy, Kennan wrote,

> On the one hand it is more sensitive to contrary force, more ready to yield on individual sectors of the diplomatic front when that force is

felt to be too strong, and thus more rational in the logic and rhetoric of power. On the other hand it cannot be easily defeated or discouraged by a single victory on the part of its opponents. And the patient persistence by which it is animated means that it can be effectively countered not by sporadic acts which represent the momentary whims of democratic opinion but only by intelligent long-range policies on the part of Russia's adversaries, policies no less steady in their purpose, and no less variegated and resourceful in their application, than those of the Soviet Union itself. (575)

Anticipating the critique of *American Diplomacy*, the central binary of X, its pivotal conflict, was not that between the United States and the USSR, but that between "the momentary whims of democratic opinion" and "intelligent long-range policies." Ivie finds in phrases like this in Kennan's work a political realism that "depends upon a lurid distortion of democratic life."[108] To be sure, there was a way in which Kennan's realism remained "in the clouds," and was thus out of touch with the conditions of the actually existing midcentury American democracy. And yet it should not therefore be forgotten that the distinction between "the momentary whims of democratic opinion" and "intelligent long-range policies" could be made *within* a democratic outlook, as the latter form of deliberative strength is central to the distinctly democratic virtue of self-rule.

Likewise, within the immediate internal context of X, the central phrase of its legendary sentence was not "containment of Russian expansive tendencies" but rather "long-term, patient but firm and vigilant." X, in its compositional structure, revealed that Kennan's strategy, called *containment*, a term recognizable in strategic circles, was in fact a strategy of constancy, which in the seventeenth-century revival of stoic thought consisted of the cultivation of reliance upon the self as a dependable, rational, and immovable force in the world.[109] Consistent with the ambition of grand strategy, which seeks to organize a nation for successful being in the world, Kennan's aims in X transcended the Soviets per se. X was a call to a form of subjectivity nurtured historically by stoicism, one that much stronger proponents of democratic self-rule than Kennan have embraced.

This was no less the case in LT. Every one of its five concluding recommendations was concerned principally with the problem of subjectivity.

Kennan claimed that whatever policies might follow, the ultimate tasks of America were subjective in nature. The first duty the United States had, he argued, was to approach the problem with the Soviets "with the same courage, detachment, objectivity, and same determination not to be emotionally provoked or unseated by it, with which the doctor studies an unruly and unreasonable individual" (708). Second was to "see that our public is educated to realities of Russian situation," in order to overcome "hysterical anti-Sovietism" (708). Third, he explained that because Communism functioned parasitically, "Much depends on health and vigor of our own society." However, for Kennan, this "public health" policy was not, as it would be for Truman in the Truman Doctrine speech, primarily a matter of prophylactics.[110] Rather it was a matter of exercise, of self-care: "Every courageous and incisive measure to solve internal problems of our own society, to improve self-confidence, discipline, morale and community spirit of our own people, is a diplomatic victory over Moscow worth a thousand diplomatic notes and joint communiqués" (708). And of "positive thinking"—for, fourth, he called upon the United States to "formulate and put forward for other nations a much more positive and constructive picture of sort of world we would like to see than we have put forward in past." And lastly, repeating once again what he had said before, he concluded by summarizing the pivotal logic of his strategic vision: "Finally we must have courage and self-confidence to cling to our own methods and conceptions of human society. After all, the greatest danger that can befall us in coping with this problem of Soviet communism, is that we shall allow ourselves to become like those with whom we are coping" (709). The clear call of the LT was a call to a type of national—and more broadly cultural—health that was synonymous with character. This was much more than a mere contingent "psychological" strategy; it was the expression of a vision of integrity and well-being that Kennan would later describe as the "profoundly positive experience" of living tragically.[111]

The picture of the Soviets that emerged from the LT and X was both logically and rhetorically subordinate to Kennan's overarching ethical concerns. Logically, because the vision he articulated did not depend on the existence of Soviet Communism per se, but upon the mere existence of anarchical instincts within human society. Rhetorically, because the pernicious and powerful picture of the Soviets that Kennan constructed in the LT and X served not merely to analyze, but to dramatize, the ethical task before the nation. What is so remarkable about these Cold War documents is that they did not so much prescribe in detail a strategic approach as they powerfully performed a normative subjective response to the disease and disorder of the world. The LT and X, in other words, were more exemplary than they were explanatory.

Kennan's arguments in the LT, echoed in X—that the Soviets are insecure and irrational, driven by impulses to defend and repress; that their Marxism is merely a "trapping," albeit an exceedingly dangerous one; and that their hostilities and insecurities are "centuries old," rooted in the land and an "atmosphere of oriental secretiveness and conspiracy"—make the Soviets titanic, intractable, and strangely awe-inspiring (700–701). They have at their disposal "infinite" means of deception (701); they are immune to "objective truth" because they do not believe in it (701); they are driven by an insatiable appetite for power (702–703); they are destructive, seeking to undermine the West at every turn and to "tear down sources of strength beyond reach of Soviet control" (702, 706); and they posses "a police regime par excellence" (706). The Soviets, in sum, are "undoubtedly the greatest task our diplomacy has ever faced and probably the greatest it will every have to face" (707).

What should be the American attitude toward this gargantuan challenge? Kennan answered by arguing, first, that "the problem is within our power to solve." The Soviets, though irrational, are "highly sensitive to the logic of force," and therefore the United States can coerce them into cooperation. Furthermore, they suffer from relative weakness when compared to the "Western world as a whole," and the internal strength of the Soviet system is still tenuous. Finally, Soviet propaganda, because it is "basically negative and destructive," should "therefore be relatively easy to combat by any intelligent and really constructive program" (707). Therefore, Kennan concluded, "I think we may approach calmly and with good heart the problem of how to deal with Russia" (708). Kennan created a monster only to stare it coolly in the face. Self-mastery was thus made evident: sober, confident, competent, and in control. In this way, Kennan demonstrated for his audiences precisely the way of seeing and being in the world he wished America and its allies would adopt.

Social Control as Self-Control

Much can be learned about public cultures by looking at the reception of texts circulated within them. Conversely, much can be learned about texts by looking at their reception in public cultures. Without question, Kennan's X struck a cultural chord, giving rise to a Cold War strategy—ostensibly *the* Cold War strategy—that took many twists and turns, providing very able historians and scholars of strategy ample material for examination. As should be apparent by now, my own study here of the stoic spirit of containment is not intended to be a contribution to the particular history of containment as it was variously implemented by the U.S. government together with its allies. Nevertheless, I do want to insist that my argument is relevant to such study. Without stoicism, I am arguing, we would never have had Kennan's containment. Kennan's thinking—through Gibbon preeminently, but also through Freud, contemporaries like Hans Morgenthau and Reinhold Niebuhr, and broader stoic sentiments pervading European and Anglo-American culture during the first half of the twentieth century—was profoundly indebted to the ancient stoic ideals of self-respect, self-realization, self-sufficiency, and self-help.[112] In this way, the oft-noted "psychological" emphases of Kennan's thought are not merely the product of the curious twentieth-century obsession with therapy, personality, and behavior, but derivatives of an older European—and indeed American—sentiment that well-being begins with the rational care of the self, that emotions (especially strong ones) and mass populations (especially hysterical ones) are to be kept in check, and that the best state, whether for self or society, is one that can look upon and act within the world without either being carried away or falling apart.

The stoic ideal is a historically dense and complex one. It entails a repertoire of practical strategies for dealing with the upheavals and disturbances of souls and societies that seem to perennially undermine social well-being, not by remaking the world, but by disciplining what "is." It was therefore ideationally and historically critical to the early-modern roots of what is now often called *Realpolitik* as well as the logics of *raison d'état*, interest, and power politics. As containment adapted and articulated this history, it drew on the vitality of a long-standing cultural common sense, one so powerful as to be a near-tautology. This common sense can be said to have functioned mythically, that is, as an enduring and compelling "pattern of events."[113] The stoic worldview, in mythic form, begins with a crisis confrontation of a self with the world, proceeds toward a reinterpretation of the confrontation as a crisis of the self, and culminates in a disciplining of the self that represents conformity to the true nature of the world. Kennan's LT and X retold this myth, adapting it, like all effective retellings, to the circumstances of a complex geopolitical crisis. LT and X did what works that are transfigured from "myth" to "literature" do—they found a new poetic form to complement and reinforce the ancient narrative pattern of events.

The LT and X were also well timed. Stoicism was in mid-twentieth-century America, despite Stillman and Pfaff's claim that it had been "lost," a particularly compelling worldview. Especially after the advent of the Soviet bomb in 1949, social-scientific research into the consequences and management of disaster dramatically accelerated. These research programs shared the goals of creating a rigorously scientific approach to disaster research and of devising means, based on scientific findings, whereby the public could be taught to act both "freely" and "rationally" in the event of a catastrophe. Driving disaster research of the period was essentially a concern to make the American public into the image of the stoic. In this vein, Edward Bernays, the nephew of Sigmund Freud, envisioned "The Manhattan Project of Social Sciences." In his supporter Hornell Hart's words, the project would produce an "ideal social science" that could "point out with high reliability who is to do what, under what circumstances, in order that civilization may survive and continue to progress" amidst the atomic crisis.[114] In 1949, Hart stressed in *The Journal of Social Issues* that a principal way by which to establish such "social control" would be, as Kennan had advised in the LT, through a public education campaign that would bring citizens to freely choose to act rationally in crisis.[115] Social control would thus be self-control writ large, as rationality confronted irrationality and freedom faced up to fanatical tyranny. Thus, to magnify the character of the crisis, Hart parroted Kennan:

> Most American students of Russo-American relations would probably agree that the effective leaders of Russia, at present, have certain

attitudes which make it extremely difficult to establish world law and order by mutual consent. Such attitudes would include the Russian belief that non-Communistic countries are incurably hostile toward Russia, that no promises made to Russia by such countries can be trusted, that the Russian people should have no access to facts and opinions except such as the Politbureau [sic] provides for them, that democratic processes in non-Communistic countries and in international agencies should be used to destroy democracy, that capitalism is headed for collapse in which Communism will triumph, and so on.[116]

What is striking about this approach to "social control" is its capacity to enlist as well as criticize the "democratic." Like the argument in Plato's *Republic* for the philosopher-king, elitism is not necessarily its first and fundamental premise. Rather, it entailed the correspondence of freedom with an ideal of a well-composed soul, thus driving a social-scientific agenda that could be presented, in spirit if not practice, within the scope of democratic self-rule. For social scientists like Hart, as for Kennan, democratic whims could be criticized even as a democratic ideal could be propagated.

Five years later, in 1954, the same journal devoted an entire issue to "Human Behavior in Disaster: A New Field of Social Research." M. Brewster Smith, general editor of the journal, described the task before social scientists as "submitting the inconceivably terrible to scientific scrutiny." Only then will social scientists live up to their responsibility as the "social guardians of rationality."[117] For these thinkers, guarding rationality meant its dissemination en masse. It therefore meant, in one respect, creating a public that could mimic the scientist's own ability to submit the inconceivably terrible to a scientific gaze. Thus, Irving L. Janis wrote in the 1954 issue of *The Journal of Social Issues* that the great problem facing the public was malign patterns of emotional behavior in the face of disaster. People's "reaction patterns" to catastrophe lead to interference with "the person's ability to perceive reality correctly, to appraise the safe and dangerous features of his environment, to plan realistically for the future, to control one's socially unacceptable impulses, to take account of the consequences of alternative courses of action, and so on."[118] At the same time, Cold War realists like Kennan, Morgenthau, and Niebuhr were urging rational but "tragic" approaches to international relations. Stoicism is a major reason why they and their successors were able to claim simultaneously that their approaches were thoroughly modern and in accord with the most rigorous methods of the social sciences *and* that their political tradition reached back all the way to ancient Greece. It is also a major reason why they could profess to be operating within the sphere of the democratic, urging self-rule even as they were deeply critical of American popular sentiment and opinion.

A 1953 *Collier's* article written by a U.S. Civil Defense administrator reveals just how powerful and flexible the call to stoic subjectivity had become. Val Peterson, in "Panic: The Ultimate Weapon?" decried that "mass panic—not the A-bomb" might be the "ultimate weapon" that could be used by the Soviets against the United States and prescribed, in response, an unambiguously stoic remedy: "Some say that the snowy owl is the most panic-proof animal in creation." "Curiously," the article continued, "tests have shown that the closest counterpart to the unpanicky owl is the cowboy of the Western high plateaus, where the lonely spaces seem to weave into men an attitude of stoic calmness."[119] The *Collier's* article reveals not only the strong emergence of a stoic attitude with respect to the Cold War in America, but the convergence of myth, science, public administration, and public rhetoric. Social scientists represented not only the hope of a rational way of dealing with the atomic crisis, but mimicked, in a strange way, the mythical stoicism of the American cowboy on the plateau. Cowboys, scientists, and soldiers together emerged as models for public emulation. Thus, by the mid-1950s Kennan's vision of an intractable and monumental enemy had become a common vision, and his stoicism a regnant Cold War attitude.

Kennan's LT and X were therefore part of a much larger historical cultural dynamic, rather than the remarkable cause of a new way of thinking about America, American subjectivity, or the life of nations. Kennan's stoicism addressed the felt-need among war-weary policymakers for a renewed attitude and outlook before a new international crisis. It did the same for a war-weary but triumphant American public. And it could do so by claiming for itself the democratic virtue of self-rule. Indeed, Kennan's articulation of containment magnified America's triumphant song, even as he would rebuke smugness, arrogance, and ignorance. It did so by holding out the image of a self-reliant, stalwart nation—a "great soul" in a world of crises.

Conclusion

Within the world of strategy, one of the merits of Kennan's stoicism was its emphasis on nonreactivity, or what the ancient stoics called *apatheia*. The deliberations of policymakers during the Truman and Eisenhower administrations were riddled with strategic and tactical logics that began with the actions or apparent actions of the Soviets and then proffered reactions: the Soviets had done X, the argument went, so we must do Y. Indeed, this was the imperative logic of the nuclear arms race, and not coincidentally Kennan would end up strongly opposing its acceleration. Among other things, the aggressive arms race violated for him the cardinal rule of nonreactivity; he envisioned basing strategy upon a rational appraisal of means and ends rather than specifically on the actions of the enemy. In the 1950s, Kennan held that too many of the Eisenhower administration's policies were grounded in a psychological tit-for-tat with the Soviets rather than *apatheia*.

Kennan's stoicism also had the virtue of cultivating self-critique vis-à-vis the nation. He advocated keeping a critical eye on the self, even before the face of an apparently intransigent and malicious enemy. This was, as we will see with John Foster Dulles, an exceedingly difficult capacity to preserve during the heat of the Cold War. And yet Kennan did preserve it, to a degree. He could see self-chastisement as a virtue, even a duty. "But there are times and situations," he wrote government officials in 1948 while still working under Truman, "when a frank confession of error is the only healthy course. We are too often inclined to forget that it is the right of any government, as any individual, to change its mind upon due reflection. But when persistence in a course of error has literally nothing to commend it but a desire to avoid embarrassment, then the change of mind is not only a right: it is a duty."[120] Thus, in the 1950s, even as he articulated what Lasch calls the "orthodox interpretation" of the Cold War—the idea that Soviet actions were primarily responsible for the global conflict—Kennan suggested that American expansionism might be more problematic than any Soviet actions. Beginning in 1957, he argued critically that the U.S. military presence in Europe was not predicated after all on the presence of the USSR in Eastern Europe.

> I have been able to see, to date, no evidence that any of the major Nato countries would be willing to agree to a withdrawal of the American military presence in Germany even if the Soviet Union were prepared to make an equivalent withdrawal of its own forces, or, in fact, even if the Soviet government were first to withdraw unilaterally as a gesture. In this respect, our position is harder than that of Moscow, because Moscow has never said anything that would foreclose with the same finality the entire possibility of a mutual withdrawal. To imply, therefore, that the American presence is necessitated by the Soviet presence seems to me to be a one-sided way of stating the problem.[121]

Stoicism encouraged a critical eye—above all a self-critical eye. Its ancient theme of "cosmopolitanism" encouraged the repression of provincialism and patriotism in favor of rational and "realistic" appraisals of the state of things.

Indeed, a third potential merit of Kennan's stoicism was closely related to this. Kennan's commitment was to a type. He was a categorical thinker; for him, as for Hobbes and Kant, rationality and abstraction were closely allied. For Kennan this meant resisting what might be called ethnocentrism. Kennan's repeatedly insisted that the United States must refrain from attempting to remake other nations and peoples in its own image. His norm for the nation was actively disassociated from any particular culture. Like his universal language of "interest," Kennan's universal type of nationhood sought to transcend any particular culture even as it took seriously the role of culture in the life of nations. Therefore, relative to the other political actors I consider in this book, Kennan's strategic thinking was the least "American" and the most abstractly universal. It meant that he could, at least theoretically, tolerate a world of difference.

It meant also that he could sharply criticize American interventionism. Kennan's stoicism, while not isolationist, represented the legitimate heir to American isolationism in the postwar world.[122] Rebutting those like James Forrestal who insisted the United States needed a "policy" on China's internal politics, a 1948 Policy Planning Staff paper Kennan designed stated,

> There is no requirement either in United States diplomatic tradition, or in the general rules which govern intercourse between states, that a government have "a policy" with respect to internal events in another country. On the contrary, it is a traditional principle of this Government, deeply sanctioned in practice and in public opinion, to refrain from interference in the internal affairs of other countries. Non-intervention in internal affairs is therefore our normal practice; and we do not consider that we are automatically obliged to take measures to influence decisively the course of internal events in other countries. There are, to be sure, instances in which such intervention has been found to be in the national interest. But these are the exceptions and not the rule.[123]

In the mid-1950s Kennan repeatedly, albeit privately, appealed to Switzerland as an apt model for the United States. His letter to his friend John Lukacs summed up his sentiment. The U.S. Cold War strategy, he argued, should be to build a protective alliance with Great Britain, Iceland, Canada, Portugal, the states of Caribbean, and to neutralize Scandinavia, Formosa, Japan, the Philippines, and parts of Africa.

> Beyond that I would like to see this country learn to mind its own business, to adopt toward others policies similar to those of the Swiss, to recognize the uniqueness of its own national experience and the irrelevance of many of its practices for the problems of others, to address itself to the ordering and sanctification of its own life—to find, in other words, its own soul, and to cultivate, with dignity and humility, the art of self-improvement, asking of others only respect, not love or understanding.[124]

Again, this approach was not isolationist. However, it preserved the outlook of American isolationists to remain, as much as possible, detached from the internal affairs of other nations.

And yet these merits conspired to produce many of the problems of containment as it came to be practiced in the Cold War. The problems of

Kennan's containment were inseparable from its strengths. Its coherent center was exclusively ethical in nature: it prescribed *how* to be in the world but not clearly *what* to do. Like the God of philosophers, which has metaphysical properties but no historical or personal ones, Kennan's containment was both liberated and limited by its philosophical commitments. Perhaps this is the lot of all truly "grand" strategies, which set before them the magnificent task of bringing together the entirety of a nation for the sake of long-term "best interests." Indeed, the notion of national "grand strategy" itself may depend quite strongly on envisioning a national society as a self. And once within the metaphor of society as self, the "how" question assumes logical preeminence, as something like the construction of national *character* is the only adequate means of devising a coherent, long-term strategy for success in an unpredictable, contingent, and often uncontrollable world.

However, even if we accept the metaphor and the logic that follows, we can still fault Kennan for leaving the means toward the "how" unclear. In foreign policy, means matter. Kennan urged strength, resilience, and constancy often without making clear, in a consistent and coherent manner, how a mass population achieves these subjective states, let alone exactly how they are translated into the objective relations among nations. What, precisely, is required for a people to achieve a stoic subjectivity? Kennan's intricate involvement in the Marshall Plan suggested that economic vitality was critical. However, he would later go on to sharply criticize proponents of "development" like Walt Rostow. Similarly, Kennan, as C. Ben Wright explored, advocated that the United States make a strong military commitment in pursuing containment, but later repeatedly insisted that the military dimension was secondary to his plan.[125] Kennan too stressed that the role of culture and tradition is the strength of the nation—such was the appeal of the conclusion of X. And yet, in arguing for the importance of a balance of powers or multiple strong states in the world, he denied any strict connection between national strength and particular cultures or traditions. Indeed, this relative inattention to the ingredients of "strength" could lead him to echo smug racist logics, as when, for example, he wrote in 1967 that while apartheid was "foolish and misconceived" and "offensive to our sensibilities," foreign pressures on South Africa to end it would make whites "feel that they were being cornered." A sudden end would be "a disaster for all concerned," he argued, because blacks "are quite unprepared" for its end, especially since South Africa is a "complex, intricate, and modern industrial establishment" and the "herdsman tribes of Southern Africa" may lack "native aptitude."[126] In short, Kennan was very clear with regard to his allegiance to a type; but beyond this his judgments regarding the ingredients of the sort of national strength he admired and advocated were exceedingly impressionistic, and sometimes reactionary.

This failure to clarify the means of national strength, whether in America or in foreign nations, meant that containment could be called upon to justify a wide array of disharmonious strategies and tactics in the Cold War. Within the strategic field, containment opened up a Pandora's box—in any given instance military, economic, personal, or propagandistic "aid" could be called upon to strengthen an anti-Communist "counterforce" against an apparent Soviet intrusion. Containment, too, could be a subtle justification for problematic domestic efforts to remedy social "diseases." Kennan, of course, opposed McCarthyism in the 1950s and the interventions in Vietnam in the 1960s, but the logic he so effectively articulated could justify both of these infamous efforts to create robust and vigorous counterforces to Soviet expansionism. Hinds and Windt go so far as to argue that through X Kennan "inadvertently supplied the theoretical reasons for searching out subversives in domestic America as well as containing communism abroad," and Ivie finds in Kennan's disease metaphor a basis of Cold War fear-mongering.[127]

Such dilemmas are not incidental to the stoic legacy. Stoicism offers us a powerful image of nationhood, but its emphasis on subjectivity can make for a national self apathetic not only before the crises of the world, but toward the more and practical dimensions of means. The eighteenth-century Italian humanist Giambattista Vico wrote of the likes of Lipsius, Hobbes, and Locke,

> The inflexibility of human behavior, the rigor of moral conscience, i.e., the duty of the individual person to be, in all of his doings and under all circumstances, consistent with himself, was excellently inculcated by the Stoics, of whom, in my opinion, modern philosophers are the exact counterpart.[128]

Indeed, Vico complained that these modern philosophers had made the art of politics a "type of physical research," abandoning "practical common sense."[129] But it was within "truth as it is," he protested, not "truth as it ought to be by nature and reason," that human affairs were conducted.[130] Hence the need, above all, for a "Practical judgment in human affairs [that] seeks out the truth as it is, although truth may be deeply hidden under imprudence, ignorance, whim, fatality, or chance"—a decidedly nonstoical approach.[131]

As Kennan rose to prominence in the field of foreign affairs, the world was in upheaval. Kennan saw in this upheaval principally a psychological problem, and conceived containment as primarily a therapy for the nations. And while he could argue that the strategic thinker must pay constant attention to flux and change, his norm for the nations, his guiding ideal, did not adjust itself in any substantial way to the upheavals of his era. Kennan was too much a skeptic to seek a radically new world order. Even as another rising star in American foreign affairs, John Foster Dulles, was melding an old Puritan rhetoric with the "dynamic" philosophy of Henri Bergson to argue that the era of the nation-state was over, Kennan was quoting lines from Gibbon to try to reinstitute for the West, and indeed the world, a stoic model of a virtuous self and society. And this, as he wrote Stephenson, was "primarily a matter of style rather than of purpose. It is more a question of the 'how' than the 'what.'"

CHAPTER 2

Protest and Power: Dulles, Massive Retaliation, and Evangelicalism

The geometry of the ancients may have provided particular solutions which were, so to say, an anticipated application of our general methods; but it never brought out these methods; the impetus was not there which would have made them spring from the static to the dynamic. . . . Now, we have just the same impression when we compare, for example, the doctrine of the Stoics with Christian morality. The Stoics proclaimed themselves citizens of the world, and added that all men were brothers, having come from the same God. The words were almost the same; but they did not find the same echo, because they were not spoken with the same accent.
—Henri Bergson, *The Two Sources of Morality and Religion*

In a September 1952 speech, "Principle Versus Expediency in Foreign Policy," John Foster Dulles, then one of presidential candidate Dwight Eisenhower's chief foreign affairs spokespersons, attacked containment as a "non-moral policy." Of Kennan, he told the Missouri Bar Association, "I respect highly his scholarship, intellectual integrity and keen insight into the Soviet Communist world. But he repudiates what he calls the 'legalistic-moralistic approach to international problems.' He believes that international difficulties should be settled by whatever practical solution will be 'least unsettling to the stability of international life.'" Echoing a criticism Dulles made days earlier that containment was rooted in a "defeatist, appeasing mood," he told the bar association that containment "assumes that we should be willing that the Kremlin should continue to rule its 800-million captive people, provided it will leave us alone." Dulles further suggested that the policy was undemocratic, even un-American. "Non-moral diplomacy inevitably makes for a break between our government and our people. Whether we like it or not—and I like it—our people are predominantly a moral people, who believe that our nation has a great spiritual heritage to be preserved."[1]

Without question, Dulles was here engaged in a good deal of political posturing. He could play rough with his political opponents. (In running for the Senate a few years earlier, he had stoked the foul flames of anti-Communist paranoia by campaigning on a promise to rid the government of Communist infiltrators.) However, his criticisms were at the same time consistent with lifelong sentiments. Dulles saw within Kennan's policy perspective an *apatheia* that appeared defeatist, a hardness that seemed insensitive to injustices, and the intimations of a wish for America just to be left well alone. Moreover, his suggestion that Kennan's views placed a "break" between the government and the people was not far off from Kennan's own conclusion in a letter written but two years earlier. Criticizing American foreign policy actions, Kennan wrote of "the seething confusion of thought which prevails among Americans in general about the nature and purpose of their own society, the character of their world environment, and the relationship between the two." "The leadership of the world," he argued, "like its thought, must be, in the last analysis, individual and not collective." Turning to the United States, Kennan continued,

If, therefore, you want to get ahead with foreign policy, take young men of high qualities of intellect and character, train them to great hardness of mind and body, to maturity and seriousness of purpose, and to a genuine understanding of our society with all its virtues and imperfections; then see to it that they function and become wise in the processes of government.[2]

This vision of stoic leadership was based on a general proposition on the nature of political leadership as such, rather than any particularly American political philosophy. It represented at best a tension within American democracy, at worst a direct challenge to it. Kennan knew this. In his mid-1960s private moment of sketching out a public philosophy, he wrote that his ideas for reforms in U.S. government were "on such a scale that mere suggestion of it would be very ill-received."[3]

Whether as an invitation to genuine dialogue or as fair forewarning of future plans (Dulles would release Kennan from his State Department duties when he became secretary of state), in the fall of 1952 Dulles sent to Kennan in Moscow a copy of "Principle Versus Expediency in Foreign Policy." Kennan replied, in turn, with a copy of one of his own speeches, given abroad, regarding the matter of morality in foreign affairs. Invoking the stoic (specifically Senecan) idea of accommodating outwardly to cultural norms even as one remains detached from them within, as well as the analogy of society as self vis-à-vis the "body politic," it read,

> I have never felt, and trust I have never said, that moral concepts have no place in the conduct of the public affairs of the United States. We Americans are a national group; our society was formed for the promotion of certain purposes which we profess to understand; we have criteria for judging what corresponds to our national spirit and purposes, what does not. We are also a body politic. Each of us bears a bit of the responsibility for our conduct as a nation. In the exercise of that responsibility each of us is free to invoke moral concepts, and is even, I think, obliged to do so. . . .
>
> But when you come to other countries, it is a different thing. For the conduct of *their* affairs, we have no responsibility; and they, in turn,

have no obligation to promote the moral principles on which *our* national society was founded.[4]

Dulles, not surprisingly, was unpersuaded by this kind of distinction between "us" and "them," and was unwilling to let Kennan have the last word. After reading Kennan's speech, he wrote back, "I do believe that there are certain basic moral concepts which all people and nations can and do comprehend, and to which it is legitimate to appeal as providing some common standard of international conduct."[5] In this way, the lines of debate between Dulles and Kennan were entrenched.[6]

In the field of strategy, these lines of debate would receive their most visible and dramatic expression in the difference between containment and massive retaliation. The latter idea remains lodged in the memory of the Cold War, along with Mutually Assured Destruction, as the most militant of U.S. security stances. If ever apprehensions that America was a dangerous nation were confirmed, it was in 1954 when Dulles publicly proclaimed, "The way to deter aggression is for the free community to be willing and able to respond vigorously at places and with means of its own choosing." "Massive retaliatory power," he argued, would let an aggressor "know that he cannot always prescribe battle conditions that suit him."[7] In one respect, this statement can be seen as a mere extension of the policy of containment: it presumed the Soviets were aggressors and proposed that the most effective and efficient means of containing them via a counterforce was through the ever-present threat of nuclear retaliation. In fact, as I will argue in chapter 4, this way of thinking was integral to President Eisenhower's approach to his New Look. Yet even as Dulles's massive retaliation emerged on the scene as an articulation of the New Look, it had a very different ethical-rhetorical genealogy than either Kennan's containment or Eisenhower's approach to nuclear deterrence. I argue that an *evangelical* worldview possessed massive retaliation and that its militancy was, first of all, a militancy of the word, rooted in the long-standing Protestant tradition of the manifesto.

My argument, therefore, is not only that Kennan's and Dulles's differences were substantive, enduring, and historic, but that Eisenhower's and Dulles's were too. This may sound like a provocation to those who still speak of the 1950s as the "Eisenhower-Dulles" years, as if the two figures combined to form a synthetic approach to foreign policy. To be sure, it must be said that Eisenhower and Dulles shared much the same perspective on international affairs and worked closely together to address important issues like nuclear arms, trade, diplomatic ties, and the ongoing drama of Soviet-American relations. Nevertheless, I find that with respect to worldview the compound "Eisenhower-Dulles" represents a compression rather than a synthesis. Like a Parisian speaking to a Haitian, the two men spoke overlapping but distinct foreign policy languages. At the heart of the distinction was an assumed image of America, and at the heart of Dulles's image was that of a moral community, a covenant community. This image, too, set Dulles's language apart from Kennan's, and in much clearer relief than with Eisenhower's. Thus, to best elaborate Dulles's distinctiveness I continue with Dulles contra Kennan.

Evangelicalism and Stoicism

Kennan and Dulles spoke as Berliner to a Londoner. While they participated in the same broad family of language, that of international affairs, they still spoke in profoundly different ways vis-à-vis the world of nations; they envisioned different ways of national being in the world; they depended on different analogies; and they embraced different mythic structures. Kennan's own effort to explain the conflict of his views with those like Dulles's as that between a "particularized" and a "universalistic" approach—the former representing an approach built upon interest, the latter upon something like legalism or moralism—captured adequately neither the depth nor the nuance of his disagreement with Dulles.[8] The same can be said for Dulles's appeal to "principle" versus "expediency." Indeed, these terminological contrasts but touched upon the thick differences between the stoic and the evangelical.

In arguing in this chapter that an evangelical spirit possessed Dulles's massive retaliation, I do not mean by "evangelical" a particular Christian set of doctrinal positions, associated with Billy Graham and having to do with a view of scripture, church, and authority. Rather, I mean to denote a broader way of seeing and being in the world, one that Graham and other modern-day evangelicals participate in, but one that is not reducible to theological distinctives. This evangelical engages in boundary disputes. She seeks to transcend limits, whether geopolitical or cultural, by redrawing them with a message that would proclaim as a means toward new social order a higher law. If the stoic confronts the world only to turn the confrontation into a crisis of the self, the evangelical has the audacity to proclaim a means of transformation of self and world. If the stoic is skeptical of the passions, placing them under the rule of reason, the evangelical seeks to cultivate unadulterated passions as motive powers. If the stoic seeks conformity to the world's true nature, the evangelical speaks of a new nature. And if the stoic establishes an exemplary moral ideal as a model for the world, the evangelical always comes back to the responsibility to bear a message. The stoic, therefore, can be content enough with the care of the self and perhaps the eventual establishment of "a city upon a hill" as an example to the world. The evangelical cannot quite be content with example: in his or her view self-reform and world-reform are equally imperative; moral example, "a city upon a hill," always also entails the imperative to "go forth."

The evangelical spirit is therefore activist, entailing a responsibility toward propagation and reformation. It is also law-oriented, appealing to a higher rule. Finally, the evangelical possesses a certain commitment to singularity, or exceptionality, typically concentrated in a community, an *ekklēsia* (Greek, for "an assembly duly summoned").[9] These facets converge in what most distinctly characterizes the evangelical worldview, the notion of a "new order." In Roman antiquity an *euangelion* was carried by a herald and entailed the celebratory announcement of the birth or accession of a king or emperor. It therefore amounted to the declaration of and a summons to a new order. As biblical scholars argue, *euangelion* was co-opted by early Christians to say, in essence, that with Jesus had come a new order for humankind.[10]

It was not until the Protestant Reformation, however, that this evangelical spirit was transformed into what moderns would recognize as radical political action. Indeed, Michael Walzer finds the roots of modern revolution in the Calvinist notion that "specifically designated and organized bands of men might play a creative part in the political world," creating a new order.[11] The "incessant activism" of Calvinists produced a covenantal politics that culminated in the Puritan Revolution in England, as well as a series of other revolutions and reforms in Europe.[12] Legitimating this activism was the possibility of political covenant. "The sectarian covenant," Walzer notes, "was a voluntary agreement taken among equals," reinforced by "a common regiment to which all the saints equally submitted."[13] Thus, as early as Calvin's Geneva, we see an attempt to bring spiritual authority, moral community, and secular law into agreement on a covenantal basis.

> It was assumed that the coincidence of believer and citizen would be a permanent feature of this new discipline. Calvin required this much cooperation from secular law: the final punishment of an unrepentant excommunicant was exile. He insisted upon this not so much because "civil death" would prefigure the sinner's spiritual death, but rather in order to maintain the moral purity of the Christian state. That purity would not be perfect, for many citizens of the state would exist in some kind of spiritual limbo while being warned or chastised by their consistorial inquisitors. But the price of final defiance was to be made clear.[14]

What this meant for Calvin's successors was an earnest attempt to reconcile moral community with state government, spiritual ends with worldly politics, and sacred covenants with positive law. The consequences were indeed revolutionary, and not strictly for political institutions, but for political speech as well. For Calvin's successors, political speech became covenantal speech.

In fact, it was to this religiously inspired political and rhetorical upheaval that those like Hobbes responded with their neostoic countervision of ethical and political order. As Quentin Skinner writes of Hobbes's 1668 *Behemoth*,

> *Behemoth* lays the blame for the catastrophe of the 1640s [the English Civil War] on two groups above all. Hobbes mainly denounces the [Calvinist] Presbyterians and other "Fanatick Ministers," going so far as to declare that the entire rebellion arose from "the incitement of Presbyterian Ministers, who are therefore guilty of the death of all that fell in that Warre." He also inculpates the democratical gentlemen in the House of Commons [allied with the ministers], insisting that they

"did no lesse desire a Popular government in the Civil State then these Ministers did in the Church."[15]

Hobbes's skepticism of the motivations of the Calvinists notwithstanding, it is striking that he blamed *less* their political theory of covenant for the upheaval of his age (which, of course, he did criticize) than their speech.[16] For Hobbes, as Skinner summarizes, "Presbyterian rhetoric is to blame for everything."[17]

In arguing that Dulles's massive retaliation fell within an evangelical tradition, I argue that it represented an essentially Protestant speech act, one consistent in many respects with the sorts of speech acts that left Hobbes, and England, troubled. Dulles's Protestant influences were significant. He was the son and grandson of Protestant ministers, and in the 1920s he worked diligently on behalf of the "modernists" within the American Presbyterian Church to defeat the "fundamentalists," arguing for more liberal criteria for the ordination of clergy and the measurement of orthodoxy.[18] In the 1940s, as I discuss below, he was heavily involved in the leadership of the Federal Council of Churches of Christ in America. However, it was just after graduating from Princeton in 1908 that Dulles was philosophically prepared to embrace an evangelical outlook on the world. Upon graduation, he went to Paris to study under the Nobel Prize–winning French philosopher Henri Bergson; Bergson's thought, especially as it developed after World War I, tracked closely with an evangelical outlook, and was widely embraced by American liberal Protestant intellectuals. Indeed, throughout the remainder of his career Dulles drew heavily on Bergson's concepts and categories.

Bergson's gift as a thinker, like his admirer William James, was to think scientifically even as he challenged materialism, mechanism, and rationalism, all of which, he held, produced a direly rigid conception of being. Bergson was above all a philosopher of life and time, and thus of change, novelty, freedom, and progress. His was an optimistic evolutionary philosophy, in contrast to the pessimistic mood of Herbert Spencer. His was also an urgent philosophy. In the aftermath of World War I, Bergson was an important figure in transatlantic efforts to achieve a League of Nations, and he was a strong admirer of Woodrow Wilson.[19] In this vein, Bergson's philosophy was revolutionary for some; it provided a framework in which to pursue radical, indeterminate, and experimental social and political change. Bergson's work especially provided theologically liberal religious thinkers with a vision of a "dynamic" faith that could move beyond rigid ecclesiastical dogmatism and oppressive mechanistic science alike to produce a vision of a progressive social order.

Bergson shaped Dulles's thinking about social and political change in a number of ways. The themes of Bergson's 1932 *The Two Sources of Morality and Religion* (translated into English in 1935) would be echoed in Dulles's speeches and writings in the late 1930s and well into the 1940s. In that work, Bergson argued that the evangelical spirit of Christianity represented a singular ethical breakthrough and a crucial stage in the moral evolution of humankind.

> Humanity had to wait till Christianity for the idea of universal brotherhood. . . . Some may say that it has been a rather slow process; indeed eighteen centuries elapsed before the rights of man were proclaimed by the Puritans of America, soon followed by the men of the French Revolution. It began, nevertheless, with the teachings of the Gospels, and was destined to go on indefinitely; it is one thing for an idea to be merely propounded by sages worthy of admiration [as in Greek and Roman philosophy], it is very different when the idea is broadcast to the ends of the earth in a message overflowing with love, invoking love in return. . . . Classical antiquity had known nothing of propaganda; its justice had the unruffled serenity of the gods upon Olympus. Spiritual expansion, missionary zeal, impetus, movement, all these are of Judaic-Christian origin.[20]

The Two Sources of Morality and Religion also argued that the evangelical spirit of Christianity represented for humankind the possibility of a political leap beyond what Bergson called the "closed society." Bergson's closed society represented humankind's primitive and primary social condition; it was grounded in "self-preservation," "interest," and identities of family, clan, and nation.[21] Christianity, Bergson argued, threw open the door to an "open soul" and thus to an open society. It introduced a new morality rooted not in "instinct" or "habit," which circle around the desire for self-preservation, but in "aspiration" and "the enthusiasm of forward movement."[22] Critically, Bergson argued that this new morality rejected the stoic analogy of self and society, forwarding instead an altogether different mode of being in the world. The society-as-self idea, he argued, is part of the order of "nature"; the evangelical spirit of Christianity creatively "outwitted nature," resulting in a qualitatively different ethic of love and universal solidarity.[23] In the context of the crises rampant in Europe in the first half of the twentieth century, Bergson's work suggested that the conflict between totalitarianism and liberalism was rooted in an evolutionary spiritual conflict between an old, even primitive, way of being and a new, revolutionary one.

It is the "new" evangelical spirit that I suggest explains the ethical-rhetorical context of Dulles's massive retaliation. While strategy can be theoretically conceived as the alignment of means with objectives, its political practice is far more complex. In the case of Dulles's massive retaliation, the complexity of its articulation lay in its public performance. Massive retaliation was less a strategic principle than a means of registering radical dissent and summoning moral outrage. It was, in other words, a Protestant speech act embedded within the discourse of strategy.

A Covenantal Summons: Dulles's War, Peace, and Change

From the perspective of stoicism, evangelicalism can look not only audacious, but arrogant, unrealistic, and, as Kennan said, "almost criminally unforgivable."[24] However, from the perspective of despair, felt by many during the interwar years, evangelicalism can look pragmatic, as a new order can appear to be the only viable alternative for the survival of the human spirit, let alone its flourishing. Indeed, the "city upon a hill" rhetoric of the Puritans has kept many since from seeing just how pragmatic the Protestant pursuit of a new order could be. Central to this pragmatism was the notion of covenant. Witness William Bradford's telling of the creation of the famous Mayflower Compact. Faced with the shores of New England, which the Puritan voyagers had not anticipated hitting, and thus with a political crisis, given that their government grant was for Virginia rather than New England, they simply formed a new covenant.

> This [the formation of the Mayflower Compact] was occasioned partly by the discontented and mutinous speeches that some of the strangers amongst them had let fall: that when they got ashore they would use their liberty, that none had power to command them, that patent being produced for Virginia, and not for New England, which belonged to another company, with which the Virginia company had nothing to do. And, further, it was believed by the leading men among the settlers that such a deed, drawn up by themselves, considering their present condition, would be as effective as any patent, and in some respects more so.[25]

As the account of the pilgrim landing indicates, the political covenant, though sacred, represented as well a pragmatic solution to the limited scope of any legal contract and the disorder of anarchy. Indeed, for the Puritans more broadly, covenant meant the institution of a solemn social and political obligation in order to fend off the twin evils of anarchy and tyranny. In this way, as Richard Tuck has shown, seventeenth-century Calvinists could use the language of "necessity" as readily as their neostoic counterparts.[26] The central difference between them in this regard was twofold: (1) for the Puritans sovereignty remained popular, whereas for neostoics it could quickly become authoritarian, and thus (2) "necessity" for the Calvinists was a social force calling for regular intervention and activism, whereas for the neostoics it was more of a primeval social force that legitimated the maintenance of social order.

In the interwar years in America, both anarchy and tyranny seemed to be ever-present threats to human survival. World War I, the Russian Revolution, the specter of aggressive nationalism in Germany, Italy, and Japan, and the vast social and economic crises of the Great Depression each seemed to put social order upon a narrow precipice between mayhem and totalitarianism. For Dulles, the precarious state of the world was felt on several levels in the mid-to-late 1930s. As a highly prized and high-priced corporate lawyer, he was quite literally invested in social order and worried about Franklin Roosevelt's apparent statism. As a political disciple and former surrogate of Woodrow Wilson, he felt that the upheavals at home and abroad were a threat "civilization" itself, and that some large-scale new measures were needed to prevent its disastrous end. Finally, especially after 1937, Dulles believed that the "spiritual legacy" of the West, especially universal norms of rights and responsibilities, was in danger of dying through a combination of erosion and attack.

The signature moment for Dulles in this last regard was his participation in a 1937 conference at Oxford University on "Church, Community, and State," sponsored by the Universal Christian Council for Life and Work, one of the antecedents to the World Council of Churches. Dulles's time at the conference represented for him something of both a spiritual reawakening and an intellectual enlightenment. He had come to it on the heels of an exceedingly frustrating and depressing experience at a League of Nations conference in Paris devoted to the subject of peaceful change. The delegates there were unable to agree on any set of principles for international cooperation. At Oxford, however, he found not only what he saw as a congenial group of interlocutors, but a conceptual breakthrough, "the conception of the church as a community that transcended the boundaries of any particular nation."[27] As one Dulles biographer writes, "The fact that, at Oxford, the discussions were built upon something deeper and more enduring than national self-interest gave Dulles a renewed hope in the possibility of 'creating an international ethos which would be essential as a foundation for any lasting political structure.'"[28]

Two years later, that ethos and the conceptual framework behind it would form the core of Dulles's most focused effort to articulate a political philosophy in his long and varied career, his 1939 *War, Peace, and Change*. Its argument called for a careful balancing of what he referred to as "ethical" and "political" solutions to the problems of state sovereignty and total war. The ethical solution, Dulles argued, had to do with the subjective states of people, their attitudes, opinions, and dispositions. Dulles wanted to overcome what he called the "deification of the nation."[29] The "political" solution concerned more formal legal frameworks by which nations could establish means of peaceful cooperation. The book advocated a type of world federalism, presenting early American federalism as a prototype (9–16, 24). Kennan would understand this approach as the fusion of moralism and legalism, respectively. From an evangelical perspective, however, the book represented an effort to renew, on a global scale, a covenantal politics in spirit as well as in letter. *War, Peace, and Change* functioned as a summons to a "new covenant" among the nations.

It was in this regard that the U.S. Constitution stood as an exemplar in the book. Importantly, what Dulles admired about the Constitution was not mainly its contribution to a solid, strong, and enduring republic, the attributes that Kennan seems to have admired, but rather the way it demonstrated "the extent to which exaggerated nationalistic conceptions can be shrunk *through the opening up of boundaries.*"[30] Dulles valued the way the Constitution fostered circulation (especially of goods and services), movement, and fluidity by mitigating the role of static state boundaries. Similarly, he admired its capacity to withstand change over a long period of time. "It prescribed a regime so elastic and was itself an instrument of such general terms that it has proved possible there-under for momentous evolutions gradually to occur" (157). The Constitution was therefore, in his estimation, a model of a dynamic covenant, capable not only of tolerating change, but also of creating an active, flexible, and indeed porous union.

In this way Dulles's *War, Peace, and Change* modified the neostoic ideal of the strong state. Like Hobbes's *Leviathan*, Dulles's book presented a portrait of a primeval scene.

> In the material field the conflict of selfish desires assumes, in its simple form, a struggle between those who primarily are satisfied and wish to retain that which they have and those who are dissatisfied and wish to acquire at the expense of others. When such conflicts arise—and they are omnipresent—some solution must be found. There must be some way of determining which of the conflicting desires shall be satisfied. The primitive method was force or the threat of force. (7)

Dulles thus largely accepted Hobbes's anthropological portrait of humans as possessed by strong but rational desires that produce social conflict and the broader problem of insecurity. Dulles, also like Hobbes, concluded in *War, Peace, and Change* that apart from a covenant and some surrender of autonomy mass violence would be inevitable. However, he went beyond Hobbes in imagining a covenant that would "cut in the boundaries of sovereignty" (127). Indeed, *War, Peace, and Change* was sharply critical of national sovereignty and, by implication, the Hobbesian "body politic," placing on it the blame for nationalist and totalitarian politics. Dulles argued that strong-state thinking was the foundation of romantic nationalism and the modern wars and revolutions that ensued. The nation had become "personified," he argued, and this personification gave rise to a perverse logic of nationalist sacrifice. A society, *War, Peace, and Change* suggested, should not be conceived as a self. Rather, it should be envisioned impersonally, as a collection of selves forming contractually based states, and then as a collection of states forming a contractually based world society. This world society, in turn, could serve as an object of proper sacrifice, serving ideals of "duty to fellow-man, without regard to propinquity, or to race, creed or nationality" (118). And as it served such ideals, it would remain flexible, open to change and revision according to exigencies.

Kennan, too, had argued for the importance of flexibility in international life. "It should be recognized that there can be no static objectives of U.S. foreign policy: complete security of perfection of international environment will never be achieved. Foreign policy will always operate in a changing environment: and the purposes of foreign policy will always be relative to a moving stream of events." Nevertheless, he insisted on certain permanencies: the inviolable logic of "interest," the primacy of security, and the need for state sovereignty.[31] Before these permanencies, "morality" had no role. To insist that it did was to be utopian. However, for Dulles the crises of the world were inextricably moral, and both morality and utopianism were deeply pragmatic: they were goads toward reform, not promises of immanent perfection. In this sense, Dulles's thinking stood squarely within the evangelical tradition of deriving social imperatives from eschatological visions. His utopianism was meant to engender a pursuit of "fundamental" solutions to the world's crises; even to, as Karl Mannheim writes of the utopian, "shatter . . . the order of things prevailing at the time."[32] He refused resignation to the supposed permanencies of interest, security, and sovereignty. The only permanency of his vision, much like the radicalism of seventeenth-century Calvinists, was that of supernal law. *War, Peace, and Change* held out the sweeping prospect of a new world order and a reformed human nature; it did not, however, propose changes in any fundamental laws of being. Indeed, its entire argument was built upon the edifice of laws of being—particularly, laws of sociality and change. It sought to derive from fundamental laws of being principles for world reform.

Reflecting Bergson's line of thought, Dulles argued in *War, Peace, and Change* for an ethic of universal solidarity and the deconstruction of "the devil characterization of another" (114). The personifications of other nations, as well as the personification of one's own nation, were not only "fictitious" constructs, he argued, but the psychological basis of the "deification" of the state and the wars that follow (110, 118). "Religions," he argued, "form the most usual vehicle for the projection of the ethical solution beyond national lines" (18). Yet, Dulles's appraisal of the potential of religious belief to foster universal solidarity was cautious.

> Few religions conceive of their deity as concerned with the welfare of all mankind. Christianity has attained, at least in theory, the concept of a god whose interest is universal. This quality of universality, when it is genuinely accepted and practiced, undoubtedly serves to increase the effective range of the ethical solution. But most religions, in theory or in practice, conceive of their deity as having jurisdiction and interest substantially coterminous with that of the social group which worships it. (19)

Additionally, in decidedly Protestant fashion, Dulles complained, "Religions, as a vehicle for universalizing the ethical solution, are further deficient in consequence of a tendency to become identified with human authorities" (19). Nevertheless, *War, Peace, and Change* argued for a form of pure religious expression as the "ethical" solution to the world's upheavals: "Christ taught that we should render unto God that which is God's. We have been rendering unto Caesar that which is God's. The finest qualities of human nature are at once too delicate and too powerful to be put blindly at the disposal of other humans who are primarily concerned with their own kingdom—not the bringing into being of the Kingdom of God" (117).

Bergson's other major influence upon *War, Peace, and Change* was seen in the book's attitude toward change. In celebrating "the enthusiasm of forward movement" Bergson aligned change not only with progress, but also with a new, more vital and promising ethic. While many in his time placed the blame for the world's upheavals on the vast changes of modernization, Bergson argued that change, far from being the source of the world's problems, was the necessary ingredient to its forward movement. In the same way, Dulles argued, "We need to develop in world affairs a feeling that change is not, *per se,* something abnormal and strange and to be avoided except as a matter of dire necessity. Rather we should look upon change, at least in certain phases of the national domains, as normal and not something about which the world must become greatly excited" (156). Consequently, Dulles could argue that the movement toward a type of world federalism could be peaceful and indeed "normal." Revolutionary change, *War, Peace, and Change* argued, need not be violent. Furthermore, once this new order was established, Dulles argued that it could adapt itself peacefully to changing circumstances, so long as the federal institution had the "moral position" by which to pursue "a periodic but measured alteration of the *status quo,* designed to strike an acceptable balance between the dynamic and static desires of national groups" (137).

Nevertheless, in following Bergson's thought in these ways, Dulles in *War, Peace, and Change* was confronted with a problem that stood between the *status quo* and change toward a world federalist system. This was what he called the "ethical" problem. The world federalist political project, Dulles confessed, "is so pure as to lack ready appeal" (118). In this way, Dulles, like Kennan, was squarely confronted with the problem of mass subjectivity. However, his imagined solution was strikingly different from Kennan's in that it was pietistic and popular in orientation. It would focus not on the establishment of social and self control of a wise ruling class, but on the cultivation of mass desires consistent with a new world federalist order. "The 'ethical' solution," he argued, "would affirmatively create desires which are susceptible of fulfillment without human conflict" (10). Dulles therefore called for the deployment of a range of cultural institutions—religious, governmental, educational, philanthropic, etc.—in the service of the reformation of mass desire.

Despite its pietistic and popular orientation, at moments *War, Peace, and Change*'s approach to reforming social desire came troublingly close to prescribing forms of social engineering. For example, it stated,

> Generally speaking, we have a choice between a condition of change which is fairly constant and which, because it is constant, can be

moderated and constructively guided, or a condition of rigidity, interspersed with violent change which is irrational and destructive.

Those of responsibility in any field of life, if they are wise, are constantly on the watch for symptoms which foreshadow the necessity for change. If detected at an early stage, adjustment can be offered which will serve to prevent a damming up of dynamic forces to a degree such that violent and drastic change becomes inescapable. Change, if skillfully induced, is almost imperceptible until viewed in retrospect. This is the ideal form of change. (139)

Yet very little in the rest of the book or in the remainder of Dulles's career smacked squarely of social engineering, technocracy, or even Kennan's class of ruling elite. To be sure, Dulles grew to be more and more a part of the power elite, and in no way did he resist this. However, his public life was consistently more religious in character than managerial. He wanted to use the various means of culture to cultivate conditions for change. He relied upon the pulpit, the lectern, the radio studio, and the press to formulate, articulate, and propagate his evangelical messages.

Well into the next decade after the publication of *War, Peace, and Change*, Dulles would call for a new world order and a commensurate conversion among the masses of people with regard to desires, attitudes, and allegiances. Increasingly, moreover, he would speak as if a covenant among the nations already existed, in spirit though not in letter. In fact, Dulles could have seen this as the implication of Bergson's thought, as Bergson argued that evangelical Christianity represented a *historical* as well as spiritual phenomenon. The spirit of Christianity, Bergson argued, had entered history; its presence was felt, experienced, and deployed. It was not a mere intellectual abstraction, but an immanent phenomenon. It lived as a real source of morality and as a present potentiality.

In this regard, one of the more revealing arguments of *War, Peace, and Change* came in defending the exemplary place and normative status of common law. Peaceful change could become the norm, Dulles argued,

> if we could develop in international affairs a viewpoint corresponding to that which is epitomized by the common law. No one knows with precision what the common law is. No one can tell at what precise moment

it changes, and the many changes which have occurred have not, in detail, been spectacular. We find here conformity with the criterion we suggested, namely, that change should preferably be almost imperceptible except in retrospect. (156)

The allusion here to the Johannine Gospel's description of the ways of the Spirit was barely cloaked (John 3:7–8). Just as Dulles had been reinspired to pursue world federalism by the ecumenical church, which transcended, at least in concept, national boundaries, so he appears to have found in the Johannine portrait of the Spirit inspiration for a universal "common law." His later invocation before the Missouri Bar Association of America's "great spiritual heritage" and insistence to Kennan that there were universally shared "basic moral concepts" represented reverberations of this thinking. Thus, while *War, Peace, and Change* proposed that both subjective "ethical" and formal "political" changes were needed before a new world covenant could be achieved, it intimated that the covenant, in some elusive spiritual sense, was already in place.

Indeed, in the almost two decades remaining in his life after the publication of *War, Peace, and Change* Dulles repeatedly spoke as if a kind of covenant was in place. Sometimes he referred to it as spiritual, other times as moral. Sometimes he spoke in ways that suggested that it was in place primarily in America, other times as if it was worldwide. But his speeches and writings in the 1940s and 1950s reveal a belief in the presence of a spiritual covenant. This faith was revealed primarily through a distinct pattern of speech Dulles adopted, first jeremiadic and eventually manifestic in character. The jeremiad and the manifesto have roots in the covenantal politics of seventeenth-century Puritans. They constituted a discrete set of rhetorical practices that were integral to the establishment and maintenance of Calvinist covenantal political culture, even as they came to develop a life of their own well after the eclipse of this political culture. In the following short section, I provide a sketch of their political and rhetorical logics, for these logics, I will argue, were integral to the spirit of Dulles's "massive retaliation." This "strategy," I will argue, was in fact primarily a manifestic speech act.

Covenantal Speech

Seventeenth-century Protestant covenantal politics had an acute relationship to public discourse, for it was in public, in the presence of the people, and through formal speech that the covenant was typically founded and renewed. Covenants were seen as constituting communities, but not just any community. Covenants constituted moral communities, bound by solemn public promises of fidelity, moral rectitude, and perdurance. Covenants therefore mitigated risk and uncertainty by casting a vision of a future that was bound by the same principles and promises that held the community together in the present. However, when covenants were broken, risk multiplied, for the covenantal community not only became vulnerable to the indeterminacies of an apparent lawlessness, but subject to divinely sanctioned punishment or judgment.[33]

Guided by the writings of John Calvin's successors like Theodore Beza, seventeenth-century Calvinists developed a sophisticated theology of legitimacy and rebellion vis-à-vis the state.[34] Integral to this theology was the idea that the covenant—the biblical archetype of which was the bond between Yahweh and Israel mediated by Moses—was the proper framework for legitimate civil governance. Subsequently, the idea of covenant informed political thought in ways that extended well beyond a distinctly Calvinist and Puritan theology, for example, in the thought of Hobbes, Rousseau, and Locke. Nevertheless, it was Calvinists who first robustly developed these ideas in the early-modern period; moreover, they created distinct and enduring forms of covenantal speech that would play a vital role in providing later more liberal polities with forms of public moral suasion.

Indeed, because covenantal communities rested on solemn promises, they required and developed specialized forms of public discourse that addressed promise breaking. Most noted among these is the jeremiad, a form of public discourse that gained strength among seventeenth-century Puritans in both England and New England. In America, the jeremiad is a rhetorical form that has endured well beyond the culmination of colonial Puritan hegemony—indeed, so much so that J. G. A. Pocock calls the jeremiad "the most American of all rhetorical modes."[35] Integral to

American culture has been the idea that the nation was founded upon a covenant and that this covenant, while giving birth to a politics, was above all moral in nature, consisting of self-evident rights vis-à-vis justice. The idea of the moral founding of the nation has persisted in the symbolic construction of America in the jeremiad. As Sacvan Bercovitch argues, the rhetoric of the jeremiad "invested the symbol of America with the attributes of the sacred," such that the nation could at once sustain a sense of its own peculiar identity and extend its moral foundation universally.[36]

The jeremiad is a rhetoric of memory, judgment, and promise: memory, because it recalls for the people the communal norms of the covenant; judgment, because it calls the people to account for violating those communal norms; and promise, because it pledges future well-being if the people repent from their violations and recommit themselves to the communal norms. Importantly, the jeremiad is a rhetoric made from *within* the community, in the sense that it seeks to bring about restoration and reform rather than revolution—in Bercovitch's terms, it aims at "cultural revitalization" rather than "social alternatives."[37] The jeremiad is thus always in this respect a conservative rhetoric, even as it may be radical in its judgment. As James Darsey writes of the jeremiadic rhetoric of "self-evident truth" in America, "It is conservative in that it has no power of invention; it can only reveal that which was already there, the sempiternal; it is always the rhetoric of the messenger. It is radical in its engagement of society at its root."[38]

There is, however, a second form of rhetoric that is also indebted to the covenantal outlook and yet is strongly revolutionary in orientation, the manifesto. The manifesto is a rhetoric of judgment that decries an irreparable breach of a covenant and reconfigures the memory of a people to cultivate strong identification with a history of resistance to oppression. The manifesto is what happens beyond the jeremiad, when communal norms have been so grievously upended that the possibility of their restoration among a people seems to have evaporated. In the manifesto, the oppressed present themselves as having been the objects of irreparable covenantal violations; they thus divide the community into "us" and "them," covenant keepers and covenant breakers, respectively. The former constitutes a community that stands outside of, and over and against, the community of the latter. In this respect, the etymology of *manifesto* is telling: the Latin *manus* and *fectus* together create the image of the fist striking, the hostile hand. Thus, in seventeenth-century Italy, a manifesto was a text that made public the purpose of a military unit or the will of a sovereign. It was, quite literally, a militant speech act.[39]

The manifesto is integral to the application of a covenantal outlook to human polity, for every humanly constituted covenant must present the possibility of an irreparable breach. Thus, Puritans of the seventeenth century produced not only jeremiads, but also manifestos, the formal features of which were carried over into a proliferation of manifestos in the eighteenth century. Janet Lyon describes these features as a "selective and impassioned chronicle of oppression that has led to the present moment of rupture," a "forceful enumeration of grievances," and an "epigrammatic style."[40] Puritan manifestos of the seventeenth century used language that was strong and even violent. In England, early Puritans opposed the practices of the state-sanctioned church in manifestos characterized by unequivocal language: "Fie upon these stinking abominations," declared the influential 1571 *A View of Popishe Abuses Yet Remaining in the Englishe Church, for the which Godly Ministers have Refused to Subcribe*, a prelude to the Puritan Revolution of the next century.[41] Importantly, Puritan manifestos like *A View of Popishe Abuses* made these declarations from without the council chamber of the church and before Parliament, thus signifying a radical breach with the established church in England.

Manifestos provided their authors with moral legitimacy, and this is the central legacy of the manifesto in modernity. As Lyon explores, by the eighteenth century the manifesto came to represent speech acts that confronted power in the name of universal truth. The manifesto expanded into a recognizable and widely used rhetorical form that chronicled oppressions and declared, in light of these grievances, a political and historical rupture, and thus a new epoch of collective being in the world. Lyon argues that the proliferation of manifestos in the eighteenth and nineteenth centuries was due to the scope of the promises of modernity itself, writing, "The promises held out by the developmental narratives of modernity—promises of universal freedom, autonomy, equality, and inclusion—are reiterated and recast in political manifestoes in the eighteenth and nineteenth centuries as the broken promises of modernity."[42] In this way, she argues, the emergence of the "ideology of a universal subject with universal rights and sensibilities" finds a counterpart in "a public genre [the manifesto] geared to contesting or recalibrating the assumptions underlying a 'universal subject.'"[43]

The manifesto, more than the jeremiad, lends itself to universalization because its moral stance is unequivocal. Whereas the jeremiad must hold before the people both the fact of a covenantal breach and the possibility of its repair—and thus maintain a degree of equivocation—the manifesto need only declare a radical breach. It therefore conjoins a morally unequivocal attitude to a revolutionary stance and solidifies the distance between the people and their oppressors. With respect to communal identity, the manifesto means writing one's group into the history of resistance to oppression. As Lyon writes, to compose a manifesto is "to participate symbolically in a history of struggle against dominant forces; it is to link one's voice to the countless voices of previous revolutionary conflicts."[44] Thus, the manifesto not only creates a distance between oppressors and oppressed, but allies the latter with the larger historical struggle of truth against false power and domination. Whereas the jeremiad invokes a particular communal history, the manifesto can expand this particular history into a universal one. The manifesto can therefore suggest that a particular breach of a covenant is but an episode in a larger historical narrative of injustice and the abuse of power.[45] As such, it can address audiences as if a universal moral law exists that transcends time and space and that divides the just from the unjust.

I have outlined here the political and rhetorical logics of the jeremiad and manifesto because, in important respects, Dulles's political career in the 1940s and 1950s was bound to these logics. In 1941—two years after the publication of *War, Peace, and Change* and, as it turned out, the beginning of the new world war—Dulles made a pivotal career decision to serve as chair of the newly inaugurated Committee on the American Church and the Peace and War Problem, under the auspices of the Federal Council of Churches of Christ in America (FCCCA). He would soon become a widely recognized American religious leader, taking his place for a time alongside figures like Reinhold Niebuhr and John C. Bennett, speaking and publishing in church venues across the country, and serving as the chief foreign affairs spokesperson for the FCCCA.[46] During this period Dulles developed with his FCCCA colleagues broadly publicized proposals for postwar peace. The proposals echoed in principle many of the concepts of *War, Peace, and Change,* but the tone of Dulles's work during this period was, for obvious reasons, even more somber. As the war culminated in 1945, Dulles ended his tenure with the FCCCA and entered a series of governmental roles as a diplomat, senator, and eventually Eisenhower advisor. However, his religio-political framework, rejuvenated if not reborn in 1937 at Oxford and developed in the years after, would endure. A covenantal political imaginary and central preoccupation with moral authority would continue to absorb his work well into his years as secretary of state. In the early days of the Cold War, these concerns were most clearly expressed in his jeremiads.

Dulles's Jeremiads

As the crafting of the United Nations Charter began in San Francisco in 1945, Dulles told fellow Protestants, "To Christians this Conference is not merely one more diplomatic conference. This Conference has been an item in their program. They have helped to bring it about. This Conference is, in a very real sense, their Conference."[47] Or, as he wrote in a draft of the speech, "The San Francisco Conference is not a political conference which we observe with detachment. It is in a sense *our* conference. It has come to pass largely through the efforts of Christian groups."[48] President Truman had appointed Dulles an official U.S. representative to the San Francisco conference, but Dulles's own sentiment was that his governmental role was continuous with his work begun in 1937 at the Oxford Conference. It was part of a larger mission to reach substantive ethical and political goals among the world of nations, to realize a new order both subjective and legal in character.

As a leader in the FCCCA, however, Dulles frequently worried that America would stand in the way of necessary change. He told the FCCCA in 1940,

> If evil is today rampant, this has a cause. Men will always differ in their appraisal of specific causes and in their apportionment of responsibility. It is certain, however, that none of us is guiltless and we who are

Americans recognize that a great burden must rest upon us. "For unto whomsoever much is given, of him shall be much required." During the period preceding, and formative of, the present wars, our nation possessed great power and influence. Through our action or non-action we exerted a profound influence upon the course of world events. That course has generated widespread unrest, great violence and immense disaster. Obviously, we have fallen short of what was required.[49]

Although America had great spiritual resources, he argued, it had failed to generate the vital spiritual power needed for world organization. In turn, the FCCCA Commission on a Just and Durable Peace thereafter produced, under Dulles's leadership, "The Six Pillars of Peace," which entailed bold call for universal human rights, international economic and diplomatic cooperation, and the liberation of subjected peoples. It was presented as a list of principles for world peace; its audience was presumably world leaders. However, it was also implicitly a list of moral demands for the American people.

The "Six Pillars" study guide, distributed widely among Protestant churches in America in 1943, began by quoting the apparently exceptionalist language of Federalist 1, "It seems to have been reserved to the people of this country, by their conduct and example, to decide whether societies of men are really capable or not of establishing good government from reflection and choice, or whether they are forever destined to depend for their political constitutions on accident and force." "The American people again find themselves in an era of critical decision," the study guide declared. "It must now be determined, this time in worldwide terms, whether men are capable of establishing good government. . . . Now, as before, it is reserved to the people of this country to play a decisive role. Now, more than ever, a wrong choice of the part we shall act will involve us in the general misfortune of mankind."[50] The study guide in this way called for Americans to engage in a new founding, worldwide in scope. The call was decidedly evangelical. "Basically the task is to ensure that God's will be done on earth as it is in heaven," Dulles explained to FCCCA supporters.[51] In a radio interview concerning the "Six Pillars," Dulles claimed, "The only road that can lead to durable peace is the way of fellowship shown us nineteen hundred years ago by Jesus of

Nazareth. Many men follow that way in the personal relations with each other. Those same standards of conduct must now be followed by peoples in their relations with each other."[52] The FCCCA, he argued elsewhere, sought "to revive in our people a sense of destiny in the performance of a great work of creation. Upon the success of our effort, with parallel efforts by others, depends the future of our nation."[53] In arguing for this evangelical mission and in blurring the boundaries between contingent political associations like the United Nations and the kingdom of God, Dulles intimated once again a spiritualized covenant to which all should, by virtue of being human, be subject.

Dulles thus drew heavily from the historic well of evangelical radicalism, calling for a new founding, a new order, and, ultimately, a new subjectivity. The type of Christian spirit Dulles propounded, however, was one that basically affirmed liberal values; its main interest was to check and qualify the apparent tendency of liberal societies toward the mere pursuit of self-interest without regard for others. Christianity, Dulles declared on the radio in 1942, had "the quality of universality," for "Christ taught that all men were children of God." Jesus taught "very simple things" like the problems of hatred and vengeance and the importance of "seeing the defects within yourself."[54] In this way, Dulles envisioned Christianity as an instrument for political and moral reform in the United States, rather than dogmatically or confessionally. His was a Christianity conceived in the service of contemporary political crises: supra-creedal, ethical, and "spiritual," binding people to a common sentiment and a common moral law. "The great obstacle to world order is the lack of any universal moral judgments about national conduct," he complained in 1944.[55] The "fallacy of world government," he declared as a delegate to the United Nations five years later, was seen in the fact that "the law-making, police-enforcing process never works unless the laws reflect the views of the community to which they apply." Christianity, Dulles suggested throughout the 1940s, once translated into basic moral principles, could provide the basis for universal moral judgments. The Christian church, he declared as early as 1937, could provide "the spiritual background" for the resolution of major world problems.[56]

Dulles's Christianity was therefore evangelical in spirit but liberal in creed. It was radical in its implications, but basically progressive in its vision. It was more than a civil religion—its scope transcended national boundaries and its content was far more demanding than most civil religious discourse in America. As such, it was profoundly vulnerable to disappointment, if not despair. In 1945, Dulles wrote Truman what he seems to have firmly believed: "There are no purely mechanistic solutions of the grave international problems which we face. Adequate international machinery can be developed only under conditions of fellowship."[57] The following year, in a speech at Princeton University, he would condemn the people of the United States for their failure to play a decisive role in world transformation. "Unhappily the fact is that at this critical juncture the people of the United States have no great faith which moves them. We are in no mood to seize on the United Nations as an agency for accomplishing some great purpose in the world." This, he further complained, would not have happened among previous generations of Americans. "Then the American people were imbued with a great faith." However, he lamented, "That mood has passed, with the result that at this critical time we may fail the world." Materially and intellectually, Dulles concluded, America is doing its part in the world; but spiritually it is lacking, and thus is "incapable of breathing into that organization the spirit needed to make it a living body."

Indeed, as late as the winter of 1952 Dulles continued to chastise the American people for their moral, and thus political, failures. In a speech before Princeton alumni in February, he forwarded three "propositions" regarding foreign policy: (1) "The dynamic usually prevails over the static," (2) "In human affairs, the non-material or spiritual element is more important than the material," and (3) "There is a moral or natural law not made by man which determines right and wrong and conformity with this law is in the long run indispensable to human welfare." Dulles asserted that the United States had failed to abide by these principles. A largely "passive" foreign policy (containment), materialistic appetites, and "the fact that our practices have been divorced from their Christian context" left America and the rest of the free world in an unpromising situation vis-à-vis the Soviets. Indeed, he argued, the Soviets had abided by the first two propositions more faithfully than their political enemies. However, Dulles urged his audience to refuse to believe that America had come to the point of losing its "sense of purpose and of mission in the world." "Surely," he declared, "that hour has not struck for us. . . . There is no reason whatsoever why we should stand frightened and on the defensive in the face of Soviet communism."[58]

Dulles thus was a Jeremiah, condemning America's vices and calling the nation back to fidelity to its evangelical essence. His liberalized Christianity granted him a strong and flexible moral vocabulary by which to judge the failings of the nation. His "ethical" solution in *War, Peace, and Change,* the transformation of subjectivity, was the basis of his complaints. Written covenants among nations, he claimed, were a good. However, in order for them to be genuine, their force must be derived not from procedure, mechanism, and legalities, but from a broad and common moral vision. True covenants, he therefore insisted, were made on a moral and spiritual level. And this could be realized only as peoples throughout the world recognized and adhered to the universal moral law, which, as Dulles wrote Henry Luce, is "objective" and "not subject to be made and remade just by ourselves to serve our own convenience."[59] If Americans, his exceptionalist logic concluded, would not have faith in the universal law and assume responsibility for its dissemination and institutionalization, then who would?

As the Cold War emerged, Dulles attempted to reinvigorate the evangelical spirit among American people vis-à-vis the universal moral law and its attendant responsibilities. Within his rhetoric, the call to national character and an emphasis on America's exemplary role had very different valences from Kennan's. Their language could be similar, but their respective worldviews were quite different. Whereas for Kennan the nation realized its traditions in sure and steady knowledge of its own purposes and an acute diagnosis of the enemy, for Dulles the greatness of America could only be realized in action. Dulles wrote in *Life* in 1946, in sharp contrast to Kennan, "It is not very profitable to speculate about what will come of the Kremlin. That is an interesting intellectual pastime, but an outsider will not, in that way, get much practical guidance. From the standpoint of action, the course is clear. We must act on the assumption that we *can* do something to bring Soviet leaders to change their foreign program. If we do not go ahead on this basis, we shall almost surely fail."[60] The only question, as Dulles wrote Walter Lippmann regarding his argument in *Life,* was "whether the American people can see the truth."[61]

During most of the 1940s Dulles seriously questioned whether Americans could "see the truth." A great deal of his energies as a public figure were devoted to recalling for the American people the norms of their founding covenant, the Constitution, calling them to account for violating the spirit of those norms, and promising future well-being if they would but feel sorrow for their violations and recommit themselves to their spiritual mission. However, as Dulles approached (with presidential candidate Thomas Dewey in 1944 and 1948) and eventually achieved (with Eisenhower) the office of secretary of state, his jeremiadic rhetoric began to subside and his public militancy vis-à-vis the Soviets increased. The reasons for this transformation, Mark Toulouse argues, are found in a change in Dulles's political outlook from "prophetic realism" to "priestly nationalism."[62] Yet here too, I suggest, there was continuity in the transformation. For in an important respect, Dulles's basic political and philosophical outlook remained continuous. What changed in the State Department were his attitudes toward the United States and the USSR. Already, by insisting in *War, Peace, and Change* that a critical part of the solution to the world's problems was "ethical"—that is, concerned with the subjective attitudes of people—Dulles had laid the groundwork for concluding that while "the truth" could be universal and absolute, the capacity to "see the truth" could be judged relatively. Indeed, his exceptionalist view of America presumed that Americans, even if they were dangerously near to failure, were somehow placed in closer subjective proximity to the truth. However, as the Cold War intensified and as Dulles's political role in America became more visible and powerful, first as a senator and then eventually as Eisenhower's political partner, this implicit map of relative subjective proximity to the truth produced a very different kind of rhetoric. Dulles began to increasingly condemn the actions and ideology of the Soviets and to place America and its liberal allies within a history of resistance to oppressive forces. Dulles's public declarations as secretary of state suggest that he had come to convince himself that, relative to the Soviets, Americans *had* seen the truth. At the same time, as his initial expectations for the United Nations were disappointed, he became less invested in what *War, Peace, and Change* called the "political" solution to the world's problems, a loose but strong world federalism. Thus, in an importance sense, spirit began to take sharp precedence over matter in

Dulles's rhetoric. That is, notions like the moral law, the spiritual foundation of society, and the universal fellowship of humankind assumed the force of historical fact even if they lacked institutional sanction. If Dulles could not be satisfied with an effective "political" solution, he could at least persist in insisting on an "ethical" one.

Whereas in the early 1940s, Federalist 1 signified a moral call to the American people to reform their own ways, by 1953 it signified the paramount responsibility Americans had to protest against the Soviet way.[63] Whereas in 1943, Dulles could say with other members of the FCCCA that Russian "anti-religious and materialistic" attitudes could "prevent a world community of spirit" but that "we need not assume that this will be the case," by the early 1950s he had concluded that it was the case.[64] Whereas in 1946, Dulles insisted in *Life* that "we *can* do something to bring Soviet leaders to change their foreign program"—and even could speak in a conciliatory manner about the USSR—by 1953 as secretary of state Dulles frequently addressed the Soviets in categorically condemnatory terms.[65] The Soviet's status as "other"—for Kennan a matter of pathology—became for Dulles a matter of a moral breach. The Soviets had gone too far; they had put themselves firmly without the bounds of a moral international community, even as they were still subject, in principle, to the universal moral law. And America's own virtue, as is the case with all radical rhetoric in a manifestic mode, had grown in proportion to the faithlessness of the USSR. Whereas in the 1940s Dulles saw the churches of the world and the Christian faith as instruments for the establishment of a world moral community, in the Department of State America became that instrument. What remained continuous throughout were a vision of world moral community, an instrumental approach toward its realization, and a commitment to public declarations as the medium of propagation.

Thus Dulles came to champion as secretary of state the "Eisenhower faith," in which, as he declared in a press conference, "the guiding spirit is liberty, not enslavement, and when human relations will be those of fraternity, not one-man domination."[66] Dulles frequently used such binaries; they served as rhetorical means of reifying the breach and of registering public moral protest. They were in form and function the vestiges of the manifestic mode of Protestant rhetoric, for their purpose was to delimit a moral world constituted by an "us" and a "them." In *War, Peace, and Change* Dulles criticized the "demonization" of other peoples and nations as counterproductive to the realization of peace. However, his argument presupposed the preeminent place of moral community, and his arguments against demonization were made on moral grounds. And within the logic of moral community there is always a limit beyond which the exclusion, if not the demonization, of the other is necessary for the preservation and integrity of the moral sense itself. In Protestant rhetoric, this limit represents the line dividing jeremiadic from manifestic speech. Dulles spoke from beyond this limit when he addressed the Council on Foreign Relations in New York in January 1954, introducing to the world what would become the strategic doctrine of "massive retaliation."

Dulles's Massive Retaliation

In the late summer and early fall of 1953, on the heels of Project Solarium, the Eisenhower administration took to focusing its strategic approach and putting its own distinctive stamp on it, culminating in NSC 162/2 of October 1953.[67] The document, packaged as the "New Look," entailed an unprecedented turn toward nuclear deterrence, and sanctioned a U.S. nuclear arsenal potent enough to "win" a nuclear war, if need be. The New Look held the potential to accomplish two strategic goals at once: "regaining the initiative while lowering costs."[68] Economic efficiency and strategic power and flexibility need not be mutually exclusive, the New Look postulated. It was a simple, if counterintuitive, formulation for a tension-riddled time in which Eisenhower was pulling ground troops out of Korea, placing "tactical" nuclear weapons in Western Europe, and trying to quell fires threatening to erupt in the Taiwan Strait, Berlin, Vietnam, and Iran, all the while trying to get his presidential feet on the ground. It was thus unfortunate for the president that the first major headline exposition of the New Look came through his verbose secretary of state, John Foster Dulles. In an address before the Council on Foreign Relations on January 12, 1954, Dulles announced a new foreign policy approach.

In that now historic speech, Dulles described, with Eisenhower's blessing, a "new strategy" of nuclear deterrence.[69] "The way to deter aggression is for the free community to be willing and able to respond vigorously at places and with means of its own choosing." "Massive retaliatory power," he argued, would let an aggressor "know that he cannot always prescribe battle conditions that suit him." This strategy would help the United States secure its role as a global police force to prevent Soviet aggression. "We keep locks on our doors; but we do not have an armed guard in every home. We rely principally on a community security system so well equipped to punish any who break in and steal that, in fact, would-be-aggressors are generally deterred."[70] In short, Dulles argued that threat of indiscriminate nuclear retaliation could keep a Soviet imperial appetite in check.

In this way, massive retaliation has been understood chiefly as a military or national security dogma—indeed, as the most notorious statement with regard to nuclear deterrence until Mutually Assured Destruction. In 1954, James Reston of the *New York Times* called massive retaliation a security doctrine "potentially graver than anything ever proposed by any United States Government."[71] In fact Dulles had been advocating such a retaliatory strategy as a means of deterrence since at least 1952.[72] However, even before the moment of its dramatic public declaration in 1954 massive retaliation suffered from an obvious set of strategic aporias. Indeed, Eisenhower himself during the 1952 campaign urged Dulles, who had explained to him the basic idea of massive retaliation, to consider the limits of the idea:

> America cannot live alone, and . . . her form of life is threatened by the Communistic dictatorship. . . . The minimum requirement of those programs is that we are able to trade freely, in spite of anything Russia may do, with those areas from which we obtain the raw materials that are vital to our country. . . . This means that we must be successful in developing collective security measures for the free world—measures that will encourage each of these countries to develop its own economic and political and spiritual strength. Exclusive reliance upon a mere power of retaliation is not a complete answer to the broad Soviet threats.[73]

Furthermore, Eisenhower had told Dulles that retaliation could do little to prevent "Soviet *political* aggression" from chipping away at the "exposed positions of the free world."[74] The concerns were not only Eisenhower's. After the Council on Foreign Relations speech that made massive retaliation well known, Hamilton Fish Armstrong pleaded with Dulles to write a follow-up article in *Foreign Affairs,* explaining, "Doubts remain in some minds both as to your meaning at some points and as to probable consequences at others." The questions were plain: Who was to decide how and when to respond? Was the United States committing to refuse to fight local skirmishes and rely exclusively on atomic retaliation? Might this have led to U.S. isolation from rest of world? What would happen when the USSR could reach the U.S. continent with its own bombs? Would massive retaliation be relevant anymore?[75] In fact, Dulles tried to clarify these points in an article in *Foreign Affairs* that spring.[76] However, rather than putting to rest the questions, the article led to their repetition. As Reston quipped in the *New York Times* after Dulles's supposed "clarification," "This 'massive retaliation' phrase has caused more trouble than any slogan since Clara Bow popularized 'it.'"[77]

There is no evidence to show that Dulles foresaw that massive retaliation would be such a snag to so many. He seems to have believed that the strategic principle behind it was clear and well established within government thinking; moreover, it does not appear that he intended to offer in massive retaliation a full-fledged security doctrine declaring that the United States would retaliate unilaterally and instantly if the Soviets started another proxy war, despite the fact that many believed this, including some who worked under him in the State Department.[78] Indeed, the broader consideration of Dulles's overall outlook I have undertaken here, together with the close reading of the Council on Foreign Relations speech, suggests that massive retaliation was never a well-composed security strategy. It was instead at its core a manifestic moral declaration. It announced, in dramatic form, a struggle against a dominant and oppressive Soviet force in light of a claim that the USSR was guilty of a dramatic breach of universal norms.

In fact, Dulles's jeremiadic complaints about America, expressed repeatedly in the 1940s, contained the seed of massive retaliation, for they presumed not only that the United States had an evangelical mission toward the establishment of a universal new order, but also that some force or power had to be put behind this mission. In the mid-1940s, Dulles envisioned the Protestant churches worldwide, the United Nations, and the United States each as agents of positive and forceful change in the world. The Protestant churches represented an already established transnational presence; the UN an emerging one; and the United States the exceptional bearer of a transnational liberal vision. The only persistent worry Dulles had during this period concerned the will of the United States, both popularly and officially, to act with positive resolution in world affairs. As Dulles expressed in a confidential memorandum to Secretary of State James Byrnes in 1946, "The United States needed to demonstrate to the rest of the world its capacity to act decisively in relation to international affairs."[79] Whether the United States would so act was a persistent question for Dulles in the immediate aftermath of the war. For a time, he spoke as if the churches and the United Nations would be far more effective forces for a new world order.

However, by the time he was in the State Department both the churches and the United Nations had fallen to the backdrop of Dulles's moral vision. This was due not only to his official governmental role, but to his commitment to an instrumental framework through which to realize new, moral, international boundaries. If power was needed as an instrument of world reform, America's power as a nation-state was manifestly greater than anything the churches or the United Nations could muster. In this respect, Dulles's approach resonated with the thought of Truman expressed in a letter to Dulles in 1945. "You represent the church militant," Truman wrote, "and there is need for your kind of militancy in this troubled world. . . . We often hear it said that spiritual values are indestructible, but I think it should be added that they are indestructible only as long as men are ready and willing to take action to preserve them."[80] Indeed, this sentiment was consistent with that used by the Truman administration to justify the dropping of atomic bombs on Hiroshima and Nagasaki but two months earlier. As Secretary of War Henry Stimson declared in a public statement on the day the bomb was dropped on Nagasaki, "No American can contemplate what Mr. Churchill has referred to as 'this terrible means of maintaining the rule of law in the world' without a determination that after this war is over this great force shall be used for the welfare and not the destruction of mankind."[81] The thinking here was indeed militant. It was also decidedly metonymic—the "whole" needed to take form in a forceful "part." For Truman, spiritual values needed to be realized in lived sacrifice and materially manifested power. For Churchill and Stimson the "rule of law" and the welfare of humankind needed a visible icon of force. National strength was as important as national purpose, for without strength, the nation could not act effectively in the world on behalf of its ideals.

For Dulles it had long been the case that power was meant to protect and cultivate moral ideals. However, his journey from the convictions of the church militant to a strong belief in the nation militant was more gradual. In fact, for him the atomic bomb was initially a false form of national power. Dulles's insistence on the priority of the nation's evangelical mission provided him with the grounds for condemning it in a speech in 1946 published as "The Atomic Bomb and Moral Law." The nation's role, he wrote, is above all to stand for "high moral principles" and then "to get power behind those principles." However, he complained, "The power that we want is the power of world opinion, not of atomic energy."[82] Frank Ninkovich argues that Cold War appeals like this to "world opinion" were part of a Wilsonian legacy.

> The struggle for world opinion, although it seemed at first sight to reflect an idealistic neo-Hegelian belief in a world spirit, was actually predicated on the belief that such controlling ideas were products of logical fantasy. Wilson and his successors recognized that there was no Cunning of Reason to guarantee automatically the progressive outcome of conflict situations; indeed, they suspected that the supposed rationality behind the balance-of-power concept was phony. . . . In their realization that history was not part of some meta-narrative, that technology and interdependence had made possible civilization's self-destruction as well as its onward march, and that the liberal sensibility in the twentieth century had suffered enormous shocks to its self-confidence, American policymakers cast off their old historicist baggage and sought to take history in hand.[83]

As a successor to Wilson, "world opinion" represented for Dulles the ethical (or subjective) side of the forces by which to take history in hand and save civilization. The conviction was not simply moralistic. It was activist, consistent with the pivotal political principle that ran through early Calvinism into Wilsonianism that new orders depend for their realization on the intentional exercise of power by political agents. In this way, Dulles's initial objection to the atomic bomb was not that it was a site of destructive power per se, but that, as far as he could see, it possessed only the negative power to create fear in people, not the positive and productive power of liberal ideas.

Yet, seven years later and six months prior to the Council on Foreign Relations speech, Dulles described a necessary, if not entirely positive, role for military might, including the atomic bomb. "The role of power," he told the graduating class of the National War College in 1953, "is to give moral ideas the time to take root." Invoking the community analogy crucial to his massive retaliation speech, he continued,

> Where moral ideas are well rooted, there is little occasion for much military or police force. We see that illustrated in our communities. Where the people accept the moral law and its great commandments, where they exercise self-control and self-discipline, then there is very little need for police power. . . . Where, however, there are many who do not accept moral principles, then that creates the need of force to protect those who do. That, unfortunately, is the case of the world community today.[84]

Dulles, I have argued, did not envision society fundamentally as a self. Rather, he saw it as moral community. Within the neostoic worldview, in which society is envisioned as a self, power tends to assume an essentialist cast—it is basic to social being as such and "symbolic" only in a secondary sense. However, within the Protestant frame (as with the romantic frame, as we will see), the symbolic is foundational and power secondary. Since its vision of moral community depends on language—in public and through speech the covenant is founded and renewed—the symbolic is basic to politics. Power, on the other hand, tends to take only an interventionist instrumental role where the integrity of the moral community is seen to be at risk. Power therein becomes both a form of raw force to address lawlessness and a persuasive symbol by which to reinforce the normative status of law. Alexis de Tocqueville observed of the Puritan uses of capital punishment, "Never was the death penalty more frequently prescribed and never more rarely enforced. The overriding concern of these legislators is the preservation of moral order and good practices in their society."[85] It was the same concern, it seems, that brought Dulles to judge the atomic bomb as useful.

The speech in which Dulles threatened massive retaliation began by commending the Truman administration for its loyalty to the United Nations, for its recognition that America's "own safety was tied up with that of others," and for its support for "Congressional bi-partisanship which puts the nation above politics." Thus, the speech affirmed what Dulles had long advocated: the notion of a world community concerned chiefly with the best interest of all, and the imperative need to transcend mere party or national politics. The speech, however, proceeded to complain that the Truman administration, for all of the good it did, succumbed to a reactive rather than a proactive mode in foreign policy. Echoing earlier complaints about containment as passive and defeatist, Dulles declared of Truman's policies, "But we need to recall that what we did was in the main emergency action, imposed on us by our enemies." Korea, the Marshall Plan, and the surge in military spending, Dulles claimed, all were initiated because the Soviets had acted first. It was the lack of a proactive policy, he insisted, that the Eisenhower administration sought to correct through the development of policies intended to serve the long haul (a basic premise of Eisenhower's New Look). He argued, however, that such a shift to a proactive and dynamic foreign policy was risky, as it could invite fear and miscalculation by other nations unclear as to U.S. purposes. Therefore, Dulles argued that it was "equally imperative" that "change should be accompanied by understanding of our true purposes. Sudden and spectacular change had to be avoided."

Dulles's speech before the Council on Foreign Relations therefore infused the broad approach sought by the Eisenhower administration, the New Look, with his own long-standing ideas about community, action, and change. Critical to the former was economy: Eisenhower's New Look sought to achieve an economically sustainable security policy by reducing military expenditures and troop numbers, decreasing production of conventional arms, and relying more on collective security and what seemed like relatively cheap nuclear weaponry. As Dulles told the Council on Foreign Relations, "We need allies and collective security. Our purpose is to make these relations more effective, less costly. This can be done by placing more reliance on deterrent power, and less dependence on local defensive power." For Dulles, critical to deterrent power, however, was the preservation of a strong sense of moral community, and this is what made Dulles's massive retaliation distinct from Eisenhower's own approach to nuclear deterrence.

While massive retaliation represented an expression of both Eisenhower's economic and Dulles's moral concerns, its logic was more closely tied to the latter. The language Dulles used to represent the doctrine of massive retaliation exposed the priority of moral community.

> We need allies and collective security. Our purpose is to make these relations more effective, less costly. This can be done by placing more reliance on deterrent power, and less dependence on local defensive power.
>
> This is accepted practice so far as local communities are concerned. We keep locks on our doors; but we do not have an armed guard in every home. We rely principally on a community security system so well equipped to punish any who break in and steal that, in fact, would-be-aggressors are generally deterred. That is the modern way of getting maximum protection at bearable cost.
>
> What the Eisenhower Administration seeks is a similar international security system. We want, for ourselves and the other free nations, a maximum deterrent at a bearable cost.
>
> Local defense will always be important. But there is no local defense which alone will contain the mighty land power of the Communist world. Local defenses must be reinforced by the further deterrent of massive retaliatory power. A potential aggressor must know that he cannot always prescribe battle conditions that suit him. Otherwise, for example, a potential aggressor, who is glutted with manpower might be tempted to attack in confidence that resistance would be confined to manpower. He might be tempted to attack in places where his superiority was decisive.

> The way to deter aggression is for the free community to be willing and able to respond vigorously at places and with means of its own choosing.

Nuclear deterrence was thus presented as an economically efficient means of international security, as "the modern way of getting maximum protection at bearable cost." However, it was also presented as an extension of a communal ethic. Dulles suggested that massive retaliation worked as a form of moral suasion, as a symbolic hedge against the power of the temptations of power itself, as a means of limiting aggressive agency. And he claimed that if massive retaliation were to be actually enacted, it would be a form of punishment.

The presumption of Dulles's articulation of massive retaliation was that the Soviet Union needed to be addressed as a moral self: not as an irrational but nevertheless self-interested actor on the world stage, as with Kennan (nor as a raw force to be controlled, as so often with Eisenhower), but as an agent responsible to moral law. Ironically, Dulles could address the Soviets as a self precisely because, in their totalitarian system, they had betrayed the liberal evangelical spirit. They were guilty, as *War, Peace, and Change* asserted, of "personification." Presumably, the virtuous moral act on their part would have been to die to their "self," submit themselves to an impersonal legal mode of authority, and to adopt the social mode of moral community. However, as long as that repentance was not achieved, a collectivity would need to stand over and against them as a deterrent threat against Soviet aggressive appetite.

Massive retaliation, therefore, entailed a claim—a claim to a right, a right "to retaliate, instantly, and by means and at places of our own choosing." It was here that the manifestic nature of Dulles's rhetoric was most apparent. In claiming the right to absolute retaliation, Dulles was claiming the right to initiate the ultimate end to the remaining solidarity of the international community *in the name of the norms of that community.* In other words, like the manifesto, the moral force of the Dulles's massive retaliation was presented as residing within the communal norms rather than without it. It was a stance, he claimed, intended to guarantee "the long-term defense of freedom," to "leave unimpaired those free world assets which in the long run will prevail," and indeed "to advance the cause of human welfare." Massive retaliation as a stance, he suggested, would in the long run "let time and fundamentals work for us."

> The fundamental, on our side, is the richness—spiritual, intellectual, and material—that freedom can produce and the irresistible attraction it then sets up. That is why we do not plan ourselves to shackle freedom to preserve freedom. We intend that our conduct and example shall continue, as in the past, to show all men how good can be the fruits of freedom.

Dulles's massive retaliation was thus presented as both the expression and protector of communal norms, norms assumed to have global reach.

Importantly, it was only after Dulles explained the doctrine of massive retaliation in the speech that the Soviets were specifically invoked. Although the identity of the accused was assumed, Dulles was careful to lay out the principle of massive retaliation in its abstract form before he explicitly named its target. Form preceded content. And, when Dulles did eventually name its target, the Soviets were addressed as a "dictatorship," a repressive power. Indeed, the peroration of the speech entailed a list of grievances against the Soviets—for denying the worship of God, the dictates of reason, and freedom of speech, and for establishing a society premised on the police state and forced labor. Dulles argued in concluding the speech that in no society can such practices be long sustained, and that the hope of the free world was that the Soviet leaders might "be dimly perceiving a basic fact, that is that there are limits to the power of any rulers indefinitely to suppress the human spirit."

> In that God-given fact lies our greatest hope. It is a hope that can sustain us. For even if the path ahead be long and hard, it need not be a warlike path; and we can know that at the end may be found the blessedness of peace.

Thus, remarkably, his infamous massive retaliation speech ended on a strongly universalistic, even benevolent, note.

Dulles's presentation of massive retaliation was a means toward the survival of a moral universe. His pronounced commitment to the United

States maintaining its right to act at the time and place of its own choosing in retaliating was presented in the speech as a necessary condition for *moral* as well as strategic initiative in the Cold War. The Communists, he claimed, had no moral scruples; they would seek their advantage wherever they thought themselves superior. Therefore it was crucial that the United States, which Dulles now portrayed as a highly moral agent, maintain both the aura of overwhelming power and the right to strategic prerogative. In this way, moral agency might endure in the Cold War world. As Dulles told the National War College, "Where . . . there are many who do not accept moral principles, then that creates the need of force to protect those who do." Security and power were envisioned not as "natural" conditions of being, but as instruments conceived to aid in the survival of a moral universe. Similarly, as the seat of world power, the United States was presented as principally moral in nature.

In Dulles's speech, the Soviets were covenant breakers. America, at least when compared to the Soviets, was a covenant keeper. Massive retaliation was a claim to moral prerogative and a declaration of resolute opposition to an oppressive dictatorship. Far more than a security strategy, massive retaliation was a means of maintaining a moral stance and a way of performing moral blame. Dulles had come to reconcile himself to the atomic bomb; he allowed it to escape strong moral purview; but he was adamant that whatever would come of its use, moral blame must fall on the Soviets.[86] Massive retaliation as a means by which to "punish" was a way of ensuring that moral blame would always fall on the Soviets and that the United States would maintain—even to the very end of humanity itself, if need be—its moral agency and superiority.

But this meant that massive retaliation was a conditional, contingent, and indeed conflicted strategy built on an inviolable logic. As Dulles told a gathering of Department of Defense chiefs in 1958, massive retaliation was a "practical concept," derived from a particular set of circumstances. But its practicality, as a summary memorandum of the meeting relates Dulles arguing, meant that its strength was limited, and indeed would "rapidly deteriorate as the consequences of putting the doctrine into action became so appalling." "Are we," Dulles asked his Defense counterparts, "becoming prisoners of our strategic concept and caught in a vicious circle?" The memorandum continues,

Secretary Dulles pointed out that the world works not unlike a small community. He pointed out that policemen didn't have machine guns. The London police for years used only sticks. He acknowledged that circumstances had forced us to depend on a strategic concept which was quite limited and one that won't work in the coming years. Fortunately, future circumstances may no longer require the doctrine as an exclusive one.

Dulles thus came to question massive retaliation *as* nuclear deterrence, but he does not seem to have questioned the underlying evangelical conception of the world that I have argued motivated the strategic statement, nor its emphasis on moral policing. Ironically, his Defense counterparts resisted his questions about nuclear deterrence by turning his infamous words of 1954 against him. As Deputy Secretary of Defense Donald Quarles argued before Dulles at the same meeting, nuclear deterrence "had a certain inevitability about it." "The best defense," Quarles insisted, "is in a strong offense at places of our choosing."[87] In this way evangelical language could be turned against the evangelical.

Conclusion

In an essay written in the thick of the Cold War on Dulles's rhetoric, Wayne Brockriede concluded that Dulles offered "symbolic appeals that did not change the fundamental United States foreign policy since 1947—containment."[88] Dulles, Brockriede argued, but offered a "new rhetoric" to justify an "old policy." Most historians of the Cold War have basically agreed, as, in many respects, do I. And yet, we might ask, why the new rhetoric? In part, to be sure, it was simply a matter of differentiating the Eisenhower administration's policies from those of Truman. Clearly there was an element of populism in it as well. Brockriede argues,

> His evangelistic advocacy of the anticommunist ideology gave him general popular and congressional support. Dulles had his performance as secretary of state evaluated not by the wisdom of his policy but by the enthusiasm of the rhetorical justification for the current United States

ideology. Dulles saw the Cold War as primarily a "moral struggle" rather than as a power political struggle.[89]

And yet to invoke a "new rhetoric" to distinguish one's approach from a prior "immoral" one, and to thus appeal to populist sentiment, is, of course, to invoke a rhetoric that is only "new" in a limited sense. For Dulles to see the Cold War as a moral struggle was to invoke an old rhetoric on behalf of a relatively new foreign policy situation wherein the United States was suddenly one of two undeniable global hegemons. It was to recast this new situation, to change, indeed transform, the register on which success and failure in the Cold War might be measured. It was to cast the nation before a different Cold War aspirational horizon by resurrecting an old image of America. Thus whatever it might otherwise mask or occlude in terms of the actual policies of the Eisenhower administration, the significance of Dulles's covenantal rhetoric should not be minimized, even on the level of policy.

In Dulles's massive retaliation, I have argued, radicalism, activism, transnationalism, instrumentalism, and moralism were combined into a manifestic speech act. To reduce Dulles's 1954 address before the Council on Foreign Relations to merely a hyperbolic and vitriolic expression of the philosophy of nuclear deterrence is to neglect the wager of the speech, which risked publicly a trajectory toward the annihilation of human society in the name of preserving the moral texture of that society. Of course, there were significant ideological and pragmatic reasons Dulles worked to preserve this moral texture, not the least the fact that his government's quest for public support to fight the Cold War gained much from the "demonization" of the USSR. Militancy needs an enemy, as Dulles himself warned in *War, Peace, and Change*. However, such axioms, while true, too often fail to acknowledge the thickness of such demonizations.

Indeed, the problem with any account of Dulles's views as *mere* political opportunism—or legalism, moralism, universalism, fanaticism, or even nationalism—is, first of all, the very same problem entailed in the notion of "grand strategy": the presumption that political actors and actions can be approached unequivocally. Strategies of security and strategies of speech always entail more than the aligning of means and ends. And it is, second of all, to neglect the thick historical traditions that have claimed, as evangelicalism has, that the symbolic is foundational to politics, power secondary. Dulles's declaratory act in massive retaliation was in this sense, in the spirit of Woodrow Wilson, an intervention in the world of *Realpolitik* strategy, both as a pragmatic attempt to reclaim the benefits of "world opinion" for the United States (this failed) and, as my discussion of his pre-1950s career suggests, as a more ideational attempt to insist, in a manner entirely consistent with Eisenhower, that the symbolic world represents the world wherein human aspirations are most fully realized (this, in collaboration with Eisenhower, succeeded).

To be sure, massive retaliation even in this symbolic register was heavily laden with equivocations: it drew upon the universality of the moral law to propose the prospect of universal annihilation; its instrumentalism exempted from the purview of moral examination both the language of protest and technologies of destruction; and its radicalism led to its conservative nationalism. In short, it lost sight of human goods in the name of rights, and so contradicted itself. Similar equivocations have been endemic to Protestant evangelicalism since the Reformation: its zeal for universal human solidarity has resulted in violence against humans; it has embraced an amoral instrumentalism in the name of achieving its moral aims; and its radicalism has produced a reactionary conservatism. Moreover, evangelicalism's history, like Dulles's history, has often been passively or actively complicit in the liberal political, technological, and commercial projects of modernity. Liberalism has often hijacked evangelicalism, turning its moral and evangelistic zeal into fervor for markets, innovations, and imperialism. Protestant evangelicalism, on the other hand, has often willingly given itself over to such projects for love of its own power or fear of its own irrelevance.

However, while evangelicalism in this way represents a dangerous spirit, it is critical to also note that more than any other worldview examined in this book—the others being stoicism, romanticism, and adventurism—evangelicalism can acknowledge the equivocations of being in the world without sliding into a stoic and skeptical removal from the world, an opportunistic nihilism, or a romantic partitioning of Being. The paradox of massive retaliation is that even as it was a dangerously equivocal idea, it contained the seeds of its own critique vis-à-vis the notion of the moral law. For all of the admirable ways in which stoicism cultivates self-critique and a type of appreciation for universal human solidarity, its ethic is strangely resistant to critiquing things in the world apart from the preeminent concern with the care of the self. Seneca could write of the virtuous life and of his brotherhood with slaves while contently working in Nero's court and owning persons as chattel. Marcus Aurelius could meditate on cosmopolitanism while leading the empire's wars. And Kennan could famously characterize the Soviets as pathological while stoutly refusing to morally judge their acts as crimes. Indeed, stoic *apatheia* can produce an indifference to the means through which lives are actually lived in the world. Even Kennan's well-known opposition to the nuclear arms race was marked by an indifferent instrumental logic. As he wrote his friend Louis Halle in 1966,

> The weapons of mass destruction have no rational political application. The aim of warfare, if it is to be anything more than sheer unreasoning panic or madness, must be to affect in some way the political realities in a given part of the world. . . . This is not done by acts of blind destruction. Stalin, I believe, had this same view. For him, as for myself (intellectually), the aim of war—the only rational aim—is to affect political realities in a manner favorable to one's self.[90]

Kennan's objection to nuclear arms reflected here was strictly a form of self-preservation, even self-care. By his logic, if nuclear weaponry could be shown "to affect political realities a manner favorable to one's self," their place in the American arsenal would be secure.

On the other hand, Dulles's career was characterized by a frenetic and too often thin but nevertheless consistent willingness to critique the objects and entities in the world before him. Of the figures I consider in this book, he is the only one who seriously questioned at one point in his career the sanctity of the nation-state. Similarly, well before 1958 his commitment to nuclear deterrence, despite the legacy of massive retaliation, was far from unequivocal. Indeed, even as he was preparing his speech before the Council on Foreign Relations Dulles was pushing hard for disarmament talks with the Soviets, however equivocally, only to be met with firm resistance in the Department of Defense.[91] In fact, as John Lewis Gaddis has written of Dulles's advocacy for greater strategic flexibility, "Dulles persistently sought to achieve this flexibility by reducing the Eisenhower administration's reliance on nuclear deterrence—only to encounter resistance for Eisenhower himself."[92] Dulles's concerns were strategic in the classical sense: he worried that American nuclear militancy would create abroad a psychological climate of "appeasement" vis-à-vis the Soviets.[93] But his reservations were also more explicitly moral: as secretary of state, he confessed to German chancellor Konrad Adenauer of the use of the bomb, "Even to contemplate it seems unchristian."[94] Dulles's evangelicalism produced a preoccupation with means and, relative to many of his contemporaries, a distinct willingness to change courses, reimagine possibilities, and advocate change. He also, much more successfully than the other figures featured in this book, persisted in approaching the Soviet leaders as moral agents.

Evangelicalism's equivocations, therefore, should not be lightly dismissed as "moralism" or smugly ridiculed as "hypocrisy," as is all too common among stoics, skeptics, and nihilists. If nothing else, the intensity of the evangelical engagement with the world provides a more useful picture of the complexity of action in the world than does stoic rationalism, or, as I will discuss in the subsequent chapters, adventurist exploit and romantic instrumentalism. Evangelicalism's equivocal radical history, including massive retaliation, evinces a fact to which liberal modernity is too frequently blind: intentional action in the world always risks creating conditions for its own disruption or undoing. Both conservative and progressive liberalisms can assume the basic obstinacy of the world, either per se or in its historical progression, respectively. Evangelicalism, in assuming that, as Walzer writes, "specifically designated and organized bands of men might play a creative part in the political world," approaches action as a wager and the world as a field of action caught between obstinacies and indeterminacies. Creative action thus can have surprisingly constructive or catastrophic consequences. Both the "optimistic" and "tragic" sensibility of the evangelical is therefore ethical and historical, rather than ontological or historicist.

With respect to grand strategy, evangelicalism admonishes its pretensions. Indeed, a policy that would orchestrate all the nation's major instruments, resources, institutions, and interest groups on behalf of "best interests" falsely assumes with neostoicism the possibility of an unequivocal national order and the straightforward nature of action. Kennan's persistent disappointment with American foreign policy stands as a vivid testimony to the profound difficulty of approaching strategy in this way. And Dulles's shifting and frenetic career offers another kind of testimony. To act at all, his career suggests, is to act in the world with others, and to act in the world with others is to submit oneself to the world's and other's obstinacies and indeterminacies. It is to risk being "carried away." Indeed, massive retaliation, as a Protestant speech act, was a supreme example of political action being carried away by a mode of speech and a type of public culture. Kennan's and Dulles's two very different ways of being in the world suggest that the ultimate question of grand strategy is not about means and ends, policy and interests, but about the nature of positive national action in the world.

In fact, it was precisely this question that preoccupied Dwight Eisenhower's discourse during his years in the White House. Whereas Kennan relied on an ethical type as a guide for positive action in the world only to be frequently frustrated and alienated by America's failure to achieve his ideal, and whereas Dulles relied on a faith in the positive potential of universal moral community only to grow more and more hostile in his rhetoric toward the Soviet rupture of that community, Eisenhower partitioned national being into two distinct realms, one material and instrumental and the other spiritual or ideal. More than a quirky feature of his rhetoric or a concession to civil religion, Eisenhower's dualism represented a romantic legacy in American foreign policy.

Yet, before I proceed to discuss Eisenhower more fully, I want to turn to a strategy that had a most ambivalent place within the Eisenhower administration, that of "liberation." Early in the Cold War, Dulles was himself known for his advocacy of liberation, specifically with regard to the Eastern European countries of the Soviet bloc. For him and others, liberation represented an aggressive policy over and against the "passive" one of containment, and it was quite consistent with his evangelical sense of moral activism. Nevertheless, Dulles did not pursue liberation with the same political energy with which he pursued moral policing; massive retaliation much more succinctly encapsulated his foreign policy attitudes and outlooks than did liberation. Similarly, Eisenhower in the end gave little credence to liberation. Nevertheless, the creed lived on in the halls of the Eisenhower White House and the Dulles State Department in the 1950s. In the next chapter, I consider its vocation by looking at the career of one of its more persistent proponents, the adventurer C. D. Jackson.

CHAPTER 3

Deeds Undone: C. D. Jackson, Liberation, and Adventurism

It is not your sin, but your moderation that cries to heaven.
—Nietzsche, *Thus Spoke Zarathustra*

Spirits die hard, but when they do it can be disastrous. Such was the sentiment that brought together an illustrious group of American intellectuals, journalists, and government brass for three days in Dedham, Massachusetts, in May 1957. The list of invitees included Alfred H. Barr (director, Museum of Modern Art), Richard M. Bissell (CIA), Lyman Bryson (Jewish Theological Seminary of America), McGeorge Bundy (then at Harvard), Joseph I. Coffey (U.S. Army), Richard Hofstadter (Columbia), Carl Jonas (a novelist), George F. Kennan (then at Princeton), Duncan Norton-Taylor (*Fortune* magazine), J. Robert Oppenheimer (Princeton), David Riesman (Chicago), W. W. Rostow (MIT), Arthur M. Schlesinger, Sr. (Harvard), and William S. White (*New York Times*). What was the occasion for congregating these power elite? *The American Style*, or so was titled the volume that emerged from the gathering.

For a number of years, MIT's Max Millikan explained in the preface to the work, the premise in U.S. foreign policy had been "that the difficulties with which we are confronted in our international relations spring primarily from the nature and evolution of the foreign countries with which we deal." However, Millikan continued,

> We have been impressed anew with the fact that the characteristics of our own society are as important as developments abroad in determining the shape of our foreign relations. Again and again we have been forced to the conclusion that a more imaginative and constructive international performance by the United States is inhibited not so much by the intransigent forces outside our borders as by our values, by the way our government functions, by the American image of the world we live in, by our historically determined national style.[1]

Therefore the meeting at Dedham (funded by the Carnegie Corporation) was called in order to take account not only of the "American style," but, as Walt Rostow wrote in the volume, "how the national style as a whole and recent changes in it strengthen or weaken the society's ability to deal with certain major problems it confronts and is likely to confront over the foreseeable future."[2] National style was thus a *strategic* concern (as Kennan had noted too), and its apparent intransigency as "historically determined" brought Rostow to treat it as if it were a natural resource needing husbanding, managing, juggling, manipulating, and, above all, renewing.

What were the features of "the national style" according to Rostow? A propensity for great ideals, a persistent pragmatism with regard to problem solving, a perpetual conflict among individual, group, and regional interests, and a sense of "participation in the special adventure of America"—such Tocquevillian commonplaces, Rostow argued, comprised "relatively stable patterns of performance" in the nation.[3] However, he warned that the culture of the Cold War presented significant challenges to America's national style. An increase in material wealth, urbanization and bureaucratization, the welfare state, and the threat of World War III each presented substantial challenges to the American ideals, practices, and sentiments that Rostow argued were integral to the nation's success before the Cold War crisis.[4] If national style was like a natural resource, the midcentury acceleration of bureaucratization, wealth, urbanization, state power, and world danger comprised something like an intricate administrative maze that hindered the ready exploitation of that resource. Indeed, for Rostow as for midcentury thinkers ranging from David Riesman to James Burnham, the first phenomenon, bureaucratization, represented not only a challenge to, but the stylistic antithesis of, traditional American national style, and in this way it was one of the nation's greatest internal disruptions.[5] The solution for Rostow was not to deconstruct the managerial revolution, but to infuse it with a spirit of old. "Somehow, finally," he argued, "we must, if we are to succeed, find ways of suffusing the national government with a sense of private adventure."[6]

My argument in this chapter is that the worldview of the would-be strategy of "liberation" in the 1950s stemmed from this selfsame sense of adventure; that while liberation suffered disrepute and was at best only covertly pursued in the decade, it represented for some the truest strategic expression of "the national style." Whereas containment could be seen as passive, and nuclear retaliation or deterrence as either militant or overly instrumental, liberation seemed to these figures to be the only strategy that faithfully articulated the essence of America as an experiment, an adventure, on behalf of liberty. Thus, during the 1950s, even as it was constrained by the long-haul instrumentalism of Eisenhower's New Look, liberation was sublimated from a martial act into a vision of a new kind of American political-economic adventurism abroad. I argue that in the decade and a half between D-Day in 1944 and President Kennedy's announcement of the Alliance for Progress in 1961, an American spirit of liberatory adventurism underwent a profound transfiguration. Ultimately, liberation became fused (or *con*fused) with liberalization. We see in this transfiguration a distinct Cold War worldview, one that rested neither on a sense of society as a stoic self, nor on the notion of moral community, nor on a romantic dualism, but on the image of America as a dramatic performer on the world stage. With this performative adventurism came the sense of irony inherent within all dramatic action, for the stage is a place where meaning is never literal, actions are always "roles," and effect always the object of orchestration. Indeed, as I will show in this chapter as well, adventurism in modern Western politics has perennially possessed an element of drama, and thus irony. Therefore, in chronicling the transfiguration of liberation in the 1950s from principally a martial idea to a political-economic one, I chart a change the direction of American adventurism, but not its basic form.

As this chapter concerns a transfiguration, I focus in it on a transitional figure. Charles Douglas (C. D.) Jackson first worked with Dwight Eisenhower in World War II as Eisenhower's psychological warfare advisor. By the end of the 1950s, after a great deal of work for the president as a Cold War strategist, speechwriter, and, in H. W. Brands's words, a "bureaucratic provocateur," Jackson dismissed much of Eisenhower's Cold War leadership as lacking opportunism, boldness, and imagination.[7] A symptom of this, he held, was the Eisenhower administration's abandonment of the idea of "liberation," made so powerful by Eisenhower's actions at D-Day. And while he harbored serious doubts that Kennedy would do any better, his close collaborator in the 1950s, Rostow, promised that the new president could and indeed would. Jackson thus represents a line of continuity between both the worldview (adventurism) and, in a certain respect, the strategy (liberation) of D-Day and Kennedy's bold political-economic initiatives.

I begin the body of this chapter with an overview of Jackson's role in the Cold War in the 1950s, arguing for his place within a history of adventurism. Then I consider important factors that helped create the strategic context for Jackson's adventurism, and subsequently, in the next section, I look at more broadly cultural and ideational factors that propelled it, especially Henry Luce's "American Century" and Rostow's modernization theory. In the penultimate section of the chapter I discuss what I see as the culmination of Jackson's approach, an ambitious proposal for a "World Economic Plan," which was envisioned as part of a broader project of liberation. I then conclude the chapter by considering both the role and the significance of American adventurism in the early Cold War, and its implications for both conceptions of strategy and conceptions of the nation in a world of nations.

In the end, this chapter explores the continuity in worldview and strategy between a deed undone by the United States in the early Cold War, the political liberation of peoples behind the Iron Curtain, and American scientific, economic, and political adventures beyond its borders. The line of continuity, admittedly, is circuitous, in at least two ways. First, as I will suggest in the conclusion, adventurism is an amorphous spirit, motivating a variety of political, economic, and scientific enterprises. This chapter will focus on the former two domains, but the legacy of adventurism in the Cold War in spectacular space exploration shows that scientific and technological outlooks were near kin to those of politics and economics during the period. Second, the circuitousness of *political* liberation is seen in its partisan and ideological travels in the 1950s: in the early 1950s it was Republicans championing liberation, whereas a decade later it was a liberal elite that claimed fidelity to the idea.[8] To be sure, the Eisenhower administration would go on to engage in a great many covert and subversive operations as part of its cold war. And yet Eisenhower approached such measures as a tactical matter, and not as a great American adventure. Soon advocates of liberation like Jackson came to see Eisenhower's approach as differing little in tone and temperament from Truman's "passive" containment policy. It would be left, they hoped, to the Kennedy administration to reintroduce adventure to America's sense of itself. And indeed even as Nikita Khrushchev was publicly declaring support for "wars of national liberation," Kennedy proclaimed in his inaugural, "Now the trumpet summons us again—not as a call to bear arms, though arms we need—not as a call to battle, though embattled we are—but a call to bear the burden of a long twilight struggle, year in and year out, 'rejoicing in hope, patient in tribulation'—a struggle against the common enemies of man: tyranny, poverty, disease, and war itself."[9] And so he urged deeds done on behalf of liberty worldwide, clearly echoing Republican calls in the early 1950s for an affirmative, proactive American foreign policy on behalf of liberty. Indeed, this trek through the transformations and transfigurations of liberation in the 1950s shows that spirits do indeed die hard, if they die at all.

Liberation and Adventurism

In June 1963, but a year and a half into the Kennedy presidency, John Steele, the Washington bureau chief for *Time* magazine, received a distressed letter from C. D. Jackson, then a Time Inc. executive. "The following is the result of quite a lot of introspective stewing over the last few weeks," the letter began. "As you know, I have been extremely interested over the years in the Free Europe Committee, not just for emotional anti-Communist reasons, but because as I look at the map of the world, the Eastern Europe satellite group is still the only real Achilles' Heel in Mr. Khrushchev's empire." Yet, Jackson worried, it seemed that the Kennedy administration "actually considers these countries nuisances." Might Kennedy, he asked, be "in the mood to sell the Eastern European satellite countries down the river"? Would Steele do some sleuthing on his behalf to find out?[10]

At the time of the letter Jackson was not only publisher of *Life* but also one of the most experienced practitioners in the United States of what Eisenhower called "psychological warfare," but what Jackson himself typically called "political warfare" or simply "cold war methods." Before Eisenhower's election, Jackson had been president of the Council for Democracy, an economic and political warfare specialist during World War II, a chief architect and director of Radio Free Europe, and a close ally of Henry Luce, overseeing at different times beginning in 1937 Luce's *Time*, *Life*, *Fortune*, and *Sports Illustrated*, and founding the international editions of *Time* and *Life*. During Eisenhower's tenure as president, Jackson was a regular if not always official advisor to Eisenhower and John Foster Dulles and one of Eisenhower's most notable speechwriters. And throughout his Cold War career he participated in both high-level government national security meetings and in the often off-the-record meetings of powerful private groups like the Advertising Council, MIT's Center for International Studies, and the Bilderberg Group—all to formulate American and European Cold War campaigns. Recollecting Jackson's career, Rostow declared of Jackson's role in the Cold War, "When the history of this decade [1950s] is written, even C.D.'s friends will be surprised to know how many of the enterprises of which the nation can be proud were sparked or colored by his initiative."[11] Indeed, as Rostow knew because of his role in both the Eisenhower and Kennedy administrations, while many of Jackson's proposals failed under Eisenhower, what he advocated—indeed, what he embodied—was taken up in the Kennedy administration with some vigor, especially with respect to economic development abroad.

Steele's reply to Jackson's letter is telling in this respect. "The Kennedy Administration in no sense of the word has consciously written off Eastern Europe," he fired back, sounding more like an administration spokesman than a journalistic sleuth. "Its policy, to use an abused phrase, is 'eventual, peaceful liberation.'" Citing private interviews with Dean Rusk, George Ball, Rostow, and others, Steele swore that liberation "does represent what the current Administration—for better or for worse—is up to." Rostow, who was working on economic development programs for Kennedy, had asked Steele to tell Jackson, "The SOBs who fought C. D. and I [in the 1950s] are at their weakest point ever." Steele reminded Jackson that Kennedy himself had said publicly in West Berlin, "The right of free choice is no special privilege claimed by the Germans alone. It is an elemental requirement of human justice. So this is our goal, and it is a goal which may be attainable most readily in the context of the reconstitution of the larger Europe on both sides of the harsh line which now divides it." The administration, Steele emphasized, "DOES . . . believe in the possibility of such change." All in all, Steele argued that Jackson's vision of an energetic, though largely nonmartial, American policy of liberation, after years of frustration under Eisenhower, was finally being realized in the Kennedy administration.[12]

Thus, while Jackson worried about the Kennedy administration's Cold War intentions, Steele, Rostow, and others were persuaded that Kennedy would at least attempt to fulfill what Jackson had stood for all along. The connection between Jackson, an Eisenhower cold warrior, and Kennedy's "eventual, peaceful liberation," is subtle but strong. It is found, I suggest, in both a circle of collaborators including Jackson and Rostow, and in a broader worldview vis-à-vis the Cold War that Jackson articulated: American adventurism, especially political-economic adventurism.

Perhaps the most important discussions of adventurism in Western political philosophy occur in Machiavelli. Cyrus, Romulus, Theseus, and even Moses, Machiavelli explains in *The Prince,* are models worthy of the admiration and imitation of princes because "they owed nothing to fortune but the opportunity which gave them matter to be shaped into what form they thought fit." The adventurism of these figures resided in their action before opportunity and their willingness to risk, for "there is nothing more difficult to carry out, nor more doubtful of success, nor more dangerous to handle, than to initiate a new order of things."[13] Machiavelli portrayed the adventurer prince as an innovator, a practitioner of state*craft,* and thus akin to an artist who masterfully makes out of available resources an extraordinary new thing. More so, the adventurer prince was for Machiavelli a performer, as his innovation was rooted in *action.* J. G. A. Pocock writes of Machiavelli's chapter 2 of *The Prince,* where the Roman strategy of what we might call "preventative war" is recommended,

> We hear for the first time the assertion that the prime necessity of strategic behavior is action. The alternative to action is delay and temporization, and once time has become the domain of pure contingency [as it is in Machiavelli] it is impossible to temporize because there can be no secure assumptions about what time will bring; or rather, the only assumption must be that, unless acted upon, it will being change to one's disadvantage. One has power, and others have not; the only change that can come is that others will gain power, to the loss of one's own.[14]

The urgency of time, the assumption of a zero-sum game, and the imperative of action—such ideas comprise the substance of the ethic of Machiavelli's adventurer. Importantly, "liberty," understood as maximum autonomy from fortune, was integral to this ethic; it entailed, above all, a quest for mastery of one's own fate and freedom from happenstance, and thus a right to glory, understood as the reward for the highest *human* achievements.

As Michael Walzer suggests, Machiavelli's adventurer prince is a progenitor to a more modern economic version of the adventurer: both share a "new [modern] consciousness of politics as a matter of individual skill and calculation." Indeed, the adventurer represents a transitional figure between antiquity and modernity. As with the ancients, the adventurer is driven largely by the prospect of *glory,* rather than "goodness" or "self-preservation."[15] Yet, with the moderns, the adventurer is "cut loose from organic, hierarchical, and particularistic ties—ambitious, calculating, irreverent."[16] Consequently, Machiavelli's adventurer preserves something of the ideal of Aristotle's megalopsychic man (the "great soul"), while rejecting the ethical Aristotelian framework of virtues, or any other strongly constraining moral framework.

In fact, the adventurer has been seen perennially as a lawless type. Machiavelli's adventurer prince gains power through exploiting opportunity by means of "force or fraud."[17] In *Democracy in America,* Alexis de Tocqueville characterizes the economic adventurer of the early American colonies as a man of "turbulent and restless spirit," fundamentally lawless and eager to profit from the new and relatively lawless world.[18] Max Weber offers a further portrait of the economic adventurer as a perennial historical figure seeking "the exploitation of political opportunities and irrational speculation."[19] The significance of the adventurer for Weber resides largely in the type's attitude, which "laughs at all ethical limitations" and is thoroughly opportunistic.[20] It is no wonder, therefore, that Federalist 11 described "the adventurous spirit, which distinguishes the commercial character of America" as exciting "uneasy sensations in several of the maritime powers of Europe."[21] Indeed, American adventurism has bled over into uneasy figures of the "frontier" as diverse as Jesse James, Daniel Boone, and J. P. Morgan, all who shared a propensity to make the great exploit their defining mark, and all who have, to different degrees, ambivalent legacies in America.[22]

In seventeenth-century Elizabethan drama Machiavelli's villain enjoyed great influence, seen in characters like Christopher Marlowe's Barabas in *The Jew of Malta* and Shakespeare's *Henry V.* Lionel Trilling suggests that such enterprising Machiavellian figures were popular in the period because they represented the possibility of social mobility "by covert acts, by guile."[23] In this way, Baldassare Castiglione's *The Book of the Courtier* shared with Machiavelli's *The Prince* not only tremendous popularity in the Renaissance, but also an emphasis on mobility through scheming. Castiglione advocated that the courtier pursue *sprezzatura,* the ability to "conceal all art and make whatever is done or said appear to be without effort and almost without any thought about it."[24] The courtier of the Renaissance imagined political identity in a distinctly aesthetic way.

> In an age of great portrait art, he paints his own portrait, as it were. He wears carefully crafted masks that help him to improve his character. He is always "on stage," always carefully monitoring how his performance

is affecting his audience, the people around him. Above all, he must appear to do everything that he does so wonderfully well without much conscious effort: This is his crowning trait. . . . The performance must never appear to be a performance.[25]

Thus social mobility was conceived as artistry and adventure, but designed in such as a way as to appear natural, lacking affectation, and even striking the cord of destiny. In fact, suggesting a further link between Castiglione's courtier and Machiavelli's adventurer prince, Machiavelli, after praising the great adventurer princes of the past as owing "nothing to fortune but the opportunity," stressed that it was the opportunities presented by fortune that "gave these men their chance." Thus, it was the opportunistic and masterful seizure of the moment that allowed both the courtier and the adventurer to succeed in their respective enterprises.

In seventeenth-century England, such means of social mobility were not merely a part of an aristocratic courtly political culture, but employed by a blossoming merchant class. In fact, seventeenth-century economic adventurism came face-to-face with evangelicalism: the *Mayflower* was boarded by two types of seventeenth-century personalities, the pious Puritan and the enterprising economic adventurer. And, as Bradford's account of the Mayflower Compact testifies, it was the guile, the amorality, and the anarchy of the latter that drove the former to form a binding, solemn covenant.[26] To be sure, the adventurer and the evangelical, although profoundly at odds with regard to their basic outlook toward the world, resemble each other in form: both are activists, ambitious, and quite eager to transgress fixed social boundaries for their respective causes. Felix Gilbert has thus suggested that a basic incongruity resides at the historical and imaginary "founding" of the New World: "The promise of financial rewards and the belief in the possibility and necessity of constructing a more perfect social order were two motives which led people to embark on the dangerous voyage to the New World. Different—almost contradictory—as these two motives were, they existed together, tightly intertwined in the development of the various English settlements on American soil."[27] As I will discuss, nowhere were these tightly intertwined spirits more pronounced in twentieth-century America than in Henry Luce's "American Century" and its champions. Luce, the son of a missionary, took the language of evangelicalism and applied it to capitalist enterprise. In so doing, I suggest, he merely exploited the common form of the evangelical and the adventurer, enveloping the motives of the latter in the language of the former.

Indeed, one barrier to discerning the worldview of adventurism with respect to *national* ways of being in the world is that it seems, at least at first glance, purely individualistic, disassociated from imagined communities. Because adventurism is enterprising, anarchic, and "heroic," it appears to be an ethic of the individual, not the group. However, Machiavelli's adventurer was a profoundly social creature. This is apparent in the opening of the first book of the *Discourses,* where he presented the writing of political theory itself as an adventure:

> Although the envious nature of men, so prompt to blame and so slow to praise, makes the discovery and introduction of any new principles and systems as dangerous almost as the exploration of unknown seas and continents, yet, animated by that desire which impels me to do what may prove for the common benefit of all, I have resolved to open a new route, which has not been followed by any one, and may prove difficult and troublesome, but may also bring me some reward in the approbation of those who will kindly appreciate my efforts.[28]

Worth noting here is the way in which Machiavelli imagines his "adventure" as both "for the common benefit of all" ("comune benefizio a ciascuno") and as potentially meriting "some reward in the approbation" of others. Thus, his adventurism, while it stressed the importance of individual feats, was not radically individualistic; quite to the contrary, it represented a *social* ethic, both in the sense that it was seen as serving a form of "common good" and in that the adventurer looked to the approbation of others for "reward." Furthermore, as an ethic of *glory,* adventurism not only depends on a social context for its realization, but lends itself to a kind of conversion to corporate dimensions. As Georg Simmel suggests, adventurers tend to make climatic feats subservient to an *idea*. The adventure, like the passionate love affair, Simmel argues, "displays two standards of time: the momentarily climatic, abruptly subsiding passion; and the idea of something which cannot pass."[29] To be sure, the quest for glory is a quest for a place in timelessness, and nations as well as individuals can aspire to such a place. In fact, in the eyes of some, the *only* permanent legacy a nation might achieve is one of glory. Made a self-conscious pursuit, glory becomes not the by-product of great national feats but their designed end. It is in this way that adventurism can be highly ironic; it is a performative and dramatic ethic paradoxically premised on a highly "realistic" perspective—either as glory becomes its own end in a world devoid of any other binding moral meaning, or as glory becomes a means of inspiring others to pursue what the strategist views as ultimately a raw power calculation.

Indeed, the need for "glory" has been connected to anxieties about American democracy. Tocqueville warned in the nineteenth century that leaders of democracies "would be wrong to seek to lull their citizens to sleep with too flat and quiet a happiness." "It is good," he urged, "occasionally to give them difficult and dangerous tasks, so as to rouse their ambition and give it a stage upon which to perform."[30] Tocqueville thus suggested that a democratic society's gains with regard to egalitarianism could be its bane with regard to enterprising collective action. In this vein, Burnham, who had published a theoretical work on Machiavellianism in 1943, insisted in his 1953 *Containment or Liberation?* that in order for the United States to win the Cold War, it would have to engender greater sacrifice from its people.[31] Yet, he wrote,

> It is perhaps the crucial defect of the policy of containment that it is incapable of meeting this moral and spiritual demand. Who will willingly suffer, sacrifice and die for containment? The very notion is ridiculous. The average man cannot even understand the policy of containment, much less become willing to die for it. . . . For a man to endure resolutely, he must believe that he is pursuing a goal—he must believe so even if the goal is in reality an illusion or a lie.[32]

Here the dangerous adventure of liberation via aggressive "political warfare"—Burnham's means of choice—and even martial attacks, was ironically conceived as a means toward, in Burnham's words, circumventing "the gravest peril," "a mortal danger."[33] For Burnham, liberation was a strategic idea ironically wrought out of the same faith in a "realistic" perspective that thinkers ranging from Tocqueville to Kennan claimed—to see the world as it is, not as we wish it to be.

Indeed, even though Burnham made Kennan his arch-political enemy, in important respects their differences were not profound: both hinged their arguments on a realistic appraisal of the world situation, both put national subjectivity at the center of their solution, and both sought to win. They differed only—and profoundly—over the correct realistic appraisal of the world situation and the resultant shape national subjectivity should take in order to win the Cold War. Kennan might be called a literalist, assuming a basic order in the world (e.g., "balance of powers") and calling for subjective conformity to this order; Burnham was an ironist, disavowing any natural order (which he criticized as rooted in "metaphysics") in the world, and contriving the performance of American liberatory "destiny" as a self-conscious design to mobilize national subjectivity in the service of raw national power.

As will become apparent, Jackson's strategic outlook paralleled Burnham's. Jackson's ideal of adventurism hinged on the accomplishment of great feats and paid relatively little heed to a "natural" order of things or a moral law. And, as an iteration of the American Century, the *idea* assumed a preeminent place in his approach, especially the idea of liberation. His was thus a form of adventurism where the adventurers were themselves quiet, indiscreetly working behind the scenes to orchestrate great national feats in order to validate and further an ideology, a "way of life," and capitalist economics. Above all, his approach was thoroughly ironic, self-consciously advocating an essentially artificial concept of the nation a dramatic actor on the world stage for aesthetic effect in the service of power and interest.

However, this artificiality vis-à-vis liberation, and indeed artifice, not only had tacit or explicit support from other Cold War cultural elite like Burnham, but was situated within the official strategic setting of the early Cold War and the broad cultural ideal, even movement, in the United States associated with Henry Luce's American Century and new economic theories. Therefore, although infused with irony and self-conscious artificiality, liberation was not merely a fanciful idea of provocateurs, disassociated from the exigencies, urgencies, and pressures of "necessity." In order to show how the Cold War idea of liberation developed in response to political and cultural exigencies, I devote the next three sections of this chapter to the particular historical context C. D. Jackson worked within with respect both to a set of strategic Cold War concerns and to an aspect of American political culture associated with Luce and the emerging notion of modernization.

The Emergence of "Peaceful Liberation"

In a campaign speech in San Francisco shortly before his election, Eisenhower argued for the centrality of psychological warfare in the conflict with the Soviets. He pledged that if elected he would place "a man of exceptional qualifications" who had "the full confidence of, and direct access to, the Chief Executive" over America's psychological warfare operations. The first of such men in the Eisenhower administration would be Jackson. His mandate, according to Eisenhower's speech, was to ensure that "every significant act of government should be so timed and so directed at a principal target and so related to other governmental actions that it will produce maximum effect." Anticipating themes in "Chance for Peace," "Atoms for Peace," and Jackson's World Economic Plan, Eisenhower placed economic assistance among a set of psychological-warfare tactics—also including propaganda, travel, and sports—that could "gain a victory without causalities."[34]

And so, as Kenneth Osgood writes, Eisenhower inaugurated a presidential administration that "ensured that psychological strategy—the shaping of policies and programs for their impact on public attitudes at home and abroad—would exert a greater influence on his foreign policies than on those of any other presidential administration."[35] Scholars like Osgood, Christopher Simpson, and J. Michael Hogan have emphasized that behind this sweeping adoption of psychological strategy was the tremendous currency of the "new" communication sciences. Social scientists like Harold Laswell, writes J. Michael Sproule, believed,

> With the advent of democracy, social control necessarily proceeded through symbols more than by force. "If the mass will be free of chains of iron, it must be accept its chains of silver." From this vantage point,

propaganda technique could be seen as a matter of efficaciously solidifying the polity as opposed to wantonly manipulating citizens.[36]

In this regard, both Osgood and Simpson look at the influence of Laswell and public relations upon the development of America's Cold War approach, and Hogan examines the new perceived power of polling through the career of George Gallup.[37] To be sure, as I discussed in chapter 1, the social sciences offered government officials a framework by which to imagine political possibilities ranging from social control to social cooperation. C. D. Jackson was no less interested in these possibilities than his more stoic contemporaries. Indeed, as Hogan shows, the Eisenhower administration's influential President's Committee on International Information Activities, to which Jackson was central, "echoed Gallup on virtually every major topic relating to the purposes, character, and media of American overseas propaganda."[38] Nevertheless, there was another, more antique, dimension to the Eisenhower administration's psychological warfare activities represented by Jackson: that of Machiavellian *activism* that defied the bedrock naturalism of the social sciences and instead embraced the sheer artificiality of the political stage.

Thus Jackson's means of addressing the contradictions of political action. The Eisenhower administration's emphasis on psychological warfare frequently put Eisenhower in a position where his public words contradicted more privately deliberated policy, not the least with "liberation" and its near synonym "rollback."[39] Indeed, both Dulles's and Eisenhower's gestures toward liberation as a policy put them in positions of contradiction. For Dulles, as I have argued, the contradiction took the form of equivocation: his discourse, which put the United States in the position of a kind of global moral police force, led to talk of "rollback" that far exceeded in its ambition both the nation's will and global support. For Eisenhower, as I will discuss further in the next chapter, the contradiction was dualistic in form: the spirit of liberation represented the essence of the nation even as its policies would be much more cautious, calculating, and conservative. For Jackson, however, the contradiction was ironic in form; "liberation" represented for him neither a moral imperative nor the essence of the nation's spiritual principles, but rather a central aspect of "maximum effect" in the Cold War. It entailed for him something profoundly "American" vis-à-vis the image of the nation and, in this way, something profoundly threatening to the Soviets. Indeed, his career in the 1950s can be understood in terms of a persistent quest to amplify the legacy of liberation as a national performance in World War II in the service of the Cold War. Yet Eisenhower's concept of "victory without causalities" made the pursuit of liberation in U.S. foreign policy a tricky affair, for while World War II had made liberation a preeminent American act, it had also made it firmly a martial, and indeed moral, act. To follow Jackson's career in the 1950s is thus to follow the evolution of the notion of liberation from the overtly martial and strongly moral to the realm of adventure.

In the few years subsequent to World War II the memory of heroic military enterprises so consumed the nation that the use of the word *liberation* in American public discourse straightforwardly denoted a form of military intervention derived from a moral mission. For example, as the North Korean army advanced south in late June 1950, leading the United States to enter the Korean War, the *New York Times* told its readers, "Like the war that ended in 1945, this also is a war of liberation."[40] And when in September 1950, MacArthur succeeded in taking Seoul, Truman congratulated the general for the city's "liberation."[41] In this way, when in the early Cold War Americans imagined the act of liberation, they were likely, given the near-history of the Allied liberation of the European continent, to imagine GIs. Indeed, America's intervention in Korea seemed to solidify "liberation" as a martial idea.

Yet, liberation could represent something more abstract, a "national purpose" not strictly tied to martial intervention, an aspect of America's long-term purpose in the Cold War. Truman's Policy Planning Staff, under Kennan's leadership, had envisioned America stimulating a "heretical drifting-away process" in the Soviet satellites that could be seen as a form of liberation.[42] In this vein, President Truman publicly told an audience in West Virginia,

> Remember that in 1941 it was President Roosevelt who refused to recognize the brutal Soviet seizure of Latvia, Lithuania, and Estonia. We have never accepted that aggressive act. Remember, too, that on Navy Day in 1945, and at the opening of Congress in 1946, and many, many

times since, I have stated that America will always work for the return of freedom and independence to the people who have been deprived of them by force or by subversion.[43]

In this way, containment could be seen as consistent with liberation, where the latter represented a long-term national purpose as well as moral commitment.[44] Yet the moral and ideological connotations of liberation could be turned sharply against containment. In the buildup to the 1952 presidential election internationalist Republicans sought to sack Democrats by accusing them of adopting in containment a defensive, passive, and indeed, as Dulles claimed, an immoral policy—"containment" became a slur. Democrats defended themselves by insisting that their party not only represented liberation more truly than the Republicans, but had a track record of success. In a radio debate with Dulles, William Averell Harriman, after Dulles lambasted Truman's "containment," retorted, "containment has never been the Administration's policy." Rather, he argued, "we have had a dynamic policy, which has rolled Communism back in many areas of the world."[45] In this way, even as containment was the regnant strategic position among policymakers, it suffered a kind of moral and ideological inferiority before liberation.

This inferiority was due in part to the power of a Protestant moral vision, like that envisioned by Dulles; but it was also due to the strength of liberal political-economic ideology. Indeed, implicit in more historic liberal forms of political and economic thought are ideas that democracy and commerce could themselves be viral liberating forces. When surmising the reasons for both of the great wars of the first half of the twentieth century, important American opinion-makers believed that illiberal political and economic policies were at least partly responsible for the horrors. More liberal trade was seen as a panacea to such crises and as a means of turning the world away from totalitarian tendencies. For this reason the third of Woodrow Wilson's Fourteen Points was, "The removal, so far as possible, of all economic barriers and the establishment of an equality of trade conditions among all the nations consenting to the peace and associating themselves for its maintenance."[46] The same idea emerged in response to World War II. In 1944, both Bretton Woods and Dumbarton Oaks proceeded according to the assumption that more liberal trade was necessary for global peace. With respect to Dumbarton Oaks, the United States successfully argued that the canopy of the United Nations should cover world economic development, and not merely security alliances. Thus when the UN was formed, the Economic and Social Council was as central to the UN as the Security Council in the minds of many, and this former council's initial outlook, as John Toye and Richard Toye write, was "broadly based on an American blueprint."[47] As the war came to an end, Americans, Britons, and other Westerners saw economic enterprise and development as having the potential to be the centerpiece of an effort to create not only global stability, but a liberalized world.[48]

Not surprisingly, therefore, liberation was a vague strategic notion, and its relationship to American intervention abroad conflicted. As the Korean War was under way as a "war of liberation," in fact two images of American intervention abroad were firmly in place: on the one hand, military interventions, as that in Korea, and on the other, large-scale economic interventions like the Marshall Plan. Both military and the political-economic forms of intervention could be addressed as broadly "liberating." Yet it was not clear if both represented means of "liberation." According to Robert Taft's logic, and that developing within the Eisenhower campaign, political-economic intervention could be envisioned as a means of liberation vis-à-vis "psychological warfare."[49] According to architects and advocates of the Marshall Plan like Kennan, however, political-economic intervention was more likely to be viewed as an act of "reconstruction" or "development" in the service of containment. Therefore, while two images of American intervention abroad were in place, one martial and the other political-economic, their respective strategic places were, on the whole, muddled. Were they both ultimately aimed at liberation? Were they both aimed at containment? Was containment merely an interim policy within an ultimate strategy of liberation? Or was liberation merely vitriolic war talk?

The 1952 U.S. presidential campaign was fought, in part, over these questions, and Republicans found what was to them a satisfactory resolution in the notions of psychological warfare and "peaceful liberation." In the 1952 election, Adlai Stevenson affirmed a clear binary between martial and political-economic interventions abroad. Largely following Kennan's template, he argued explicitly that Democrats believed in an approach to the war against Communism that was characterized by two distinct fronts, defense through localized armed conflicts, as in Korea, and U.S.-sponsored economic development in areas free of internal political strife, as in India.[50] Stevenson thus preserved the sense of liberation-as-martial-action energized in World War II, but presented Korea as more about containment than liberation, even as he argued for economic aid in stable but economically underdeveloped areas. Indeed, in 1952—amidst increasing concern about the advent of Soviet atomic power—"liberation" was lambasted by some Democrats: "Talk of liberation under present circumstances is war talk," Truman shot back at Republicans.[51]

Republicans, in fact, were more than sensitive to this accusation, Eisenhower not the least. Eisenhower, to be sure, wanted to steer clear of any substantial armed conflict that might escalate out of control into a general war fought with atomic weapons.[52] Thus, his campaign began to speak of "peaceful liberation," which they presented as a new form of Cold War effort. For example, having urged in public a policy of "rollback," John Foster Dulles later qualified his approach: "No responsible person that I know of has advocated a war of liberation or an effort now to stir up the captive peoples to violent revolt. I myself have categorically rejected that idea," he told the Chicago Council on Foreign Relations while campaigning for Eisenhower in 1952.[53] Instead, he and other Republicans were in favor of "peaceful liberation." Indeed, Eisenhower call for psychological warfare in the 1952 campaign represented a unified and integrated approach to the conflict with the Soviets—as opposed to Stevenson's basic two-front approach—that supposedly could achieve liberation without resorting to full-scale war.

Upon taking office, Eisenhower oversaw the centralizing and militarizing of propaganda in the White House.[54] This centralizing and militarizing, however, went much further than propaganda operations. Under Eisenhower's vision of psychological warfare all U.S. interventions abroad would be part of a unified Cold War effort. The president's notion of psychological warfare "extended beyond the official propaganda agencies of the American government to embrace any word or deed that affected the hearts and minds of the world's peoples."[55] C. D. Jackson was instrumental in shaping this vision. He was a pivotal member of the seminal committee of the administration with regard to psychological warfare, the President's Committee on International Information Activities (also called the Jackson Committee after its chair William Jackson). Indeed, this committee was itself in part the product of a preelection secret conference on psychological warfare held at Princeton, discussed below, which had been organized by C. D. Jackson. The "Jackson Report" urged a unified and militarized approach to psychological warfare, stating, "Psychological activity is not a field of endeavor separable from the main body of diplomatic, economic, and military measures by which the United States seeks to achieve its national objectives. It is an ingredient of such measures."[56] This unified approach was retained in spirit, if not always in practice, well into the Eisenhower years.

In effect, the Eisenhower administration was pointing to a kind of reversal of a Clausewitzian formula: the "political" became war by other means. Far from being restricted to pacific strategies, the Eisenhower administration—not the least Jackson—substantially broadened the meaning of "war." It became "total," part of what Robert Ivie describes as a culture-wide transformation in America toward the institutionalization of an "age of peril."[57] Thus eventually references to "psychological warfare" were displaced by "political warfare." "Words like 'propaganda' and 'psychological warfare,'" warned one statement in Eisenhower's circles in 1952, "have apparently obscured from American view the fact and significance of *political* warfare."

> Political warfare may be defined as "coordinated governmental action in the international field in time of cold war." *Political warfare is an alternative, not a preliminary, to armed warfare.* It is the sum of the activities in which a government engages for the attainment of its objectives without unleashing armed warfare. But it is a description which applies to none of those activities when each of them is carried on independently of the others. In that case they become "mere" diplomacy, intelligence, propaganda, economic negotiation, armament production, and so on. The essence of political warfare is that it is planned and the means employed to carry it on are coordinated.[58]

This spacious and ambitious conception of political warfare contrasted sharply with neatly delimited definition of "political strategy" being offered at the National War College in the winter of 1952: "'Political strategy' is considered to include those measures employed to change policies of foreign governments and the position and aims of elite groups of foreign governments rather than to influence large masses of peoples." Such "political strategy" was distinguished from "economic strategy" and "psychological strategy," the former having to do with "economic pressures to disrupt the enemy" and the latter with "measures taken against masses."[59] In the Eisenhower administration, on the contrary, "political warfare" represented a comprehensive, integrated "alternative" to armed warfare—but with respect to means, not ends. As such, it purportedly could resolve the tension within the notion of "peaceful liberation." "Peaceful liberation" was more than a slogan of the Republican's 1952 campaign. It represented an attitude and a strategic orientation. It brought together what to the postwar mind was typically kept apart, representing the conflation of all forms of American international action and intervention into the act of war—albeit now unconventional war.[60]

The turn to "peaceful liberation" was a way to give purpose to a new unified and forceful Cold War strategy. It gave activists within the administration like Jackson and Dulles a framework for a more aggressive Cold War policy. And yet it did it in a way that could pacify Eisenhower's anxieties about risking general war or overspending on defense—key components of the New Look.[61] "Peaceful liberation" represented the delicate attempt of the Eisenhower administration to avoid general war and show economic restraint even as the United States pursued a "bold" and "dynamic" Cold War policy.

Containing Liberation

It was the subjects of political warfare and liberation that Jackson (then sitting atop *Fortune* magazine), Abbot Washburn, and Arthur Page addressed at a private meeting with over twenty other men in Princeton in May 1952. Attendees included representatives from the State Department, the CIA, Radio Free Europe, the Psychological Strategy Board, Princeton University, and MIT, including Rostow. Steered by Jackson, conversation at the secret meeting centered on liberation via political warfare. "No clear statement had been made by the President or the Secretary of State," Jackson complained of the Truman administration, "to the effect that it is the policy of the nation 'that the 100,000,000 people enslaved by the Russian Communist regime behind the Iron Curtain shall be free.'"[62] America, Jackson argued, had simply failed to seize opportunities to engage in political warfare. "What we are here for," he concluded, "is to determine whether or not an American *will* to engage in political warfare can be stimulated; if it can, the objectives and the means will be forthcoming without too much difficulty."

Despite this expression of confidence in the relative ease of political warfare itself, Jackson and others at the conference knew that "peaceful liberation" could be very complicated. Charles Bohlen, representing Truman's State Department, decried Jackson's call for the United States to announce an explicit policy of liberation: "If you say that as the Government, you say your policy is the overthrow of the Soviet regime." Robert Joyce, of Truman's Policy Planning Staff, retorted that the question of armed conflict was not merely one Americans were worried about. Europeans "were troubled by American lack of patience, fearful that we may pull the trigger, unsure that we are 'politically mature enough' to attain our aims without war." Thus, a political war of liberation required a level of political discipline and virtue that the United States had yet to effectively display (Kennan's worry, too). Even Allen Dulles, already working with the CIA, felt the need to remind the conference participants, "We should clearly state that peaceful means are envisaged." The question remained, then, how the nation could go about liberation or talk of liberation without inaugurating another world war. And even as this question was tossed about, Rostow made the matter even more complicated: liberation in Eastern Europe, he argued, was about seeing "that part of the world move without war towards a shape which is in the American interest." Liberation, therefore, had to serve American interests—not necessarily a given, as Tito had dramatically demonstrated in 1949.

In this way, the 1952 Princeton conference contemplated a template of American Cold War strategy that was (1) explicitly centered on "liberation," (2) restricted to "political" means, and (3) committed to staying within the bounds of American interests (however defined). Washburn, in a memo written to Eisenhower summarizing the majority sentiment at the conference, stated, "The policy of mere 'containment' or holding of the line against further Soviet expansion has outlived its usefulness and should be replaced with a more dynamic and positive policy of ultimate liberation of the enslaved nations, in line with our fundamental American concept of man's God-given right to individual freedom." However, he continued, liberation did not mean conventional war; political warfare could "win World War III without our having to fight it."[63] It was exactly this sentiment that Eisenhower expressed in his campaign speeches.

The Princeton conference helped give birth to the Eisenhower administration's 1953 "Jackson Report," which was squarely marked with C. D. Jackson's thought. The document asserted, "Soviet rulers will be most reluctant to run deliberately a grave risk of general war." It added, "However, we agree with the estimate that 'the USSR will continue its efforts to undermine and destroy the non-communist world by political warfare.'"[64] Counteroperations against the Soviet system, the report advised, should include economic embargoes and use of agencies like the Voice of America—that is, as long as the U.S. government could accept responsibility for their actions. Otherwise, it urged that private organizations be used, which could secretly operate with the support and supervision of government agencies like the CIA but appear to be purely civilian agencies, therefore freeing the government from having to accept responsibility for their actions. In this way, the Jackson Report placed a strong emphasis on state-private networks in fighting the most provocative battles of political warfare.[65] Overt interventions of the United States within the Soviet bloc or otherwise neutral areas had to be designed so as to not bear the traces of overt U.S. hostility or aggression. Whatever subversive or liberatory actions the United States might take, the nation must maintain the appearance of being basically pacific in its intentions.

The October 1953 NSC 162/2—the first major security statement of the Eisenhower administration, which stressed nuclear deterrence—constrained the enterprise of liberation even more. Echoing Joyce's concern about the attitude of Europeans toward America's ability to exercise military restraint and political wisdom, as well as something of the perspective of Task Force A in Project Solarium, NSC 162/2 warned that American militancy threatened to weaken the confidence of allies in America's leadership.

> Many consider U.S. attitudes toward the Soviets as too rigid and unyielding and, at the same time, as unstable, holding risks ranging from preventative war and "liberation" to withdrawal into isolation. Many consider that these policies fail to reflect the perspective and confidence expected in the leadership of a great nation, and reflect too great a pre-occupation with anti-communism.[66]

Consequently, the document suggested, Cold War tactics of the United States had not only to appear pacific, but positive. It was not enough for the nation to appear merely nonaggressive. America had to instill constructive confidence in its allies while still taking "feasible political, economic, propaganda and covert measures designed to create and exploit troublesome problems for the USSR, impair Soviet relations with Communist China, complicate control in the satellites, and retard the growth of the military and economic potential of the Soviet bloc."[67] Yet perhaps the greatest constraint put on liberation in the Eisenhower administration was the emphasis of the New Look on budgetary restraint in the name of economic stability and long-term U.S. vitality in the conflict with the Soviets. NSC 162/2 rested on the supposition that U.S. success in the Cold War depended on a strong and expanding American economy capable of sustaining the "long pull." Consequently, under its purview, whatever liberation might be, if it was to be it must not cripple the nation economically, invite wartime catastrophe, or otherwise put too great a risk upon the nation.

Therefore, by the time Eisenhower established his Cold War policies, three emphases were clear: the avoidance of general war, an emphasis on America creating for itself the appearance of peaceful purposes, and the emergence of the U.S. economy as a pivotal front in the Cold War. In this climate, liberation, where it survived at all as a relevant strategic concept, was sublimated into the activities of state-private networks, American economic enterprises, covert actions, and other forms of American action abroad aimed at vindicating and furthering the American way without risking America's "peaceful" image.

For Jackson, liberation survived, and potentially could thrive. However, the constraints presented placed on it by the Eisenhower administration meant that for him liberation required a transfiguration into a kind of political artistry reminiscent of Machiavelli's adventurer prince and Castiglione's courtier. That Jackson preferred "political warfare" to "psychological warfare" was not merely incidental—it suggested a vision of the world of nations dominated by Machiavellian notions of power and action, rather than by psychological and social-scientific notions of social control through balancing the forces of cognition and affect. Communication scholars and historians have attended to the social-scientific inspirations behind America's psychological warfare; they have not yet well reckoned with this older political spirit.

Like Burnham, Jackson was a "new Machiavellian," possessed by a spirit of political artistry and adventure. America's actions in and before the world needed to be of such character as to forward the superiority of the *American* economic and political way. An element of striking spectacle was in this regard critical, for global audiences needed to come to associate the United States in particular with the promise of their own well-being. On the other hand, U.S. propagation of its way had to be designed so as to not draw attention to its aggressive and contrived character. It must appear "natural." Otherwise the United States could appear at best as a disingenuous manipulator upon the world stage, and at worst as a careless and unlawful antagonist. This demand meant the invention of efforts on behalf of ideological ideas that could not seem to be anything but natural expressions of America's pacific purposes. As Martin J. Medhurst has shown, "Chance for Peace" and "Atoms for Peace" were conceived in this vein, and as J. Michael Hogan has shown, so was "Open Skies."[68] Jackson was an integral part of all three of these speeches. However, Jackson, consistent with the vision of his mentor Luce's "American Century," pushed for an even more expansive and adventurous approach to combating the Soviets than these captivating speeches. He urged large-scale international programs, believing them to be both entirely in line with the psychological and economic concerns of Eisenhower, and critical to the United States' long-term success. Jackson believed liberation should motivate a grand American policy, but one that did not appear militantly aggressive and dangerous to the world. He believed, in other words, that the drama of liberation should be performed on the world stage with great effect but without the least bit of affectation.

Jackson and the Artistry of the American Century

In 1959, by then quite frustrated with the Eisenhower administration's Cold War designs, Jackson wrote Allen Dulles, "Were we really smart in abandoning the policy of liberation and carefully never mentioning the word again?" "Liberation," he continued, "is not an ugly word; it is a good word: it is an American word; it is an unambiguous word. It is the one word the Kremlin fears."[69] Indeed, Jackson measured the progress of the Cold War not on a scale of world stability or a balance of powers, but on one of world opinion vis-à-vis the contagion of the idea of liberty. As much as any of his contemporaries in the Eisenhower administration, he retained the ideological emphases seen in the Truman administration. Like Truman's NSC 68, Jackson believed that the conflict with the Soviets was principally ideological in nature and needed to be approached as such.[70] For Soviet successes, as Jackson measured them, were derived from the combination of a well-organized political system with a compelling ideology.

In fact, the efficiency of the former, he believed, was due to the power of the latter. "We are always amazed," he wrote Rostow,

> at the way in which Communist officials and organizations are able within a brief space of time—24 hours—to say the same thing simultaneously in hundreds of languages all over the world in response to some event or action. The unsophisticated assume that a message of instruction on the Party line has been flashed from the Kremlin to all parts of the world. You and I know that that is not true, even if it were technically possible to cover that many bases in that short a time with a coded message.
>
> What we actually witness is the operation of the "diamat," [dialectical materialism] the ideological and operational Litmus paper to which a trained Communist applies any stimulus. Given a worldwide uniform dogma, an identical set of goals, and few carefully worked out overall limitations, practically every half-way intelligent professional Communist anywhere in the world can almost instantly come up with the same answer.
>
> We do not seem to have worked out our "diamat."[71]

For Jackson, the *strategic* gains and losses of America in the Cold War depended on the power of ideology. Jackson's view of human psychology was strongly ideational, as well as, with the social scientists, quite behavioristic. Convince a people of an idea and you can manage their actions and reactions. And yet such control depended on orchestrating political action, rather than merely numbing the masses with the buzz of propaganda.

Jackson sought what he described, retrospectively, to Rostow in 1962 as a "Orchestrated, total, long-term program" for U.S. victory through political warfare in the Cold War.[72] To be sure, *orchestrate* is a revealing word for understanding the tensions of Jackson's approach to political warfare. It was for him, a patron of the Metropolitan Opera, more than a term to describe coordinated effort; it was a metaphor of artistic virtuosity. "If this is not properly orchestrated, and these things are dribbled out without organized impact," Jackson warned Sherman Adams in 1953 about Eisenhower's "Atoms for Peace" proposal, "we will fritter away what is probably the greatest opportunity we have had yet."[73] Or, as he argued in a secret panel report of the Quantico meetings of 1955, gaining public support for foreign policy in a democracy, as opposed to dictatorship, was "a matter of orchestration."[74] Indeed, *orchestrate* is a word that contains a tension that was ever-present in his work with Eisenhower, that between "order" and "artistry." Shawn J. Parry-Giles describes how Eisenhower, following aspects of Truman's precedent and consistent with the basic recommendations of the Jackson Report, pursued "a propaganda pyramid of operations [that] allowed Eisenhower to serve as commander-in-chief of the propaganda program, with the White House functioning as the central command post."[75] This "militarization" of propaganda through the establishment of a command-and-control model achieved one aspect of C. D. Jackson's vision, the integration of all aspects of U.S. foreign (and often domestic) policy into a coordinated political warfare model. But at the same time it tended to militate against other equally vital aspects of Jackson's approach, creativity and adaptability. While the more streamlined bureaucratic structures Parry-Giles chronicles could serve to "orchestrate" through coordination and integration, they could work against the inventiveness and nimbleness of the U.S. propaganda apparatus. This tension was a constant point of frustration for Jackson, one that was sharpened in his pursuit of "liberation."

Therefore, as we have seen, Jackson held that America's success before Communism depended on thoroughly integrating political warfare into every diplomatic, security, and economic policy. He argued everyone in authority should take "responsibility for at least elementary psywar thinking." Political warriors were not "magicians manipulating some mysterious device, but were to be considered specialists in assisting the Departments and Agencies to achieve the desired impact abroad."[76] Political warfare, in other words, could not be partitioned into a distinct realm of the Cold War. It was at the very heart of "cold" war. It was politics-as-war. And for Jackson an idea at the heart of political warfare remained liberation. Liberation, Jackson believed, could be the United States' "diamat."

But this meant that for Jackson liberation entailed a kind of artistry, specifically the translation of the American Way into other countries and cultures. It was part of the comprehensive image of America envisioned by his mentor, archliberal internationalist Henry Luce, in 1941 in "The American Century":

> America as the dynamic center of ever-widening spheres of enterprise, America as the training center of the skillful servants of mankind, America as the Good Samaritan, really believing again that it is more blessed to give than to receive, and America as the powerhouse of the ideals of Freedom and Justice—out of these elements surely can be fashioned a vision of the 20th Century to which we can and will devote ourselves in joy and gladness and vigor and enthusiasm.[77]

Luce's vision was strongly ideological, but not strictly so. It claimed self-interest as well as a national historical mission as principal motives. "America," Luce explained, "is responsible, to herself as well as to history, for the world-environment in which she lives.... [I]f America's environment is unfavorable to the growth of American life, then America has nobody to blame so deeply as she must herself."[78] For Luce and Jackson praise and blame could only be measured in terms of an epochal and revolutionary American imperative demanding the expansion, rather than the maintenance or diminution, of the American Way. Luce and Jackson held an explicitly nation-centered rendering of internationalism.

Jackson's vision of liberation represented the perdurance of the

American Century into the Cold War. Consistent with Luce's American Century, liberation under Jackson's oversight hinged on notions of political and economic virtuosity: adeptness at accomplishment, articulation, production, performance, and profit on the world stage. And it demanded that America be what it represents. The abundance wrought by capitalism, Jackson believed, gave America a profound advantage in the Cold War both with respect to establishing a free world order and generating favorable sentiments from other nations. Yet, unlike Eisenhower in his more fiscally conservative moments, Jackson tended to envision economic expansion less in terms of sustaining the American way of life than in terms of fulfilling an adventurous American mission. Free enterprise was the product of artful innovation and intervention. In this sense, Jackson became not only champion of liberation but also of "development."

It was in collaboration with Rostow that Jackson had opportunity to refine his approach to development. In the early 1950s Rostow, an economist who had been involved in the formation of the Marshall Plan, served as an advisor and speechwriter to Eisenhower, working with Jackson on "Chance for Peace" (a speech that, as Robert Ivie has shown, hinges on adventurous notions of "quest" and "crusade").[79] Simultaneously Rostow was developing an approach to economic development that came to be known as the "take-off model." The model was at once structural and contingent. It theorized development as proceeding from "traditional societies" through four subsequent discrete stages culminating in an "age of high mass consumption" associated with science and technology. Importantly, the model relied neither on historical determinism nor exclusively on impersonal economic forces for its theory of development. Development sometimes needed to be managed, massaged, or otherwise supervised by expert authorities. Economic epochs, much like Luce's vision of historical epochs, rested on contingencies. And Rostow placed ideology at the center of these contingencies—Communism, no matter if it was embraced in Russia, China, Cuba, or Antarctica, represented a monolithic approach to economic modernization and political control, captured in the notion of dialectical materialism, and a similarly monolithic democratic capitalism represented its only viable alternative. Thus, Rostow's model stressed the role political actors could play in political-economic coordination and the propagation of an ideology.[80]

Through his collaboration with Luce and Rostow, as well as through his experience in mass media and his impression of the stunning success of Soviet propaganda, Jackson seems to have grown increasingly convinced in the 1950s that the success of America in the Cold War depended on a strategy of aggressive but adept intervention in world affairs. "In this business of political warfare," he exhorted attendees of the 1952 secret Princeton conference, "it does no good to stand still. Somebody is going to move into the vacuum; and if we don't, the enemy will; not only will, but is doing it every day of the week."[81] Jackson's vision of the zero-sum dynamism of the Cold War world engendered a strong belief in opportunism. In seizing or not seizing the moment, America would win or lose the fight with the Soviets.

The consequence was a good deal of historicism, repeated attempts by Jackson to read the times. In a memo to Luce and several other Time Inc. executives dated June 21, 1955 (the day after an Eisenhower's speech at United Nations in San Francisco in which the president declared, "But the summer of 1955, like that one of 1945, is another season of high hope for the world")[82] Jackson argued that 1955 would likely be, in the eyes of historians, "the year 'things began to get unstuck' internationally." For the Soviets, he continued, "the summer of 1955 represents the moment when the ratio of their weakness to our strength became very plain to them and assumed practical military, political, and economic meaning to them." Referencing an article in the *New York Times*, he insisted that the paper was wrong when it urged the free world to see the summer of 1955 as a time to "stand firm." Such an approach was "defeatist." Rather, "This is the moment of all moments when our diplomacy, our military posture, and our economic actions should not give them what Walt Rostow refers to as 'options for fussing around.'" "*Our* problem, *our* challenge, *our* responsibility, is to see to it that this moment is not just a passing point on a graph, but a continuing line through the immediately coming years."[83]

To see the moment as a point on a graph upon which depends the trajectory of history is to invoke both Luce's revolutionary and Rostow's structuralist narratives. History is characterized by epochal shifts formed out of quiet actions taken within condensed auspicious moments, or crises. Political actors carry the weight of history itself as the future rests upon the quality of their response to the opportune moment. The deep structure of such a worldview hinges on the ideal of political virtuosity as the right word or action at the right time (what the ancient Greeks called *kairos*). "Time," as Jackson wrote in a philosophical mood in the June 1955 memo to Luce, "is the essential common denominator that runs through everything."[84]

Jackson thus worked behind the scenes on project after project and plan after plan to take advantage of opportune moments. The "Jackson Report" articulated an adventuristic worldview, as it suggested that Stalin's death represented an auspicious moment in the U.S. propaganda offensive.[85] Following the report, Jackson, working on "Atoms for Peace," wrote Eisenhower regarding the need for a candid speech about nuclear war, declaring, "The need for a frank speech on the atomic age and Continental Defense is, if anything, greater than ever. . . . The speech should be given as soon as possible—certainly before Congress reconvenes, and preferably during October or not later than the first week in November."[86] Indeed, this fixation with the moment helped generate Eisenhower's most memorable speeches. The dramatic announcements of "Chance for Peace," "Atoms for Peace," and "Open Skies" were fueled by Jackson's penchant for creating what he once referred to as "absolutely electrifying" effects on the world stage.[87]

Yet, because ideology was primary, such effects often depended on strategic deception.[88] Jackson was nearly as satisfied with fostering illusions of American political-economic virtuosity as he was in seeing the nation take more muscular steps in foreign relations. For example, as a follow-up to "Atoms for Peace," Jackson suggested to Eisenhower and the CIA's Frank Wisner that the United States start an international rumor of plans to build an atomic reactor in Berlin for economic-development purposes. A rumor, he argued, "is almost as good as actual [sic] getting on with the work." What was critical for Jackson was that United States follow "Atoms for Peace" with "symbolic evidence" of its intentions to spark the global economy with the infusion of nuclear energy, irrespective of the feasibility of plans. "In this work" he continued, "as you know, the emotional and psychological impact of a small and relatively unimportant piece of action is as great, and frequently greater, than a vague realization that something tremendous is being cooked up behind closed doors which *might* be unveiled months hence."[89] Jackson was convinced that more concrete and material actions were needed as well—especially with regard to opening up foreign markets and encouraging trade—but economic enterprise was always for him principally a symbolic action, no matter what the material correlative.

Liberation, too, was wrought into this image under his care. It was, as he expressed to Allen Dulles, a "word" the Kremlin feared. By amplifying liberation into a "word" akin to Luce's "freedom," liberation operated on a strongly symbolic plane. Thus, when in 1956 the Hungarian revolt was quashed by the Soviets, Jackson—who had worked with organizations and efforts that helped propel the revolt—centered his complaint to the Eisenhower administration on the United States' poor symbolic response to the crisis: in light of this quashing, why, he demanded to know, had not the United States led an effort in the United Nations to reject the credentials of Soviet-backed Kadar government?[90]

In this way, Jackson urged an approach focused on dramatic political and economic maneuvers that preserved, above all, the image of America as liberator. As such, he represented a political style analogous to Robert Hariman's discussion of the "courtly style," where power is "entirely crafted . . . but dependent on the thousand contingencies of audience response."[91] Jackson saw the world aesthetically and, in an important sense, hierarchically. He wanted the position of the nation to move up relative to the Soviets. Global public opinion was for him like the king's body—it was the seat of power before which psychic proximity was crucial for political success. It was also like Machiavelli's *Fortuna* a fickle but powerful force in the destiny of nations.[92] Success was contingent on the way America composed itself before the world in word and action through the force of public opinion, and power would follow virtuoso performances. Jackson imagined America as an actor in the court of public opinion, profiting as it outwits and outmaneuvers opponents to move up the ladder of world esteem. In this enterprise, everything depended on the virtuosity of America's performances in opportune moments. Jackson's America thus bore both the energy and the anxiety of the courtier, displaying "incessant plotting for higher rank and constant anxiety about the precariousness of one's position."[93]

However, Jackson's approach was principally cultivated within the spheres of economic enterprise rather than aristocratic circles or popular culture (the two loci of Hariman's discussion of the courtly style). It is thus more helpful, with respect to typical historic social types, to envision it as a form of economic adventurism where the discursive, aesthetic, and public dimensions of such enterprise were acutely felt. Indeed, as Simmel argues, there is a "profound affinity between the adventurer and the artist."[94] As publisher for Luce's various periodicals, as founder of Luce's international publications, and as a practitioner of economic warfare during the war, Jackson approached his work artistically, valuing both the imagination and adaptability of the courtier and the freedom, mobility, innovation of the adventurer.

Jackson's artistic approach was not merely subconscious. As he explained to Ambassador George Allen, "there is a basic dilemma which throws the problem [of propaganda] into the area of taste and intuition, rather than into a book of rules."

> By that I mean that these American publications, particularly TIME and LIFE International, become immediately suspect if the overseas reader gets the impression that they are being carefully edited to or for him. Their entire usefulness, propaganda-wise, depends on the credibility, and they achieve maximum credibility if the foreign reader thinks that he is simply looking over the shoulder of an American reader, seeing the news of the world and of the U.S. freely presented with no punches pulled, instead of seeing what is "good for him."[95]

This emphasis on "taste and intuition" was at the core of Jackson's accent on an artistry that appears natural, manipulation that appears genuine, and contrived enterprises that appear authentic expressions of pacific and benevolent American purposes. An artistic frame provided Jackson and his close collaborators with an activist programmatic vision prone to bold proposals and ambitious adventures. This vision was reflected in a 1956 retrospective celebrating Time-Life's first ten years overseas, produced by the editorial staff at Time-Life International (TLI), which Jackson had founded and with whom he remained involved throughout the 1950s. Touting TLI's fast success, the retrospective echoed a paean to the economic adventurer: "Establishing this kind and this much of an audience for *Time* and *Life* overseas entailed pioneering in transport, distribution, international finance, direct mail, market research, advertising sales, and private encouragement of world trade."[96] But the report also looked forward, trumpeting a new age,

> Given peace, TLI believes that the next decade will see a continuation of present tendencies: more industrialization of countries now primarily agrarian, a higher standard of living for the whole world, and a gradual removal of barriers to free world trade. As transportation improves and tourism increases, TLI looks toward an era of better understanding among peoples brought about by more personal contacts.
> In such an atmosphere the world will prosper—and with it, TLI.[97]

Time-Life International thus found in its own postwar adventures the seeds of a new order of things. But it was not in this venture only that Jackson's political-economic adventurism came to fruition. It was apparent in a far more ambitious effort, the World Economic Plan.

A Political-Economic Adventure: The World Economic Plan

For Jackson, a logical outcome of Eisenhower's sense of the "inseparability of political economy and strategic concerns," seen most dramatically in "Atoms for Peace," was the World Economic Plan (WEP).[98] Indeed, the WEP capitalized on the psychological and symbolic thrust of "Atoms for Peace." As an early outline of the plan stated, "What can be immediately and effectively shared—or rather, stimulated—is not the isotope but all that the isotope stands for, namely an age of material abundance made possible by tremendous culmination of scientific and technological knowledge and expertise."[99] In this way, Eisenhower's speech ballooned into all-out program for the liberalization of smaller, less materially prosperous nations.

In 1954 Jackson formulated with Rostow and Rostow's colleague at MIT, Max Millikan, a proposed "Partnership for Economic Growth." Purportedly, the plan was developed in response to John Foster Dulles's 1954 worries about the apparent aggressive growth of the Soviet economy, which Dulles feared would lead poorer nations to embrace the Soviet system.[100] However, the seeds of the plan can be seen earlier in Jackson's approach to "Atoms for Peace," and, even earlier, in Rostow and Jackson's collaboration on "Chance for Peace." With respect to "Atoms for Peace," immediately after the speech Jackson argued for a serial and comprehensive follow-up, "a series of actions—repeated actions."[101] "Atoms for Peace" was for him and others in the administration the inauguration of a Cold War offensive, not the culmination of one. And the nature of this offensive was already indicated in "Chance for Peace," written by Jackson and Rostow, which addressed both the legacy of liberation and the need for world economic development.[102] Thus, as Jackson argued to state and private officials regarding the WEP, "In both of these speeches he (Eisenhower) was leading into a Foreign Economic Policy."[103] Such a policy, he proposed, could supplement, and perhaps supplant, "military symbolism" with a "weapon of peace."[104]

The WEP conjoined liberation with liberalization in envisioning an expansive long-term American economic adventure abroad. As a July 1954 WEP proposal stated, "In the short run, then, Communism must be contained militarily. In the long run we must rely on the development, in partnership with others, of an environment in which societies which directly or indirectly menace ours will not evolve. In the long we must free security from dependence on military strength."[105] The WEP, as Jackson, Rostow, and Millikan wrote in a draft of a presidential speech proposing the plan, was aimed at "An expansion, not a contraction, of the area of freedom."[106] Through the infusion of capital and technical expertise in "underdeveloped" areas of the world, they proposed the United States could ultimately win the Cold War without resorting to arms. The WEP was therefore tailor-made to fit the guiding foreign policy principles of the Eisenhower administration: it avoided general war, it preserved and indeed sought to expand a strong U.S. economy, and it was consistent with "peaceful purposes."

The WEP was proposed at a time of significant challenges to the vision of the American Century. Beginning in 1953, under the leadership of Dag Hammarskjöld, the United Nations raised economic development to the center of its concerns. Simultaneously, so-called underdeveloped nations were gaining more and more power in the General Assembly, exercising greater independence with respect to U.S. or USSR hegemony, calling into question economic dogmas, and seeking greater economic equity. Indeed, with regard to American Century–style economics, a quiet but forceful revolt against free-trade doctrine was brewing among economists inside the United Nations.[107] The WEP therefore came at a time not only when the Soviets seemed to be succeeding economically but also when free trade and American prestige were under fire in the UN.

To create momentum in the administration for the WEP Jackson convened under the auspices of Time Inc. a secret, off-the-record conference at Princeton in the spring of 1954—much like the one he had composed to create momentum for "psychological warfare" in 1952.[108] Jackson opened the conference with a short speech in which he reminded the attendees that the president had said in "Chance for Peace" that the U.S. government was ready to help "other peoples to develop the underdeveloped areas of the world." The offer, Jackson argued—tacitly recognizing and challenging Eisenhower's romanticism—was an example of "the dream," but one he complained that was without follow-through. Jackson hoped to use the gathering at Princeton to "narrow the gap between intelligent dreaming . . . and action" that had opened up under Eisenhower. Otherwise, the United States could ultimately be stuck with a militant image and expensive military-aid packages. "In other words," he summed up starkly, "is it to be cannons, or is it to be growth? Is it to be a functioning partnership in an expanding area of freedom, or a shrinking area of freedom on the American dole? We are right up against it."[109]

The United States, he argued, needed a foreign economic policy designed to marry the needs of America and Europe to those of poorer nations.

> I have been sitting in the Executive Office Building across the street from the White House for a year, and one thing has really struck me; that is, we have two kinds of economic headaches in the Free World. The first is countries that cannot find markets large enough for their own goods to buy what they need without our help. That is the plight of Great Britain, it is the plight of Germany, it is the plight of Japan. It is the plight of others whom we need as strong and not as resentful partners.

Then, second, we have in the world a host of what has gotten to be underdeveloped countries that badly need exactly what Britain, Japan, Germany, and the United States can export. But because they cannot get those things, they become increasingly vulnerable politically.

As I see the big job of a Foreign Economic Policy, it is to marry up these two Free World weaknesses into a functioning partnership, to make a tremendous asset out of two liabilities.[110]

In this way, Jackson proposed that the United States make a macro-intervention in the world through a kind of political-economic matchmaking. Through capital investment, diplomatic efforts, presidential speech-making, government-coordinated publicity, and the ample use of state-private networks, he argued, the United States could turn the tide of world opinion, as well as the fortunes of the U.S. economy, in a dramatic new direction.

Jackson's belief in the feasibility of world economic matchmaking rested upon the edifice of the work of Rostow and Millikan. In an outline of the WEP the two economists expressed concern about the "terrible disparity between the U.S. and the rest of the world" economically. The American economy, in the short fifteen-year period leading up to the postwar period, expanded fivefold. Why, they asked, could not such growth be realized in economies elsewhere? In "an age of high culmination of Science and Technology" there was no reason it could not.[111]

Thus Rostow and Millikan evoked an older and more ambitious form of economic theorizing, inscribed preeminently in the works of Adam Smith and Karl Marx. Political economy, and not simply economics, was their avowed domain.[112] "Because we mention Science and Technology first," they explained in their WEP outline, "let it not be thought that we have anything but scorn for any narrow and shallow philosophy of 'technocracy.'" "It is not possible to label or catalogue," they explained, "all the dynamic (and often conflicting) elements which go into the making of America and the Western World generally. But, however the causative elements are classified, one result is self-evident: manking [sic] has arrived at a point where material abundance for vast numbers of people is quite plainly possible." Indeed, Rostow and Millikan stressed the spectacular simplicity of their plan, even in a complex world, arguing that it could be reduced to basic propositions "comprehensible to all literate men and women."[113] What was important for America to see, they argued, was not economic calculations and detailed plans, but that "The moment is propitious for mobilization of all capitalistic sentiments and techniques."[114] The problem with "technocracy" in their view was not the extent of its claim to be able to manage economic factors to realize general prosperity, but the limits of this claim. Nations and their economies, Rostow and Millikan protested, were at once as complex and as simple as people themselves, and the problems of the world economy could be overcome as leaders took a direct and aggressive approach to the historical, psychological, and material realities of the world's political economy. Jackson's image of matchmaking was therefore not merely a convenient trope; it carried the tenor of an ambitious revitalization of political economics in the name of global capitalism.

The Princeton Economic Conference resulted in a formal proposal to the Eisenhower administration for a "Partnership for Economic Growth," written by Jackson, Rostow, and Millikan. The proposal so thoroughly blended the historical, psychological, political, and economic that its premises could have appeared fantastic to Eisenhower, who wrote to Jackson upon receiving it that he feared it would only be seen as "bigger and better give-aways."[115] In addition to the scope of the plan's premises, Eisenhower could also have been put off by the tone of crisis the proposal set, evoking a sense of time quite adverse to a "long haul" approach, and something of the "crisis" style of the Truman administration's security policy writings. It began by describing "The Crisis of 1954," claiming that the free world was growing more and more fragmented, threatening to leave the United States "essentially a beleaguered island." Above all, it argued, the crisis was "political and psychological. . . . [T]he roots of the crisis lie in the minds of men and women throughout the Free World." Still, the proposal argued that this crisis was a fantastic opportunity for U.S. action. "Indeed," it claimed, "it is a part of our national character that crises evoke from us our best and most creative performances." The United States could be not merely an example of abundance, but its source. "We must find the words and deeds which will restore and strengthen the image of the United States not merely as the military bulwark of the Free World but as the major source of its democratic faith, its constructive energy, and its initiative in the pursuit of peace."[116] Thus the proposal argued that by meeting the crisis of 1954 with creative world political and economic action, the United States could restore its ideological hegemony over the free world and "expand the area of freedom."

America, as the paragon of the ultimate stage of science and technology, represented for Jackson, Rostow, and Millikan a way of not simply being, but *acting*, in the world. At the center of a national virtuoso performance was the seizure of opportune moments. Failure in such moments amounted to a kind of aesthetic catastrophe: "If the rest of the Free World is in a mood to move along 'free enterprise' lines, then the responsibility of the U.S. is simply to promote what it itself profoundly believes in. To fail to respond to so simple a responsibility would be a tragic rejection of opportunity."[117] Indeed, once the WEP finally failed to gain Eisenhower's approval, Jackson registered and remembered the failure in aesthetic terms. "We both know that I failed," he wrote Rostow in 1962 when the latter was working for Kennedy. "I still hope that you will succeed." "An all-important element of my failure," Jackson explained, "was my inability to enlist *positive* and *continuing* and *dynamically meshed* acceptance and support by the President and the Secretary of State of a total program. One-shot, crisis projects—*sí*. Orchestrated, total, long-term program—*no*."[118] Thus, while Jackson was hardly a solemn character, he took upon himself extraordinarily weighty burdens with respect to American foreign policy. He sought to orchestrate coordinated, ambitious, and extensive programs that he knew would be met with a great deal of reticence. He was not only a bureaucratic provocateur, as Brands describes him, but a bureaucratic adventurer.

The Princeton Economic Conference was one case in point. The conference itself, like so much Jackson did and imagined the nation doing, was a strategic deception, a premeditated ruse, meant for political effect rather than serious deliberation. Jackson, Rostow, and Millikan had developed a detailed sketch of the WEP well before the meeting, and their plan was not open to significant revision. Rather, the role of the conference was to navigate the idea through the labyrinth of Washington bureaucracy, like a courtier working to gain an audience with the sovereign. A month before the conference, Jackson wrote Luce, "Millikan agrees with you that the actual Plan could be written in 48 hours out of the heads of two or three of us, without the conference stage setting. On the other hand, I feel that this little bit of theatre has a certain importance, and, on the basis of previous experience, will make a definite contribution."[119] Indeed, Millikan, echoing Jackson's sentiment, wrote Jackson a week later,

> Walt and I believe that it will desirable to have our thoughts pretty clearly in mind beforehand as to what we want to come out of this first meeting, but we feel that the thing has got to be so stage managed that the other participants all believe that at least some the ideas were originally theirs. I am sure that you are even clearer about this than we are, and I feel a little foolish even mentioning this point except that it does bear on the question of how much you can expect to accomplish in this meeting.[120]

Thus, the Princeton Economic Conference was staged; its invitees, for the most part, were unknowing actors; its agenda was the performance of a script; and its aim the artful orchestration of American foreign economic policy. The state-private network Jackson so freely exploited was, in his view, nearly as susceptible to the techniques of "political warfare" or artful stage-managing as he imagined general publics to be.

Conclusion

Ironically, the means toward liberalization and liberation presumed by the World Economic Plan resembled those of the socialist vision to which it was ideologically opposed. Far more than mere liberalization, the WEP asserted that a bold and proactive economic policy was needed in order for the peoples of the "under-developed" world to advance toward liberty, that some "plan" and bureaucratization was integral to economic progress. It thus embraced a conception of economy and freedom seemingly illiberal in its assumptions. (Eisenhower's concern that the proposal would be seen as "bigger and better give-aways" spoke to the "planned economy" undertones of the WEP.) What, then, was liberal about the WEP? Precisely that which Rostow advocated: "suffusing the national government with a sense of private adventure."[121] It was the spirit of adventurism in the WEP that made it liberal. It was its assertion that America needed to *act* positively, progressively, dynamically, and daringly that tied the WEP to the economic and political adventurers of old. In this way, the WEP was principally an *aesthetic* challenge to Soviet-style socialism—for on the level of economic planning and development, it merely sought to do better and more scientifically what it imagined the Soviets already doing, but on the level of style, it sought an antithetical approach to Soviet planning and bureaucratization. It sought fidelity to an imagined "American style."

Adventurism in its early-modern form was predicated on a principle of liberty understood as freedom before external obstacles to action like fortune, fate, or even fidelity to a moral law. It therefore shared with stoicism the ideal of "freedom of action" that suffused, and continues to suffuse, the discourse of American foreign policy. And yet adventurism too suffers from a similar dilemma stoicism faces—just as stoicism is motivated not simply by an aspiration to realize a true self, but by a desire to become subjectively invulnerable to the chaos and incertitude of the world around, and therefore is a reactive ethic, so adventurism as an ethic of freedom of action cannot help but be reactive, committed as it is to *opportunistic* action and a vision of an ever-changing field of political chance. In fact, Jackson's career illustrates a Machiavellian tension: if the adventurer princes "owed nothing to fortune but the opportunity which gave them matter to be shaped into what form they thought fit," the adventurer prince was nevertheless a hostage to opportunity, constantly on the alert for openings, occasions, and chance developments. Incessant activism thus can become obsessive activism. Action can become a never-ending series of reactions.

Indeed, the reactivity of Jackson was doubled, as it became not only reactive in the sense of a hyper-concern with opportunity, but ideologically reactionary. A strategy is not de facto an ideology, but a strategy can become an ideology if the material and political conditions that once made its practice plausible are eviscerated. Indeed, it is often the case that ideologies grow stronger rather than weaker when the material conditions they would support erode. And so a strategic idea may grow stronger, and even be transfigured into an ideology, as the conditions for realizing the strategic objective grow weaker. Such was the fate of liberation as seen in Jackson's career. As the thought of World War III became more and more dangerous, the martial pursuit of liberation in Eastern Europe and in other parts of the world by American-led forces became increasingly implausible. Concurrently, liberation became progressively more ideological, representing simultaneously three distinct aspects of America's Cold War:

1. The watchword of right-wing American cold warriors like Burnham, for whom "liberation" represented the only true means of confronting the monolithic Soviet threat.
2. A motivating principle (but not the only one) behind virulent covert activities, led especially by the CIA.
3. A framework for envisioning the Cold War as a prolonged occasion for the expansion of liberalization and the "American Way."

I have focused in this chapter on the last aspect, but all three were reactionary. The evolution (or devolution) of liberation in the early Cold War shows vividly the way in which strategic successes (America's success with liberation in World War II) can later fuel ideologies that justify actions of a very different order. Of course, this is not done indiscriminately. Some continuity between a former historic action and a later agenda must be in place, and this continuity will often be the spirit of the action. Adventurism represents the spirit that bound together D-Day, the World Economic Plan, Kennedy's "decade of development," and even his moon shot. And all were deeds done (or left undone in the case of the WEP) in the name of liberty, liberation, and liberalization.[122]

Foreign aid provided by United States—which became firmly entrenched in U.S. policy only under Kennedy—was motivated by a range of factors that can be understood variously in terms of interests, ideology, exploitation, globalization, norms, and/or domestic politics.[123] But we must add to these ways of understanding the advent of a strong U.S. foreign aid program a worldview: the restless, enterprising, and often-dangerous spirit of American adventurism. The WEP, as the forerunner to a new era in American foreign aid, was not merely a "development" plan. It was envisaged as an adventure. Indeed, it was conceived in the spirit of America's martial heroics of World War II: both were envisioned as great American adventures abroad on behalf of the liberation of captive peoples. The WEP represented a transfiguration of World War II's liberation not only because it made political economy its medium, but because it self-consciously approached national action as a performance on the dramatic stage of world opinion. It thus subordinated personalities to processes, was opportunistic even as it was grounded in a metanarrative of historical progress, assumed a reactive and strongly ideational sense of human psychology, and rested on the maintenance of ambiguity vis-à-vis agency in U.S. geopolitical action. The artistry of foreign aid was meant to provoke positive worldwide sentiments that in turn would provide the affective ground for broader worldwide ideological commitments to American-style free enterprise and liberal politics. In this way, America could win the Cold War without having to "fight" it.

Adventurism, unlike stoicism and evangelicalism, but with romanticism, is a heroic ethic, requiring for its performance an inhospitable field of play. Both stoicism and evangelicalism presuppose in some way that the material world is ultimately a fitting place for the self's peace—stoicism through resignation to the cosmic order, evangelicalism through the divine redemption and recreation of the worldly order. Romanticism and especially adventurism, however, risk a basic nihilism vis-à-vis the self and the material world, asserting not merely that the material world is a field of struggle and indeterminacy, but that social order is ultimately the product of the coercive assertion of a sovereign will. Romanticism, as we will see, compensates for this rather stark situation through acts of interpretation that reconfigure social meaning around a symbolically manifested transcendent order. Adventurism, on the other hand, keeps higher meaning within the purview of the coercive assertion of a sovereign will. The achievement of "glory" in Machiavelli is a self-conscious human pursuit, the substantive product of human action. If the subject of glory is the nation, then the nation is not conceived metaphorically as a self, nor metonymically as moral community, nor synecdochally as a mystical self, but ironically as a performer. The nation within the adventurist worldview is both the agent and result of "propaganda." The glory of nation, to use more contemporary parlance, is ultimately an "image event," the product of its own creative action. "Strategy" within this worldview must be *essentially artifice,* aimed not at the restoration of a natural "balance of powers," nor at the inauguration of a new order in accordance with transcendent moral truth, nor at the preservation of a reified "way of life," but at the fabrication of a nation, and a world environment conducive to its glory.

Spirits die hard in part because they are amorphous, adaptable, translatable from one epoch to another, and from one domain of human action to another. Adventurism, more than any of the other worldviews I consider in this book, has, like its type, a restless and nomadic quality. "Given the vigour of adventure," Alfred North Whitehead wrote, "sooner or later the leap of the imagination reaches beyond the safe limits of the epoch, and beyond the safe limits of learned rules of taste. It then produces the dislocations and confusions marking the advent of new ideas for civilized effort."[124] I have focused in this chapter on the way in which adventurism transformed a particular strategy, liberation, into a push for U.S. political-economic interventions, helping to create a new epoch in American foreign policy. Indeed, as the Cold War continued into the early 1960s, through science and technology *adventure* more and more came to displace stoic *apatheia* and evangelical moralism on the Cold War political stage, seen in Kennedy's Alliance for Progress, and most spectacularly in the space race. But I suspect that Jackson, if he had lived through the 1960s, would have still been disappointed, for the 1960s did not in fact bring what he imagined, a new world order wrought by America's great feats, but rather only the high age of the *romance* of adventure. Indeed, as I argue in the next chapter, it was Eisenhower, under the pressure of the horrible logic of nuclear deterrence, who set in motion, as much as anyone, a new age of romance.

CHAPTER 4

The American Sublime: Eisenhower, Deterrence, and Romanticism

He diffuses a tone and spirit of unity that blends and (as it were) *fuses*, each into each, by that synthetic and magical power to which we have exclusively appropriated the name of imagination. This power, first put in action by the will and understanding and retained under their irremissive, though gentle and unnoticed, control (*laxis effertur habenis*) reveals itself in the balance or reconciliation of opposite or discordant qualities.

—Coleridge, *Biographia Literaria*

Some three decades before the premature 1989 provocation by Francis Fukuyama associating the end of the Cold War with the "end of history as such," the Eisenhower administration brought a literal end to human history firmly within America's material capabilities by stockpiling thermonuclear weapons.[1] Indeed, one month before Dulles's massive retaliation speech, Eisenhower vividly described the nuclear retaliation scenario to the United Nations in his "Atoms for Peace" address:

> Should such an atomic attack be launched against the United States, our reactions would be swift and resolute. But for me to say that the defense capabilities of the United States are such that they could inflict terrible losses on an aggressor—for me to say that the retaliation capabilities of the United States are so great that such an aggressor's land would be laid waste—all this, while fact, is not the true expression of the purpose and the hope of the United States.[2]

Thus Eisenhower articulated an approach to nuclear retaliation similar in form but different in kind than Dulles's punitive Protestant one. For Dulles, I have argued, the symbolic and instrumental functions of nuclear warheads were presented within the historic framework of a universal covenantal worldview. Massive retaliation was in an important respect merely the extension of an ethic of community policing via moral spectacle, its declaration a reiteration of covenantal moral protest. Retaliation as "punishment" presupposed the regulative presence of a transcendent moral law. Punishment was thus a moral right (much less so, a duty). The deterred was morally accountable. Therefore, retaliation *would have been* "the true expression of the purpose," if not the hope, "of the United States." The result was both a pronounced moral vigor vis-à-vis deterrence and an ultimate moral equivocation. Eisenhower, however, presented the possibility of a nuclear retaliation with a different motive force, one explicitly disassociated by the president from "the true expression of the purpose and the hope of the United States." Retaliation appeared as a calculated necessity, not a moral right. Deterrence was consequently not a product of moral policing, but of utilitarian calculus, instrumental control, and of heeding the logic of a material order only loosely tied to moral order.

The distinction, admittedly, might be merely a rhetorical one. For those who would be subject to American nuclear retaliation, it would matter little if the bombs were motivated by moral law or utilitarian calculation. But to say that the distinction is rhetorical is not to say that it is merely subjective, let alone inconsequential.[3] To those constructing nuclear policy such a distinction must matter, for moral law and utilitarian calculation entail two distinct forms of prudential deliberation, and indeed two distinct forms of historical action. Thus, they present two distinct sets of possibilities for nuclear legitimation. And states, beginning with the United States, have taken refuge behind what can rightly be called the *rhetorical* force of nuclear weapons much more so than their limited tactical use. As one Eisenhower-era report from the Department of Defense insisted,

> Effective deterrent weapons systems must be shaped by political and psychological considerations as well as military effectiveness. . . . They should combine just the right balance—and it can be very subtle balance—of threat and assurance. What deters is not the capabilities and intentions we have, but the capabilities and intentions the enemy thinks we have. The central objective of a deterrent weapons system is, thus, psychological. The mission is persuasion.[4]

Thus the question of legitimacy is accentuated, as this particular form of persuasion rests on the ability of nuclear weapons possessors to gain support for their belligerency from "friendly" publics while appearing to be a credible but controlled threat to enemies. Therefore deterrence is a rhetoric, possessing objectivity and subject to rhetorical distinctions.

I have argued that the dilemma for Dulles with regard to nuclear weapons culminated in the problem of moral equivocation. For Eisenhower, the dilemma was different. It was, in sum, a *historical* problem: specifically, how to reconcile political and economic liberalism with militancy, the democratic state with the rudiments of a garrison state, a free society with a military-industrial complex. The dilemma was not only that these disjunctions represented two contrary societal aspirations; it was that for Eisenhower *both* were vital to the historical survival of the nation. As he explained in his 1957 State of the Union address,

> National security requires far more than military power. Economic and moral factors play indispensable roles. Any program that endangers our economy could defeat us. Any weakening of our national will and resolution, any diminution of the vigor and initiative of our individual citizens, would strike a blow at the heart of our defenses.[5]

The reasoning behind this rather typical Eisenhowerian statement was layered and complex. It rested on a theory of modern martial mobilization. As General Eisenhower told an audience of veterans in 1946, "One atomic missile could paralyze a city and blot it out of the national economy for all effective purposes. By bacterial warfare a ruthless enemy might seek to destroy our nation, using our own citizens as human weapon-carriers to bring the germs of death into every home in the country. More than ever before it is certain that there is no separate air, sea or ground warfare—just as a whole nation is the potential objective, so is the whole nation and everything and person in it the only organism by which a successful war can be waged."[6] And intricate to such martial mobilization was a productive economy. Thus, General Eisenhower concluded in a speech that same year, "National strength is note exclusively or even principally measured in guns and airplanes and ships and tanks, necessary as these are in the current conditions of the world. Our strength is represented in the uninterrupted productiveness of our mines and farms and factories and in the efficient performance of transport and communication systems."[7] But while mass martial mobilization depended on a productive economic base, Eisenhower's appeal to "economic and moral factors" in 1957 yet implicated another layer of national strength he had long summoned, the psychological, symbolic, or "spiritual." "We are either," he told the veterans in 1946, "going to take, or fail to take, our natural position in the world as a rallying point for those who yearn for the way of life you and the nation fought for in this past war. Myriads of hopeful but fearful ridden eyes are watching us to mark our posture."[8] Thus, as Ira Chernus writes, Eisenhower's formula for the historical survival of the nation looked this like this: security = spiritual force × economic force × military force.[9]

But as only the latter two factors were subject to objective measurement, and indeed could quite readily be countervailing objective forces (such that in Eisenhower's conception of the garrison state, military force ~ economic force), the modality of *spiritual force,* I argue in this chapter, was exceptional in Eisenhower's formula for security, such that

$$\frac{\text{spiritual force}}{\text{economic force} \times \text{military force.}}$$

Especially if we look closely at the logic of Eisenhower's nuclear deterrence, we find that spiritual force was not, strictly speaking, but another factor in the equation of security, but another calculus altogether: one that (super-)supplemented the delicate "economic force × military force" base formula of security.

With respect to this base formula, nuclear bombs (and eventually missiles) were for Eisenhower functionally analogous to utilitarian philosopher Jeremy Bentham's central tower in his *Panopticon*: an economical technology of control. As Michel Foucault famously described the *Panopticon*, "Bentham laid down the principle that power should be visible and unverifiable. Visible: the inmate will constantly have before his eyes the tall outline of the central tower from which he is spied upon. Unverifiable: the inmate must never know whether he is being looked at any one moment; but he must be sure that he may always be so."[10] So too, Eisenhower made nuclear weapons symbolically visible but strategically unverifiable with respect to their extent and the exact circumstances in which America might use them (and even, as when the *Polaris*-armed submarine set sail, the exact location of American nuclear arms). Nuclear stockpiles conspired with strategic ambiguity in an effort to institute a new Cold War calculus.

However, such a stark base formula constantly threatened to jeopardize not only America's status as the "free world" leader, but the United States' claim to be legitimate manufacturers, possessors, and users of nuclear weapons—for here militancy confronted liberalism, as necessity ~ freedom. For ideological, pragmatic, and propagandistic reasons the nation, as Eisenhower himself asserted in his Farewell Address, could not be both monumentally militant and liberal at the same time.[11] As Dulles wrote as secretary of state in *Foreign Affairs* in 1954, "It is no answer to substitute the glitter of steel for the torch of freedom."[12] It was in addressing this particular dilemma that Eisenhower's "Atoms for Peace" drew a distinction between the "fact" of massive nuclear retaliation capabilities, that sphere of necessity, and "the true expression of the purpose and the hope of the United States." Eisenhower here, as elsewhere, presented nuclear warheads as representing something *other* than the norms and aspirations of their creators and possessors. In "Atoms for Peace" he presented deterrence as if it stemmed from a substratum of politics determined by brute inevitability, harsh facts, and inviolable logics of action, but the true nature of America as if it resided in a superstratum of hope, aspiration, and ideals of peace and well-being.

Indeed, while this bifurcation had been anticipated in NSC 68, the last major strategic document of the Truman administration, and was endemic to America's Cold War, at no point in the history of political rhetoric had the gap between fact and value been so unequivocally pronounced as in Eisenhower's rhetoric.[13] The gap emerged from a stark dualism that was integral not only to Eisenhower's presidential rhetoric, but to his strategic worldview. And I do not mean, precisely, a moral dualism (which, to be sure, characterized Eisenhower's discourse as well),[14] but rather an *ontological* one. For at the heart of Eisenhower's approach to nuclear deterrence was a communicative wager far more severe than Bentham's *Panopticon,* not only because it depended on a technology so much more brutal in its potential, but also because the subjects of that technology needed to be able to see "beyond" it in order to reconcile themselves to it. Eisenhower staked the future of the Cold War, and indeed of human society itself, on the ability of national and international audiences to discern and internalize a militant threat without at the same time confusing that threat with American ideals. He elevated the difference between political necessity and national purpose to near-ontological status. For a thinker like Kennan, failure to abide by this distinction was not ultimately a failure at all, but a sober acknowledgment of "reality" and "necessity" as the true determinants of national purpose within the world of nations. Similarly, for Dulles America's militancy was part and parcel of its moral identity. And Jackson could hold together political necessity and national purpose through irony. By Eisenhower's light, however, a stable distinction between necessity and purpose provided a framework for articulating the nature of nuclear deterrence. To discern America's deterrent role in the Cold War aright was for Eisenhower to heed the incommensurate logics of both something like natural necessity and spiritual teleology.

It was therefore to be firmly ensconced within the most complex but unequivocal of modern dualistic worldviews, romanticism.[15] Romanticism, Louis Dupré writes, was one manifestation of "essentially a *dialectical* movement" between the naturalistic rationalism of the Enlightenment and the advent of a new subjective, spiritual expressivism.[16]

In the romantic vision, "nature" found its supersupplement in "spirit," as necessity was reconciled with freedom through *interpretation*. Such romanticism, seen especially in its American transcendentalist instantiation, represented not so much a political program as an attitude toward meaning and a broad approach toward interpreting and speaking about the world. It was, in important respects, the accentuation rather than the counterforce to the utilitarian tendencies of the Enlightenment, accepting at its core the fact/value distinction but arguing that values are ultimately of greater import than facts, that freedom is superior to necessity, and that spirit is supreme over nature. Romanticism thus produced a *heroic* ethic (seen in its tie to *romance*): before the overwhelming force of necessity or nature, the romantic hero, indeed the romantic poet, could act with extraordinary courage in the name of freedom, principally through acts of interpretation. The poet, Emerson wrote, "is a sovereign, and stands on the center. . . . [P]oets, are natural sayers, sent into the world to the end of expression."[17] Or as Thomas Carlyle wrote in a text Eisenhower very well could have read as a schoolboy, "Heroes: Universal History consists essentially of their biographies."[18]

Eisenhower's rhetoric represents a historical development of romanticism shaped by two societal changes. First, there was a gradual turn in the twentieth century away from the nineteenth-century preoccupation with heroic individuals as the motive force of history toward the prioritization of social units, like class or nation, and social processes, like collectivization or liberalization. Second, in the twentieth century "nature" assumed a magnitude virtually proportionate to "spirit" through theoretical and institutional advances in the natural sciences. While for nineteenth-century romantics, the mechanistic framework of Newtonian science could seem variously mundane, remarkable, or revolting, in the twentieth century Newtonianism was giving way to Einsteinianism, and scientists were becoming more like poets, prophets, and priests, offering theories of time, energy, and matter that possessed all the sublime wonder, or horror, of the romantic poem. As physicist Charles Critchfield once commented on the behavior of his colleague at Los Alamos, Robert Oppenheimer, he "didn't talk about weapons or physics. He talked about the mysteries of life."[19]

Indeed, Eisenhower too sometimes approached nuclear bombs with an awe as great as that which he brought to the liberal promises of spirit. *Technology* was the difference, and it represented nearly as profound a threat to liberal order and "free world" morale as it did to earth. The nuclear bomb was in his view a doomsday technology for which the spiritual counterpart was freedom, seen in the inexorable, if slow, social processes of liberalization. For Eisenhower, Cold War leadership therefore required not only that a distinction be made habitually between one order and another, necessity and freedom, the technological and the historical, but that the meaning of each order be delimited. The challenge of Cold War leadership within this framework was therefore profoundly hermeneutical, preoccupied with the art of interpreting symbols with regard to their utilitarian technological significance and their "higher," and in an importance sense, "truer" meaning. It was also rhetorical, as the mission was persuasion.

In this chapter I argue that Eisenhower's approach to nuclear deterrence draws on a romantic poetics and hermeneutics wherein the juxtaposition, so endemic to Eisenhower's rhetoric, between spirit and matter, and value and fact, was not merely a form of presidential pietism, but a strategic structure that allowed *the state* to accelerate its production of nuclear weapons in the name of "necessity," all the while professing, *as a nation,* intentions of an entirely different order. Romanticism provided a worldview that could hold together, in dualistic balance, state and nation. As an inquiry into the political power of romanticism for a nuclearized America, this chapter begins with heroism and culminates with priesthood, delving into romanticism's history and Eisenhower's presidential leadership as it proceeds. This chapter, more than the others, approaches its subject from multiple angles, because more than the others it addresses a value rationality that was also a value ideology—an ambitious and often unwieldy discourse that created the conditions for the operations of power under false, and indeed deeply problematic, premises.

Eisenhower's Heroic Balance

If interpretation presumes, at a minimum, a call for explanation, then is arguable that no U.S. president, saving Lincoln, has needed so much interpretation as Eisenhower. That Eisenhower's rhetoric has enjoyed nearly as much recent scholarly attention as Lincoln's, though the latter was far more profound in speech, is in part due to the variety of ways that the historical record has shown Eisenhower to be a president that stood amidst paradoxes. For example, as Blanche Wiesen Cook showed in the early 1980s, Eisenhower stood between a massive infrastructure of surreptitious (often CIA-led) covert Cold War operations and repeated overt efforts at détente, if not peace, with the Soviets.[20] Similarly, as scholars like Fred Greenstein, J. Michael Hogan, Scott Lucas, Kenneth Osgood, and Shawn Parry-Giles have each shown in various ways, Eisenhower stood between complex "hidden hand" maneuverings and public expressions of comparatively straightforward policies.[21] Or, as Robert Ivie, Ira Chernus, H. W. Brands, and Guy Oakes each have discussed, Eisenhower claimed to represent the best in national security and yet still cultivated in the nation a profound sense of insecurity.[22] Or, as Chernus has explored elsewhere, Eisenhower put tremendous faith in liberal economies and capitalist markets, even as he premised much of his political philosophy on overcoming the self-same selfish impulses that motivated capitalism.[23] There is, as these studies together show, little left in Eisenhower's historical legacy that remains straightforward.

Furthermore, at least since revisionist historians recognized that Eisenhower was an active participant in the politics and policy of his administration, his performance has consistently been measured not only against such paradoxes, but against the extremities of possible historical experience: economic depression, statism, isolationism, Communist global dominance, total war, nuclear apocalypse, all are recurring themes in accounts of Eisenhower's presidential career. And this gravitation toward extremes is not incidental to Eisenhower's own self-portraiture, as it was against extremes that he measured himself. As Martin Medhurst writes, "If there is any one topic or theme that can be said to be uniquely Eisenhower's, that theme is the need for balance. For as far back as Eisenhower's views can be traced, the theme of balance has been present."[24] In this regard, Eisenhower publicly espoused a philosophy of the "middle way," wherein *catastrophes*, not merely opposing philosophies, constituted navigational coordinates. As he noted in a speech before the American Bar Association in 1949,

> When the center weakens piecemeal, disintegration and annihilation are only steps away, in a battle of arms or of political philosophies. The clearsighted and the courageous, fortunately, keep fighting in the middle of the war. . . .
>
> The middle of the road is derided by all of the right and the left. They deliberately misrepresent the central position as a neutral, wishy-washy one. Yet here is the truly creative area in which we may obtain agreement for constructive social action compatible with basic American principles and with the just aspirations of every sincere American.[25]

In the view of a historian like Steven Wagner, Eisenhower's middle way was principally focused on pragmatic rather than ideological means of addressing questions of government. As Wagner writes, "In American political culture those who describe themselves as 'middle of the road' are often portrayed as unwilling to take a stand or lacking in political sophistication. This was not the case with Eisenhower. The 'middle way' was a carefully considered political philosophy similar to Theodore Roosevelt's cautious progressivism."[26] But we can see in the ethical equation of his American Bar Association speech—that between "fighting in the middle of the war," "the truly creative area," "constructive social action," and "just aspirations"—a supplement to that pragmatic, cautious progressivism. For Eisenhower not only put the military or political (or military-political, as was the case) actor in the middle of historical progression, but made the effective historical actor heroic: indeed, he presented history itself as a field of battle, at the center of which was a sphere of creative, constructive, and courageous possibility. Despite the fact that, as I will discuss shortly, Eisenhower repudiated the larger-than-life ethos of men like FDR and MacArthur, his middle way was a heroic ethic.

Heroism, of course, was not foreign to Eisenhower's public persona as he entered the White House. As the supreme commander of the Allied Forces in Europe during World War II, he had gained international status for leadership and valor. Still, it was not an image he merely accepted *tout court*. Rather, he worked to convert the heroic ethos into an image of a nation. Indeed, his 1948 memoir *Crusade in Europe* began with the story of the nation. The first few pages told the story of the "revolutionary transformation of America."[27] "In the space of three and a half years, the United States produced the fighting machine that played an indispensable role in beating Germany to its knees, even while our country, almost single-handed, was conducting a decisive war against the Japanese Empire."[28] And so the narrative was established. It was only at the end of page 4 that the "I," the narrator, General Eisenhower, was introduced: "On the day the war began, in 1939, I was in the Philippines, nearing completion of four years duty as senior military assistant to General Douglas MacArthur."[29] In this way *Crusade in Europe* balanced its author and subject's heroism by making it but a part of a whole, America, and this not only in evident contrast with MacArthur, but with the hero-cults that precipitated the world wars, the Holocaust, and emerging Cold War Communist states. Eisenhower's balanced heroism, in fact, re-created the form of the romantic hero of the nineteenth century that aspired, as Simon Williams writes, "to transform the society of which they are, however tragically, a member."[30] But this in an anti-Napoleonic mode. As Williams continues: "Such a change can occur through their [the romantic heroes'] arousing a transcendental vision of beauty among and within those who are imprisoned by the obligations, obsessions, and petty desires of everyday life."[31] The romantic hero, as opposed to the Napoleonic hero, sought to fashion a heroic image *in relation* to a transcendental whole.

As Eisenhower entered the White House, heroic questing and crusading, as Robert Ivie has shown, constituted "the conceptual imagery guiding the administration's rhetorical choices."[32] But, as Ivie argues, in the 1950s it was no longer German fascism and Japanese imperialism that stood as the peril against which American heroism would be realized. Rather, it was the nuclear age, which presented for the Eisenhower administration both existential and moral dangers. Existentially, nuclear weapons, with their massively destructive potential, increasingly threatened to render war itself pointless. And as they threatened to render war pointless, they threatened to overwhelm the moral logics that had legitimated America's costly military interventions in the first half of the century. However, in aggressively pursuing nuclear stockpiling, the Eisenhower administration stared bravely into the existential and moral abyss of modern nuclear war. As Gaddis writes,

> He believed that the best way to avoid an all-out nuclear war was *to make that the only military option available to the United States*. His reasoning was Clausewitzian: in his classic work, *On War*, the great Prussian strategist had coupled a vision of total and hence irrational violence with a demonstration of how difficult—and how foolish—it would be to attempt it. Clausewitz's "absolute war" was an abstraction, set up as a contrast to what military force, in reality, could feasibly accomplish. By the 1950's, though, "absolute war" had become an all too real possibility, a fact that made his argument, from Eisenhower's perspective, all the more relevant. The point was not to design a strategy, which implied getting from here to there. It was rather to hold out a horror, in the interests of *not* getting there.[33]

Eisenhower thus held that necessity demanded that the United States build a nuclear arsenal that would so overawe the world that self-preservation and social stability would ensue (and, to be sure, if it did not, the United States could still somehow have the upper hand in the event of nuclear war). For Eisenhower, nuclear deterrence was the product of a radical form of instrumental rationality, wherein both the fate of human existence and the bounds of human violence would be held in the balance.

What, we might ask, could grant such audacity? An ease with the wager, to be sure.[34] But a philosophy of history as well. For Eisenhower, Medhurst writes, "freedom was the entelechic principle that propelled mankind toward its *telos*."[35] Thus the middle way implied progression.

> Important to Eisenhower's thought . . . is the idea of keeping everything in balance as one advances toward the goal. For Eisenhower, the ultimate goal was to win the Cold War and usher in a true era of peace. . . . Part of Eisenhower's great "faith" in the future was his belief that it ultimately could not turn out any other way inasmuch as it was the very nature of man to be free. The task of leadership in a nuclear world, then, was that of preventing outside forces from interfering with the natural evolution of humanity toward peace and freedom.[36]

Or, as Robert Bowie and Richard Immerman attest, "He never swayed from his conviction that the free world was stronger than the Soviet bloc and that Communist Russia itself would inevitably explode—or implode. . . . In this regard Eisenhower believed as firmly in inexorable historical processes as did any Marxist."[37] The historical antecedents to such a view of human history are found at the foundations of romanticism in the thought of the eighteenth-century thinkers like Rousseau and Johann Gottfried Herder. At its origin was a crisis in empiricism, which could not scientifically demonstrate the existence of a *self,* but only of fragments of thought, feeling, memory, and experience.[38] Jean-Jacques Rousseau, the German idealists, and then full-fledged romantics, all who accepted such problem offered by early empiricists, posited in turn an essentially spiritual self. As Rousseau wrote in his "Second Discourse,"

> Man experiences the same impression, but he recognizes himself free to acquiesce or resist; and it is mainly in the consciousness of this freedom that the spirituality of his soul exhibits itself: for Physics in a way explains the mechanism of the senses and the formation of ideas; but in the power of willing, or rather of choosing, and in the sentiment of this power, are found purely spiritual acts about which nothing is explained by the Laws of Mechanics.[39]

If Rousseau in this way provided a picture of a dualistic self, Herder offered a portrait of history that later full-fledged romantics transformed. For Herder the "end of history" was, as Dupré writes, "the *moral* ideal of *Humanität,*" realized in "a universal, moral community."[40] Thus romantics identified the agent of such a history with, as Isaiah Berlin wrote, "some super-personal entity . . . which then becomes a huge intrusive forward-marching will." In this way romantics blended a philosophy of the self, especially a collective self, with a philosophy of history.[41]

Such romantic portraitures could have come to Eisenhower in any number of ways. While Eisenhower is remembered for his midcentury achievements, it should not be forgotten that he was educated nearer to the turn of the century, an age in which the likes of Emerson, Goethe, and Carlyle permeated schooling. And then their was Clausewitz himself, held in such esteem by Eisenhower, who while remembered today as a preeminent strategist and thus "realist," in his own time, as Peter Paret writes, stood in between Herder and unbridled romanticism, disparaging the latter's hyperemotional infatuation with the German state, but admiring the quest of the Sturm und Drang for internal and external harmony.[42] Indeed, the culture of romanticism provided Clausewitz with some of his pivotal themes: the interplay between variety and universality, or parts and whole; the dynamics of change; the dialectic between necessity and freedom in enacting war, and abstraction and realities in theorizing war; the vital importance of the "spiritual" animation of a state, morale as well as material might; and perhaps above all the centrality of "genius."[43]

In this vein, "balance" for Eisenhower hinged on interplay, dialectics, and dualisms. It entailed, perhaps above all, a means of advancement toward a historical destiny *as* a form of heroic rational crisis management. In its most extreme form, it entailed what Chernus calls "apocalypse management."[44]

> Its basic premises are simple and familiar: The United States faces enemies who wish to, and very may, destroy the nation and its way of life. Thus every confrontation with these foes is an apocalyptic struggle. But the traditional apocalyptic solution of eliminating evil is ruled out. The enemy threat is now a permanent fact of life. The best to hope for is to contain and manage it forever. As long as every apocalyptic danger is skillfully managed, preserving the precariously balanced status quo, the nation will be secure. Enduring stability—preventing dangerous change—is the only kind of victory to hope for, and the only kind of permanent peace.[45]

To be sure, echoes of such a view can be found in the thought of Kennan, except that Kennan was preoccupied with the *limits* of the nation, including the limits of instrumental action and the limits of history. For Eisenhower, balance—because it was measured against extremes, even apocalyptic ones—was in an important respect *limitless* in is application. Balance entailed an interminable form of management and indeed control within a romantically construed arc of history.

But this balance was not only aimed at managing history; it aimed at overcoming ideology. Indeed, it represented a quasi synthesis of competing worldviews. As a general stands upon a platform surveying a battle, so Eisenhower's "middle way" stood above the contesting worldviews of his age, intermixing rational appraisal, subjective states, worldly acts, and moral aspiration together in a would-be synthesis. And here we come upon a remarkable but little discussed aspect of Eisenhower's middle way, its *liberality*. Nowhere is this better seen than in the peroration of his 1953 State of the Union address, quoted here in full:

> We have surveyed briefly some problems of our people and a portion of the tasks before us. The hope of freedom itself depends, in real measure, upon our strength, our heart, and our wisdom. We must be strong in arms. We must be strong in the source of all our armament, our productivity. We all—workers and farmers, foremen and financiers, technicians and builders—all must produce, produce more, and produce yet more. We must be strong, above all, in the spiritual resources upon which all else depends. We must be devoted with all our heart to the values we defend. We must know that each of these values and virtues applies with equal force at the ends of the earth and in our relations with our neighbor next door. We must know that freedom expresses itself with equal eloquence in the right of workers to strike in the nearby factory, and in the yearnings and sufferings of the peoples of Eastern Europe. As our heart summons our strength, our wisdom must direct it.
>
> There is, in world affairs, a steady course to be followed between an assertion of strength that is truculent and a confession of helplessness that is cowardly.
>
> There is, in our affairs at home, a middle way between untrammeled freedom of the individual and the demands for the welfare of the whole Nation. This way must avoid government by bureaucracy as carefully as it avoids neglect of the helpless.
>
> In every area of political action, free men must think before they can expect to win.
>
> In this spirit must we live and labor: confident of our strength, compassionate in our heart, clear in our mind. In this spirit, let us together turn to the great tasks before us.[46]

Action; aspiration; expression; production; strength; spirit; universality; freedom; devotion; individuality; welfare; compassion; wisdom; wholeness;

eloquence; victory—such ideas and ideals were collected here into an effusion of just under 300 words. Such liberality warrants an interpretation in addition to the two dominant frames rhetorical scholars have brought to Eisenhower, strategy and ideology.

Of course, as rhetorical strategy, such profuseness is consistent with Eisenhower's conscious effort to navigate the middle way, and indeed to transcend petty and partisan differences.[47] For Eisenhower, Medhurst has repeatedly argued, "Communication, whether written or oral, was an instrumental art meant to accomplish a purpose."[48] In this way, Medhurst would tend to argue that behind Eisenhower's words, whether pointed or purple, was a strategic appraisal of the rhetorical situation, and the search for a fitting response. Thus, in accounting for one aspect of Eisenhower's liberality, his overwhelming charisma as a public figure in the 1952 presidential race, Medhurst concludes:

> Behind the promise, the pledges, and the partisan platform stood the imposing image of "Ike." That people liked Ike as a direct result of the image they had constructed of him before he ran for public office. That image, as we have seen, was one of a warrior for peace, an apostle of cooperation, an exemplar of duty, and a purveyor of human warmth and sincerity. Eisenhower's essentially strategic nature was oftentimes masked by this public persona, hidden in the twinkle of his blue eyes and the kindly nodding of his head, the broad expanse of his smile. He was a man recognizable, or so it seemed, from a decade of portraiture—imagery that proved to be a great asset not only in a race for the presidency, but also in the conduct of a Cold War.[49]

To be sure, liberality—seen here in Eisenhower's multiple public personae and subtle but charismatic gestures—had its domestic political advantages. And it had, as well, definite geopolitical advantages as Eisenhower took his presidential personae to a global stage. "Eisenhower's rhetoric of unrequited devotion to worldwide cooperation and global harmony," Ivie shows, was a vital "instrument for bracing public morale over a prolonged period of Cold War."[50] Indeed, whereas Kennan's rhetorical strategy could be summed up in "Be true to yourself," Dulles's in "The pen is mightier than the sword," and Jackson's in "The right word at the right time,"

Eisenhower's often seemed to live by the maxims, "A word for everyone" and "More is better."

Nevertheless, there was more to this rhetorical liberality than a stratagem. There was an ideology. Indeed, Chernus finds in Eisenhower less a strategic communicator than an "ideologue" who for better and worse, but mostly worse, remained tirelessly committed to a vision of the world that fused realism, idealism, and apocalypticism in a way that allowed Eisenhower to remain a militant cold warrior while liberally professing "peace," and in some sense believe that his policies could realize it.[51] To be sure, Eisenhower embraced not only a "middle way" but endorsed the productive potential of countervailing forces in a manner commensurate with a hefty liberal ideology. As he quoted his own 1949 American Bar Association speech in his memoir *Mandate for Change,* "We instinctively have greater faith in the counterbalancing effect of many social, philosophic, and economic forces than we do in arbitrary law."[52] But while Chernus stresses the illogic of such discourse, I want to attend to its liberal logic further here; specifically its romantic lineaments and the ensuing ways in which it opened up aspirational horizons even as it created the conditions for particular forms of instrumental action. Indeed, in this aspect, the liberality of Eisenhower's discourse was not the product of strategic communication at all, nor even fully explained by the contradictory pressures of an ideology, but was, as Eisenhower might have had it, an "expression" of the nation. For somewhere between strategy and ideology resides what Kenneth Burke describes as an "intermediate area of expression that is not wholly deliberate, yet not wholly unconscious. It lies midway between aimless utterance and speech directly purposive."[53] And this might be called the "spirit" of speech.

To return to the 1953 State of the Union address, the form of national expression that Eisenhower articulated aspired to synthesize, integrate, even reconcile aspects of the contesting worldviews of American foreign policy. He insisted on the importance of rational calculation. "In every area of political actions free men must think before they can expect to win." But while he presented rational calculation as necessary, it was insufficient. Affect and action were called for as well: for it is "our heart," he declared, that "summons our strength." Central to Eisenhower's rhetoric, therefore, was an aspiration toward *wholeness*: "In this spirit we live and labor: confident of our *strength,* compassionate in our *heart,* clear in our *mind.*" Thus Eisenhower sought to synthesize not only contrary political, philosophical, and historical forces, but the interior and subjective with the exterior and objective. But it was not so much a synthesis as it was a balance: for inasmuch as his aspiration toward wholeness was an achievement, it was one reached through the construction of *distinct* realms of American being. Indeed, the apt analogy for Eisenhower's view of America was not the integral "one body, many parts" or "society as a self," but the dualistic one of "body and soul," "mind and matter," even "the ghost in the machine." In this regard, as I will discuss, romanticism has long sought an elusive wholeness that has tended to instead produce dualisms. But first, having considered the relationship between Eisenhower's heroic balance and his liberality, I want to return to the particular concern of this chapter, Eisenhower's approach to nuclear deterrence. For here we see the preeminent expression of Eisenhower's liberality, one that would seem grossly out of balance . . . except for its spirit.

Nuclear Stockpiling

As Gaddis argues, Eisenhower saw the nuclear age as one in which "absolute war" was an imminent threat; it was a practical reality, even though it was as yet counterfactual. This practical reality, Eisenhower held, might be circumvented not through aggressive efforts to abolish nuclear weapons and thereby return the world to a prenuclear political and strategic era, but by projecting American nuclear power as an ultimate deterrent and by aggressively holding out the hope of progress even amidst this doomsday technology. Relative to Kennan and Dulles, therefore, Eisenhower's approach was remarkably modern in its outlook, built almost completely on three propositions: (1) the epochal significance of nuclear weaponry with regard to the impossibility of any more keeping large-scale war within rational bounds, (2) the inexorability of the historical process if unimpeded by large-scale war, and (3) the virtually unimpeachable "spiritual" superiority of "the American way of life" vis-à-vis this historical process. America, quite simply, was on the right side of history. His strategic outlook, consequently, was reducible to two commitments: avoidance of any major war and the political promotion and rhetorical amplification of liberal American politics and economics. These can be seen as corresponding to nuclear deterrence and "psychological warfare" respectively, and indeed for Eisenhower, these were two central elements of his New Look policy.[54]

Yet they should not be understood as distinct elements. As Kenneth Osgood writes, Eisenhower had a "deeply held conviction that psychological forces were critical elements in American leadership in the world." Eisenhower's notion of psychological warfare "extended beyond the official propaganda agencies of the American government to embrace any word or deed that affected the hearts and minds of the world's peoples."[55] Indeed, deterrence meant that the fate of the world hung on what might be called symbolic instrumentalism. Both the avoidance of war and the protection and amplification of "the American way of life" depended on audiences at home and abroad interpreting America's purposes in a way advantageous to his two policy commitments. To be sure, other factors were crucial to his New Look, especially strategic superiority, collective security, and a U.S. economy unburdened by massive defense budgets and thus purportedly free to be prosperous (apart from which Eisenhower believed both the military infrastructure and domestic public morale would erode).[56] However, even these factors depended on the interpretation of audiences abroad. As I quoted earlier, Eisenhower wrote Dulles during the 1952 presidential campaign,

> America cannot live alone, and . . . her form of life is threatened by the Communistic dictatorship. . . . The minimum requirement of those programs is that we are able to trade freely, in spite of anything Russia may do, with those areas from which we obtain the raw materials that are vital to our country. . . . This means that we must be successful in developing collective security measures for the free world—measures that will encourage each of these countries to develop its own economic and political and spiritual strength. Exclusive reliance upon a mere power of retaliation is not a complete answer to the broad Soviet threats.[57]

The United States depended on a broader political-economic order, and thus support via "morale" abroad. The nation's fate therefore hung on a world audience discerning the nuclear threat correctly, as essentially pacific rather than militant in its intent, so as to not put off or scare away allies or potential allies. Consequently, the interpretation of American actions and aims—indeed of "America" as an entity in the world—was central to Eisenhower's cold war against the Soviets.

A central aspect of the Eisenhower administration's strategic approach illustrates just how profound a role interpretation was seen as playing. Tremendous energy was invested by the administration in shaping for publics at home and abroad the symbolic significance of the atom. "Atoms for Peace" was just the tip of the iceberg. Indeed, "Atoms for Peace" publicly inaugurated "a systematic and sustained effort to publicize the peaceful applications of atomic science and industry."[58] This effort was central to the larger vital, though tension-filled, alliance between science, the state, and the ideology of national security.[59] One vivid example of the concerted effort by the Eisenhower administration to promote this alliance is found in a 1956 Atomic Energy Commission script for a television program. In it, AEC head Lewis Strauss was to sit down with Eisenhower and a kilogram of natural uranium. Strauss would claim that the small amount of uranium could replace "thousands of carloads of coal" in energy production. "What this means," Eisenhower was scripted to say, "is this: When the day comes, as we all so earnestly hope, that the threat of nuclear war is banished, we can quickly convert the fissionable materials in our weapons stockpile to peaceful uses?" "Yes," Strauss would say, America would be "Beating swords into plowshares."[60]

This simple script performed a complex symbolic dance. The kilogram of uranium stood in for the invisible atom, and the invisible atom for utopian possibility. Mediating this possibility was a combination of technocratic (Strauss) and political (Eisenhower) American leadership. Under Eisenhower's atoms-for-peace program, the atom represented what for nineteenth-century romantics was "sublime science." As Eric Wilson writes,

> Romantics like Goethe, Coleridge, and Emerson thrilled in harvesting disparity into unity, the many into one. Division, atomization, alienation: all were conditions of the Romantic hell, the universe of death. Shoring

fragments against their ruin, the poets, philosophers, scientists of the Romantic age dreamed of a universal science that would reveal a force binding the most diffuse phenomena, gathering the specimens of the biologists, the elements of the chemist, the thinker's arguments, the tropes of the writer. Bifurcation of mind and matter, words and things, poetry and science were to the Romantic unnatural severings destined to dissolve the cosmos into its former chaos. Redemption lay in the demiurgic activity of forgoing chaotic energy into dynamic forms, the transformation of facts of science into figures of poetry.[61]

Indeed, Eisenhower's words before the United Nations two years after "Atoms for Peace" expressed a romantic vision of sublime science as explicitly as anything Goethe, Coleridge, or Emerson ever penned.

It cannot be a mere stilling of the guns—it must be a glorious way of life. In that life the atom, dedicated once as man's slayer, will become his most productive servant. It will be a peace to inspire confidence and faith so that all peoples will be released from the fear of war. Scientists will be liberated to work always for men, never against them. Who can doubt that in the next ten years world science can so beat down the ravages of disease and the pangs of poverty that humankind will experience a new expansion of living standards and of cultural and spiritual horizons. In this new kind of peace the artist, teacher and philosopher, workman, farmer, producer, and scientist will truly work together for the common welfare.[62]

Eisenhower's discourse concerning the peaceful use of the atom consistently relied on such progressive pictures of the fruit of science, entailing the conversion of this powerful but purportedly neutral entity, the atom, into an instrument of wide-reaching social, and indeed quasi-religious, achievement. Brute matter took on spiritual significance.

Central to this project was a delicate rhetorical task that Guy Oakes has described as "emotion management."[63] Indeed the control of public emotions was pivotal to its logic. Eisenhower sought to assuage panic, fear, and anxiety regarding nuclear technology, all the while keeping publics at home and abroad alert, vigilant, and cooperative. However, as

Eisenhower's 1955 United Nations speech shows, more than emotions were involved in this rhetorical task. A picture of history was at stake, as well as a whole set of ideas about America and liberal order. Nuclear stockpiling strongly threatened to undermine the global perception of the "American way of life" as an object of admiration and imitation, and as representative of and concomitant with the inexorable historical process of political and economic liberalization. If the nation failed to positively project itself, Cold War orthodoxy held, Soviet expansionism would grow more aggressive and America's own domestic morale could be eviscerated. Therefore, the management task of the government was charged with shaping people's interpretations of the nation and its technologies.

The Truman administration's Psychological Strategy Board (PSB) squarely addressed this problem in the winter of 1952 with NSC 126. On December 5, 1950, Truman had issued a directive instructing government agencies to "take immediate steps to reduce the number of public speeches pertaining to foreign or military policy," and set up channels of official clearance. "The purpose of this memorandum is not to curtail the flow of information to the American people," Truman wrote his government, "but rather to insure that the information made public is accurate and fully in accord with the policies of the United States." However, by the time the PSB released more elaborate instructions in 1952, emphasis was placed not on accuracy and consistency, but on rhetorical effect. Statements, NSC 126 instructed, had to be carefully crafted to consider their impacts. NSC 126 asked three questions:

1. Will this information strengthen the morale of the free world?
2. Will this statement at this time help the American public to understand and accurately appraise the capabilities of these weapons?
3. Will this statement create the fear that the U.S. may act recklessly in the use of these weapons?

In the balance was the psychological state of the "free world," both with respect to fear and complacency. On the one hand, Truman's PSB worried that poorly conceived statements could generate alarmism abroad; on the other hand, they imagined "ill-considered statements about these weapons may create a false sense of security, lead to expectations of

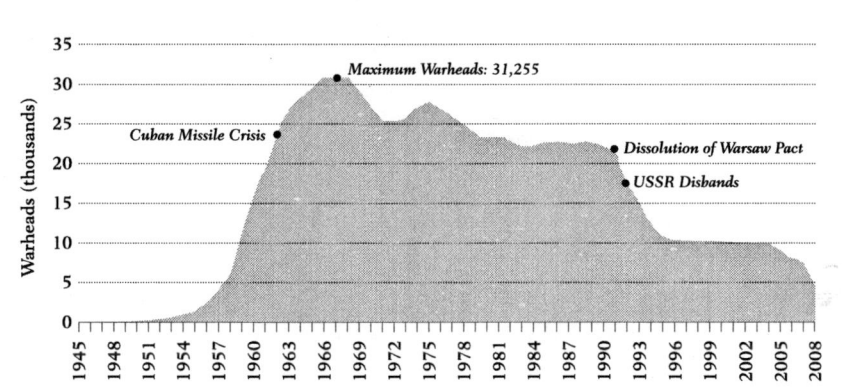

U.S. Nuclear Weapons Stockpile, 1945–2009*

*Includes active and inactive warheads. Several thousand additional nuclear warheads are retired and awaiting dismantlement.
Source: Graph reproduced from "Fact Sheet: Increasing Transparency in the U.S. Nuclear Weapons Stockpile," U.S. Department of Defense Nuclear Posture Review, updated May 3, 2010, http://www.defense.gov/npr/docs/10-05-03_Fact_Sheet_US_Nuclear_Transparency_FINAL_w_Date.pdf.

miracles in war and possibly jeopardize the maintenance of a balanced defense program, both military and civil."[64]

In fact, whereas the Truman administration focused on the potential and problems of public statements about atomic weapons, it is arguable that Eisenhower's approach to the *material* production of these weapons was shaped as strongly by symbolic considerations as by more overtly material ones, if not more so. Indeed, Eisenhower's commitment to America's nuclear superiority adhered more closely to a symbolic logic than a strict material one: by strict material calculations nuclear stockpiling quickly reaches a point of diminishing returns with regard to ensuring, in the words of "Atoms for Peace," that "an aggressor's land would be laid waste." When the uses of technologies are more or less constrained by criteria of material instrumentalism, for example, ten nails are needed to secure one beam, they are subject to relatively straightforward calculation with respect to sufficiency, for example, ten beams require one hundred nails. However, once technologies become objects of symbolic instrumentalism, calculating sufficiency can become elusive; for example, how many police on the street are sufficient to make people feel the police force is strong enough to ensure their safety? As a Department of Defense chart suggests (figure 1), the course of the nuclear arms race, which Eisenhower "dominated . . . in a way no other president has before or since," strongly implies that it operated according to this symbolic instrumentalism rather than a material one.[65]

Of course, deterrence always hinges on psychological effects, and therefore always makes the symbolic central. However, even terror (the etymology of "deterrence" reaches back to the Latin word for "terror,"), as the twenty-first century's wave of terrorism has shown, can need very little in the way of stockpiling in order to be effective.

At issue in Eisenhower's pursuit of nuclear stockpiling seems rather to be the elusive nature of rhetorical calculation, or strategic communication. To be sure, the near-vertical assent in the nuclear stockpile Eisenhower inaugurated was due in part to economies of scale, institutional momentum, and the aggressive competition among the branches of the military to lead the way in nuclear technologies. But these institutional phenomena were rooted in debates and decisions that inevitably revolved around essentially communicative questions, not the least when debating deterrent policies (for example, the respective merits of "finite" versus much more aggressive approaches to nuclear stockpiling). Such communicative questions include those of quantity and quality within messages, the polyvalent and polysemous nature of signifiers and symbols, the relative predictability versus the relative autonomy of audiences, and the difficulties of even recognizing, let alone addressing, the many contextual and cultural factors which indirectly but profoundly influence the dynamics of communication between persons. Eisenhower's default position vis-à-vis nuclear stockpiling seemed to have followed the same logic that most communicators follow when worried that their message is not clear: more is better. Indeed, the problem of calculating sufficiency is profound when the purpose of a technology is symbolic. Eisenhower's choice was to invest America's nuclear arsenal with profound symbolic weight as a deterrent; a stockpiling mentality was consistent with this choice, if not the product of it.

However—to return to the script featuring Eisenhower, Strauss, and the kilogram of uranium—Eisenhower's "peaceful" message of atomic energy forwarded a symbolic logic obverse to that of nuclear stockpiling: out of a little can come plenty. Agriculture, industry, medicine, and even the quality of the wax on America's kitchen floors would be the beneficiaries of little shipments of isotopes sent out from Oak Ridge, Tennessee (a principal site of the Manhattan Project), according to Strauss and Eisenhower. This was the *moral* economy of the atom, so to speak, that Eisenhower publicly endorsed. But this moral economy could not penetrate nuclear stockpiling. Even as he aggressively pursued a program of nuclear stockpiling, Eisenhower's script ended with the prompt: "In brief closing statement [the president] says that with all these blessings which the atom stands ready to give us—and is now giving us, in greater measure each passing day—we and all peoples must reject atomic energy as an instrument of destruction, etc."[66] It was as if Eisenhower lived in two worlds, one where he could denounce atomic weaponry as immoral and another where he could approach it as an instrumental necessity.

Nuclear stockpiles and atomic pools for peaceful purposes therefore inhabited different spheres of being—fact and value—with the latter entailing the moral rejection of the former but nevertheless incapable of materially affecting it. What they shared, however, was a preeminent status as symbols, and consequently an intense connection to form. As a symbolic enterprise, Eisenhower's deterrence followed the form of repetition, which comported not only with a "more is better" approach to communication, but also with the material form of manufacturing. Thus a kind of homology existed between the symbolic and the material with respect to nuclear stockpiling. Eisenhower's atoms-for-peace program, however, rested not on repetition, but on "conversion"—both in the sense of converting military technologies to peaceful ones, and in the sense of "out of a little can come plenty." The plenty, according to Eisenhower's rhetoric, was ultimately peace, prosperity, and general human flourishing. Thus the form of atoms-for-peace was ultimately not simply conversion, but what Kenneth Burke calls "conversion upwards."[67] And in the fusion of repetition and conversion we find liberality.

It was therefore on the symbolic that Eisenhower hung the pursuit of his two main policy commitments, the avoidance of any major war and the political protection and rhetorical amplification of liberal American politics and economics. This is not quite the same as saying that he relied on "psychology," although the discourse of psychology dominated both his time and ours with respect to deterrence and propaganda. The practical principles of psychology tend to follow theories of human personality and nature, and are focused on internal states or processes. They aim at the emotional, cognitive, and social management of human life based upon scientific theories of human subjectivity and sociality. Kennan's containment was in this sense "psychological," as it presumed certain stable realities about human nature and human societies and derived from recognition of these realities a practical sense of the best means for coping with the life of nations in the Cold War crisis. Eisenhower's deterrence, however, did not adhere as closely to a clear conception of the intransigent features of human personality and society as it did to distinct discursive patterns. (Indeed, as we will see, Eisenhower addressed "human nature" as a thing that itself needed to be reshaped according to the great changes wrought in the postwar world.) His approach was therefore not strictly psychological, but rather hermeneutical, concerned with right interpretation. And this hermeneutical approach was pursued rhetorically. His was a hermeneutical rhetoric characterized by a distinct discursive form: the "conversion upward" of mundane objects and entities into "higher" forms of life that represented the "true" nature of America. Upon such conversion upwards depended the success of his approach to nuclear deterrence.

Therefore, I suggest that Eisenhower's approach closely mirrored aspects of nineteenth-century romanticism. At issue for him was not specifically a theory of human nature or even social order per se, but an *interpretative commitment* to an ultimate synthesis—a kind of historicist vision of a whole to which every human action, human technology, and human being was a part. Both Eisenhower and many nineteenth-century romantics were existentially committed, in a kind of leap of faith, to a "whole" that historically, normatively, and symbolically gave meaning to the part. Both also were simultaneously worried about and participants within the modern processes of science and industrialization.

Romanticism, Sublimity, and Synecdoche

Nineteenth-century romanticism was marked by paradox. On the one hand, it represented a cultural effort to reintegrate what had been atomized, fragmented, and disintegrated by Enlightenment philosophy and science. It strove after a new synthesis, a reenchantment of the holism of medieval great chain of Being. On the other hand, it relied on an acute epistemological split between, in Coleridge's terms, the Understanding (the rational faculty) and Reason (the intuitive faculty), which respectively corresponded to the natural and spiritual orders of Being. Every encounter with the world—or the word, as American romanticism began with debates about scriptural exegesis—consisted of two senses, one rational, even mechanical, and the other intuitive, even mystical. Consequently, rather than being strict critics of modern science and its counterpart, industrialization, romantics urged that scientific inquiry be supersupplemented with an intuitive sense of the higher significance of objects and objectification. Within this romantic way of being, one could proceed rationally in the world while insisting that rational knowledge could not itself exhaust the world's (or the word's) significance. A full encounter with the world around (or the text before) required a "poetic" and "spiritual" supersupplement to rational inquiry.

Thus, romanticism is connected to the romance. As Hayden White writes, "The Romance is fundamentally a drama of self-identification symbolized by the hero's transcendence of the world of experience, his victory over it, and his final liberation from it. . . . It is a drama of the triumph of good over evil, of virtue over vice, of light over darkness, and of the ultimate transcendence of man over the world in which he was imprisoned by the Fall."[68] Thus in one sense romanticism's genealogy cannot be easily disassociated from stoicism. Both have sought forms of mastery of the world around. Stoicism's prescription, however, rested on self-mastery, whereas romanticism turned toward world-mastery, especially through heroic interpretations of historical processes. Stoicism is in this way epistemologically skeptical, whereas romanticism is epistemologically optimistic. Contrast, for example, Seneca's approach toward death and disaster with that of Ralph Waldo Emerson's: the wise man, Seneca writes, even amidst great distress and disaster, "will still consider what is valuable in life to be something wholly confined to his inner self." For he "does not regard as valuable anything that is capable of being taken away."[69] Entailed here is not only an attitude of *apatheia*, but a subtle skepticism about the possibilities of intimate knowledge of the objective world. On the other hand, writing of Lincoln's assassination, Emerson concluded, "There is a serene Providence, which rules the fate of nations, which makes little account of time, little of one generation or race, makes no account of disasters."[70] Here Emerson turned optimistically toward a historical consciousness as means of encountering the objective world, interpreting death and disaster according to a higher historical order of being, Providence.

This "serene" historicism allied nineteenth-century romanticism with ideologies of science, industry, and technology. As Walter Ong has commented, romanticism's supersupplemental approach to modern scientific inquiry was part of a broader affinity with the Enlightenment. "Romanticism manifests a feeling of control over nature based ultimately on noetic advance which allies it strangely with the technological spirit. Before romanticism, as has so often been pointed out, mountains were hostile masses and other comparable manifestations of nature were regarded with similar misgivings. Upon the accession of romanticism, mountains are still awesome enough, but their hostility is gone."[71] Indeed, romanticism's "sublime science" tended to approach all natural phenomena, and even historical phenomena, as approachable and manageable—not exclusively or even primarily through instrumental control, but through acts of interpretation and poetic representation.

As Philip Gura shows, in antebellum America, romanticism—articulated chiefly through transcendentalism—grew largely out of debates regarding the scientific criticism of scripture. Transcendentalists like Emerson, Henry David Thoreau, George Bancroft, Theodore Parker, and Elizabeth Palmer Peabody did not so much reject the "empirical, rational reading of the Bible" of their Unitarian fathers and mothers as seek more poetic and yet still heterodox approaches to it—and not just to scripture, but toward language more broadly (which had been restricted by Locke to a merely conventional and instrumental vehicle for communication) and toward the natural world (which had been mechanized by Newtonian physics).[72] "Emerson believed that the literal, contextual meaning of scriptural language was not as important as its more symbolic function."[73] Similarly, "Nature" could function as a text that symbolically communicated higher meanings. Intuition, self-consciousness, and subjectivity rose to the fore of interpretation. American romantics thus helped to create "a novel theory of literary symbolism that placed individual consciousness front and center."[74] In this way, Gura suggests that transcendentalism was at the center of "a culture-wide shift toward a more symbolic ordering or reality," and this well before the age of propaganda, psychology, and soft power.[75]

In its influential Emersonian vein, this symbolic ordering of reality envisioned society as a mystical self. Emerson declared in "The American Scholar" (1837) a "doctrine ever new and sublime": "There is One Man,— present to all particular men only partially, or through one faculty; and that you must take the whole society to find the whole man. Man is not a farmer, or a professor, or an engineer, but he is all."[76] Whereas stoicism helped give rise to a strong notion of society as a self, and evangelicalism to society as covenantal moral community, romanticism, in its quest for ultimate synthesis, posited a notion of society not so much as a self but as a *soul*, even a *nation*—a spiritual, immaterial, unified Being. Thus for a thinker like Emerson, pivotal to society was a kind of hermeneutical leadership in an ideal teacher, scholar, or poet who would interpret the mundane symbols of the world in light of their ultimate spiritual, and national, significance.

And so arose what cultural historians and literary scholars of the period have referred to as the "American sublime," that habit in American rhetoric of positing the immeasurable being of the nation. Rather than rehearse here the variegated history of the American sublime, I want to focus on the issue of *form*, for, as I argued above, form was central to Eisenhower's approach to nuclear deterrence. There is an important distinction to be made within the rhetoric of the American sublime with respect to form, a distinction between "concentration" and "conversion," or—in the language of ancient and modern linguists, literary scholars, and rhetorical theorists—between metonymy and synecdoche. These two distinct forms have constituted two different ways of interpreting the significance of symbols. They have entailed diverse symbolic logics.

Kenneth Burke argues that metonymy entails the concentration of meaning in a singular object, whereas synecdoche depends upon a network of symbolic associations and interrelated meanings. Both metonymy and synecdoche involve association between a whole and a part. However, metonymy seeks "to convey some incorporeal or intangible state in terms of the corporeal or tangible," whereas synecdoche works more bilaterally, stressing "a *relationship* or *connectedness* between two sides of an equation, a connectedness that, like a road, extends in either direction, from quantity to quality and from quality to quantity."[77] Metonymy therefore works through reduction or concentration, whereas synecdoche operates through movement between part and whole, microcosm and macrocosm, corporeal and incorporeal. Synecdoche often works by "conversion upwards," which Burke describes as "a one-way process of magnification, a *writing large*," such that corporeal objects take on spiritual significance. With respect to political rhetoric, the metonymic sign is relatively stable via reduction and concentration, whereas the synecdochal sign must remain unstable to be effective, as the flow of its signification is multidirectional. Metonymy creates a centralized and concentrated order, whereas synecdoche creates a dispersed and interconnected one. To contemporary eyes, the former may look somewhat Fascist, whereas the latter may look Liberal. Metonymy tends to put great value on the corporeal object, whereas synecdoche tends to devalue the corporeal object in favor of more incorporeal objects like process, system, or spirit.

Metonymic representations in political rhetoric have enjoyed great influence in American history. In his essay on the death of Abraham Lincoln, for example, Walt Whitman echoed a common metonymic idea by suggesting that Lincoln's death represented not just the end of a presidency, but the end of a national history: "A long and varied series of contradictory events arrives at last at its highest poetic, single, central, pictorial denouement. The whole involved, baffling, multiform whirl of the secession period comes to a head, and is gather'd in one brief flash of lightning-illumination—one simple, fierce deed."[78] In this way, Whitman presented the historical energies of the nation as so concentrated in Lincoln's figure that his death *was*, in a certain sense, the death of the nation. "Strange," he continues, "(is it not?) that battles, martyrs, agonies, blood, even assassination, should so condense—perhaps only really, lastingly condense—a Nationality."[79] As such, Whitman's metonymic sublime, although democratic, was partial to iconographies of exceptional figures, still prevalent in and around World War II. And James McDaniel has noted, in 1940s America representations of Franklin Roosevelt took on a quality eerily akin to representations of Fascist leaders like Hitler and Mussolini. The iconography of FDR in political cartoons pointed to "the irresistible and charismatic Leader" in the face of a great threat. FDR "occupied the place of sublime object by being represented as 'larger-than-life,' titanic and strong," such that "staples of the Fascist sublime are recuperated in the Democratic sublime."[80] In this way, FDR's death produced national anxieties similar to those generated by Lincoln's death. Had the nation died too?

To be sure, this metonymic sublime was crucial to U.S. political culture, at least at the presidential level, from the latter years of the Gilded Age through World War II. Theodore Roosevelt's "Rough Rider" persona entailed a concentration of national energies into both his own figure and into the awe-inspiring landscapes his figure was imaginatively set against. Indeed, his place in the history of American expansionism cannot be easily separated from this persona and the image of the frontier he cultivated. Later, even Woodrow Wilson's cerebral figure took on metonymic form at a crucial juncture: determined to stress the U.S. role in the Allied victory in World War I, he crossed the Atlantic and marched in a victory parade down the streets of Paris. Similarly, when faced with Republican resistance to the League of Nations treaty, he took to an ambitious whistle-stop tour, which infamously came to an abrupt and miserable end when he suffered physical exhaustion culminating in a stroke. Headlines proclaiming his "nervous breakdown" seemed to draw a metonymic relationship between his body breaking under the weight of his democratic aspirations and America's inability to bear a League of Nations. Subsequently, Herbert Hoover's appeal to "rugged individualism" drew upon vocabulary that in one sense anticipated Eisenhower's discourse—pitting a decentralized "American system" against "centralized despotism" while celebrating "ordered liberty, freedom, and equal opportunity"—but Hoover reduced such liberal notions to, and thus concentrated them within, the image of the adventurous, enterprising individual signifying "unparalleled greatness," something Eisenhower was reticent to do.[81]

Eisenhower's discourse relied instead on the synecdochal variation of the American sublime, which has been strongly resistant to concentrated form. Seen preeminently in Emerson's rhetoric, and connected historically to the Pietism that influenced the religion of Eisenhower's parents, it has represented a more distinctly spiritual and integrative strain of the

American sublime, depending on a synecdochal principle of mystical univocity.[82] For Emerson, the virtue of democracy was that it functioned as a powerful sociopolitical means by which to see the transcendental "One Man." Democracy emphasizes the whole, all the while valorizing "the near, the low, the common" by making them contingent signifiers of an absolute incorporeal reality.[83] Thus what Emerson said of nature, he could have said of American democracy: "show me the sublime presence of the highest spiritual cause lurking, as always it does lurk, in the these suburbs and extremities of nature; let me see every trifle bristling in with the polarity that that ranges it instantly on an eternal law."[84] Here every particular body becomes a contingent "sign" of the quality of the whole, while no particular body reductively represents the whole. This symbolic structure makes particulars exchangeable, even dispensable, all the while embellishing them with sublime significance. Emerson's synecdochal signs were like currency: symbols of nationhood easily exchangeable as long as accounted for within a common standard of national value.

Within this synecdochal logic of "conversion upwards," where no single body can tightly circumscribe the whole, no particular death, tragedy, or disaster can radically disrupt the course of history. Emerson's "serene Providence" "makes no account of disasters."[85] Indeed, as Harold Bloom has observed, Emerson's synecdochal sublime may have been a response to national disaster, a way of coping with it:

> Emerson delivered *The American Scholar: An Oration,* at Harvard on August 31, 1837. A few months before, in the spring of 1837, there was a business crash, banks suspended nearly all payments, and a general economic depression dominated society. It is noteworthy, and has been noted, that Emerson's two great prophetic outbursts coincide with two national moral crises, the Depression of 1837 and the Mexican War of 1846, which Emerson, as an Abolitionist, bitterly opposed. The origins of the American Sublime are connected inextricably to the business collapse of 1837.[86]

It is not unfair to say that Emerson sought to move beyond, not so much the collapse of Jacksonian America, as the possibility of such a disaster fundamentally disrupting American identity.

Therefore, what I have distinguished as the metonymical and synecdochal versions of the American sublime have at their core differing perspectives on the nature and history of American democracy. The metonymic approach has valorized the Great Individual as the exemplary product of democracy. Positively, metonymy has structured political and social crises as objects to be overcome via appeals to heroic figures, the generations of which may correspond to epochs in history. But the metonymic approach, by investing the hero with such significance, has also risked tragedy—for heroes, too, fall. Metonymy thus enjoys a kinship with both adventurism and stoicism, which emphasize either singular acts or bodies. The synecdochal sublime, conversely, would find tragedy not in failed historic adventures, but in all those ways in which the mundane world—Emerson's "the near, the low, the common"—was not seen by people in light of its transcendental aspect. We might say that hermeneutic failures, rather than historical ones, constitute the synecdochal sense of tragedy, for under synecdoche's auspices historical disasters are seen providentially as events to be transcended.[87] Evangelicalism in this sense resembles synecdochal romanticism with respect to a shared distaste for the strong concentration of identity in singular figures in favor of more spiritual loci of meaning. As Dulles himself reminded audiences during World War II, "All power does not need to be vested in a single personification."[88] However, a romantic approach to the great society finds its apogee in the transcendence of the empirical world, in the supernal significance of the seemingly mundane, whereas evangelicalism has historically remained within the world, attempting in its revolutionary mode to reform and reconstruct it according to a higher order.

In belaboring here the differences between metonymy and synecdoche vis-à-vis American romanticism, I risk inviting the epithet of "literary criticism," which for political scientists, historians, and indeed rhetorical scholars is too often a term of disparagement. But Eisenhower *spoke,* and indeed was, as Osgood argues, preoccupied with exploiting "the fourth weapon"—the massive media and information networks that exploded during the early Cold War. "Mass media, mass politics, mass movements, mass ideologies, and mass societies had a totalizing effect on the Cold War."[89] To imagine otherwise is mere wish fulfillment. Eisenhower not only spoke, he acted, and indeed reacted, in ways conceived "to have an impact on public perceptions."[90] And his words and deeds bore a form; they could not do otherwise. My turn to tropology, therefore, attempts to reckon with the effective structure of public form, rather than to dismiss it as incidental.

Thus, I belabor the differences between metonymy and synecdoche vis-à-vis American romanticism to present a sense of what Eisenhower's discourse put at stake when he told the world in "Atoms for Peace" that massive nuclear retaliation, "while fact, is not the true expression of the purpose and the hope of the United States." To be sure, for him, nuclear weaponry put the existence of human society itself at stake; yet, to deter as much as possible the catastrophic nuclear scenario, Eisenhower's nuclear stockpiling placed something altogether different at stake: the reputation of America at home and abroad, and concomitantly, the attitudes of peoples toward the possibilities of liberal society. Eisenhower therefore consistently strove to steer the image of America at home and abroad along a synecdochal route, pointing habitually to the "true" quality of the nation over and against any reductive concentrations. Indeed, Eisenhower resisted the concentration of meaning in corporeal objects, historical events, or singular entities and institutions. He even consciously cultivated a rhetorical atmosphere around the White House that resisted concentration on his own potentially powerful presidential persona.[91] And he found events that concentrated national energies in profound ways among the most difficult to handle as president, for example, Little Rock, Sputnik, and, above all, the Bomb.[92] Characteristic of Eisenhower's leadership was an effort to keep people from concentrating their attitudes toward and interpretations of America on singular events or entities and instead focus on values, purposes, and spirit. His objection to an exclusive reliance on massive retaliatory power in his 1952 letter to Dulles was in keeping with this.

This effort was caught between strategy and ideology. On the one hand, it can be seen as strategic in motive rather than ideological: in a crucial strategic sense, nuclear stockpiling had to find a supersupplement of "values" in order to preserve the morale of liberal states and present a robust alternative to the historical narratives of Communism. Eisenhower's symbolic amplification of the Bomb vis-à-vis deterrence, derived from a commitment to economic sustainability and a resolution to avoid major war altogether, backed him into a rhetorical corner, so to speak, where he had to work to undermine efforts at symbolic concentration simply because one of the most obvious candidates for such concentration was the Bomb. Yet the course of Eisenhower's prepresidential as well as presidential career suggests that the contrary was the case as well: Eisenhower's ideological predilections helped create the atmosphere, so to speak, in which a strategy of nuclear deterrence via nuclear stockpiling could seem tolerable. With respect to his sense of America, Eisenhower, in romantic fashion, habitually looked beyond the corporeal object to a higher spiritual significance.

Eisenhower and National Leadership

Commentators have more than once commented on two striking central aspects of Eisenhower's outlook: an affinity for the "spiritual" and a dislike of partisan politics, charismatic political figures, and political popularity contests. With regard to the former, Eisenhower's speechwriter Emmet Hughes wrote of the president, "Perhaps no adjective figured so prominently in his political vocabulary as 'spiritual,' and his spontaneous speeches were rich with exhortations on America's 'spiritual' strength."[93] This rhetorical habit, I suggest, was intimately related to his distaste for "politics." The "political" for Eisenhower had less to do with arts of negotiation and compromise than with publicity and publics, which tended to concentrate mass energies in singular objects, events, or institutions. By Eisenhower's reckoning, politics in this form worked against the maintenance of good political-economic order in a politically and economically interconnected world. A relatively early indication of his distaste for politics was evident in a 1942 diary entry, written before the invasion of North Africa that he oversaw. The entry reflected on the problems the Allies faced. Timing, forces, and strategy were issues, but the sharpest problems, he surmised, were political in nature. First, there were the difficulties Washington and London were having in agreeing on a plan. Then there were the unpredictable responses of "neutral" France and Spain to the Allied invasion. And finally, there was the problem of psychological reaction to the attack: if victorious, it would result in a boon of confidence for the Allies, but if a failure it would be devastating for morale. All in all, Eisenhower concluded, the undertaking was of "a quite desperate nature." "We are simply sailing a dangerous political sea, and this particular sea is one in which military skill and ability can do little in charting a safe course."[94] Indeed, the "desperate nature" of the North African invasion seems to have been for him strongly connected to the problems of the concentration of public attention, both with respect to the ambitions of egotistical politicians and with regard to the ways in which the invasion itself would concentrate world attention.

During his presidency, "politics" continued to present a problem to Eisenhower. C. D. Jackson wrote somewhat incredulously in 1954 that the president "is still mystified in a sincere and uncomplicated way at the maneuvers of politicians." Jackson imagined Eisenhower thinking, "With all there is to be done for this country, for the American people, for the whole world, how can any responsible man in the public life afford to waste God's time in being a conniving bastard."[95] And after his presidency, politics continued to represent something Eisenhower either willfully or subconsciously found alien. Stephen Ambrose has written of his discussions with Eisenhower, "while he had a sharp memory, he was not much interested in politics. The selectivity of his memory, in fact, was a good key to his feelings. He remembered relatively little about the political issues of World War II, or even about his own actions when they had been political. . . . When we discussed something he had done as a soldier he would make detailed and highly quotable comments, but when we discussed politics he would usually shake his head and dismiss the subject."[96] Eisenhower's distaste for "conniving bastards" and selective memory with regard to politics disclosed a more encompassing concern with the concentration of public power.

A second entry in Eisenhower's diary during the North Africa period is illuminating in this regard, as it revealed a distinction in Eisenhower's thought between order and politics, organization and the public.

> Through all of this, I am learning many things: (1) that waiting for other people to produce is one of the hardest things a commander has to do; (2) that in the higher positions of a modern army, navy, and air force, rich organizational experience and an orderly, logical mind are absolutely

essential to success. The flashy, publicity-seeking type of adventurer can grab the headlines and be a hero in the eyes of the public, but he simply can't deliver the goods in high command. On the other hand, the slow, methodical, ritualistic person is absolutely valueless in a key position.[97]

Terms of value for Eisenhower in the war were *organization, order, logic, method,* and *ritual.* His terms for censure, however, were not the mere opposites of these. They were represented by a type (no doubt embodied by Douglas MacArthur, under whom Eisenhower served in the 1930s): "The flashy, publicity-seeking type of adventurer can grab the headlines and be a hero in the eyes of the public." Here, concentration seemed to be the issue: Eisenhower held that as the publicity-seeking type concentrated mass attention on his figure, so organization, order, and logic were forfeited in leadership. This type depended for success on "the eyes of the public," and therefore surrendered the opportunity for real leadership.

Indeed, in the postwar years, Eisenhower made repeated calls for genuine national leadership in public speeches throughout the United States. *Leadership,* as Ira Chernus writes, was virtually a "god term" in Eisenhower's postwar rhetoric.[98] And his ideal for national leadership, like military leadership, meant transcending the whimsical winds of publicity-filled political seas. "Leadership," he declared in a July 1946 speech to the American Alumni Council, meant that one would "help produce, foster, and sustain . . . unity of purpose and action—to promote clear understanding of the relationships between domestic unity and the future peace of the world."[99] Leadership, he said in another speech two months later, entailed "widened knowledge and . . . increased comprehension of human relationship."[100] Leadership meant "firmness in the right, uncompromising support of justice and freedom, respect for all, and patience and determination in winning over any that through fear, hope for revenge or any selfish purpose, are blinded to their own national, as well as the world's, best interest."[101] Leadership, in sum, entailed the orderly, logical mind and the capacity for broad-minded oversight, the qualities Eisenhower esteemed in the military commander.

Importantly, it was also during these years that Eisenhower repeatedly rebuffed calls for him to pursue political office. Courted initially by

Democrats to pursue the presidency, and then much more so by Republicans, Eisenhower refused. A New Years' Day 1950 diary entry, written while he was president of Columbia University, attempted to justify why. His situation, he wrote, was exceptional with respect to national leadership, even as it was profoundly typical with respect to what he referred to as the "American system":

> My basic purpose is to try, however, feebly, to return to the country some portion of the debt I owe her. My family, my brothers and I, are examples of what this country with its system of individual rights and freedoms, its boundless resources, and its opportunities for all who want to work can do for its citizens—regardless of lack of wealth, political influence, or special educational advantage. Nowhere else on earth has this type of material, intellectual, and spiritual opportunity been so persistently and so successfully extended to all. Regardless of all faults that can be searched out in the operation of the American system, I believe without reservation that in its fundamental purpose and in its basic structure it is so far superior to any government elsewhere established by men, that my greatest possible opportunity for service is to be found in supporting, in renewing public respect for, and in encouraging greater thinking about these fundamentals. Since I believe that all Americans, even though they do so unconsciously or subconsciously, actually support these basic tenets of Americanism, it follows that in the field in which I should work (that is, the bringing of these basic tenets to our conscious attention) there is no difference between the two great parties.[102]

The reflection—characterized again by a penchant for liberality—is noteworthy for what it shows Eisenhower professed at the time not only about his own role in national leadership, but about the nation itself. America was seen as a place of "material, intellectual, and spiritual opportunity" that made his ascent to national leadership from modest roots typical—Eisenhower thus presented his very unusual life as essentially expressive of the American system. Such opportunities, he asserted, were "extended to all." Furthermore, whatever faults the American system evinced (which had to be "searched out") were minimal compared to the exceeding superiority of the American system. Finally, he held that "all

Americans" concurred with this assessment, albeit many did so "unconsciously or subconsciously." Hence, his role was to transcend partisanship and politics and to devote his life to a kind of consciousness-raising with respect to "the tenets of Americanism." His was a mission of converting upwards.

It is critical at this juncture to note that what apparently was a dramatic change of direction in Eisenhower's career as a public figure, his decision to run for the presidency, was connected by Eisenhower to the same sensibility that initially seemed to have driven his distaste for a pursuit of the presidency. Eisenhower included three great national and international problems among the reasons that conspired to give him reason to run for the presidency: the New Deal, Communism, and (mostly Republican) isolationism. In practice, for Eisenhower and other like-minded Americans, the New Deal and Communism shared a form: statism. In Eisenhower's view, Communism was Stalinism, and Stalinism was statism. The New Deal appeared to him to be a form of statism as well, centering national energies in a "paternalistic state" and paternalistic figure, FDR.[103] Therefore, from Eisenhower's perspective Stalin and FDR, while holding dramatically different political policies and practices, shared a similar political form, both (self-)styled as world-historical figures and easily subject to accusations of being power mongers. Eisenhower, as Hughes wrote, approached the presidency as "a studied retort and rebuke to a Roosevelt. Where Roosevelt had sought and coveted power, Eisenhower distrusted and discounted it: one man's appetite was the other man's distaste."[104] Similarly, Eisenhower's third problem, isolationism, tended to metonymically concentrate national identity, but in a geographical space rather than a paternalistic state. Such concentration, Eisenhower believed, was not only contrary to Americanism, it was fundamentally illogical, for it suggested that America could act unilaterally and in relative isolation from the rest of the world. Geopolitics and economics, he held, worked otherwise. America's vitality depended on world interdependence. The nation's leaders, he felt, must lead accordingly.

Therefore, what apparently led Eisenhower to run for the presidency was connected to the same proclivity that had earlier brought him to rebuff political aspirations: a "distaste," as Hughes puts it, for the metonymic concentration of power and a "taste" for a more spiritual or value-oriented apperception of the nation. Again, Eisenhower's distaste for the concentration of power was both strategic and ideological in nature. Strategically, Eisenhower held that, especially with respect to the economy, the concentration of power would lead to ruin—statism could simultaneously drive up taxes and government debt as well as generate a public environment controlled by a cult of personality. Ideologically, Eisenhower upheld "free enterprise" and the virtue of national spiritual strength; and thus believed that too much attention to the singular figures or events would undermine economic enterprise and national morale. All in all, as Chernus correctly notes, Eisenhower would have "taken it for granted that spiritual and pragmatic motives naturally reinforce one another."[105] In his presidency, synecdoche was a symbolic mode that could resist the concentration of power he opposed, while reinforcing notions of economic interdependence, free enterprise, and, as I will now further argue, nuclear deterrence.

Legitimizing Nuclear Deterrence

Robert J. Art describes deterrence as "the deployment of military power so as to be able to prevent an adversary from doing something that one does not want him to do and that he might be otherwise tempted to do by threatening him with unacceptable punishment if he does it."[106] Deterrence can thus be caught between certainty and faith. On the one hand, deterrence can be said to work if the threat of retaliation successfully manages the behavior of an adversary, introducing, in the words of Lawrence Freedman, "a certainty into adversary calculations."[107] Yet, on the other hand, as Steve Fetter has written, "It is theoretically impossible to prove that deterrence works, since it is always possible that the other side had no intention of using that which they were supposedly deterred from using. Only failures of deterrence can be verified." The pursuit of deterrence therefore rests on "*faith* in the power of the threat of retaliation in kind."[108] Deterrence via punishment always entails a wager that the increase and/or manifestation of one's own capacity to wreak destruction on another will lead to greater certainty, stability, and security in international affairs rather than less.[109] This is all the more the case with nuclear deterrence, where the scale of destruction is potentially so vast.[110]

The significant power of the idea of deterrence, therefore, cannot be said to rest either on the manifest evidence of empirical data, or on rationalistic proof. Rather, the widely shared faith in the power of modern military arsenals, even nuclear arsenals, to bring greater certainty and stability to the relations of nations can be attributed to probabilistic calculation reinforced by a profound cultural tradition, a historic "spirit" that possesses a wide swath of people. This spirit is clearly what Ong calls the technological spirit, which posits not only the possibility of control over nature, but positions human action in an instrumental relationship to the world around.[111] In this way, twentieth-century deterrence, especially nuclear deterrence, Oliver O'Donovan writes, is the product of "a century or more of cultural preoccupation with rendering human action infinite."[112]

However, the distinct approaches to nuclear deterrence represented by Dulles and Eisenhower suggest that the modern technological spirit is split with respect to the question of *legitimacy*. For someone like Dulles, the "punishment" of deterrence represents not only a technological strategy to prevent an adversary from taking certain actions, but a *moral* right. Punishment represents something one is morally justified in doing, as well as an instrumental means of persuasion. Within this framework, human action remains at least theoretically accountable to moral law, if not limited by it. Technology is modified by moral order, as we saw in Dulles both with respect to his advocacy of world federalism and with regard to his approach to the Bomb. The notion of human agency here is connected to the Puritan idea that peoples might construct and reconstruct society according to the Word of God, and that the moral character of human action determines the fate of human societies. What characterizes the Protestant mode of technological legitimation, therefore, is an appeal to a moral order.

For others like Eisenhower, however, deterrence is more thoroughly an instrumentalist enterprise, built on the foundation of utilitarian calculus and economic efficiency. Technology here is modified only by economy. While resources may be scarce, the faith in the capacities of human technological action is theoretically infinite. O'Donovan argues that this idea is traceable to German Idealism that followed Herder and contributed so significantly to romanticism. Idealism helped create the intellectual conditions in which to imagine the limitless possibilities of human thought and action. O'Donovan thus describes transcendence as the "inner fortress of deterrence-theory." The deterrent state assumes that it "can transcend the belligerent content of its threats in the pacific intent of its threatening. The state's will to deter, it is claimed, is at arms-length from the disproportion contained in the threat; it deploys it only hypothetically to yield a prospect of disaster that will ensure the keeping of peace."[113] Deterrence thus depends on a hierarchy of intention where the significance of the state's corporeal sign (the Bomb) is rendered insignificant relative to the transcendent purposes of the nation (world peace). In this way, the Bomb is said to be a necessary aspect of state security, but a penultimate symbol of nationhood.

This Idealist line of thinking coincided with the emergence of the industrial revolution, and, as I have already discussed, strongly influenced romantic thought in antebellum America. Within this romantic worldview, the ascent of spirit and the ascent of science and industry were often thought of as historically coordinated movements. Science provided evidence of the profound mysteries of the universe, summoning the human spirit to greater heights; and where science and industry failed or fell short, the human spirit could be invoked to summon technology to achieve its true potential. What characterizes the romantic mode of technological legitimation, therefore, is a distinct dualism—that between spirit and matter—and a hermeneutically oriented belief in the possibility of ultimate synthesis.

Legitimacy may be elusive, but it is crucial to the governance of liberal societies. During the 1950s, the legitimacy of a U.S. strategy of nuclear deterrence was precarious for several reasons. First there was the ever-present challenge of the moral legitimacy of the Bomb, critical even to an otherwise amoral strategic perspective because of the need to keep at least a portion of world opinion confident in the basic "good intentions" of America.[114] Second, and related to this, there was the problem of the legitimacy of American political culture itself: a large nuclear arsenal and a formal commitment to nuclear deterrence threatened to make America a warfare state in the eyes of others, even allies, and thus make America something other than a liberal city upon a hill.¹¹⁵ Then there was the profound problem, already discussed, of the general calmness of liberal societies before the Bomb: a strategy for the long haul of nuclear deterrence meant not only that hopes for a worldwide peaceful order had to be deferred but that the nation and its allies had to grow accustomed to living in an "age of peril." Finally, there was the question of the freedom of liberal societies: as nuclear stockpiling could only be justified as a "necessity," it could not help but challenge the freedom, above all the freedom of action, cherished by liberal societies. All four of these problems threatened to undermine the legitimacy of, and the public support for, of nuclear deterrence. The question of a "better way" was always lurking.

Indeed, a huge portion of the Eisenhower administration's energies was devoted to addressing the problems of nuclear legitimacy. Dulles's answer was to assert the moral right America had to stockpile nuclear weapons as a deterrent; his approach assumed that the moral canopy could cover issues of U.S. militancy and the prolongation of an age of peril. But this approach, as I argued, culminated in evangelical moral equivocation. Moreover, it metonymically drew attention to America's militant action, even as it presented this militancy as fundamentally moral in nature. Eisenhower's answer, thus, was profoundly different in form. It rested on a dualism rather than equivocation and entailed the synecdochal "conversion upward" rather than metonymic concentration in militant action, as his postwar speeches attest.

Immediately after World War II, General Eisenhower spoke as though the world was embarking on a new era of creativity, expression, and peace. For example, he opened an address at the Metropolitan Museum of Art in 1946 with these words: "We have recently emerged from a bitter conflict that long engulfed the larger nations of the globe. The heroism and sacrifice of men on the fighting lines, and the moral and physical energies of those at home, were all devoted to the single purpose of military victory. Preoccupation in a desperate struggle for existence left time for little else." He continued, "Now we enter on an era of widened opportunity for physical and spiritual development, united in a determination to establish and maintain a peace in which the creative and expressive instincts of our people may flourish."¹¹⁶ This emphasis on physical (especially economic) and spiritual development, a new era of peace, and the aesthetic expression of instinct was a reiteration of a liberal-developmentalist ideology and the idea of American exceptionalism, but with a new emphasis.[117] Historically, the idea of American exceptionalism was positioned over and against feudal Europe. America, it was held, was exceptional because it was free of the traditions, genealogies, and material ossification of old Europe. This freedom meant the possibility of radical innovation and experimentation both with respect to self and society. It meant infinite possibility and the boundless expression of creativity. Eisenhower's characterization at the Metropolitan Museum of Art of a new, widened epoch for development and expression reiterated this American exceptionalism, but in a different key. It was far less bound to the American landscape than its progenitors, and it came not on the heels of European feudalism but rather before "the golgotha of a Third World War."[118] Indeed, Eisenhower's enthusiasm must be read in light of atomic weaponry. Hiroshima and Nagasaki represented for him "a brink from which the prospect—if we turn not into sure paths of peace—is a thousand times more terrifying than anything yet witnessed."[119] In Eisenhower's discourse, atomic warfare displaced feudal Europe as the disaster to which America was a political as well as an aesthetic response. America itself was a "middle way" between the archaic European society that had finally been destroyed in World War II and total nuclear war.

This was not a sentiment unique to Eisenhower in the postwar years. We see it in Henry Luce's "American Century," and even in the artistic avant-garde. Indeed, a similar postwar appeal to a new era of creativity and instinctive expression was apparent in 1948 in artist Barnett Newman's influential reiteration of the idea of American exceptionalism with respect to artistic practice. Sounding very much like his nineteenth-century American romantic predecessors, and indeed like Eisenhower, Newman described in "The Sublime is Now" how a few American artists had finally succeeded in breaking free of European aesthetics and were articulating "a new way of experiencing life."[120] Like Eisenhower, he spoke of instinct, expression, creativity, and nationhood in universal terms free from corporeal boundaries, that is, landscape.

> We are reasserting man's natural desire for the exalted, for a concern with our relationship to the absolute emotions. We do not need the

obsolete props of an outmoded and antiquated legend. We are creating images whose reality is self-evident and which are devoid of the props and crutches that evoke associations with outmoded images, both sublime and beautiful. We are freeing ourselves of the impediments of memory, association, nostalgia, legend, myth, or what have you, that have been the devices of Western European painting.[121]

In his 1963 essay, "The American Sublime," Lawrence Alloway argued that Newman and others were expressing a wish, in the romantic tradition of the American sublime, for "psychic greatness."[122]

Eisenhower, too, sought for the nation a kind of psychic greatness, which he referred to as "spiritual" greatness. In his prepresidential rhetoric "America" was a preeminently spiritual being, and this carried over into his first inaugural address. In that speech, Eisenhower vividly assumed what can only be called a priestly role, becoming the first president ever to include in his address a public prayer. Indeed, throughout his presidency Eisenhower performed a kind of priestly role as defined by Max Weber: he was an institutionalized mediator, absolver of the nation, an interpreter of signs, and a vanguard of change.[123] Weber writes, "The full development of both a metaphysical rationalization and a religious ethic requires an independent and professionally trained priesthood," and notes that state officials can function as a kind of priesthood.[124] Eisenhower's priestly role depended on dualisms between the mundane and transcendent, the exterior and interior, and the static and transformative, where transcendence, interiority, and the transformative represent the truer dimension of the nation. These dualisms were integral to Eisenhower's answer to the three problems of nuclear legitimacy: moral culpability, militancy, and a kind of tranquility before the Bomb. With regard to the first problem, Eisenhower attempted to symbolically perform a kind of national absolution; with respect to the second problem, he argued for hermeneutical complexity; and with regard to the last problem, he called for human transformation.

In what follows, I provide a more detailed account of these strategies of nuclear legitimacy. My overarching argument is that they were not at all secondary to his approach to nuclear deterrence, but rather integral to it. In the conclusion to this chapter I will argue that without this rhetorical infrastructure, Eisenhower's approach to nuclear deterrence, by his own standards, would have been self-defeating. There is strong reason to argue, in other words, that without a romantic vision, Eisenhower's nuclear deterrence would have been crumbled under the weight of moral, material, and psychological pressures.

Eisenhower's Romantic Rhetoric

America of the 1950s was a montage of images, events, and personalities. The nation was possessed by suspicion, controversy, and conflict even as it took part in a reassuring rhetoric of democratic faith and economic optimism. In the 1950s isolationism waned, the New Deal's legacy grew suspect, McCarthyism thrived only to crash, serious racial crises were met with a mixture of sensationalism, moral outrage, and apathy, and Eisenhower was elected twice to the presidency under slogans as jarring as "dynamic conservatism," "progressive, dynamic conservatism," "progressive moderation," "moderate progressivism," and "positive progressivism."[125] Most dramatically, Eisenhower cast the nation as on a mission for world peace even as he and others in his administration spoke of the horrors of nuclear war and added substantially to its inventory of thermonuclear warheads.

However, the image of America that emerged from Eisenhower's presidential rhetoric acknowledged little of the tension or contradiction of this montage. Instead, especially as it addressed the purposes and essences of America, the nation was cast in language that evoked spiritual univocity. Eisenhower synecdochally "converted" the nation not only upward but inward, placing in his discourse about America a firm line dividing its incorporeal essence from its corporeal equivocations. Eisenhower addressed America penultimately as a "realistic" self-interested actor in the world but *ultimately* as a benevolent mystical national self. In his first speech act as president, his 1953 inaugural address, Eisenhower established this prototypical pattern of addressing the nation, distinguishing spirit from matter, and aligning the former with subjectivity, values, and true purposes and the latter with corporeal facts, contingent necessities, and instrumental technologies.

At the outset of his first inaugural, Eisenhower did two things that were new in the history of inaugural addresses. First, he asked permission to pray, and then he did so. His speech began, "My friends, before I begin the expression of those thoughts that I deem appropriate to this moment, would you permit me the privilege of uttering a little private prayer of my own."[126] The particular language of this request was significant. First of all, he addressed his audience simply as "friends." FDR had done the same in his 1945 inaugural, but only as the third term in a list featuring a more formal mode of address: "Mr. Chief Justice, Mr. Vice President, my friends."[127] Truman had not addressed his audience as "friends." Eisenhower's exclusive use of "friends" to begin his inaugural address suggested, however subtly, that the beginning point of his relationship with the citizenry was ideally one of felicitous fellowship rather than mere political convention. Indeed, this simple address evinced what was evident throughout Eisenhower's discourse: an idea that underlying the Union was a civic bond centered on a "spiritual" essence that transcended constitution and contract. In fact, later in the first inaugural speech, Eisenhower explicitly credited this felicitous mystic bond for the seamlessness of the presidential transfer of power. Having described at some length a common "faith," he concluded, "It is because we, all of us, hold to these principles that the political changes accomplished this day do not imply turbulence, upheaval, or disorder. Rather this change expresses a purpose of strengthening our dedication and devotion to the precepts of our founding documents, a conscious renewal of faith in our country and in the watchfulness of a Divine Providence." The friendship of faith, he claimed, made harmonious political change possible as it held back a more "natural" human tendency to make political changes disruptive events.

Second, in asking permission to pray, Eisenhower described the speech that was to follow as "the expression of those thoughts that I deem appropriate to this moment." The language of "expression" and "thought" and his use of "I deem" were significant: they associated the oration with his contemplations. Importantly, Eisenhower made no claim to be able to definitively read the moment before him. He did not say something like "those words appropriate to this moment," which would imply a kind of ability to know what words are indeed needed. Instead, he stated in the speech, "We find ourselves groping to know the full sense and meaning of these times." Thus, Eisenhower presented himself as bound to sense and intuition, describing the speech as emanating up through layers of the self: it would be the expression (top layer, that of language) of a thought (intermediate layer, that of contemplation) he deemed (bottom layer, that of judgment and will) appropriate.[128]

Thus the significance of the language used to describe the prayer itself, "a little private prayer of my own." In one sense, the description was misleading. There simply was nothing "private" about the prayer Eisenhower uttered. It was made in the most public of places and it concerned the most public of issues: government. Furthermore, it was in one way a brazen presidential act, as no president had ever opened an inaugural speech with a prayer. And yet the phrase "my own" shifted the meaning of "private" from that which is the antonym of "public" to that which is the synonym of "personal." Again, Eisenhower grounded his utterances, whether the inaugural address or the prayer that preceded it, in his interior self, hidden from the public eye not by virtue of a social boundary between public and private, but in the way that a spiritual leader's meditations can be "private" because their ultimate significance always exceeds conventional language. Eisenhower suggested in these seemingly simple and straightforward phrases that he spoke from an interior private realm somehow connected to the transcendent.

Indeed, the priestly resonances of Eisenhower's first inaugural speech were not accidental. As he wrote in his memoir,

> Religion was one of the thoughts I had been mulling over for several weeks. I did not want my Inaugural Address to be a sermon, by any means; I was not a man of the cloth. But there was embedded in me from boyhood, just as it was in my brothers, a deep faith in the beneficence of the Almighty. I wanted, then, to make this faith clear without creating the impression that I intended, as the political leader of the United States, to avoid my own responsibilities in an effort to pass them on to the Deity. I was seeking a way to point out that we were getting too secular.[129]

While Eisenhower here sought to separate himself from a priestly office per se, he stressed his desire to reestablish as sense of connection to the transcendent. To be sure, this can be understood as a mere reflection of a vague worry about the nation becoming "too secular," and it was clearly a part of a more political concern that the nation look distinctly different from "materialistic" Soviet Communism. Even so, the language of this reflection on the first inaugural should not go unnoticed: it was characterized by disjunction—"I was not a man of the cloth. . . . *But*" and "I wanted, then, to make this faith clear *without* creating the impression." The language itself moved disjunctively between a realm of "faith" on one hand and that of "responsibility" on the other. This disjunction repeated again the prototypical form of Eisenhower's presentation of the Cold War.

The essence of the Cold War, Eisenhower declared in his first inaugural, was "no argument between slightly different philosophies." On the contrary, "This conflict strikes directly at the faith of our fathers and the lives of our sons. No principle or treasure that we hold, from the spiritual knowledge of our free schools and churches to the creative magic of free labor and capital, nothing lies safely beyond the reach of this struggle. Freedom is pitted against slavery; lightness against dark." In this way, as many commentators have noted, Eisenhower presented the Cold War as diabolical conflict, best viewed from the perspective of the "spiritual." His rhetorical presidency was therefore charged with the mediation of spiritual realities. Consequently, he attended frequently to the incorporeal basis of corporeal phenomena. At the heart of the presidential office vis-à-vis rhetorical leadership was, in his view, a hyperspiritual and moral vocation, one that brought people to see material phenomena—be they political, social, or economic—as mere signs of a higher and more real immaterial reality. He approached America poetically, adding a spiritual supersupplement to the rational and "realistic" dimension of the nation.

This approach reinforced the immense interpretive liberality Eisenhower exercised in his speeches. He could draw a direct connection, as he did in his first inaugural, between "the grower of rice in Burma and the planter of wheat in Iowa, the shepherd in southern Italy and the mountaineer in the Andes . . . the French soldier who dies in Indo-China, the British soldier killed in Malaya, and the American life given in Korea"— for all, he claimed, in Emersonian fashion, were possessed by the same "faith." This faith was not only a universal "common bond," it was itself expansive in its expression, from the "faith of our fathers" to "the spiritual knowledge of our free schools and churches to the creative magic of free labor and capital." Eisenhower's rhetoric presented a conception of an American liberal faith that had as its only bounds that which was its complete opposite, described variously in the first inaugural as "tyranny," "slavery," "darkness," and "imperialism." He thus not only furthered the image of an unequivocal bipolar world vis-à-vis the Cold War, but rhetorically performed a priestly role, indeed a heroic one, absolving America's true spirit from culpability.

The result, moreover, was a preeminently priestly one, a kind of national absolution. In Eisenhower's presidential discourse, America was absolved from serious culpability with respect to two types of crises, both of which were potential threats to the nation's moral leadership of the world. First, in the domestic realm, Eisenhower's approach to describing social disparity in his first inaugural made equality essentially a matter of spirit: "the virtues most cherished by free people . . . all are treasures equally precious in the lives of the most humble and the most exalted." This spiritual egalitarianism comprised Eisenhower's equivalent to Emerson's One Man. Not surprisingly, subsequent to the first inaugural *The Nation* complained that Eisenhower "completely ignored the domestic scene."[130] This was not quite true. Rather, he addressed the domestic scene in a manner that assumed the justness of the nation from the vantage point of spirit, as American principles of equality, liberty, justice, and so on were made essentially transcendental. As James Reston commented in the *New York Times* the day after the first inaugural, "The thing that impressed most observers here about President Eisenhower's first state paper was that he spoke almost entirely in universal terms." Policy solutions to domestic problems, Reston concluded, would have to wait.[131] What Eisenhower argued in the first inaugural was repeated throughout his presidency: the essence of the nation resided in its principles, and these principles had a spiritual foundation, and adherence to these principles comprised a universal liberal ethos.

This position, in turn, was integral to his presentation of the nuclear crisis, and it was when addressing this topic that the significance of his "conversion upward" was most acute. A persistent theme in the discourse of the Eisenhower administration was the horrifying specter of a surprise nuclear attack. In his early "Chance for Peace" address, he spoke of "weapons of war now capable of inflicting instant and terrible punishment on any aggressor."[132] In "Atoms for Peace" he claimed, "even a vast superiority in numbers of weapons, and a consequent capability of devastating retaliation, is no preventive, of itself, against the fearful material damage and toll of human lives that would be inflicted by surprise aggression." And in 1955 at the Geneva Conference he declared, "Surprise attack has a capacity for destruction far beyond anything which man has yet known."[133] In his speeches and public statements Eisenhower repeatedly pointed to the day when the United States would be suddenly attacked by Soviet bombs and, in turn, instantly respond with a massive nuclear reprisal. This dreaded day, as he said in "Atoms for Peace," would culminate the confrontation between "two atomic colossi," producing a "civilization destroyed—the annihilation of the irreplaceable heritage of mankind handed down to us generation from generation."

However, this catastrophic scenario rarely stood starkly by itself in this rhetoric, as it did in Dulles's massive retaliation address. Rather, Eisenhower would present an opposite vision. As he said in "Atoms for Peace," nuclear annihilation "is not the true expression of the purpose and the hope of the United States"—that purpose and hope was one of world peace. "Against the dark background of the atomic bomb, the United States does not wish merely to present strength, but also the desire and the hope for peace." In this way visions of catastrophe in Eisenhower's discourse were repeatedly followed by millennial visions of world peace and harmony, and these visions were tied to the interior, which was also the transcendental, realm of "hope" and "faith." America's faith, he announced in "Atoms for Peace," is "the faith which can bring to this world lasting peace for all nations, and happiness and well-being for all men." The United States would "devote its entire heart and mind to find the way by which the miraculous inventiveness of man shall not be dedicated to his death, but consecrated to his life." This language of faith and spirit made the opposite of catastrophe not merely relative peace or general concordance, but the consummate expression of a transcendental human condition.

Nevertheless, for Eisenhower the emphasis was not on the historical telos so much as the transcendent ideals, principles, and spiritual truths realized in this telos. Thus while, as the work of Medhurst as well as Bowie and Immerman has shown, Eisenhower's discourse and decision making was shaped by a powerful historical teleology, scholars like Chernus and Ivie are correct in emphasizing that it was a teleology indefinitely deferred.[134] While some have therefore concluded that Eisenhower was a tragic figure caught between the desire for peace and freedom and the horrible necessities of a nuclear arms race, and while others find in Eisenhower profound ironies, we cannot neglect the ways in which Eisenhower himself actively worked to overcome, indeed transcend, tragedy and irony.[135] For he insisted repeatedly that the transcendent ideals, principles, and spiritual truths realized by his historical telos existed *irrespective* of historical eventualities or material realities. In this way, Eisenhower refused to see the essence of "America" in the visage of the Bomb, all the while maintaining the state's prerogative to produce, control, and indeed detonate this destructive technology. The nation was absolved inasmuch as one took little account of its material manifestation with respect to the meaning of America. In a sharp dualism, spirit stood over matter and hope over necessity, and—critically—the essence of America was presented as ultimately a matter of spirit and hope. Eisenhower symbolically relegated the corporeal world to an inferior level vis-à-vis the true and ultimate meaning of the nation state that was America.

Yet it was clear to Eisenhower and others that it was within the corporeal world that America would thrive or fail in the Cold War. The corporeal world thus remained a locus of political and material, if not moral, accounting. The corporeal buildup of nuclear weaponry risked putting the nation in the position of an immoral warfare state with respect to world opinion. Thus, as I have discussed, he stood amidst incongruities, paradoxes, and even contradictions.[136] On the one hand, he presented the Cold War as a diabolical conflict between two entities: America as a benign, spiritual, and principled nation, the Soviet Union as malign, materialistic, and irrational. This frame was unequivocal and metaphysical, and demanded a kind of prophetic stance, akin to Dulles's in attitude.[137] On the other hand, Eisenhower's pragmatic emphases on global interdependence, economic complexity, and strategic (and often secretive) geopolitical interventions suggested a "realist" stance, more like Kennan's than Dulles's in attitude. At the very least, he held that the United States needed to show sensitivity to various complex geopolitical contexts and make a great deal of economic and military investment. Thus, in one respect Eisenhower stressed the metaphysical essence of the Cold War, whereas in another more pragmatic way he saw it strictly in terms of the nation's strategic and material resources.

Yet the tension between Eisenhower's transcendentalism and his realism—or between interpretations of Eisenhower as ideologue or a pragmatist—may not be as acute as they appear. Robert Hariman argues that political realism has a characteristic style, which "begins by marking all other discourses with the sign of the text"—as "mere rhetoric"—because realism can assume that "political power is an autonomous material force."[138] Yet there is more than one way to mark discourse with the "sign of the text." One need not dismiss the symbolic to be a "realist." One can adhere to the logic of realism and idealism simultaneously via conversion upward, asserting that meaning of material entities ultimately resides in a transcendent realm and that, with respect to political leadership, national purpose ultimately entails a kind of autonomous spiritual force. One then approaches the corporeal world as a realm of "mere signs" reflecting governing spiritual forces. As Weber says of highly abstract forms of religious life, "Spirits may be regarded as invisible essences that follow their own laws, and are merely 'symbolized by' concrete objects." In such a hermeneutical system, political leadership entails, among other things, a kind of spiritual interpretation, pointing out the transcendent thrust of the corporeal sign.[139]

Eisenhower in fact spoke in precisely this way. Two speeches he delivered in the winter of 1957 are representative: his Eisenhower Doctrine address and his State of the Union speech. Each address took the contingent particulars of the Cold War conflict and translated them into what Eisenhower called a "universal phenomenon." In almost priestly fashion, Eisenhower discerned the ultimate meaning, the spiritual sense, or the sublime trajectory of material signs. Accordingly, in his State of the Union address, Eisenhower called for "vision and wisdom and resolution" in "all echelons of government," and presented as the assumption of his policy the connection of all sociopolitical phenomena to a singular reality. "You meet in a season of stress that is testing the fitness of political systems and the validity of political philosophies. Each stress stems in part from causes peculiar to itself. But every stress is a reflection of a universal phenomenon." Eisenhower described the universal phenomenon to which he referred as "the spirit of freedom," which ("sometimes dangerously," he noted) was propelling a global "persistent search for the self-respect of authentic sovereignty and the economic base on which national independence must rest." The "spirit of freedom" was expressed worldwide; however, he claimed that the U.S. Constitution had the particular privilege of giving it distinct proclamation when it affirmed the founding principles of human liberty, human welfare, and human progress. Consequently, he argued, the United States must be committed to "a high role in world affairs: a role of vigorous leadership, ready strength, sympathetic understanding."[140] Then, a hierarchy of spirit over matter firmly in place, Eisenhower proceeded to argue in the State of the Union address for increases in U.S. material investment abroad. Such a role for the United States in the Middle East had been outlined five days earlier in his Eisenhower Doctrine. That speech asked Congress to sanction increased U.S. military, economic, and "moral" (i.e., psychological warfare) intervention in the Middle East.

In the Eisenhower Doctrine speech, Eisenhower argued that Russia's dealings in the world were motivated neither by security nor economic gain. Rather, "The reason for Russia's interest in the Middle East is solely for power politics. Considering her announced purpose of Communizing the world, it is easy to understand her hope of dominating the Middle East." Thus he argued that ultimately the Middle East entailed dynamics that "transcend the material." For Eisenhower, these dynamics were not simply moral, for example, Russia's greed for power. Rather, they involved a metaphysical "supremacy." He stated,

> The Middle East is the birthplace of three great religions—Moslem, Christian and Hebrew. Mecca and Jerusalem are more than places on the map. They symbolize religions which teach that the spirit has supremacy over matter and that the individual has a dignity and rights of which no despotic government can rightfully deprive him. It would be intolerable if the holy places of the Middle East should be subjected to a rule that glorifies atheistic materialism.[141]

Eisenhower here made topography, the Middle East, a kind of text, and then this text yet a mere sign: Mecca and Jerusalem were "places on the map," yet they were more than this. On a register of the ultimate, they were symbols of a spiritual truth, that of the supremacy of spirit. Eisenhower thus marked them as symbols and then converted upward. Importantly, Eisenhower linked this metaphysical hierarchy to a political vision described as the positioning of "individual rights" over "despotic government." Thus, Islam, Christianity, and Judaism—blithely conflated and reduced to symbols of the spiritual—validated the essentially metaphysical thrust of Eisenhower's American liberalism.

Clearly, this emphasis on the metaphysical was politically risky inasmuch as it could have minimized the importance of the material. To avert this risk, Eisenhower's conversion upward needed also to make a "return" to the corporeal, for otherwise he could have divested himself of the support required to marshal and manage the nation's material infrastructure. Indeed, a great portion of Eisenhower's 1957 State of the Union address was devoted to pragmatic concerns about the future of the U.S. economy, and the central demand made by the Eisenhower Doctrine was for congressional support for budgetary expenditures in foreign aid and military output. However, the interpretive purchase of what I have referred to as the synecdochal sublime became apparent here, as through it the corporeal was, however contingently, made to signify the sublime.

For the 1957 State of the Union address argued that the nation's economic prosperity was a sign of the transcendent spiritual basis of America. "Principles" of the Constitution like human liberty, human welfare, and human progress—described as "lighting fires in the souls of men everywhere"—were presented in the speech as the true basis of U.S. economic prosperity. Of course, the idea that liberty gives birth to prosperity has a robust lineage within liberal thought. But in Eisenhower's speech, the idea was performed as a hermeneutical strategy for mitigating the apparent contradiction between the metaphysical essence of the Cold War and a pragmatic call for more money and resources, and between the benevolent transcendental essence and pacific intent of the United States and its aggressive, militaristic, and often stealthy geopolitical actions. Accordingly, Eisenhower introduced *complexity* into his perspective, a notion in sharp tension with the unequivocal bipolarity of so much of his Cold War rhetoric. He stated, "We must take into account the complex entity that is the United State of America; what endangers it; what can improve it." This reckoning, he argued, began with the economy, for "The visible structure (of the United Sates) is our American economy itself." Complexity thus addressed economic questions, but in what sense was the economy complex, given that Eisenhower had argued in the same speech that economic prosperity was but the sign of the transcendental?

Complexity, I suggest, characterized primarily the nature of American *interpretative fidelity* with respect to the Cold War. It was difficult, challenging, and complex, Eisenhower repeatedly stressed, to see the primacy of transcendent principles when the corporeal world appeared so contradictory, tension-filled, and multifarious. His presidential role entailed spiritual reinterpretation, making fidelity more felicitous by disclosing the transcendental sources of corporeality. It was in this vein that Eisenhower linked the economic prosperity of 1956 and 1957 to spiritual fidelity: "At home, the application of these (spiritual) principles to the complex problems of our national life has brought us to an unprecedented peak in our economic prosperity and has exemplified in our way of life the enduring human values of mind and spirit." Thus the tension between Eisenhower's appeal to the fundamental spiritual basis for American domestic and international action and the primacy of material investment and strategy in policy was mitigated. By foregrounding the spiritual Eisenhower was able to establish a perspective on America that justified national action within the corporeal world in spiritual terms: Eisenhower legitimated technological instrumentalism by asserting an essentially romantic hermeneutical imperative.

It was this same kind of approach that Eisenhower took with respect to the problem of American militancy that his symbolic instrumentalism vis-à-vis nuclear deterrence engendered. His argument was that nuclear bombs did not represent the full and true aspirations of the nation, that America's intent was quite distinct from its material actions. His argument, in other words, was that while a motive of state self-preservation was real and compelling, it did not at all exhaust America's purposes in the world. "The theory of defense against aggressive threat must comprehend more than simple self-preservation," Eisenhower once wrote. "The security of spiritual and cultural values, including national and individual freedom, human rights, and the history of our nation and our civilization, are included."[142] What Eisenhower proffered in this way was quite different from both what Kennan and Dulles professed. Eisenhower followed *both* the logic of national self-preservation and that of spiritual national purpose; each was operative, but on different levels. Hence, the primacy of state sovereignty would never be questioned even as Eisenhower spoke of higher national purposes. In stockpiling nuclear weapons, Eisenhower claimed both as justification, but the latter had priority with respect to the problems of legitimacy. America was acting on behalf of spiritual and cultural values, he essentially told the world, not merely on behalf of self-preservation. Accusing America of militancy would thus, from his perspective, entail a misreading of America's purposes. The world needed to recognize the complexity the United States faced in defending the values of the human spirit, and interpret accordingly.

Ironically, this ultimately meant for Eisenhower that something more than a kind of interpretative advance was needed in the Cold War. It meant that a transformation of human subjectivity itself was in order. The "realities" of the world had so far outrun traditional modes of being in the world that only a transformation in those modes of being, Eisenhower claimed, would satisfactorily reconcile subjective attitudes with world conditions. Whereas Kennan suggested that a kind of traditional stoic subjectivity might bring about a return to general geopolitical stability and a proper balance of powers, Eisenhower suggested that an altogether new phase in human subjectivity was needed in order to "catch up," so to speak, with reality. Eisenhower's romanticism was most pronounced in his calls for human transformation; and these calls were strongly tied to his discourse about nuclear weapons.

Eisenhower was not prone to present "political philosophies" as such, but one of his most succinct early public statements of a kind of political philosophy came in an address to an airplane industry group in New York in May 1947. In it, he praised the power of industry, seen in the airplane, to achieve "conquest" over the environment. "Vision and magnificent faith in human capacity have mastered the ancient obstacles of time and space." However, Eisenhower warned early in the speech that "Technological advance has out-distanced . . . the social progress that it induces or, more accurately, it demands." This "lag," he claimed, "is a dangerous condition that can invite disaster." Consequently, he concluded,

"Scientific developments must be matched by fundamental changes in human attitudes."[143] In the postwar years, especially when speaking to religious groups, Eisenhower sometimes used the phrase *moral regeneration* to describe the fundamental change he sought.[144] Much later, in 1954, after it was made public that the United States had tested a usable hydrogen bomb in Operation Castle, Eisenhower used similar language in a radio and television address: "Now, this transfer of power, this increase of power from a mere musket and a little cannon, all the way to the hydrogen bomb in a single lifetime, is indicative of the things that have happened to us. They rather indicate how far the advances of science have outraced our social consciousness, how much more we have developed scientifically than we are capable of handling emotionally and intellectually."[145] Eisenhower thus subtly, but nevertheless directly, suggested that alarm before the hydrogen bomb was rooted in a kind of failure of human consciousness. Human capacities had not yet reached a point of intellectual, emotional, and moral commensurability with technology. He therefore called for a transformation in human consciousness.

Weber notes that "priests may find ways of interpreting failures in such a manner that the responsibility falls, not on the god or themselves, but on the behavior of the god's worshipers."[146] Eisenhower's calls for a transformation in human orientation vis-à-vis the Bomb followed this approach, as the real problem of the Bomb, he publicly claimed, was located within public consciousness. In his 1954 post–Operation Castle address Eisenhower used the image of the family to exemplify a more proper national response: "It meets these problems courageously. It doesn't get panicky. It solves these problems with what I would call courage and faith, but above all by cooperation." Such words were consistent with what Eisenhower by 1954 had been advocating for years. Americans needed to come to see their interdependence and their need for cooperation. Change in human consciousness meant a dramatic realization of and commitment to social, and especially economic, interconnectedness and an ability to see the transcendent spiritual significance of empirical objects and events in the world.

Human transformation is very near the heart of the romantic American sublime. Romantics addressed the gap between American hope and practice by calling for transformations in human subjectivity commensurate with those in human technologies. Indeed, this call became part and parcel of a broader modern ideology of democracy. As Patrick Deneen notes, democratic citizens often underperform with respect to their ideals. They are, as Eisenhower himself noted on more than one occasion, too often self-centered, shortsighted, or less than vigilant about their responsibilities. Thus, Deneen argues that a "democratic faith" with Rousseauian roots rests on

> the possibility of *democratic transformation*. In particular, by advancing a conception of human beings as both infinitely malleable and ameliorable, along with an accompanying belief in the compatibility or malleability of nature and the universe to such perfectionist inclinations, the impulse to 'perfectibility' [subtly embedded within modern notions of democracy] becomes an integral component of democratic faith.[147]

Recalling Eisenhower's address at the Metropolitan Museum of Art, the aesthetic of the sublime has been crucial to the sustenance of this nationalized democratic perfectionist impulse because the sublime represents, even if only momentarily, a transformation in human consciousness. To confront the sublime object is to be dramatically, if even momentarily, subjectively transformed. The sublime thus holds out the possibility of the transformation of human consciousness.

In his first inaugural, Eisenhower used remarkably perfectionist language to describe his dreams and aspirations. After declaring that "whatever America hopes to bring to pass in the world must first come to pass in the heart of America," he concluded, "The peace we seek, then, is nothing less than the practice and fulfillment of our whole faith among ourselves and in our dealings with others. This signifies more than the stilling of guns, casing the sorrow of war. More than escape from death, it is a way of life. More than a haven for the weary, it is a hope for the brave." In the Cold War cultural climate, such perfectionist language was readily understood by American politicians and press publications as representing America's *motives* in the conflict with the Soviets. Lyndon Johnson called Eisenhower's first inaugural speech "a dignified statement of the dreams and aspirations that motivate millions of people."[148] *Newsweek* described the address as a "moving statement of the nation's destiny as leader of the free world."[149] The *New York Herald Tribune* celebrated it as a speech "shot through with gleams of idealism—the kind of idealism that has characterized America in its greatest undertakings."[150] The *Dallas Morning News* declared, "Dwight Eisenhower sent his voice across two oceans Tuesday to bring reassurance to those sorely afflicted and afraid. He ended all fear that the new President will fail to appreciate this nation's position in the hopes of free men."[151] And Republican senator Alexander Wiley was quoted in the *St. Louis Post-Dispatch* as saying, "There is not a line it that all Americans can not heartily indorse [sic]."[152] These were indeed polite political celebrations, masking a world of political competition and dissent. However, that Eisenhower's transcendental language vis-à-vis America's purposes in the world was so readily celebrated and repeated by the press and politicians suggest that the romantic spirit found a home in American political culture in 1953.

Conclusion

Dulles's "massive retaliation" caused great public consternation. Yet Eisenhower had presented virtually the same scenario in "Atoms for Peace" a month prior to his secretary's speech, comparatively producing next to no consternation and quite a bit of celebration. The difference between the two speeches resided in part in context, focus, and the respective public images of the speakers. But they also were distinguished by a divergence in rhetorical mode, the way of being in the world they put forth, and the worldview from which they communicated. Judging by the response to each, we can surmise that Dulles's militant Protestantism was out of step with American culture in 1954, and indeed trans-American liberal culture, whereas Eisenhower's romantic vision had struck profound cultural and ideological chords.

The *romantic* nature of those chords in America's rise as a deterrent state is not incidental. In this way, I differ from Chernus, who argues that a Christian apocalypticism rooted in a tragic "Augustinian vision of life as a struggle between selfishness and self-restraint" constituted the wellspring of Eisenhower's nuclear state.[153] To be sure, as Chernus argues, "Responsibility, self-discipline, and self-sacrifice remained the core of Eisenhower's religious views," but if these were at the core, we must ask, *on behalf of what?*[154] Here Chernus touches upon a pivotal aspect of Eisenhower's discourse that neither Christian apocalypticism nor "Augustinian" (in fact, Niebuhrian, at best) realism can well account for.[155] "The key to preventing 'the Kremlin's control of the entire earth,'" Chernus writes of Eisenhower, "was the average American's willingness to sacrifice personal ambition for *the good of all.*"[156] Or, as Chernus quotes Eisenhower's 1957 State of the Union address, every American should "truly dedicate himself to *the good of the whole* and not merely to the satisfaction of personal ambition."[157] The pivotal issue is *how is "the good of the whole" constructed?* For Eisenhower, it was as a unity. But in a democratic society (and arguably in any society), such a unified conception of the good is not realizable, let alone perceptible, in actual political practice. Thus there is pressure in Eisenhower's discourse to make the "good of the whole" a matter of spirit, requiring transcendent vision and indeed the transcendence of the given world. But this leaves us with yet another question: *Who has access to such a vision, who mediates it?* Those figures who truly exercise "leadership."[158]

Thus Eisenhower's worldview was rooted in a kind of cultural renewal, an approach endemic to various iterations of English and American romanticism from Coleridge and Ruskin to Whitman to Waldo Frank and Lewis Mumford (all of whom began from a profound sense of the tragic condition of modern life). But unlike most of these figures, cultural renewal was for Eisenhower not a means of confronting the state, but rather a means of "nation/state" making, especially as it provided a potential cultural context through which to legitimize a strong commitment to amoral instrumentalization in geopolitics. As Michael J. Hogan writes of the ideology of national security in the early Cold War, "National security discourse was essentially a discourse in state making, and the challenge . . . was to remake existing institutions or create new ones without wrecking the democratic foundations on which they were erected."[159] For many, and Eisenhower preeminently, the means by which to do this was encapsulated in a disjunction between "spirit" and "matter." Indeed, many believed with Eisenhower, as Will Herberg wrote in the thick of the Cold War, that "only a transcendental faith that finds its absolutes beyond the ideas, institutions, or allegiances of the world could meet the challenge of the demonic idolatry of Communism without falling into idolatry itself."[160] While such sentiments might seem to lead in the direction of an antimaterialism, on the contrary for Eisenhower a "transcendental faith" created room, a distinct political space, for a liberal, aggressive reliance on "matter" by refusing it ultimate moral status. Eisenhower's liberality was in this way related to his amoral instrumentalism, whether with armaments or words. Eisenhower made the "nation-state" the "nation/state."

Thus romanticism. Indeed—if we recall that the young Eisenhower was educated at the turn of the century—romanticism made available to Americans of the nineteenth and twentieth centuries not only a "transcendental faith" but a utopian tradition, a deferred idealism, and a tragic basis from which to act according to an ethic of liberality. With regard to this ethic, romanticism's most powerful aspect for an American leader in the 1950s was the possibility of a quasi synthesis of contesting worldviews. It could draw liberally from various traditions. Thus, Eisenhower could use the language of "self-control" that Kennan relied on, the language of moral purpose (and even apocalypse) to which Dulles appealed, and the language of heroic acts Jackson returned to again and again.[161] But the central question, wherein is found the central differences of Eisenhower's discourse from these worldviews, is, again, on behalf of what? In each of these cases, the answer to the question underwent a transformation within the romantic worldview through "conversion upward" toward the transcendental.

In fact, as Robert Wuthnow has demonstrated, an emphasis on the spirit's supremacy over matter was in harmony with broader trends in the nation's transforming religious sense of self in the 1950s. Whereas dissent, dissension, and sharp divisions (attributes of Dulles's discourse) characterized the religious culture and indeed broader culture of the interwar years, the postwar years inaugurated an era emphasizing unifying values and principles over distinctives, differences, and debate: or, spirit over matter. And, as Wuthnow eloquently writes, this restructuring of American religious culture was profound in its power to set the contours of discourse and debate about the policies and agendas of the nation.

> Public religion, as an element of the political culture, consists in part of public utterances about the nation and in part of unspoken assumptions

that provide the background for these utterances. On the one hand, a measure of how America defines itself is present in the kinds of arguments that intellectuals, public officials, and religious leaders deem appropriate to include in public discourse about the nation. It is in the context of such discourse that policies actually become articulated, defended, and debated. On the other hand, the unspoken assumptions prevailing in the culture broadly (often elicited only by poll takers) constitute the matrix of shared understandings that make possible the meaningful and plausible utterance of particular statements.[162]

The Eisenhower administration did not invent the idea of nuclear deterrence—it inherited it from the Truman administration. Yet, as Hogan writes, the administration did turn "the emphasis on nuclear deterrence into a formal doctrine."[163] Eisenhower thus put the legitimacy of the doctrine of nuclear deterrence in the balance. His success in this regard was to speak in step with the dominant spirit of his time and to articulate an approach to nuclear deterrence that perpetuated it: spirit over matter, values over facts, nation over state. In other words, that, as Medhurst writes, Eisenhower "was a true civil religionist" and that he formalized the doctrine of nuclear deterrence are not mere coincidences.[164]

To Eisenhower's approach to deterrence can also be attributed another kind of success. As Robert Jervis explains, the advent of nuclear weapons into international politics meant that the nuclear state otherwise suffering defeat in a war could decide to destroy its conqueror even as it was itself destroyed—an unprecedented scenario in strategic history. Therefore, in a strict sense, neither the security of the United States nor that the Soviet Union depended on the relative military strength of one over the other, which had been the traditional mode of deterrence. Rather, the security of nuclear states depends on cooperation of one kind or another, a tacit or explicit decision not to destroy the other.[165] In a curious but consistent manner, Eisenhower's approach to nuclear deterrence seems to have taken cognizance of something like this new strategic logic, for his implicit argument in "Atoms for Peace," unlike Dulles's massive retaliation speech, was that America would not *purpose* in a normative sense to destroy the Soviet Union—that if American nuclear bombs landed on Soviet soil it would be a consequence of necessity rather than strategic aims. It would be a fatalistic coup de grâce, not punishment. It would be suicide, not defense.[166]

Yet, these two "successes" in mind, in quite another sense, Dulles's massive retaliation was far more successful, for it positioned America as a morally accountable actor in the world—precisely what Eisenhower's (and indeed America's) romanticism overcame vis-à-vis dualism. In terms of what might be called "the common good," Dulles's evangelical vision kept America's material being within a moral purview, equivocations and all. Whatever one may argue about the irreversible revolutionary change wrought in international politics with the advent of nuclear weaponry, the preservation of an operative concept of justice is sometimes the only adequate counterforce to the use of force. Technological instrumentalism, symbolic or otherwise, is a runaway train, as Vietnam would reveal but a few years after the Eisenhower era. Sometimes only a "just" politics, as O'Donovan argues, can instill the forms of discipline "that constrain force to the service of the common good."[167] That Eisenhower ramped up America's nuclear arsenal to near-infinite dimensions bespeaks not rational calculation in strategy, but captivity to technological instrumentalism in the service of liberal ideology. Indeed, there is profound truth within Gaddis's suggestion that Eisenhower's approach to nuclear deterrence was in a certain sense a nonstrategy. Firmly ensconced within it was a romantic refusal of the world of *mere* necessity but not necessity per se, via a refusal to take full national responsibility for use of nuclear weapons. And concomitant with this refusal was a vigorous effort to use America's nuclear weapons as a symbolic deterrent while absolving "the American way of life" itself from any ill repute associated with the possession of, and intimate historical connection to, these doomsday technologies.

In the Eisenhower administration "conversion upward," far more than a mere stylistic habit, was a political art of transcendence through which a thoroughly technological approach to nuclear deterrence came to make public sense, and thus gain legitimacy. Synecdoche was the form that made sense of a statement such as, "For me to say that the retaliation capabilities of the United States are so great that such an aggressor's land would be laid waste—all this, while fact, is not the true expression of the purpose and the hope of the United States." Eisenhower's approach to nuclear deterrence depended on the transcendental projection of the nation. The presidency became during his tenure a kind of priestly institution through which America's sublime essence was projected as a condition of possibility for a thoroughly technological idea of deterrence in a liberal society. Via an American synecdochal sublime, Eisenhower could sufficiently explain and justify a doomsday technology even as he could indefinitely defer the realization of a millennial counterpart, by claiming that liberal values of freedom, justice, equality, and opportunity were at work in essence, even if not fully in fact. Thus, part and parcel of the establishment of the first and foremost deterrent state in a nuclear world was establishment of the nation/state, and so it has been ever since.

Conclusion

> Do I contradict myself?
> Very well then I contradict myself,
> (I am large, I contain multitudes.)
> —Walt Whitman, "Song of Myself"

I have examined four worldviews discernable within the early Cold War, the classical age of American security strategy. I have argued that stoicism, evangelicalism, adventurism, and romanticism were articulated in containment, massive retaliation, liberation, and Eisenhower's nuclear deterrence respectively. Contests in the early Cold War over strategy, I have thus argued, entailed as well contests over worldviews. Instrumental rationality intermingled with value rationality to produce strategic outlooks that depended on world-outlooks for their cogency and legitimacy.

Worldviews, to reverse the formula cited in the introduction, are language-views. Thus, worldviews are discerned by looking at the ways in which the world is addressed, constructed, and (re)formed in language. This approach to worldviews is not a form of willy-nilly social constructivism, but rather the product of the fact that language is the bedrock of the human sciences, especially the political sciences. Divorcing the study of human action in the political sphere from the study of language makes no more sense than divorcing the study of fowl from that of feathers. Language is not only the means by which humans act with others in the political world, it is the "body" within which they act. In language, humans move, live, and have their political being.

To reprise, therefore, stoicism represents a worldview and a language-view. Stoicism in political rhetoric represents a general way of talking about the nation and the world of nations. Stoicism sees the nation as a self. It centers on the rational control of irrational forces (especially subjective forces), the inextricable and universal power of "interest," and the tragic dimension of "necessity." When faced with tensions and contradictions, stoicism calls for self-critique, believing that a more thorough mastery of the self is the key to mitigating discordance in the world. Sometimes stoicism develops into a cosmopolitan language, sometimes into a fiercely statist one—both approaches based on a "balance of powers"—but often it seeks some intermediate state, a world order based on strong states that is neither purposefully cosmopolitan nor determinedly statist. Such is the world that George F. Kennan envisioned, and it was this worldview that helped bring both compelling strategic form and suasive public force to his "containment."

Evangelicalism is embedded in a highly moral language that motivates an activist stance toward the world. Evangelicalism sees the nation, and indeed the world, as a moral community. Thus in the political world it seeks to bring about through speech and action, as much as possible, a "new order" that rests on universal moral law. While evangelicalism can slide into "moralism" and "legalism," it can be remarkably pragmatic. Indeed, its pragmatism—its insistence on speaking into and acting upon the world in such a way that its moral vision is extended—can render it surprisingly morally equivocal. This equivocation was dramatically evident in John Foster Dulles's "massive retaliation." In massive retaliation we have a strategic doctrine rooted in a pragmatically oriented moral vision that threatened to destroy that which it aspired to preserve. Evangelicals like Dulles, it seems, would rather live with such moral equivocations than surrender a morally authoritative voice.

Adventurism is nihilistic and opportunistic. It entails a language of national advancement rooted in metaphors of statecraft as stagecraft. In its worldview, the nation is a dramatic actor on the world stage—political actors are indeed *actors*. They perform, and upon the *perception* of their performance, adventurism holds, rests the advancement of the nation. Adventurism thus takes the modern emphasis on the centrality of "world opinion" to a kind of logical extreme. It assumes that the world is ultimately morally void, and that it is artifice, convention, and dramatic action that grant it what substance it has. Adventurism is therefore thoroughly at home in irony. It wryly calls for bold acts that define the nation in the eyes of the world, and, indeed, in the nation's own eyes. "Liberation" as advocated by C. D. Jackson would be just this sort of "staged" bold act. It rested on the presupposition that if America could but transform its image in the world, it could transform the world.

Romanticism, in a sense, represents a worldview built to overcome both moral equivocation and nihilism. Romanticism fosters a dualistic rhetoric that divides "spirit" from "matter," urging that the latter be seen ultimately in terms of the former. Romanticism sees the nation as a great soul. Nevertheless, it would be pragmatic, open to the use of instrumental action in the world. Unlike evangelicalism, however, romanticism's pragmatism cannot ultimately compromise its purity. Romanticism transcends the moral equivocations of mundane action through "conversion upward." Eisenhower's approach to nuclear deterrence was entrenched in this romantic vision. He presented the essence of the nation as ultimately spiritual and benevolent in nature, even as he enforced material actions that made this essence difficult to see for many. His strategy of nuclear deterrence therefore rested on a complex hermeneutic, calling for American and world audiences to see the noble spiritual principles behind troubling material signs.

These worldviews, I suggest, are products neither of conscious discipline, nor of the unconscious. They are embedded in and stem from the various habitual ways in which Americans talk about themselves and the world. Worldviews are thus both contingent and in a certain sense *givens,* just as "history" is both contingent and in a certain sense given. Worldviews are, in fact, linguistically mediated ways of seeing and being in the world given in the *historical* use of language. The ways in which we come to talk about self, society, and world position us in greater or lesser degrees of proximity to relatively coherent ways of seeing and being in the world.

Of course, if worldviews are givens just as history is given, then they are given as objects of contention, debate, dialogue, or even domination. Worldviews are no less problematic than history when it comes to the question of what to do with them. Neither determinate nor radically indeterminate, worldviews share history's epistemological, social, and political volatility. They also share history's paradoxical traits of intransigence and malleability. As motive forces in human action, they will not easily go away; but neither do they resist glib or pernicious manipulation for political and ideological ends. Worldviews are thus *objects* of contestation, *motive forces* behind other forms of political contestation, and, in some sense, a *substance* of all significant political contestation.

The Grand Synthesis of a Grand Strategy

There is one more aspect to these worldviews that is particularly relevant to the United States in the Cold War: *power*. Here I do not mean strictly the raw "power politics" or *Machtpolitik* of interstate relations. I mean as well its "soft" counterparts, which gained preeminence in U.S. foreign policy in the twentieth century and were centered on what Frank Ninkovich calls "symbolic interventionism."[1] Especially in the Cold War, Ninkovich suggests, power became a "language" as much as, if not more than, a matter of material force.[2] Indeed, in the ideologically charged Cold War American power became as much about American identity, with all the indeterminacies of the latter, as about the particularities of gross domestic product, military arsenals, and diplomatic deal-making. And it is here I would suggest that a worldview approach to America's grand strategies has special purchase, for worldviews are not just *out*looks, they entail, as I have argued, self-images, or identities. In this way, a worldview is near to what the philosopher Charles Taylor has called a "social imaginary." By "social imaginary," Taylor writes,

> I mean something much broader and deeper than the intellectual schemes people may entertain when they think about social reality in a disengaged mode. I am thinking, rather, of the ways people imagine their social existence, how they fit together with others, how things go on between them and their fellows, the expectations that are normally met, and the deeper normative notions and images that underlie these expectations.[3]

For Taylor, one site for the formation of modern social imaginaries has been "inventing the people," particularly in the form of modern nation-states.[4] And integral to such inventions, I would suggest, is the question of limits, for limits are integral to the constitution of national identity. Even when they are denied, they function constitutionally in their deniability. To argue that an entity has no limits is to make a kind of definitional argument—it is to say X is *limitless*.

The worldviews I have engaged here each have a statement to make about the limits of America, beginning with stoicism's emphasis on "natural" limits (incorporating limits as broad as geographic features, cultural realities, or economic resources). America has limits, stoics say. Honor these limits, and let no moral code, legal framework, or acquisitive desire keep you from doing otherwise. Evangelicalism responds with a chorus that declares the presence of *higher* limits, above and beyond worldly natural ones. Evangelicalism thus *relativises* natural limits by subordinating them, in a moral hierarchy, to a higher law. Nevertheless, both stoicism and evangelicalism represent ethics and rhetorics of living within limits. Their dispute, profound though it is, is not about the normative, guiding force of limits, but about the ultimacy or relativity of natural limits for the life of nations.

Not so with adventurists and romantics. Adventurism denies limits, in the way suggested above. It thus envisions a nation that is limitless in its possibilities, and insatiable in its appetite for negation: it negates limits, whether natural, moral, or legal, by spectacularly pushing through them. Adventurism is thus aggressive. Romanticism is subtler. It, like evangelicalism, transcends limits by relativizing them, but it relativizes not by positing a higher limit, but by—like adventurism—claiming that the nation is ultimately limitless. Romanticism thus does not offer a strict denial of limits in the way adventurism does—it does not approach boundaries as obstacles to be heroically overcome. It can be content to give limits their due at one moment, or to push through them at another. Its approach to limits is situational because it denies them ultimacy, such that romanticism is not an ethic and rhetoric of living within limits (natural or supernal), but one of the limitless. Whereas the effect of evangelicalism's relativizing of "natural" limits is to insist on a higher order of boundaries for human action, the effect of romanticism's relativizing is to grant "natural" boundaries something like a tactical status, affirmed or pushed through according to the exigencies of the moment.

In this way, I want to argue in conclusion that romanticism is not merely one contesting American worldview among others, but a prevailing one. Indeed, given the long history of conscious thought in the Euro-American cultures about limits vis-à-vis state relations, romanticism seems absurd in its assumption of supernal limitlessness—*except* that romanticism provides a unique flexibility and a quasi-synthetic capacity particularly well suited to an age of American power that accentuates the "soft" symbolic reach of the nation among other nations. Ninkovich has argued that Woodrow Wilson stands at the provenance of this new form of American power, because Wilson—as I addressed in my discussion of Dulles in chapter 2—realized that the material bases of *Machtpolitik* could destroy civilization as easily as save it, and thus "American policymakers cast off their old historicist baggage and sought to take history in hand," especially by "pushing policy in a symbolic direction."[5] And yet Wilson in important respects failed, especially in his call for a League of Nations, and this in part because of his willingness (much like his successor, Dulles) to cast off America's "historicist baggage." In the Cold War of Eisenhower we see the reclamation of the baggage, but cunningly so. An inexorable historical process was summoned as a means of *justifying* taking history in hand. No longer is one caught between Providence and human purposefulness, or the inevitable progress of civilization and the need to manage modernity; rather, the former are reclaimed on behalf of the latter, and in a way that incorporates and accounts for the deeper norms and images of the contesting worldviews of stoicism, evangelicalism, and adventurism. For the power of Eisenhower, indeed his symbolic power, resided largely in his capacity to create at once spaces for the language and limited policies of "balance of powers," "moral mission," and "enterprise," while granting none of them preeminence.

This will to synthesis was seen from the very beginning of his presidential strategic deliberations with the creation of Project Solarium. As I discussed in the introduction, as a policy exercise Solarium deferred judgment, such that it would seem to represent the height of strategic deliberation, but did so in a way that necessarily reduced fundamental strategic differences to contesting tactical principles. The exercise thus structurally embraced contradictions by ultimately diminishing their substance, a process quite different from hearing all sides of an argument in order to judge the best of the available options. Thus whereas, for example, Truman and Acheson had presided over the tensions between Kennan and Paul Nitze in a way that resulted largely in the institutional and ideational displacement the former with the latter (with Nitze pursuing a much stronger strategy of militarization), Eisenhower worked toward "consensus" through synthesis. The significant and substantive differences among the three task forces were largely elided, rendered a kind of strategic potpourri from which to pick and choose.

For Eisenhower this was no egoistic project. Indeed, as I have discussed, Eisenhower constructed a model of leadership in contrast to the cult of personality.[6] Medhurst calls it a "group-centered view of leadership," writing, "Under this view, the leader is not set apart from the group but is an integral part of it."[7] Thus Eisenhower wrote his son, "The idea is to get people to working together, not only because you tell them to do so and enforce your orders but because they instinctively want to do it for you."[8] Consequently, Eisenhower sought group harmony centered on what he called "complete solidarity of faith in ideas and ideals."[9] The parts were aligned with the whole through an "instinctive" consensus, an extraordinarily powerful approach with regard to the tactical embrace of contradictions in a way that maintained an overarching "unity" in the midst of significant differences, and which had the not unimportant additional effect of maintaining the power and prestige of the leader, if only as a priestlike mediator.

This is an aspect of the texture of the so-called Cold War consensus that has largely been neglected. That consensus has been described in a number of different ways, but virtually all accounts hinge on some form of "us versus them" thinking. Thus Ira Chernus presents the consensus as Manichean in character: "The U.S. road would lead to peace, justice, freedom, prosperity, and hope, while the Soviet road could lead only to war, injustice, slavery, poverty, and fear."[10] Indeed, Lynn Hinds and Theodore Windt present "cold war" itself as the product of such a consensus, transforming as it did "mundane complexities of the existential world into a transcendental political reality in which ideological angels do moral and moral combat with ideological devils."[11] But as Hinds and Windt suggest, such an unequivocal dichotomy depends on a transcendental transformation—essential to the power of the Manichean outlook is a popularized Gnosticism, where those aligned with the "good" are placed unequivocally. The only means by which to achieve such univocality amidst the complexities of the mundane world is through a turn—a conversion upward—to principles, ideals, and values that have an indeterminate yet vital relationship to actually existing members of the "good." Intent, essence, and aspiration displace manifest actions as the locus for making value judgments about the political world. More than a form of rhetoric versus reality, this process—essentially an interpretative process—was the means by which the realities of the Cold War in the United States were constructed and perpetuated.

In the language of romanticism, the means for such a transformation were readily available and indeed firmly entrenched in American culture well before the onset of the Cold War. Eisenhower reasserted and adapted the romantic worldview to a nuclear world. In doing so, he participated in a long-established cultural language, but his was a particularly consequential participation, and not only because he sanctioned a nuclearized America but also because he rendered the Cold War as a romance. Indeed, from Eisenhower until Reagan, the romantic worldview was normative: all other worldviews were either distinguished from or integrated into it, and the relative "success" of Cold War elites with respect to public suasion depended in part on their ability or inability to successfully negotiate with the romantic hegemon. Thus, the adventurism of the 1960s—from the space race, to Vietnam, to Nixon's détente with the Soviets and breaking into China—was celebrated or disparaged largely in accordance with the capacity of leaders to incorporate their adventures into a narrative of American romance.[12] Similarly, Carter's stress on overcoming the tit-for-tat logic of the Cold War, his focus on deescalating American militarization, and his emphasis on human rights abroad, though initially popular, came to sound moralistic and unrealistic to a public, however weary of misadventures, that had been accustomed to the relentless Cold War dualism of aggressive instrumental action in the name of the good intentions of historical destiny.[13] With respect to American political culture, that Reagan effectively "ended" the Cold War (whether as a product of stratagem or accident, or both) meant, quite simply, that the romance was real, that what Reagan had declared in the wake of the *Challenger* disaster must be all the more true lesson of America's Cold War victory: "The future doesn't belong to the fainthearted; it belongs to the brave."[14] Such is the story of romance.

"Character Types" in the Analysis of American Foreign Policy

Romanticism, of course, is rarely indexed in books on American foreign policy discourse. Thus I suggest that the terms that have had currency— terms like *idealism, realism, security, interest*—need supplementing. While there may be two great forces at work in American foreign policy, idealism and realism, there are at least four elements that constitute something like the rhetorical roots of national being. These roots—the worldviews I have explored—ground American foreign policy discourse, and occasionally, when the debate grows fierce, their substantive differences are evident, differences that are arguably thicker and deeper than the countervailing forces of idealism and realism.

In this respect, two gatherings of strategic thinkers in the 1950s that I have discussed are outliers for my introduction of a worldview approach toward American foreign policy discourse. The first is Project Solarium, which in 1953 raised the disquieting prospect that visions of America are sufficiently pliable as to become mere putty in the hands of strategists and power elite. Solarium produced not only three considerably divergent strategic visions but also three conflicting visions of America among the world of nations. Is "America," I asked in the introduction, so malleable as to be made in any image that suits the strategic framework of those in power? The second gathering, the 1957 conference at Dedham, Massachusetts, on "the American style" resolutely said *no*. That conference explored America's "historically determined national style," arguing it was integral in "determining the shape of our foreign relations" and thus a significant difficulty for policymakers and strategists.[15] Yet one may have asked the participants at Dedham, what of Project Solarium and of the disparate ways America could be plausibly envisioned? And if a national style determines the shape of American foreign relations, then why address it as a subject to be instrumentally exploited, as the participants at the Dedham conference did? A critical problem thus emerges from the juxtaposition of Solarium and Dedham: to what degree is "America" an ad hoc invention and to what degree is it "historically determined"? How pliable or recalcitrant is "the national style"?

I have suggested here a middle ground between strong indeterminacy and determinacy, and thus have offered an additional terminology with regard to the problem, long-standing now, of addressing and analyzing the attitudes, outlooks, and styles of American foreign policy.[16] Both the approach suggested by Solarium and that suggested by Dedham suffered from what might be envisioned as distortions of the notion of history as "drama." In its strong form, ad hoc instrumentalism (represented here by Solarium) presumes that the plots of history are written ex nihilo by powerful actors, whereas historical determinism (represented here by Dedham) presumes that history is a script to which actors must submit or vainly resist. Both suffer from similar problems: the former minimizes the power plot has in shaping character, whereas the latter minimizes the power characters have in shaping plot. In positing a worldview approach, I suggest a terminology that approaches the analysis of American foreign policy discourse according to something like "character types."

Indeed, "drama" is the operative metaphor in Reinhold Niebuhr influential 1952 *The Irony of American History*, which, along with Kennan's *American Diplomacy*, helped firmly entrench the historical typology of realism versus idealism in the classical period of American security strategy—and both of which can be read as positing a weak form of historical determinism. *The Irony of American History* entailed an extensive reprimand of American idealism. "Nations," Niebuhr wrote, "as individuals, may be assailed by contradictory temptations," either as they disavow any of "the responsibilities of their power" or as they "refuse to recognize the limits of their possibilities and seek greater power than is given to mortals."[17] It was the latter temptation, Niebuhr argued, to which America had too widely succumbed. "That idealism," he wrote, "is too oblivious of the ironic perils to which human virtue, wisdom and power are subject. It is too certain that there is a straight path toward the goal of human happiness; too confident of the wisdom and idealism which prompt men and nations toward that goal; and too blind to the curious compounds of good and evil in which the actions of the best men and nations abound."[18] Niebuhr argued for a more chastened approach to American foreign policy, which blended power and responsibility, but which refused illusions of grandeur. "It is easy to forget," he warned, "that even the most powerful nation or alliance of nations is merely one of many forces in the historical drama; and that the conflict of many wills and purposes, which constitute that drama, give [sic] it a bizarre pattern in which it is difficult to discern a real meaning."[19]

Niebuhr's reproach is felt whenever the dilemma of American foreign policy is seen as one of maintaining the sober use of power in a dangerous world and of finding a middle way between realism and idealism. Niebuhr was possessed by a confidence in power of reality, understood in terms of the "tortuous historical process," to chasten us toward this middle way.[20] Historical reality, he held, was recalcitrant, as any "practical statesman" knew "intuitively."[21] The "tortuous historical process" would prevail, no matter what the idealistic aspirations of a people. The question therefore for America was would it conform to historical reality willingly or disastrously? Would the nation accommodate itself to historical process or deceive itself into catastrophe through a pretentious idealism?

To be sure, to refer to history as "drama" is more often than not to stress plot, a series (typically a sequence) of events having some identifiable form. Nevertheless, drama need not be plot driven. It can also be character driven. Indeed, the dramatic nature of a character-driven drama inheres in the logic of the character and his or her life story rather than in a sequence of represented events. While most dramas depend for their dramatic effect on some combination of plot elements and character explication and/or development, one element will be stressed over the other. Plot-driven dramas, because they depend for their effects on the intensity of the pattern of a series of events, tend to rely on stylized characters, often antithetical types: a hero versus villain, lover and potentially beloved, as well as some twist or turn in the plot that reorients the relationship between the two central types. Such starkly contrasting characters serve to intensify the plot as agon and/or erotic play. Character-driven dramas, on the other hand, tend to rely for their dramatic effect on the complexity of the character or characters—subtleties of thought, action, feeling, and speech—and on the story of the character, which always exceeds the events represented in the drama.

Historical typologies like those of Niebuhr's are strongly plot-driven, rooted in a sense of the inextricability of historical progress. They may be quite fatalistic, calling for resignation, but more often they tend to be tied to a progressive social vision, presenting history as a field of social action from which societies should learn and aspire to do better.[22] On the other hand, many biographical and more focused historical accounts of American foreign policy represent character-based dramas. These accounts are more or less tied to a notion of statecraft that sees individual actors and actions as constituting the pivotal center of political progress or regress.

As a supplement to both approaches, one can posit a character-based approach that is not premised on the unique virtue of the individual political actor, but on types. In Greek antiquity, dramatic art was conceived by Aristotle as plot driven; simultaneously, political life was seen as resting primarily on the political constitutions and character of a people. Along with the rise of modernity, however, plot took an exaggerated place. As Hayden White has discussed at length, "history" by the nineteenth century "was considered to be a specific mode of existence," and historians relied on "emplotment" to explain historical data.[23] Implicit in this historical consciousness was a "synchronic structure"—history was viewed as a "story," "a *completed* diachronic process."[24] If it is the case that plot-driven dramas tend to rely on stylized antithetical character types, and if the history of a people, nation, or civilization is strongly emplotted, it follows that that history will often be conceived in a way that relies on simple, contrasting types. Politics and progress will be conceived as a tension, conflict, or "war" between dramatically different "characters," one sometimes representing "good" and the other "evil." If the drama is complicated and conceived ironically, as Niebuhr did in *The Irony of American History*, then it may be that evil characters turn out to be at least partly good, and noble characters indirectly villainous. But the plot will nevertheless still depend on a basic contrast between two different types. History will therefore be seen in an evolutionary (progress through agon), dialectical (progress through conflict and reconciliation), or Manichean manner (progress through good defeating evil). The implicit typology of such views will either be dualistic or tripartite. History as process (and/or progress) will cultivate this relatively stark typology. Historical knowledge and historical consciousness will hinge on a contrasting set of archetypes.

Niebuhr implicitly recognized that the stronger the emplotment of history, the more the plot of history relies on strong archetypes. Writing of poetic versus philosophical or scientific knowledges, he argued,

> The unique and irreplaceable individual . . . with his private history and his own peculiar mixture of hopes and fears, may be delineated by the poet. The artist-novelist may show that his personality is not only unique but subject to infinite variation in his various encounters with other individuals; but all this has no place in a strictly scientific account of human affairs. In such accounts the individual is an embarrassment.[25]

Indeed, even as Niebuhr extolled "the mystery of the individual's freedom," he put forth an essentially "scientific" account of American history, relying on notions of contradiction, conflict, contrast, opposition, or antithesis, which are resolved only imperfectly through instrumental means of control.[26] *The Irony of American History* foregrounded a basic conflict in American history between American idealism and "innocence" and a more "realist" strain, advocating "Christian realism" as a kind of middle way.

In a certain respect, Max Weber's work has played a crucial role in the "scientific" account of history and therefore in the cultivation of stark antithetical typologies and the plot-driven view of history. And yet, in a more fundamental manner, his work (set as it was partly against Marx) sought to undermine a plot-driven historical perspective in favor of a character-driven one. Weber's work suggests the form an *ethical typology* might take: rejecting social Darwinism, Marxism, and other plot-driven approaches to social history, he focused on character types possessed by a certain view of the world and corresponding ethical qualities that produced the "spirit" of social phenomena. This character-based approach, which imagined the history of societies as contingent and tied to specific but still generalizable social phenomena, presumed the polyvocity rather than univocity of "society," even if one spirit rose to the fore with respect to a specific sociological phenomenon. In this way Weber's work echoed Aristotle, who in his *Politics, Nicomachean Ethics,* and *Rhetoric* suggested that something like a communal ethic would be the driving force of a polis. Habits, customs, ways of being constitute the structure of the polis, and as Aristotle's *Rhetoric* makes tediously clear, habits, customs, and ways of being vary not only from polis to polis, but to different degrees within a polis, based on such "demographic" aspects as wealth, education, age, occupation, etc. For Aristotle, a collective ethos can reverberate through a polis in speech and action, determining the fate of the polis. Similarly, for Weber, an ethos can reverberate into the spirit of a social practice, becoming institutionalized, proceduralized, even raised to the level of ideology as it is transfigured into a dominant plot.

One of the goals of typological analysis, Weber notes, is to show that "processes of action which seem to an observer to be the same or similar may fit into exceedingly various complexes of motive in the case of the actual actor," something dialectical historical typologies, because they are plot-driven, for the most part fail to do.[27] An ethical typology, in this regard, represents an attempt to sharpen our analytical vision. It entails as well as an implicit renunciation of the idea that history moves dialectically. In this sense, it is "postmodern," as when Jean-François Lyotard writes, "The social bond is linguistic, but is not woven with a single thread. It is a fabric formed by the intersection of at least two (and in reality an indeterminate number) of language games, obeying different rules."[28] Lyotard seems to take this view to an extreme that might undermine all typological approaches as impossible. I would hold that collective meaning is predicated on some degree of determinacy, and that while we need to expand our typologies, if we do so radically we end up not only eradicating the value of typologies, but doing violence to the character of public meaning, which rests on common knowledges, shared abstractions, generalizations, and, as Robert Hariman notes, "the concreteness of anonymous formulations."[29] There is both a kind of scarcity and a kind of clarity about such overarching publicly shared ideas and languages—the terms of nationhood are relatively limited and delimited. Thus, neither pacifists nor masochists have gotten much hearing in foreign policy deliberations in America because neither speaks an ethical language that is tacitly or explicitly recognized as "American." On the contrary, it is generally incumbent upon the American policymaker to present policies that can be recognized as consistent with an established national way of being in the world.

We will achieve further explanatory clarity with regard to American foreign policy discourse if we reengage ethical typologies. I have written at length of four strategies, finding in Kennan's "containment," Dulles's "massive retaliation," Jackson's "liberation," and Eisenhower's "deterrence" cogent distillations of American worldviews. However, my typology of stoicism, evangelicalism, adventurism, and romanticism should ultimately suggest that the different ways Americans have envisioned their nation are less like a debate between two sides, or even among four distinct outlooks, than like Chinese checkers, with multiple players competing, each moving in a different direction, toward different ends, and sometimes forming curious intentional or unintentional alliances. Or to use another analogy, it can be approached as a mathematician might approach a set of numbers, which can be approached both as independent entities standing in relation to other entities, or put within a potentially infinite series of structures of interaction. Analogously, an ethical typology can be seen as a set of "objects"; history can be seen as an infinite realm of potential structures. An ethical typology therefore allows for indeterminacy and continuities, or at least strong affinities.

Arts of War, Arts of Speech

Strategy in the first decade of the Cold War was infused with worldview in the sense of ethos, "character," a way of seeing that is also a way of being. My argument rests on the idea that strategies have what Weber called "motive force," and motive forces are embedded worldviews, and thus language-views.[30] Perhaps counterintuitively, it is *not* one thing to rationalize a strategic approach, and another to motivate others to adopt it. These two strategic tasks—one part of the "art of war" and the other the "art of speech"—overlap. Both represent what Hans Morgenthau, citing Abraham Lincoln, called the "official duty" of political actors.[31] Some repertoire of attitudes, outlooks, assumptions, ideas, and terms is essential to the motive force of strategy, and it would be purely academic to devise a strategy of war (or cold war) that did not already in some way take into account the fact that motive force must be communicable. Therefore (excepting perhaps pure academic strategy) while no particular worldview is inherent to a particular strategy, some worldview or worldviews always inhere in the social practice of strategy.

This is especially true with strategies formed in a society guided by the norms of liberal democracy, republicanism, or other forms of broad-based political support, as in such societies worldviews must not only have a linguistic basis, but broad collective appeal if a political actor is to be successful. Even if we take "grand strategy" as an ideal abstraction, aspired to but never actually realized, it is apparent that integral to even its partial achievement is the summoning of shared motive forces. Grand strategy, to paraphrase Paul Kennedy, depends on the ability of a nation's leaders to conjoin military and nonmilitary resources of a society to maintain and further a nation's long-term best interests.[32] This can be accomplished only if leaders are able to draw upon or engender broad motive forces, capable of orienting and inspiring a people to pursue a particular course of action. Therefore, to write of the worldview of a strategy is to delineate something of its rhetorical force. It is to focus on the relationships among national seeing, national being, and national action, and to consider the ways in which the latter shape the former vis-à-vis strategy as social action.[33]

The human sciences and their antecedents have long established means of critically cataloguing and scrutinizing the ethical alternatives before a nation, even with regard to such a seemingly instrumental matter like strategy. Plato and Aristotle were both concerned with discerning types of individual and collective souls, a concern that was kept alive in the tradition of teaching and theorizing rhetoric. Much later Vico found in the rhetorical tradition the resources for philosophies of history and society, and in Vico's wake German thinkers—from Herder, through Hegel, to Weber—turned their attention to *Geist,* to ways of being in the world that suffuse historical action. More recently, Alasdair MacIntyre has relied on something like the concept of ethos to explore competing understandings of justice and rationality, as have Robert Bellah and his coauthors in their analysis of competing understandings of America's purposes and goals.[34] To be sure, scholars should continue to seek to understand the role of interests, ideologies, processes, crises, and political traditions in studying strategy, but we also need a means by which to account for common aspirational forms. To approach national action in terms of worldview is to discern ways of speaking about the world that pass through particular contexts, interests, ideologies, and politics. It is therefore to place strategy and other forms of national action within history and society without thereby making history or society determinative of them.

Notes

Preface

1. F. M. Barnard, *Herder on Nationality, Humanity, and History* (Montreal: McGill University Press, 2003), 6.
2. Barnard, *Herder*, 7–8.
3. Thus what Wilhelm Dilthey, revising Hegel, referred to as "objective spirit"—the objectification and perdurance of the past in the present in language, custom, and styles of life. See Wilhelm Dilthey, *Dilthey: Selected Works*, vol. 3 in *The Formation of the Historical World in the Human Sciences*, ed. and trans. Rudolf A. Makkreel and Frithjof Rodi (Princeton, NJ: Princeton University Press, 2002), 170–174.
4. The title of this book suggests an equivalence between "spirit" and "worldview," one that I am more or less comfortable with. The further equivalence I draw with "ethics" is one I am also more or less at peace with. These equivalences are rooted in the history of Republican thought, which has long associated spirit with outlook, and outlook with virtue, as in Montesquieu's *De l'esprit des lois* (1748). Much later, Weber's *The Protestant Ethic and the Spirit of Capitalism* drew similar equivalences,

associating the terms *ethic*, *spirit*, and *worldview*. Nevertheless, my use of these equivalences does not mean that I am equally at peace with the early Republican idea that, as Quentin Skinner states in volume 1 of his *Foundations of Modern Political Thought*, "what matters most in good government is not the fabric of the institutions, but rather the spirit and outlook of the men who run them" (New York; Cambridge University Press, 1978, 46). This book, to be sure, hinges on the premise that "spirit and outlook" matter a great deal, but not over and against the importance of institutions and material structures ranging from geography to economy. I offer in this book an analysis of but one vital piece of the larger complex field we call American foreign policy.

5. On "Jacksonians" versus "Wislonians," "Hamiltonians," and "Jeffersonians," see Walter Russell Mead, *Special Providence: American Foreign Policy and How It Changed the World* (New York: Routledge, 2002).

6. For just one example, see Yannis S. Stivachtis, "U.S. Foreign Policy and International Order," in *International Order in a Globalizing World*, ed. Yannis S. Stivachtis (London: Ashgate, 2007), 39–66. I do not mean to suggest that such analyses are entirely unhelpful, but rather only that they have their limits.

7. Charles Sanders Peirce, *The Essential Peirce: Selected Philosophical Writings, 1893–1913* (Bloomington: Indiana University Press, 1998), 224, 232, 106.

8. James Jasinski, "The Status of Theory and Method in Rhetorical Criticism," *Western Journal of Communication* 65 (2001): 256.

9. Charles Douglas Jackson, Walt Rostow, and Max Millikan, "Proposal for a New United States Foreign Economic Policy," July 23, 1954, Charles Douglas Jackson Papers, Dwight D. Eisenhower Presidential Library (hereafter "CDJ Papers"), Box 32, "Beaver—Foreign Economic Policy (2)."

10. The seminal study of the U.S.'s "Open Door" policy is found in William Appleman Williams, *The Tragedy of American Diplomacy* (New York: Delta, 1962).

11. Aristotle, *On Rhetoric*, trans. George Kennedy (New York: Oxford University Press, 1991), 36. Kenneth Burke, *A Rhetoric of Motives* (Berkeley: University of California Press, 1969), xiii.

Introduction

1. Reinhold Niebuhr, *The Irony of American History* (New York: Charles Scribner's Sons, 1952).

2. Quoted in Robert Bowie and Richard Immerman, *Waging Peace: How Eisenhower*

Shaped an Enduring Cold War Strategy (New York: Oxford University Press, 1998), 124. My brief account of the off-the-record meeting is adapted from Bowie and Immerman's book (124–125).

3. Bowie and Immerman, *Waging Peace*, 125.
4. Memo to the National Security Council by James S. Lay, Jr., Executive Secretary, July 22, 1953, Dwight D. Eisenhower Presidential Library, White House Office of the Special Assistant for National Security Affairs NSC Series: Subject Subseries, Box 9, "Project Solarium, Report to the NSC by Task Force 'A' [1953] (1)."
5. "A Report to the National Security Council by Task Force 'A' of Project Solarium on a Course of Action Which the United States Might Presently or in the Future Undertake with Respect to the Soviet Power Bloc—Alternative 'A,'" July 16, 1953, Dwight D. Eisenhower Presidential Library, White House Office of the Special Assistant for National Security Affairs NSC Series: Subject Subseries, Box 9, "Project Solarium, Report to the NSC by Task Force 'A' [1953] (3)." Page citations hereafter are given parenthetically in the text, indicating the pagination within the report.
6. "A Report to the National Security Council by Task Force 'B' of Project Solarium on a Course of Action Which the United States Might Presently or in the Future Undertake with Respect to the Soviet Power Bloc—Alternative 'B,'" July 16, 1953, Dwight D. Eisenhower Presidential Library, White House Office of the Special Assistant for National Security Affairs NSC Series: Subject Subseries, Box 9, "Project Solarium, Report to the NSC by Task Force 'B' [1953] (1)." Page citations hereafter are given parenthetically in the text, indicating the pagination within the report.
7. Citations regarding Task Force C in this paragraph reference two different documents, the official report (referred to in parenthetical citations as "Report") and a summary outline (referred to in parenthetical citations as "summary outline"). For the report see, "A Report to the National Security Council by Task Force 'C' of Project Solarium on a Course of Action Which the United States Might Presently or in the Future Undertake with Respect to the Soviet Power Bloc—Alternative 'C,'" July 16, 1953, Dwight D. Eisenhower Presidential Library, White House Office of the Special Assistant for National Security Affairs NSC Series: Subject Subseries, Box 9, "Project Solarium, Report to the NSC by Task Force 'C' [1953] (1)." For the "summary outline" see "Task Force C" in documents following Lay memo of July 22, 1953, Dwight D. Eisenhower Presidential Library, White House Office of the Special Assistant for National Security Affairs NSC Series: Subject Subseries, Box 9, "Project Solarium, Report to the NSC by Task Force 'A' [1953] (1)."
8. See introductory letter to "A Report to the National Security Council by Task Force

'B' of Project Solarium on a Course of Action Which the United States Might Presently or in the Future Undertake with Respect to the Soviet Power Bloc—Alternative 'B.'"

9. Hans-Georg Gadamer, *Truth and Method*, 2nd ed., trans. revised by Joel Weinsheimer and Donald G. Marshall (New York: Continuum, 1989), 442. Gadamer is here invoking Wilhelm von Humboldt.

10. "Strategy," *The Random House Dictionary of the English Language*, ed. Jess Stein (New York: Random House, 1966), 1404.

11. "Strategy," *Oxford English Dictionary Online*, 2nd ed. (1989) (New York: Oxford University Press, 2009).

12. Martin J. Medhurst, "Eisenhower's Rhetorical Leadership: An Interpretation," in *Eisenhower's War of Words*, ed. Martin J. Medhurst (East Lansing: Michigan State University Press, 1994), 288.

13. Martin J. Medhurst, "Rhetoric and Cold War: A Strategic Approach," in *Cold War Rhetoric: Strategy, Metaphor, and Ideology*, ed. Martin J. Medhurst, Robert L. Ivie, Philip Wander, and Robert L. Scott (New York: Greenwood Press, 1990), 19.

14. Medhurst, "Eisenhower's Rhetorical Leadership," 289.

15. See Max Weber, *Economy and Society*, vol. 1, trans. Ephraim Fischoff et al., ed. Guether Roth and Claus Wittich (Berkeley: University of California Press, 1978), 24–26. Weber also adds to this list "affectual" and "traditional" types of social action, noting that the latter "may shade over into value rationality" or *Wertrational* action (25). For a discussion of this typology of social action in Weber's thought see Raymond Aron, *Main Currents in Sociological Thought*, vol. 2 (New Brunswick, NJ: Transaction Publishers, 1999), 220–221.

16. Francis A. Beer and Robert Hariman, "Realism and Rhetoric in International Relations," in *Post-Realism: The Rhetorical Turn in International Relations*, ed. Francis A. Beer and Robert Hariman (East Lansing: Michigan State University Press, 1996), 24. Especially important contributions to poststructural theories of international relations have been David Campbell, *Writing Security: United States Foreign Policy and the Politics of Identity*, rev. ed. (Minneapolis: University of Minnesota Press, 1998), James Der Derian, *Antidiplomacy: Spies, Terror, Speed, and War* (Malden, MA: Blackwell, 1992), and Michael J. Shapiro, *Language and Political Understanding: The Politics of Discursive Practice* (New Haven: Yale University Press, 1981).

17. Beer and Hariman, "Realism and Rhetoric," 22.

18. Robert L. Ivie, "Cold War Motives and the Rhetorical Metaphor: A Framework of Criticism," in Medhurst et al., *Cold War Rhetoric*, 71, 73.

19. Philip Wander, "The Rhetoric of American Foreign Policy," in Medhurst et al., *Cold War Rhetoric*, 155.
20. Shawn J. Parry-Giles, *The Rhetorical Presidency, Propaganda, and the Cold War, 1945–1955* (Westport, CT: Praeger, 2002), xix–xx.
21. Robert L. Scott, "Cold War and Rhetoric: Conceptually and Critically," in Medhurst et al., *Cold War Rhetoric*, 13–15.
22. See F. M. Barnard, "Accounting for Actions: Causality and Teleology," *History and Theory* 20 (1981): 291–312, especially 307–308.
23. Carl von Clausewitz, *On War*, trans. Michael Howard and Peter Paret (Princeton, NJ: Princeton University Press, 1984), 149.
24. Clausewitz, *On War*, 177, emphasis added.
25. Clausewitz, *on War*, 184.
26. Karl Marx, *The Eighteenth Brumaire of Louis Bonaparte*, trans. Daniel De Leon (Chicago: Charles H. Kerr, 1907), 5.
27. Barnard, "Accounting for Actions," 301.
28. Hannah Arendt, *The Human Condition* (Chicago: University of Chicago Press, 1998), 80, 94.
29. Burke, *A Rhetoric of Motives*, xiii.
30. Karlyn Kohrs Campbell, "Agency: Promiscuous and Protean," *Communication and Critical/Cultural Studies* 2 (2005): 5.
31. In effect, I reverse the polarity of the ideal type method by seeing the general instantiated in the particular. Weber's ideal type was a composite picture, more like a synecdoche; for me it is a kind of metonym, as the general is concentrated in the particular.
32. Weber, *Economy and Society*, 9.
33. In particular, I am indebted to Kenneth Burke's early work, *Permanence and Change: An Anatomy of Purpose*, 3rd ed. (Berkeley: University of California Press, 1984) and *Attitudes toward History*, 3rd ed. (Berkeley: University of California Press, 1984); as well as Hayden White, *Metahistory: The Historical Imagination in Nineteenth-Century Europe* (Baltimore: Johns Hopkins University Press, 1973). But more fundamentally, I am indebted to the works of Vico and Herder.
34. I have carefully chosen *society* over *state* or *nation* or even *civic/civil community* in order to denote a form of human association that is recognizably ordered and organized—sometimes, but not necessarily, through official structures (state), through ideological identification and mediated imaginings (nation), through civic association, or some combination of these.

35. White, *Metahistory*, xi. Burke's essay "Four Master Tropes" can be found in his *A Grammar of Motives* (Berkeley: University of California Press, 1969), 503–517.
36. Claude Lévi-Strauss, *The Savage Mind* (Chicago: University of Chicago Press, 1966); White, *Metahistory*.
37. Thus Irving L. Janis's classic *Victims of Groupthink: A Psychological Study of Foreign Policy Decisions and Fiascos* (Boston: Houghton, Mifflin, 1972).

Chapter 1. The Care of the Self: Kennan, Containment, and Stoicism

1. John Lewis Gaddis, *Strategies of Containment: A Critical Appraisal of American National Security Policy during the Cold War*, rev ed. (New York: Oxford University Press, 2005), viii.
2. Paul Kennedy, "Grand Strategy in War and Peace: Toward a Broader Definition," in *Grand Strategies in War and Peace*, ed. Paul Kennedy (New Haven: Yale University Press, 1991), 2.
3. Kennedy, "Grand Strategy," 5.
4. George F. Kennan ("X"), "The Sources of Soviet Conduct," *Foreign Affairs* 25 (July 1947): 575, 581. Hereafter I cite the page numbers parenthetically.
5. This confusion was almost immediate upon the publication of X. In the fall of 1947 Walter Lippmann penned a set of columns criticizing containment as it was articulated in X. His columns were thereafter published as a book, *The Cold War: A Study in U.S. Foreign Policy* (New York: Harper, 1947).
6. George F. Kennan, *Memoirs 1925–1950* (New York: Pantheon, 1967).
7. Charles Gati, "What Containment Meant," *Foreign Policy* 7 (Summer 1972): 23–24, 36.
8. C. Ben Wright, "Mr. 'X' and Containment," *Slavic Review* 35 (March 1976): 8–9, 16.
9. Frank Costigliola, "'Unceasing Pressure for Penetration': Gender, Pathology, and Emotion in George Kennan's Formation of the Cold War," *Journal of American History* 83 (March 1997): 1311.
10. Costigliola, "Unceasing Pressure," 1328.
11. Robert L. Ivie, "Realism Masking Fear: George F. Kennan's Political Rhetoric," in Beer and Hariman, *Post-Realism*, 56.
12. Ivie, "Realism Masking Fear," 71.
13. Richard Tuck, *Philosophy and Government, 1572–1651* (New York: Cambridge University Press, 1993). Tuck is picking up where Quentin Skinner left off. Skinner has

argued that stoic sources provided much of the political vocabulary of the Renaissance, sometimes complementing, sometimes challenging Platonic and Aristotelian normative languages. See his *Foundations of Modern Political Thought*, vol. 1. See also the foundational work of Gerhard Oestreich, *Neostoicism and the Early Modern State* (New York: Cambridge University Press, 2008).

14. American republicanism, which became an object of vibrant scholarly interest only in the 1970s and 1980s, has been exceedingly difficult for scholars to consistently conceptualize. Its interpretations have so varied, its histories so proliferated, and its importance been so widely debated, that a precise conception of republicanism has been elusive. (For a somewhat dated but nevertheless very insightful and helpful review of this literature see Daniel T. Rodgers, "Republicanism: The Career of a Concept," *Journal of American History* 79 [June 1992]: 11–38.) Therefore, in saying anything general about republicanism one must rely on rather broad notions like civic virtue; political participation; the dangers of vice, corruption, and conspiracy; the virtues of mixed constitution; and the importance of the rule of law. As my discussion of stoicism and neostoicism will reveal, there are overlaps between stoicism and republicanism. However, I would posit this basic difference: whereas republicanism in its American forms operates on a plane of the "ideal"—a republican order is the *best* of all possible orders—stoicism operates on the plane of the "real"—it is concerned with orders and attitudes *necessary* to self-preservation. I do not mean to make this distinction in terms of political idealism versus political realism, but rather mean to suggest that what motivates republican versus stoic discourse is "what is best" versus "what is necessary or feasible," respectively. This is not at all to say that stoicism does not represent an ideal; rather, the argumentative ground for this ideal tends to be distinct from that beneath republicanism.

15. George Washington, "Final Manuscript of the Farewell Address," September 19, 1796, in Felix Gilbert, *To the Farewell Address: Ideas of Early American Foreign Policy* (Princeton, NJ: Princeton University Press, 1961), 144–145.

16. I am indebted to John Durham Peters for helping me initially to see the influences of stoicism in modern social and political thought. See his *Courting the Abyss: Free Speech and the Liberal Tradition* (Chicago: University of Chicago Press, 2005).

17. Kennan, "Sources of Soviet Conduct," 582.

18. The Chargé in the Soviet Union (Kennan) to the Secretary of State, February 22, 1946, *Foreign Relations of the United States*, 1946, VI, 709. From here on I will refer to *Foreign Relations of the United States* as FRUS. Hereafter I cite the page numbers of LT parenthetically.

19. Wilson D. Miscamble, *George F. Kennan and the Making of American Foreign Policy, 1947–1950* (Princeton, NJ: Princeton University Press, 1992), 282.
20. Kennan, "Sources of Soviet Conduct," 575; "Basic Factors in American Foreign Policy," Lecture at Dartmouth College, February 14, 1949, George F. Kennan Papers, Princeton University, Box 17.
21. Kennan, "Basic Factors."
22. George F. Kennan, "Containment Then and Now," *Foreign Affairs* 65 (Spring 1987): 889.
23. John Lukacs, *George Kennan: A Study of Character* (New Haven: Yale University Press, 2007), 131.
24. As I address presently, Ivie in "Realism Masking Fear" claims Kennan's "quest for civility" compounds "the problem by insinuating a turn toward authoritarianism" (64). Kenneth W. Thompson writes, "Kennan is a romantic as well as a realist" (see his foreword to Richard L. Russell, *George F. Kennan's Strategic Thought* [Westport, CT: Praeger, 1999], x); John Lamberton Harper calls Kennan a "romantic egoist" in his *American Visions of Europe: Franklin D. Roosevelt, George F. Kennan, and Dean G. Acheson* (New York: Cambridge University Press, 1994), 142; and Anders Stephanson, in an excellent book on Kennan, describes him as an organic conservative within the romantic tradition. I have some disagreements with Stephanson, taken up later in this chapter. However, as I discuss in chapter 3, romanticism shares a family resemblance to stoicism. My disagreement with Stephanson is therefore not a sharp one. See his *Kennan and the Art of Foreign Policy* (Cambridge: Harvard University Press, 1989), chapter 8.
25. Plato, *Gorgias*, The Loeb Classical Library, vol. 3, ed. Jeffery Henderson, trans. W. R. M. Lamb (Cambridge: Harvard University Press, 2001), 482b.
26. Plato, *Gorgias*, 458a.
27. Plato, *Republic*, in *The Dialogues of Plato: Republic, Timaeus, and Critias*, trans. Benjamin Jowett (London: Macmillan, 1892), Book VII, 220–221.
28. Karl Popper, *The Poverty of Historicism* (New York: Routledge, 2002), 66–69.
29. See A. A. Long, "The Socratic Imprint on Epictetus' Philosophy," in *Stoicism: Traditions and Transformations*, ed. Steven K. Strange and Jack Zupko (New York: Cambridge University Press, 2004), 10–29.
30. Epictetus, *Discourses*, 2.5.6–10, in *Hellenistic Philosophy*, 2nd ed., trans. Brad Inwood and L. P. Gerson (Indianapolis: Hackett, 1997), 233.
31. Martha C. Nussbaum, *The Therapy of Desire: Theory and Practice in Hellenistic Ethics* (Princeton, NJ: Princeton University Press, 1994), 5.

32. Margaret R. Garver, *Stoicism and Emotion* (Chicago: University of Chicago Press, 2007), 81–82.
33. Nussbaum, *Therapy of Desire*, 353.
34. Steven K. Strange, "The Stoics on the Voluntariness of the Passions," in Strange and Zupko, *Stoicism*, 35.
35. Nussbaum, *Therapy of Desire*, 318.
36. Strange, "Stoics on Voluntariness," 37–38.
37. Nussbaum, *Therapy of Desire*, 3.
38. Nussbaum, *Therapy of Desire*, 316.
39. Firmin DeBrabander, "Psychotherapy and Moral Perfection: Spinoza and the Stoics on the Prospect of Happiness," in Strange and Zupko, *Stoicism*, 198–213.
40. Marcus Aurelius, *Meditations*, trans. A. S. L. Farquharson (New York: Oxford University Press, 1989), 10.
41. Immanuel Kant, *Critique of Judgment*, trans. J. H. Bernard (New York: Hafner Press, 1951), 102. See also Nancy Sherman, *Stoic Warriors: The Ancient Philosophy behind the Military Mind* (New York: Oxford University Press, 2005).
42. Justus Lipsius, *Politica: Six Books of Politics or Political Instruction*, ed. and trans. Jan Waszink (Assen: Koninklijke Van Gorcum, 2004), 301.
43. Thomas Hobbes, *De Homine*, in *Man and Citizen*, ed. Bernard Gert, trans. Charles T. Wood (Indianapolis: Hackett, 1991), 55.
44. Even as deliberative strength, or right reason, is for Hobbes the basis of a stable and effective state, Hobbes argues, again following Lipsius, that the sovereign of the state is not so much a head to a body, as a soul to a body. This is because the soul is seen by Hobbes as the locus of the will, and the will for Hobbes is the site of "supreme power," conceived by him as ultimately a capacity to *act* (see *De Cive*, in *Man and Citizen*, 188). Yet, this voluntarianism does not undermine the primacy of right reason in Hobbes's thought so much as represent its logical outcome. And here we come to a dilemma of neostoic political thought and its successors: rationality does not guarantee the capacity to act, and a "self" incapable of acting is in danger of losing its status as a self altogether, since action seems to be a constituent aspect of selfhood. Therefore, the will can take primacy over reason; in order to preserve a sense of selfhood, it can become more important to act at all than to act rationally, and thus we are met with the possibility of realism dissolving into adventurism.
45. John of Salisbury, *Policraticus*, ed. and trans. Cary J. Nederman (New York: Cambridge University Press, 1990).

46. Daniel Philpott, *Revolutions in Sovereignty: How Ideas Shaped Modern International Relations* (Princeton, NJ: Princeton University Press, 2001), 77–78, 97.
47. Lipsius, *Politica*, 299.
48. Marcus Aurelius, *Meditations*, 10. See as well Martha Nussbaum, "Kant and Stoic Cosmopolitanism," *Journal of Political Philosophy* 5.1 (1997): 10.
49. 1 Corinthians 12:12, New International Version.
50. Thomas Hobbes, *Leviathan, or the Matter, Forme, and Power of a Commonwealth Ecclesiastical and Civil* (New York: Macmillan, 1962), 19.
51. Hobbes, *Leviathan*, 137.
52. John M. Cooper, "Justus Lipsius and the Revival of Stoicism in Late Sixteenth-Century Europe," in *New Essays on the History of Autonomy*, ed. Natalie Brender and Larry Krasnoff (New York: Cambridge University Press, 2004), 12.
53. George F. Kennan, "In the American Mirror," in *At a Century's Ending* (New York: Norton, 1996), 212.
54. John Locke, *Two Treatises of Government* (New York: Cambridge University Press, 1960), 454.
55. Locke, *Two Treatises of Government*, 456.
56. Tacitus, *The Annals of Imperial Rome*, trans. Alfred John Church and William Jackson Brodribb (New York: Barnes and Noble, 2007), 1.
57. Edward Gibbon, *The Decline and Fall of the Roman Empire*, 3 vols. (New York: Heritage Press, 1946). Hereafter I cite the page numbers parenthetically. Gibbon's influence on Kennan is discussed in Walter L. Hixson, *George F. Kennan: Cold War Iconoclast* (New York: Columbia University Press, 1989), 8–9; and in Stephanson's *Kennan and the Art of Foreign Policy*, chapters 6–8. Lest one too quickly dismiss this neostoic ideal as pretext for opportunistic power politics or the *libido dominandi* (which it certainly can be), I want to stress that the neostoic ideal of the state was formulated in part as a response to the problem of pluralism, or difference. Indeed, in contemporary thought, stoicism has had a strong practical kinship with difference-based ethics, in that it emphasizes the primacy of the care of the self over the (legal) enforcement or constitutional authorization of universal rules. This is why, historically speaking, stoicism has been quite amenable to skeptics, relativists, or just plain old pragmatic pluralists. At the level of ethics, thinkers like Emmanuel Levinas and Michel Foucault, though taking different ethical positions, are both indebted to the stoic ideal. Underlying their thought is a concern with ethical freedom, obligation, and otherness divorced from universal legal code—this was the basic concern, although in a dramatically different context and with quite

dissimilar aims, of the neostoics of the late sixteenth and seventeenth centuries and of George Kennan.

58. James Madison, "Federalist No. 10," in *The Federalist Papers* (Whitefish, MT: Kessinger Publishing, 2004), 41.

59. Alexander Hamilton, "Federalist No. 11," in *The Federalist Papers*, 51.

60. Abraham Lincoln, "Speech of Abraham Lincoln, Springfield, June 16, 1858," in *Lincoln-Douglas Debates of 1858*, ed. Robert Johannsen (New York: Oxford University Press, 2008), 14, 21. Importantly, in his rejoinder to Lincoln's "House Divided" speech, Stephen A. Douglas argued that Lincoln was treating a domestic issue, slavery, as if it were a national security concern: "I assert that it is neither desirable nor possible that there should be uniformity in the local institutions and domestic regulations of the different States of the Union. The framers of our government never contemplated uniformity *in its internal concerns*. . . . [F]or that reason it was provided in the Federal Constitution that the thirteen original States should remain sovereign and supreme within their own limits *in regard to all that was local, and internal, and domestic*, while the Federal Government should have certain specified powers which were *general and national*, and could be exercised only by federal authority." Stephen A. Douglas, "Speech of Stephen A. Douglas, Chicago, July 9, 1858" in *Lincoln-Douglas Debates*, 29. Obviously, the question of slavery was in part one of its status as either a "local" and "internal" matter, or a "general" and "national" one.

61. The (neo)stoic aspect of Lincoln's political thought is evident throughout his speeches and writings, but perhaps most complexly expressed in his Temperance Address of February 22, 1842: "Happy day, when, all appetites controlled, all poisons subdued, all matter subjected, *mind*, all conquering *mind*, shall live and move the monarch of the world. Glorious consummation! Hail fall of Fury! Reign of Reason, all hail!" This nearly ecstatic celebration of Reason captures neatly Lincoln's seemingly paradoxical political outlook, which approached the stoic commitment to law, impassioned reason, and impersonality with almost religious enthusiasm. In fact, as Lincoln makes most evident in the Temperance Speech, this "paradox" was rooted in a belief that while Reason should reign supreme, especially in political matters, humans are motivated—that is *persuaded,* to use Lincoln's term—not by "naked truth itself" but by sympathy, friendship, heart-felt devotion, or "benevolence and charity." For Lincoln, Reason's reign hung on chords of affection and devotion, law on "public sentiment," social order on the subjective state of society's members. The key to the political rule of Reason rested on what he called

"practical philanthropists," who "glow with a generous and brotherly zeal, that mere theorizers are incapable of feeling," rather than on moral zeal and condemnation. See his Temperance Speech in *Lincoln: Speeches and Writings, 1832–1858*, ed. Don E. Fehrenbacher (New York: Library of America, 1989), 81–90.

62. Marcus Aurelius, *Meditations*, 19.
63. Edmund Stillman and William Pfaff, *The Politics of Hysteria: The Sources of Twentieth-Century Conflict* (New York: Harper and Row, 1964), 252.
64. Sigmund Freud, *Civilization and Its Discontents*, trans. James Strachey (New York: W. W. Norton, 1961), 23.
65. Freud, *Civilization and Its Discontents*, 24–25. Hobbes, *Leviathan*, 100.
66. DeBrabander, "Psychotherapy and Moral Perfection," 210.
67. Howard L. Kaye, "Rationalization as Sublimation: On the Cultural Analyses of Weber and Freud," *Theory, Culture, & Society* 9 (1992): 47.
68. Peters, *Courting the Abyss*, 207.
69. Aurelius, *Meditations*, 17.
70. Seneca, *Letters from a Stoic*, trans. Robin Campbell (New York: Penguin, 1969), 87.
71. See Bruce Kuklick, *Blind Oracles: Intellectuals and War from Kennan to Kissinger* (Princeton, NJ: Princeton University Press), 2006.
72. Drafts for a Possible Lecture Course on the Subject of Politics, 1964, Kennan Papers, Box 27.
73. Hixson, *George F. Kennan*, 154.
74. Ivie, "Realism Masking Fear," 55.
75. Kennan to Louis Halle, January 3, 1956, Kennan Papers, Box 31.
76. Kennan to Arthur Schlesinger, October 17, 1967, Kennan Papers, Box 31.
77. Kennan to R. Gordon Wassen, February 4, 1947, Kennan Papers, Box 28.
78. Kennan to Marion Grafin Donhoff, March 15, 1965, Kennan Papers, Box 31.
79. Stephanson, *Kennan*, 230. Stephanson argues that romanticism rests on "a strong feeling that some elementary values of precapitalist society have been lost in the process [of commodity production]. Natural harmony of the whole is a central notion, and the object of the romantic critique is therefore typically the ills of society in toto, not the doings of, say, individual classes. Historically it has no specific political identity. There have been romantics both right and left" (230). I will address romanticism at some length in chapter 4. My view of romanticism is a bit different from Stephanson's, in that it takes into account rhetorical and hermeneutical dimensions as well as its ideational structure.
80. Stephanson, *Kennan*, 224.

81. "Where do we stand?" National War College, December 21, 1949, Kennan Papers, Box 17.
82. Stephanson, *Kennan*, 214. The best Kennan could do with respect to the United States, Stephanson argues, was contrive an "amalgam" as a solution to the nation's ills (214).
83. A clear example of Kennan's commitment to a system of strong states, and corresponding rejection of the romantic concept of nationhood as a basis for that system, is found in NSC 20/1 (August 18, 1948), a document that Kennan produced while leading the Policy Planning Staff. The document expressed sympathy for the plight of Baltic nations (Estonia, Latvia, Lithuania) behind Soviet borders (toward whom the United States had a recognition policy, formally denying the USSR's right to dominion over them), but it ultimately rejected any "peacetime" effort to free these areas from Soviet control, as this would involve "the dignity and the vital interests of the Soviet State as such," and could only be brought about through war. In the event of war, however, the liberation of the Baltic region could be a legitimate U.S. aim, NSC 20/1 argued (178). Yet—and importantly—the document argued that even in war, U.S. aims vis-à-vis liberation of peoples behind the Iron Curtain should be restricted to the Baltic peoples, as they "happen to be the only peoples whose traditional territory and population are now entirely included in the Soviet Union and who have shown themselves capable of coping successfully with the responsibilities of statehood" (184). The Ukrainians, on the other hand, it argued, showed "no signs of being a 'nation' capable of bearing successfully the responsibilities of independence in the face of great Russian opposition." "The Ukraine is not a clearly defined ethnical or geographical concept. . . . The real basis of 'Ukranianism' is the feeling of 'difference' produced by a specific peasant dialect and by minor differences of custom and folklore throughout the country districts. The political agitation on the surface is largely the work of a few romantic intellectuals, who have little concept of the responsibilities of government" (199). Kennan therefore rejected claims to statehood based on "identity" and instead made "responsibility" and/or "ability" the legitimate basis. In this way, NSC 20/1 stated, "It should be added that while, as stated above, we would not deliberately encourage Ukrainian separatism, nevertheless if an independent regime were to come into being on the territory of the Ukraine through no doing of ours, we should not oppose it outright. To do so would be to undertake an undesirable responsibility for internal Russian developments" (200). If, in other words, Ukrainians could somehow stand up to the Kremlin and moreover prove that they had the capacity

to handle the responsibilities of statehood, then the United States should not deny them this right. See NSC 20/1, document 22 in *Containment: Documents on American Policy and Strategy, 1945–1950*, ed. Thomas H. Etzold and John Lewis Gaddis (New York: New York University Press, 1978), 173–203.

84. Kennan to Elim O'Shaughnessy, October 29, 1952, Kennan Papers, Box 29.
85. For a discussion of the metaphorical versus literal uses of the "organic" in political thought, see Barnard, *Herder*, 52–62.
86. "Where do we stand?" National War College, December 21 1949, Kennan Papers, Box 17.
87. Christopher Lasch, *The World of Nations: Reflections on American History, Politics, and Culture* (New York: Vintage, 1972), 219.
88. Gibbon, *Decline and Fall*, vol. 1, 43–44.
89. George F. Kennan, *American Diplomacy, 1900–1950* (New York: New American Library, 1951), 9. Hereafter page numbers of *American Diplomacy* are cited parenthetically.
90. Immanuel Kant, "To Perpetual Peace: A Philosophical Sketch," in *Perpetual Peace and Other Essays* (Indianapolis: Hackett, 1983), 108. Kant's indebtedness to stoicism is explored in Martha Nussbaum, "Kant and Stoic Cosmopolitanism." As I read him, Kant represents an effort to overcome the skepticism of neostoicism vis-à-vis "Enlightenment" while retaining the central metaphors, concepts, and attitudes of both ancient and neostoicisms with respect to political thought.
91. In describing "realism," Kenneth W. Thompson would later argue, "Sometimes, in politics, as in life, enlightened self-interest is man's highest moral attainment." See Thompson, *Ethics, Functionalism, and Power in International Politics: The Crisis in Values* (Baton Rouge: Louisiana State University Press, 1979), 22.
92. Kennan to Arnold Toynbee (London), April 7, 1952, Kennan Papers, Box 29.
93. Kennan to Isaiah Berlin, April 26, 1950, Kennan Papers, Box 29.
94. Kennan to Adlai Stevenson, March 28, 1956, Kennan Papers, Box 31. Kennan wrote the same thing to Chester Bowles on October 16, 1955 (see Box 31 of Kennan Papers).
95. Kennan to George Kateb, December 15, 1967, Kennan Papers, Box 31.
96. Kennan to Isaiah Berlin, April 26, 1950, Kennan Papers, Box 29.
97. Kennan to Cyrus Vollmer, May 14, 1944, Kennan Papers, Box 28.
98. Gaddis, *Strategies of Containment*, 18–19.
99. See chapters 3 and 4 of Lynn Boyd Hinds and Theodore Otto Windt, Jr., *The Cold War as Rhetoric: The Beginnings, 1945–1950* (New York: Praeger, 1991).

100. Kennan, "Sources of Soviet Conduct," 566.
101. Lippmann, *The Cold War*.
102. See E. Wilder Spaulding (Department of State) to Kennan, April 8, 1947, Kennan Papers, Box 28.
103. Kennan to the Secretary of State, April 23, 1945, *FRUS*, 1945, vol. 7, 344.
104. Kennan to Lippmann, April 6, 1948, Kennan Papers, Box 17. This letter, apparently, was never sent to Lippmann, but it may have been shown to him briefly.
105. Robert L. Ivie, "Fire, Flood, and Red Fever: Motivating Metaphors of Global Emergency in the Truman Doctrine Speech," *Presidential Studies Quarterly* 29 (1999): 573.
106. Hinds and Windt, *Cold War as Rhetoric*, 79, 81, 190.
107. It is not hyperbolic to argue that Kennan believed that the Soviets suffered from castration anxiety. See Costigliola, "Unceasing Pressure."
108. Ivie, "Realism Masking Fear," 71.
109. Jacqueline Lagrée, "Constancy and Coherence," in Strange and Zupko, *Stoicism*, 148.
110. See Ivie, "Fire, Flood, and Red Fever."
111. Drafts for a Possible Lecture Course on the Subject of Politics, 1964, Kennan Papers, Box 27.
112. John Lamberton Harper adds to this list of influences Anton Chekhov, describing Kennan's detachment as "Chekhovian" in *American Visions of Europe*, 154–160.
113. C. S. Lewis, preface to *George MacDonald*, ed. C. S. Lewis (New York: Macmillan, 1947), xxvii.
114. Hornell Hart, "Social Science and the Atomic Crisis," *Journal of Social Issues*, Supplement Series, No. 2 (April 1949): 15.
115. Hart, "Social Science," 23.
116. Hart, "Social Science," 24.
117. M. Brewster Smith, preface, *Journal of Social Issues* 10.3 (1954): 1.
118. Irving L. Janis, "Problems of Theory in the Analysis of Stress Behavior," *Journal of Social Issues* 10.3 (1954): 20.
119. Val Peterson, "Panic: The Ultimate Weapon?" *Collier's*, August 21, 1953, 107.
120. Explanatory Notes by Mr. George F. Kennan, March 25, 1948, *FRUS*, 1948, vol. 6, 717.
121. Kennan to Adam Watson, October 30 1967, Kennan Papers, Box 31.
122. In a *Meet the Press* interview, November 5, 1967, Kennan said, "The older I get, the more sympathy I have for the isolationist principles of my forefathers. I don't say

that I am isolationist in their sense, but I understand much better than I did 20 or 30 years ago why a country like ours should exercise a great deal of prudence before it involves itself in complicated affairs far from its own borders." See Kennan Papers, Box 13.
123. Memorandum by the Policy Planning Staff, November 23, 1948, *FRUS*, 1948, vol. 8, 208.
124. Kennan to John A. Lukacs October 31, 1955, Kennan Papers, Box 31.
125. See Wright, "Mr. 'X' and Containment."
126. Kennan to Waldemar A. Nielsen, October 19, 1967, Kennan Papers, Box 31.
127. Hinds and Windt, *Cold War as Rhetoric*, 202; Ivie, "Fire, Flood, and Red Fever."
128. Giambattista Vico, *On the Study Methods of Our Time*, trans. Elio Gianturco (Ithaca, NY: Cornell University Press, 1990), 43.
129. Vico, *On the Study Methods*, 37.
130. Vico, *On the Study Methods*, 43.
131. Vico, *On the Study Methods*, 43.

Chapter 2. Protest and Power: Dulles, Massive Retaliation, and Evangelicalism

1. John Foster Dulles, "Principle Versus Expediency in Foreign Policy," Missouri Bar Association, St. Louis, MO, September 26, 1952, John Foster Dulles Papers, Princeton University, Box 308. Dulles's claim that containment was rooted in a "defeatist, appeasing mood" can be found in "Address by John Foster Dulles before the World Affairs Council of Seattle," September 18, 1952, Dulles Papers, Box 308. From here on I will cite documents in the John Foster Dulles Papers at Princeton University simply as "Dulles Papers."
2. Kennan to James Russell, October 11, 1950, Kennan Papers, Box 29.
3. Kennan, "Drafts for a Possible Lecture Course on the Subject of Politics," 1964, Kennan Papers, Box 27.
4. Kennan's lecture can be found in Box 71 of the Dulles Papers.
5. Dulles to Kennan, October 19, 1952, Dulles Papers, Box 71.
6. For Kennan the debate became personal. "Foster Dulles," Kennan wrote his friend Louis Halle some years after Dulles's death, "in my deep conviction and in that of people much more closely associated with him than I ever was, did not have an ounce of real piety in his system[;] the hypocrisy was pure, as was the ambition. Both were unadulterated by any tinges of genuine Christian charity or obligation."

Kennan to Louis Halle, April 20, 1966, Kennan Papers, Box 31.
7. Dulles, "Evolution of Foreign Policy," Council on Foreign Relations, New York, NY, January 12, 1954, Dulles Papers, Box 322. My reference to America as a "dangerous nation" is indebted to Robert Kagan's *Dangerous Nation* (New York: Alfred A. Knopf, 2006).
8. For Kennan's distinction between a "particularized" and a "universalistic" see Policy Planning Staff Paper "Review of Current Trends U.S. Foreign Policy," February 24, 1948, *FRUS*, 1948, vol. 1, 526–527.
9. Henry George Liddell and Robert Scott, *A Greek-English Lexicon*, revised and augmented by Henry Stuart Jones and Roderick McKenzie (Oxford: Clarendon Press, 1940). Accessed at http://www.perseus.tufts.edu/hopper/text?doc=Perseus%3Atext%3A1999.04.0057%3Aentry%3De%29kklhsi%2Fa .
10. See N. T. Wright, "Gospel and Theology in Galatians," in *Gospel in Paul: Studies on Corinthians, Galatians and Romans for Richard N. Longenecker*, ed. L. Ann Jervis and Peter Richardson (London: Sheffield Academic Press, 1994), 222–239; and N. T. Wright, *What Saint Paul Really Said* (Cincinnati: Forward Movement Publications, 1997), chapter 3.
11. Michael Walzer, *The Revolution of the Saints* (Cambridge: Harvard University Press, 1965), 1.
12. Walzer, *Revolution of the Saints*, 18.
13. Walzer, *Revolution of the Saints*, 221.
14. Walzer, *Revolution of the Saints*, 55.
15. Quentin Skinner, *Reason and Rhetoric in the Philosophy of Hobbes* (New York: Cambridge University Press, 1996), 431–432.
16. On Hobbes's alternative to the sectarian theories of covenant, see Skinner, *Reason and Rhetoric*, 311–315.
17. Skinner, *Reason and Rhetoric*, 435.
18. Mark G. Toulouse, *The Transformation of John Foster Dulles: From Prophet of Realism to Priest of Nationalism* (Macon, GA: Mercer University Press, 1985), 3–26.
19. See Philippe Soulez and Frédérick Worms, *Bergson: Biographie* (Paris: Flammarion, 1997), especially chapter 8.
20. Henri Bergson, *The Two Sources of Morality and Religion*, trans. R. Ashley Audra and Cloudesley Brereton (Garden City, NY: Doubleday, [1935] 1956), 78.
21. Bergson, *Two Sources*, 37–38.
22. Bergson, *Two Sources*, 51.
23. Bergson, *Two Sources*, 56–58.

24. Kennan, Drafts for a Possible Lecture Course on the Subject of Politics, 1964, Kennan Papers, Box 27.
25. William Bradford, *The History of Plymouth Colony* (New York: Walter J. Black, 1948), 99–100.
26. Tuck, *Philosophy and Government*, chapter 6.
27. Toulouse, *Transformation of Dulles*, 52. Toulouse offers a much more thorough account of the impact of the Oxford conference on Dulles than I am able to here.
28. Toulouse, *Transformation of Dulles*, 53.
29. John Foster Dulles, *War, Peace, and Change* (New York: Harper and Brothers, 1939), 9–16, 118. From here on I cite pages from *War, Peace, and Change* parenthetically.
30. See Kennan's 1986 review of Arthur Schlesinger's *The Cycles of American History* in "In the American Mirror"; Dulles, *War, Peace, and Change*, 124, emphasis added.
31. Kennan, "Comments on the General Trend of United States Foreign Policy," August 20, 1948, Kennan Papers, Box 23. See also "Morality and Foreign Policy" in *At a Century's Ending*, 269–272.
32. Karl Mannheim, *Ideology and Utopia*, vol. 1 in the *Collected Works of Karl Mannheim*, trans. Louis Wirth and Edward A. Shils (New York: Routledge, 1997), 173.
33. For theological backdrop to such "covenantal speech," see Christopher Hill, *The Collected Essays of Christopher Hill*, vol. 3, *People and Ideas in 17th Century England* (Amherst: University of Massachusetts Press, 1986), especially chapter 14.
34. See John Witte, *The Reformation of Rights: Law, Religion, and Human Rights in Early Modern Calvinism* (New York: Cambridge University Press, 2008).
35. J. G. A. Pocock, *The Machiavellian Moment: Florentine Political Thought and the Atlantic Republican Tradition* (Princeton, NJ: Princeton University Press, 1975), 513.
36. Sacvan Bercovitch, *The American Jeremiad* (Madison: University of Wisconsin Press, 1978), 179.
37. Bercovitch, *The American Jeremiad*, 179.
38. James Darsey, *The Prophetic Tradition and Radical Rhetoric in America* (New York: New York University Press, 1997), 20.
39. Janet Lyon, *Manifestos: Portents of the Modern* (Ithaca, NY: Cornell University Press, 1999), 13.
40. Lyon, *Manifestos*, 3.
41. John Field, *A View of Popishe Abuses Yet Remaining in the Englishe Church, for the which Godly Ministers have Refused to Subcribe*, (1571), in *Puritan Manifestoes: A*

Study of the Origin of the Puritan Revolt, ed. W. H. Frere and C. E. Douglas (London: SPCK, 1907), 32.
42. Lyon, *Manifestos*, 30.
43. Lyon, *Manifestos*, 32.
44. Lyon, *Manifestos*, 3–4.
45. See Lyon, *Manifestos*, especially 39–44.
46. Dulles was described as a "religious leader" by the host of CBS Radio's "The People's Platform," December 19, 1942, Dulles Papers, Box 290.
47. Dulles, "The Beginning of World Order," San Francisco, April 22, 1945, Dulles Papers, Box 291.
48. Dulles, "Speech [Draft]: San Francisco Conference," March 29, 1945, Dulles Papers, Box 291.
49. Dulles, "Proof of Statement to be submitted at the Biennial Meeting of The Federal Council of Churches of Christ in America at Atlantic City, December 10–13, 1940," Dulles Papers, Box 290.
50. The Commission on a Just and Durable Peace of the Federal Council of the Churches of Christ in America, *Six Pillars of Peace: A Study Guide based on "A Statement of Political Propositions"* (New York: Federal Council of the Churches of Christ in America, 1943), 1.
51. Dulles, draft speech, Dulles Papers, Box 292.
52. Dulles radio interview, "Beyond Victory," produced by the World Wide Broadcasting Foundation, Dulles Papers, Box 291.
53. Dulles, "Christian Mission," November 4, 8, 9, and 10, 1943, Dulles Papers, Box 291.
54. CBS Radio, "The People's Platform," December 19, 1942, Dulles Papers, Box 290.
55. Dulles, "The Dumbarton Oakes Proposal," Biennial Meeting of Federal Council of Churches of Christ in America, November 28, 1944, Dulles Papers, Box 291.
56. Dulles, "Radio Talk," NBC radio, May 20, 1937, Dulles Papers, Box 289.
57. Dulles to Harry S. Truman, November 8, 1945, Dulles Papers, Box 27.
58. Dulles, "Speech: Princeton National Alumni Luncheon," Princeton, NJ, February 22, 1952, Dulles Papers, Box 306.
59. Dulles to Henry Luce, September 29, 1943, Dulles Papers, Box 22.
60. Dulles, "Thoughts on Soviet Foreign Policy and What to Do About It," *Life*, June 10, 1946, 119.
61. Dulles to Walter Lippmann, June 4, 1946, Dulles Papers, Box 29. Dulles and Lippmann corresponded off and on into Dulles's tenure as Eisenhower's secretary

of state. In 1946, however, they seem to have felt a special affinity for each other with respect to foreign policy. In September of that year Dulles wrote Lippmann, "When I read your piece this morning in the Tribune, I was somewhat embarrassed because some of the ideas and phrases which I have used are so close to yours that it may seem that I have been a plagiarist." See Dulles to Lippmann September 5, 1946, Dulles Papers, Box 29.

62. Toulouse, *Transformation of Dulles*, xxiii–xxix.
63. Dulles, "The Power of Moral Force," First Presbyterian Church, Watertown, NY, October 11, 1953, Dulles Papers, Box 319.
64. Pamphlet, "A Christian Message on World Order," from the International Round Table of Christian Leaders, Princeton, New Jersey, Federal Council of the Churches of Christ in America, July 1943, Dulles Papers, Box 283.
65. Dulles relatively conciliatory posture toward the Soviets in 1946 was also reflected in a NBC *University of the Air* broadcast regarding "Problems Facing the United Nations." Dulles explained that it was critical that "tolerance" should be practiced internationally, and argued that fanatical faiths only will lead to violence. He argued that Communism and Christianity could exist side by side, "if we both renounce the use of violent methods to make our faith prevail. It is necessary to make clear to the Soviet Union that the United States does not intend to use violence—for example the atomic bomb—to crush out the Soviet experiment. Also the Soviet Union must give up using force, coercion and purge to make its faith prevail in the world." Dulles did complain, however, "The difficulty arises from the fact the Soviet government does not believe in tolerance." He urged that the same show that the armaments race between the United States and the USSR should end. "Our basic conclusion," he told the radio audience, is "war with Russia can be avoided and it can be avoided without compromise of basic convictions." See Dulles, NBC "University of the Air," November 2, 1946, Dulles Papers, Box 293.
66. Dulles, Statement at press conference at United Nations Headquarters, March 9, 1953, Dulles Papers, Box 311.
67. NSC 162/2, October 30, 1953, NSC Series, Box 6, Dwight D. Eisenhower Library.
68. Gaddis, *Strategies of Containment*, 144.
69. The January 1954 "massive retaliation" speech, according to Dulles, "was cleared with President and principal NSC members." See memo from John Foster Dulles to Allen Dulles, undated, sometime winter 1954, Dulles Papers, Box 80. In fact, Eisenhower himself made edits to the speech before Dulles presented it (Ira Chernus, *Apocalypse Management: Eisenhower and the Discourse of National Insecurity*

[Stanford, CA: Stanford University Press, 2008], 78).

70. This and all the following references to the speech are from John Foster Dulles, "Evolution of Foreign Policy," Council on Foreign Relations, New York, NY, January 12, 1954, Dulles Papers, Box 322.
71. James Reston, "Washington: 'Massive Atomic Retaliation' and the Constitution," *New York Times*, January 17, 1954, E8.
72. Wayne Brockriede, "John Foster Dulles: A New Rhetoric Justifies an Old Policy," in *Rhetoric and Communication*, ed. Jane Blankenship and Hermann G. Stelzner (Urbana: University of Illinois Press, 1976), 190.
73. Dwight D. Eisenhower to Dulles, June 20, 1952, Dulles Papers, Box 60.
74. Quoted in Gaddis, *Strategies of Containment*, 126, emphasis added.
75. Hamilton Fish Armstrong to Dulles, February 5, 1954, Dulles Papers, Box 78.
76. Dulles, "Policy for Security and Peace," *Foreign Affairs* 32.3 (1954): 353–364. "Flexibility" in retaliation was the emphasis of this article, and thus the means-ends strategic logic of Dulles's deterrent approach was clearer in it than it had been in his speech before the Council on Foreign Relations. Nevertheless, the ethical-rhetorical context was strongly consistent with the sort of evangelicalism I describe in this chapter. Dulles, for example, advocated "the creation of power on a community basis" (355), and put at the forefront of the article the notion of the "great American experiment" as "a source of hope and inspiration to men everywhere, and especially to those living under despotism." America could thus "exert a liberating influence everywhere" (353).
77. James Reston, "Washington: 'Massive Retaliation' Is '2X' Now," *New York Times*, January 9, 1955, E8.
78. With regard to Dulles's statement that "The way to deter aggression is for the free community to be willing and able to respond vigorously at places and with means of its own choosing," Dulles no doubt felt that he was not only restating Eisenhower administration doctrine, but rephrasing a well-established assumption vis-à-vis policy of the United States since the early 1950s. Indeed, he had made virtually the same claim in May 1952 in *Life* magazine ("A Policy of Boldness," *Life*, May 19, 1952, 146–160), and the general notion he posited was echoed in more official venues. For example, a draft 1950 NSC statement stated plainly, "The certainty of retaliation of a kind still beyond the capability of an aggressor is today a potent safeguard for the peaceful efforts of democratic peoples," and likewise the so-called Oppenheimer Report, written in the twilight of the Truman administration (January 1953) stated as a matter of fact, "The United States is heavily

committed to a swift and almost unlimited use of atomic retaliation in the event of major Soviet aggression" (for the draft NSC statement, see Papers of Harry S. Truman, PSF: Subject File, 1940–1953, National Security Council, Box 176, Harry S. Truman Presidential Library; for the "Oppenheimer Report" see *FRUS*, 1952–1954, vol. 2, National Security Affairs, 1063). The report of Task Force A in Eisenhower's Project Solarium stated, "In addition to the military threat posed by conventional Soviet armaments there is increasing evidence that the Soviet union [sic] is developing a strong capability in the field of weapons of mass destruction. If this process continues unimpeded, the Soviet leaders will soon have it in their power to inflict massive damage on the cities, industries and facilities of this country and its major allies, although presumably not without suffering retaliation in kind" (White House Office of the Special Assistant for National Security Affairs NSC Series, Subject Subseries, "Project Solarium, Report to the NSC by Task Force 'A' [1953] (1)," Box 9). And the Eisenhower administration's NSC 62/2 (October 1953) claimed that "U.S. capability to retaliate massively" made the likelihood of the USSR inaugurating a general war unlikely, spoke of an "emphasis on the capability of inflicting massive retaliatory damage by offensive striking power" and "the manifest determination of the United States to use its atomic capability and massive retaliatory striking power" if Western Europe was attacked, and envisioned a "stalemate" between the United States and USSR based on the prospect of "major atomic retaliation" if one side attacked the other (NSC 162/2, October 30, 1953, NSC Series, Box 6, Dwight D. Eisenhower Library, 4, 5, 12). Eisenhower himself in "Atoms for Peace" (December 8, 1953), declared, "Should such an atomic attack be launched against the United States, our reactions would be swift and resolute." "The retaliation capabilities of the United States," he went on to say "are so great that such an aggressor's land would be laid waste" (Dwight D. Eisenhower, "Address Before the General Assembly of the United Nations on Peaceful Uses of Atomic Energy, New York City, December 8, 1953," also known as "Atoms for Peace," *Public Papers of the Presidents of the United States* (Washington, DC: United States Government Printing Office, 1953), document 256, 1953; available from John Woolley and Gerhard Peters, *The American Presidency Project* (online), Santa Barbara: University of California (hosted), Gerhard Peters (database), http://www.presidency.ucsb.edu/ws/?pid=9774). And Arthur W. Radford, chairman of the Joint Chiefs of Staff in 1953, told the National Press Club on December 14, 1953, "We must be ready for tremendous, vast retaliatory and counteroffensive blows in the event of a global war"(Dulles Papers, Box 74).

Confusion in the State Department about the significance of massive retaliation for relations with the Soviets was apparent in the winter of 1954. In a February 1954 interaction between Key (assistant secretary of state for UN affairs) and Lodge (U.S. representative at the UN) regarding what to tell the Soviets in diplomatic negotiations regarding what the United States understood by "self-defense," Lodge stated that he wanted to tell the Soviets that the United States would not use atomic weapons other than for purposes of "self-defense." Key, however, expressed reservations about making such a statement: "The difficulty with a statement that we would agree not to use atomic weapons except in 'self-defense' rests in the ambiguity of the term 'self-defense.' If, in the event of another Korea, we choose to retaliate directly against the source of aggression with atomic weapons, would that be 'self-defense?' This is the type of situation we have to envisage in the light of Secretary Dulles' speech of January 12 in which he said: '. . . Local defenses must be reinforced by the further deterrent of massive retaliatory power. A potential aggressor must know that he cannot always prescribe battle conditions that suit him. . . .' '. . . The basic decision was to depend primarily upon a great capacity to retaliate, instantly, by means and at places of our choosing . . .' The Secretary's speech is, of course, based on recent decisions taken in the National Security Council" (*FRUS*, 1952–1954, vol. 2, National Security Affairs, 1359). A Policy Planning Staff study two months later explained the way in which public declarations about nuclear retaliation presented profound problems vis-à-vis disarmament. The study argued that if the United States signed an agreement with the Soviets outlawing the use of nuclear weapons, even while this would not keep either nation from breaking the agreement and using nuclear weapons, it *would* prohibit any declarations about possible uses of nuclear weapons: "Thus, even thought the declaration might impose no inhibition which does not now exist upon strategic planning or military action on our part, it might impose a new inhibition on our diplomatic freedom of action, so far as diplomacy consists of making clear, where appropriate for deterrent purposes, what one is prepared to do in case of trouble" (*FRUS*, 1952–1954, vol. 2, National Security Affairs, 1390). Both the Key-Lodge interaction and the Policy Planning Staff report illustrate the profoundly confusing implications of Dulles's massive retaliation speech even for those within the State Department.

79. Dulles to James Byrnes, October 9, 1946, Dulles Papers, Box 28.
80. Harry S. Truman to Dulles, November 6, 1945, Dulles Papers, Box 27.
81. "Stimson's Memo to Press," August 9, 1945, document 83 in *The Manhattan Project: A Documentary Introduction to the Atomic Age*, ed. Michael B. Stoff, Jonathan F.

Fanton, and R. Hal Williams (New York: McGraw-Hill, 1991), 239.
82. Dulles, "The Atomic Bomb and Moral Law," *Christian News-Letter*, January 9, 1946, Dulles Papers, Box 284.
83. Frank Ninkovich, *Modernity and Power: A History of the Domino Theory in the Twentieth Century* (Chicago: University of Chicago Press, 1994), 318.
84. Dulles, "Morals and Power," National War College, June 16, 1953, Dulles Papers, Box 314.
85. Alexis de Tocqueville, *Democracy in America* (New York: Penguin, 2003), 49.
86. Special assistant to the president C. D. Jackson, in a memo written to Eisenhower on October 2, 1953, summarized Dulles's belief with respect to any disarmament proposal made or pursued by the United States as one focused on "moral blame." Dulles held, Jackson told Eisenhower, that a U.S. disarmament proposal "must be of such a nature that its rejection by the Russians, or even prolonged foot-dragging on their part, will make it clear to the people of the world, not just to the Governments, that we must all prepare for the worst, *and the moral blame for the armaments race, and possibly war, is clearly on the Russians."* See "Memorandum to the President, by the Special Assistant to the President (Jackson)," C. D. Jackson, October 2, 1953, *FRUS*, 1952–1954, National Security Affairs, vol. 2, part 2, 1225, emphasis added.
87. "Memorandum of Conversation, 7 April 1958, with 20 June 1969 cover letter from Gerard C. Smith, Top Secret," accessed at The National Security Archive's "The Nuclear Vault," "Special Collection: Some Key Documents on Nuclear Policy Issues, 1945–1990," ed. William Burr. Accessed at http://www.gwu.edu/~nsarchiv/nukevault/special/index.htm , August 7, 2010.
88. Brockriede, "John Foster Dulles," 198.
89. Brockriede, "John Foster Dulles," 197.
90. Kennan to Louis Halle, April 20, 1966, Kennan Papers, Box 31.
91. See The Special Assistant to the President (Charles Douglas Jackson) to the President, *FRUS*, 1952–1954, National Sec. Affairs, vol. 2, part 2, 1315, where Jackson claims that the differences between state and defense on this matter "lies very deep."
92. Gaddis, *Strategies of Containment*, 172.
93. Gaddis, *Strategies of Containment*, 172.
94. Quoted in Ninkovich, *Modernity and Power*, 208.

Chapter 3. Deeds Undone: C. D. Jackson, Liberation, and Adventurism

1. Max F. Millikan, preface to *The American Style: Essays in Value and Performance*, ed. Elting E. Morison (New York: Harper and Brothers, 1958), vii.
2. W. W. Rostow, "The National Style," in Morison, *The American Style*, 247–248.
3. Rostow, "The National Style," 248–259.
4. Rostow, "The National Style," 299–300.
5. See James Burnham, *The Managerial Revolution* (New York: John Day, 1941) and David Riesman, Reuel Denney, and Nathan Glazer, *The Lonely Crowd: A Study of the Changing American Character* (New Haven: Yale University Press, 1952).
6. Rostow, "The National Style," 309.
7. H. W. Brands, *Cold Warriors* (New York: Columbia University Press, 1988), 117.
8. In 1952 Taft called for "an affirmative policy which will constantly extend the doctrine and the power of liberty" and proposed "an underground war of infiltration in Iron Curtain countries." Quoted in Divine, *Foreign Policy and U.S. Presidential Elections, 1952–1960* (New York: New Viewpoints, 1974), 9.
9. William Taubman, *Khrushchev: The Man and His Era* (New York: W. W. Norton, 2003), 487. John F. Kennedy, "Inaugural Address," January 20, 1961, available from John Woolley and Gerhard Peters, The American Presidency Project (online), Santa Barbara: University of California (hosted), Gerhard Peters (database), http://www.presidency.ucsb.edu/ws/?pid=8032.
10. C. D. Jackson to John Steele, June 17, 1963, "Free Europe Committee, 1963 (3)," CDJ Papers, Box 53.
11. Quoted in W. W. Rostow, *Concept and Controversy: Sixty Years of Taking Ideas to Market* (Austin: University of Texas Press, 2003), 394 n. 40.
12. John Steele to C. D. Jackson, July 5, 1963, "Free Europe Committee, 1963 (3)," CDJ Papers, Box 53.
13. Niccolò Machiavelli, *The Prince*, trans. Luigi Ricci and E. R. P. Vincent, in *The Prince and the Discourses* (New York: Modern Library, 1950), 20–21.
14. Pocock, *The Machiavellian Moment*, 166. Pocock continues, interestingly, by contrasting this mode of activism with "deterrence." "What Machiavelli would have said of modern deterrent strategies of 'buying time' we can only guess; perhaps that they make sense only a collusive strategy between powers aiming to stabilize and legitimize their relations."
15. See Arendt, *The Human Condition*, 77, and Tuck, *Philosophy and Government*, 57–58.

16. Walzer, *Revolution of the Saints*, 9–10.
17. Niccolò Machiavelli, *The Discourses*, trans. Christian E. Detmold, in *The Prince and the Discourses*, 318 (book 2, chapter 13).
18. See Tocqueville, *Democracy in America*, book 1, chapter 2.
19. Max Weber, *The Protestant Ethic and the Spirit of Capitalism*, trans. Talcott Parsons (New York: Dover, 2003), 76.
20. Weber, *The Protestant Ethic*, 58.
21. Alexander Hamilton, "Federalist Number 11," *The Federalist Papers*, 49.
22. See James McDaniel, "Figures for New Frontiers, from Davy Crockett to Cyberspace Gurus," *Quarterly Journal of Speech* 88.1 (2002): 91–111.
23. Lionel Trilling, *Sincerity and Authenticity* (Cambridge: Harvard University Press, 1972), 13.
24. Baldesar Castiglione, *The Book of the Courtier*, trans. Charles S. Singleton, in *The Rhetorical Tradition: Readings from Classical Times to the Present*, 2nd ed., ed. Patricia Bizzell and Bruce Herzberg (New York: Bedford / St. Martins, 2001), 661.
25. Patricia Bizzell and Bruce Herzberg, introduction to Baldesar Castiglione's *The Book of the Courtier* in *The Rhetorical Tradition*, 653. Bizzell and Herzberg rely here on the work of Wayne Rebhorn's *Courtly Performances: Masking and Festivity in Castiglione's "Book of the Courtier"* (Detroit: Wayne State University Press, 1978).
26. Bradford, *History of Plymouth Colony*, 99–100.
27. Gilbert, *To the Farewell Address*, 4.
28. Machiavelli, *Discourses*, 103.
29. Georg Simmel, *On Individuality and Social Forms*, ed. Donald N. Levine (Chicago: University of Chicago Press, 1971), 197.
30. Tocqueville, *Democracy in America*, 734.
31. James Burnham, *The Machiavellians* (New York: John Day, 1943).
32. James Burnham, *Containment or Liberation?* (New York: John Day, 1953), 41–42.
33. Burnham, *Containment or Liberation?* 250.
34. Dwight D. Eisenhower, "Text of Gen. Eisenhower's Foreign Policy Speech in San Francisco," October 8, 1952, *New York Times*, October 9, 1952, 24.
35. Kenneth Osgood, *Total Cold War: Eisenhower's Secret Propaganda Battle at Home and Abroad* (Lawrence: University Press of Kansas, 2006), 47.
36. J. Michael Sproule, *Propaganda and Democracy: The American Experience of Media and Mass Persuasion* (New York: Cambridge University Press, 1997), 69.
37. Osgood, *Total Cold War*, 15–45. Christopher Simpson, *Science of Coercion: Communication Research and Psychological Warfare* (New York: Oxford University Press,

1994), 26–27, 82; J Michael Hogan, "The Science of Cold War Strategy: Propaganda and Public Opinion in the Eisenhower Administration's 'War of Words,'" in *Critical Reflections on the Cold War: Linking Rhetoric and History*, ed. Martin J. Medhurst and H. W. Brands (College Station: Texas A&M University Press, 2000), 134–168; Parry-Giles, *Rhetorical Presidency*.

38. Hogan, "Science of Cold War Strategy," 152.
39. See Chris Tudda, *The Truth Is Our Weapon: The Rhetorical Diplomacy of Dwight D. Eisenhower and John Foster Dulles* (Baton Rouge: Louisiana State University Press, 2006), 77–78.
40. Editorial, "For the Sake of Koreans," *New York Times*, July 1, 1950, 9.
41. Harry S. Truman, "Message Congratulating General MacArthur on the Liberation of Seoul," September 29, 1950, available from John Woolley and Gerhard Peters, The American Presidency Project (online), Santa Barbara: University of California (hosted), Gerhard Peters (database), http://www.presidency.ucsb.edu/ws/?pid=13635.
42. Quoted in John Lewis Gaddis, "Containment: A Reassessment," *Foreign Affairs* 55 (July 1977): 879.
43. Truman, "Parkersburg, West Virginia Speech" September 2, 1952, available from John Woolley and Gerhard Peters, The American Presidency Project (online), Santa Barbara: University of California (hosted), Gerhard Peters (database): http://www.presidency.ucsb.edu/ws/?pid=14242.
44. Gaddis, "Containment: A Reassessment," 880.
45. "Pick the Winner, CBS Radio Program, Dwight Cooke, Moderator," broadcast August 24, 1952, Dulles Papers, Box 308. Indeed, Harriman felt a great deal of ambivalence about "liberation." In 1949 Harriman wrote that he was "frankly worried" at Winston Churchill's talk of "liberating" the peoples of Eastern Europe. While such a policy was "theoretically desirable," he wrote, it would entail (unacceptable) "offensive action." See Richard Toye, "The Churchill Syndrome: Reputational Entrepreneurship and the Rhetoric of Foreign Policy since 1945," *British Journal of Politics and International Relations* 10 (2008): 367.
46. Woodrow Wilson, "Address to a Joint Session of Congress on the Conditions of Peace," January 8, 1918, also known as "Fourteen Points," *Public Papers of the Presidents* (hereafter *PPP*), available at http://www.presidency.ucsb.edu/ws/?pid=65405.
47. John Toye and Richard Toye, *The UN and Global Political Economy: Trade, Finance, and Development* (Bloomington: Indiana University Press, 2004), 18.
48. This was obviously connected to the United States' "Open Door" policy as described

in Williams, *Tragedy of American Diplomacy* and in Christopher Layne, *The Peace of Illusions: American Grand Strategy from 1940 to the Present* (Ithaca, NY: Cornell University Press, 2006).

49. On Taft and liberation, see Divine, *Foreign Policy*, 9–10.
50. See Adlai Stevenson, "The Contest of Freedom and Tyranny," September 9, 1952, in *Documents on American Foreign Relations*, ed. Clarence W. Baier and Richard P. Stebbins (New York: Harper and Brothers / Council on Foreign Relations, 1953), 94–99.
51. Truman, "Parkersburg, West Virginia Speech," September 2, 1952.
52. Gaddis, *Strategies of Containment*, 173–174.
53. John Foster Dulles, "Our Foreign Policy—Is Containment Enough?" Chicago Council on Foreign Relations, October 8, 1952, Dulles Papers, Box 309.
54. Parry-Giles, *Rhetorical Presidency*, 136–140.
55. Osgood, *Total Cold War*, 47.
56. "The President's Committee on International Information Activities: Report to the President," June 30, 1953, William H. Jackson, Chair. Accessed through the Declassified Documents Reference System (hereafter DDRS) (Farmington Hills, MI: Gale, September 2007).
57. Osgood, *Total Cold War*, 3. Robert Ivie, "Eisenhower as Cold Warrior," in Medhurst, *Eisenhower's War of Words*, 8.
58. Untitled document marked "Strictly Confidential." See "Princeton Meeting, May 10–11, 1952," CDJ Papers, Box 83.
59. "Political, Economic, and Psychological Strategy: Outline of a Course," February 1952, Harry S. Truman Papers, SMOF: Psychological Strategy Board Files, Box 30, Harry S. Truman Library.
60. Here I concur with Osgood's "post-revisionist" assessment of Eisenhower as more committed to "shrewd Cold War calculations" and "waging and winning the Cold War" than to what revisionist historians had presented as an "altruistic desire for world peace" or détente (*Total Cold War*, 6–7).
61. See Gaddis, *Strategies of Containment*, chapters 5 and 6, especially 130–132, 146, 159, 165, and 173.
62. This and all following quotations from the meeting are taken from "Princeton Meeting on Political Warfare," May 10–11, 1952, summary compiled by Lewis Galantiere of Radio Free Europe, CDJ Papers, Box 83.
63. Abbot Washburn to Dwight D. Eisenhower, no date, but sometime after May 1952 and prior to November 1952. CDJ Papers, Box 83.

64. "The President's Committee on International Information Activities: Report to the President," 4.
65. My reference to "state-private networks" is indebted to Scott Lucas, *Freedom's War: The American Crusade Against the Soviet Union* (New York: New York University Press, 1999).
66. NSC 162/2, October 30, 1953, NSC Series, Box 6, Dwight D. Eisenhower Library, 12.
67. NSC 162/2, 25.
68. See Martin J. Medhurst, "Eisenhower's 'Atoms for Peace' Speech: A Case Study in the Strategic Use of Language," in Medhurst et al., *Cold War Rhetoric*; and J. Michael Hogan, "Eisenhower and Open Skies: A Case Study in Psychological Warfare," in Medhurst, *Eisenhower's War of Words*, 137–155. Hogan "Eisenhower and Open Skies."
69. Quoted in Richard Aldrich, "Liberation: Rolling Back the Frontiers of Clandestine Cold War History?" review essay, *Cold War History* 1.2 (2001): 132.
70. Truman's NSC 68, the pivotal Cold War security document of Truman's tenure and a statement of political philosophy in its own right, argued that U.S. "policy and actions must be such as to foster a fundamental changes in the nature of the Soviet system," and that such changes are best realized "as a result of internal forces in Soviet society." This position rested upon an explicit opposition between the "idea of freedom" and the "idea of slavery." "In relations between nations," it declared, "the prime reliance of the free society is on the strength and appeal of its idea, and it feels no compulsion sooner or later to bring all societies into conformity with it." Nevertheless, the idea of freedom "is the most contagious idea in history." In this way, NSC 68 suggested that contagion rather than compulsion was the key to U.S. success in the Cold War. Through strategic contagion, the United States might convince the Kremlin "of the falsity of its assumptions," so as to create the "pre-conditions for workable agreements." See NSC 68, "A Report to the President pursuant to the President's directive of January 31, 1950," April 7, 1950, 5. Accessed on the website of the Harry S. Truman Library and Museum, http://www.trumanlibrary.org/whistlestop/study_collections/korea/large/week2/nsc68_1.htm, December 2007, 1–2, 5.
71. Jackson to Rostow, September 28, 1962, "Rostow, Walt W., 1962," CDJ Papers, Box 92.
72. Jackson to Rostow, September 28, 1962, "Rostow, Walt W., 1962," CDJ Papers, Box 92

73. Quoted in Medhurst, "Atoms for Peace Speech," 46.
74. C. D. Jackson, "The U.S. Public—A Matter of Orchestration," Paper 6 in *Psychological Aspects of United States Strategy: Source Book of Individual Papers*, November 1955, CDJ Papers, Box 88, accessed through DDRS, September 2007.
75. Parry-Giles, *Rhetorical Presidency*, 131.
76. Jackson to Edgar R. Baker (a Time Inc. executive), January 4, 1961, "Baker, Edgar," CDJ Papers, Box 31.
77. Luce, *The American Century*, 39.
78. Luce, *The American Century*, 24.
79. Robert L. Ivie, "Dwight D. Eisenhower's 'Chance for Peace': Quest or Crusade?" *Rhetoric & Public Affairs* 1.2 (1998): 227–243.
80. A summary of this model and a synthesis of the World Economic Plan appears in Walt Rostow and Max Millikan, *A Proposal: Key to an Effective Foreign Policy* (New York: Harper and Brothers, 1957).
81. "Princeton Meeting on Political Warfare."
82. Dwight D. Eisenhower, "Address at the Tenth Anniversary Meeting of the United Nations, San Francisco, California," June 20, 1955; accessed through John T. Woolley and Gerhard Peters, The American Presidency Project (online). Santa Barbara: University of California (hosted), Gerhard Peters (database), http://www.presidency.ucsb.edu/ws/?pid=10261.
83. Jackson to Luce et al., June 21, 1955, "Beaver—Foreign Economic Policy (2)," CDJ Papers, Box 32.
84. Jackson to Luce et al., June 21, 1955.
85. "The President's Committee on International Information Activities: Report to the President," 12.
86. Jackson to Dwight Eisenhower, October 2, 1953, "Atoms for Peace—Evolution (7)," CDJ Papers, Box 30.
87. "The President's Atomic Proposal before the UN," December 29, 1953, "Atoms for Peace—Evolution," CDJ Papers, Box 29.
88. I borrow the term *strategic deception* from Gordon Mitchell, *Strategic Deception: Rhetoric, Science, and Politics in Missile Defense Advocacy* (East Lansing: Michigan State University Press, 2000).
89. The letter to Wisner was forwarded by Jackson to Eisenhower. See Jackson to Eisenhower, March 8, 1954, "Eisenhower, Dwight D.—Correspondence, 1954," CDJ Papers, Box 50.
90. For Jackson's response to the Hungarian crisis see Jackson to John Foster Dulles,

February 9, 1959, "Dulles, John Foster (1)," CDJ Papers, Box 48.
91. Robert Hariman, *Political Style: The Artistry of Power* (Chicago: University of Chicago Press, 1995), 73.
92. In this respect, Walter Lippmann stands between the two sources of modern political realism, Lipsius the stoic (Kennan) and Machiavelli the adventurer (Jackson), arguing in *The Phantom Public* for an understanding of "public opinion" that echoes Machiavelli's *Fortuna*, but insisting on the possibility of its rational discipline: "Public opinion, in this theory, is a reserve of force brought into action during a crisis in public affairs. Though it is itself an irrational force, under favorable institutions, sound leadership and decent training the power of public opinion might be placed at the disposal of those who stood for workable law as against brute assertion. In this theory, public opinion does not make the law. But by canceling lawless power it may establish the condition under which law can be made. . . . Public opinion in its highest ideal will defend those who are prepared to act on their reason against the interrupting force of those who merely assert their will." Walter Lippmann, *The Phantom Public* (New Brunswick, NJ: Transaction Publishers, 2004), 59.
93. Hariman, *Political Style*, 57.
94. Simmel, *Individuality and Social Forms*, 189.
95. Jackson to Allen, August 26, 1949, "AL-Misc.," CDJ Papers, Box 27.
96. Editors of Time-Life International (anonymous), "So We Went Abroad," unpublished manuscript available in the library of the University of Illinois, Urbana-Champaign, 2.
97. Editors of Time-Life International, "So We Went Abroad," 30.
98. Bowie and Immerman, *Waging Peace*, 51.
99. "World Economic Policy: A Simple Outline of a Great Opportunity for the United States," May 1954, "Princeton Economic Conf—5/54 Draft Papers," CDJ Papers, Box 82.
100. See "Proceedings of the Off-the-Record Conference Held Under the Auspices of Time, Inc.," May 15–16, 1954, Princeton Inn, Princeton, NJ, "Princeton Economic Conf., 5/54-Transcript (2)," CDJ Papers, Box 83, 3; and Toye and Toye, *The UN*, 166.
101. "The President's Atomic Proposal before the UN," December 29, 1953, "Atoms for Peace—Evolution," CDJ Papers, Box 29.
102. "Chance for Peace" spoke of the Western Allies and Russians meeting in Europe as "triumphant comrades in arms." With respect to development, the speech

imagined "the dedication of the energies, the resources, and the imaginations of all peaceful nations to a new kind of war. This would be a declared total war, not upon any human enemy but upon the brute forces of poverty and need, and, "This Government is ready to ask its people to join with all nations in devoting a substantial percentage of the savings achieved by disarmament to a fund for world aid and reconstruction. The purposes of this great work would be to help other peoples to develop the undeveloped areas of the world, to stimulate profitable and fair world trade, to assist all peoples to know the blessings of productive freedom." See Dwight D. Eisenhower, "Chance for Peace," delivered before the American Society of Newspaper Editors, April 16, 1953, *PPP*, document 50, 1953, available at http://www.presidency.ucsb.edu/ws/?pid=9819.

103. "Proceedings of the Off-the-Record Conference Held Under the Auspices of Time, Inc.," 4.
104. "Proceedings of the Off-the-Record Conference Held Under the Auspices of Time, Inc.," 6.
105. C. D. Jackson, Walt Rostow, and Max Millikan, "Proposal for a New United States Foreign Economic Policy," July 23, 1954, "Beaver—Foreign Economic Policy (2)," CDJ Papers, Box 32.
106. "Draft of Presidential Speech," July 22, 1954, "Beaver—Foreign Economic Policy (4)," CDJ Papers, Box 32.
107. See Toye and Toye, *The UN*, 2, 5, 11. The new strength of "underdeveloped" nations meant that the United States believed Communist expansion in these areas was increasingly likely. In the mid-1950s, the CIA contracted with MIT's Center for International Studies (Millikan and Rostow's outfit) to produce a study on effective measures by which to counter "Communist expansion" in poorer nations. The study was described by the CIA as intended to "explore . . . ways in which political, economic, military (including paramilitary), and informational assets of the Government [of the United States] can be most effectively integrated to forestall and to counter communist inspired disorders and communist rebellions in underdeveloped areas when necessary in the interest of U.S. national security." See the CIA's response to the recommendations of the June 8, 1955, Killian Report in the document labeled "Tab C" in Eisenhower Presidential Library, White House Office, National Security Council Staff: Papers, 1948–1961, Disaster File, Box 42.
108. Among the twenty-four in attendance at the 1954 Princeton Economic Conference were Allen Dulles and Richard Bissell of the CIA, Robert Bowie of the State Department, Robert Cutler and Gabriel Hauge of the White House, Samuel Anderson

of the Commerce Department, H. Chapman Rose of the Treasury Department, Robert Garner of the International Bank, David McDonald of the United Steel Workers, Thomas McKittrick of Chase National Bank, John Jessup and Charles Stillman of Time, Inc., and Rostow, Millikan, and some academic colleagues from MIT and Harvard.

109. See "Proceedings of the Off-the-Record Conference Held Under the Auspices of Time, Inc.," 4, 5, 7.
110. "Proceedings of the Off-the-Record Conference Held Under the Auspices of Time, Inc.," 9.
111. "World Economic Policy: A Simple Outline of a Great Opportunity for the United States," May 1954, "Princeton Economic Conf—5/54 Draft Papers," CDJ Papers, Box 82.
112. Kimber Charles Pearce, *Rostow, Kennedy, and the Rhetoric of Foreign Aid* (East Lansing: Michigan State University Press, 2001), 30; Toye and Toye, *The UN*, 169.
113. "World Economic Policy: A Simple Outline of a Great Opportunity for the United States," May 1954, "Princeton Economic Conf—5/54 Draft Papers," CDJ Papers, Box 82.
114. "World Economic Policy: A Simple Outline of a Great Opportunity for the United States."
115. Eisenhower to Jackson, April 16, 1954, "Eisenhower, Dwight D.–Correspondence, 1954 (1)," CDJ Papers, Box 50.
116. "Proposal for a New United States Foreign Economic Policy," July 23, 1954, "Beaver—Foreign Economic Policy (2)," CDJ Papers, Box 32.
117. "World Economic Policy: A Simple Outline of a Great Opportunity for the United States," May 1954, "Princeton Economic Conf—5/54 Draft Papers," CDJ Papers, Box 82.
118. Jackson to Rostow, September 28, 1962, "Rostow, Walt W., 1962," CDJ Papers, Box 92. Rostow replied, "I am with you 100 percent," and told Jackson to come to Washington, DC, so they could talk details (ibid.).
119. Jackson to Luce, April 9, 1954, "Princeton Economic Conf., 5/54—Misc. Correspondence, etc. (2)," CDJ Papers, Box 83. The "previous experience" had been the 1952 Princeton conference on Psychological Warfare, which was also orchestrated by Jackson.
120. Millikan to Jackson, April 15, 1954, "Princeton Economic Conf., 5/54—Misc. Correspondence, etc. (2)," CDJ Papers, Box 83.
121. Rostow, "The National Style," 309.

122. Of course, the spirit of adventurism was more prolific in the Kennedy years than just the decade of development. Indeed, the trip to the moon inaugurated by Kennedy displayed much more vividly America's adventurism in a Cold War context. The similarity in form between the iconic image at Iwo Jima of soldiers planting an American flag and that of Neil Armstrong and Buzz Aldrin planting the same flag is not merely coincidental. Both images represent the ideological height of a liberation wrought from adventure.
123. See the overview approaches to understanding the motivation of foreign aid in Carol Lancaster, *Foreign Aid: Diplomacy, Development, and Domestic Politics* (Chicago: University of Chicago Press, 2007), 3–4.
124. Alfred North Whitehead, *Adventures in Ideas* (New York: The Free Press, 1933), 279.

Chapter 4. The American Sublime: Eisenhower, Deterrence, and Romanticism

1. Francis Fukuyama, "The End of History?" *National Interest* 16 (Summer 1989): 4.
2. Dwight D. Eisenhower, "Address Before the General Assembly of the United Nations on Peaceful Uses of Atomic Energy, New York City," also known as "Atoms for Peace," *PPP*, doc. 256, December 8, 1953, http://www.presidency.ucsb.edu/ws/?pid=9774.
3. Ivie, "Eisenhower as Cold Warrior," 8.
4. Weapons Systems Evaluation Group Report No. 42, 53–54, n.d., but content places it between 1953 and 1959. Accessed at the Office of the Secretary of Defense and Joint Staff online "Reading Room" on August 5, 2010, http://www.dod.gov/pubs/foi/ncb/.
5. Dwight D. Eisenhower, "Annual Message to the Congress on the State of the Union," *PPP*, document 8, January 10, 1957, http://www.presidency.ucsb.edu/ws/?pid=11029.
6. Dwight D. Eisenhower, "Address before Convention of Veterans of Foreign Wars, Boston, Massachusetts, September 3, 1946," in *Eisenhower Speaks*, ed. Rudolph L. Treuenfels (New York: Farrar, Straus, 1948), 129.
7. Eisenhower, "Address before the American Alumni Council upon Presentation of the Council's Award of Merit, Amherst, Massachusetts, July 11, 1946," in *Eisenhower Speaks*, 118.
8. Eisenhower, "Address before Convention of Veterans of Foreign Wars," in

Eisenhower Speaks, 128.
9. Ira Chernus, *General Eisenhower: Ideology and Discourse* (East Lansing: Michigan State University Press, 2002), 257.
10. Michel Foucault, *Discipline and Punish*, trans. Alan Sheridan (New York: Vintage, 1977), 201.
11. Eisenhower, "Farewell Radio and Television Address to the American People," *PPP*, document 421, January 17, 1961, http://www.presidency.ucsb.edu/ws/?pid=12086. By 1961, the dilemma of the "garrison state" was as old as the Cold War. See Michael J. Hogan, *A Cross of Iron: Harry S. Truman and the Origins of the National Security State, 1945–1954* (New York: Cambridge University Press, 1998), 1–22.
12. Dulles, "Policy for Security and Peace," 355.
13. NSC 68 presented a strong antithesis between freedom and necessity, justifying military power (including, but not exclusively or even specifically so, nuclear weapons) as a realm of necessity that creates the conditions for the pursuit of freedom. "For us the role of military power is to serve the national purpose by deterring an attack upon us while we seek by other means to create an environment in which our free society can flourish" (12). Yet NSC 68 subtly recognized the moral quandary of this position, explicitly argued against a mentality of strict expediency, and insisted that "The resort to force, to compulsion, to the imposition of its will" should be only a last resort "for a free society" (11). Its logic was that "freedom" could not be achieved through force. War, it held, is "an act which cannot definitively end the fundamental conflict in the realm of ideas. The idea of slavery can only be overcome by the timely and persistent demonstration of the superiority of the idea of freedom" (11). NSC 68 has been derided as offering an untenable strategic outlook that presumed unlimited means and advocated symmetrical responses to Soviet or Communist aggression (see Gaddis, *Strategies of Containment*, 87–124). While it may be the case that it failed to offer a coherent vision of the relation of means to ends, it, far more than the security documents that succeeded it in the Eisenhower administration, wrestled with the dilemmas of value-rationality in foreign policy, and thus deserves more credit than Gaddis gives it.
14. Chernus, *General Eisenhower*, 34–36, and *Apocalypse Management*, 27.
15. Indeed, Isaiah Berlin describes romanticism as "the greatest single shift in the consciousness of the West that has occurred, and all the other shifts which have occurred in the course of the nineteenth and twentieth centuries appear to me in comparison less important, and at any rate deeply influenced by it." Berlin, *The Roots of Romanticism* (Princeton, NJ: Princeton University Press, 1999), 1–2.

16. Louis Dupré, *The Enlightenment and the Intellectual Foundations of Modern Culture* (New Haven: Yale University Press, 2004), 13, 25.
17. Ralph Waldo Emerson, "The Poet," in *The Heath Anthology of American Literature*, ed. Paul Lauter, 2nd ed., vol. 1 (Lexington, MA: D.C. Heath, 1994), 1568.
18. Thomas Carlyle, *On Heroes, Hero-Worship, and the Heroic in History*, ed. John Chester Adams (New York: Houghton Mifflin, 1907), 339.
19. Quoted in Charles Thorpe, *Oppenheimer: The Tragic Intellect* (Chicago: University of Chicago Press, 2006), 11.
20. Blanche Wiesen Cook, *The Declassified Eisenhower: A Divided Legacy* (Garden City, NY: Doubleday, 1981).
21. Fred I. Greenstein, *The Hidden-Hand Presidency: Eisenhower as Leader* (New York: Basic Books, 1982); Hogan, "Eisenhower and Open Skies"; Lucas, *Freedom's War*; Osgood, *Total Cold War*; and Parry-Giles, *Rhetorical Presidency*.
22. Ivie, "Eisenhower as Cold Warrior"; Chernus, *Apocalypse Management*; H. W. Brands, "The Age of Vulnerability: Eisenhower and the National Insecurity State," *American Historical Review* 94 (1989): 963–989; and Guy Oakes, *The Imaginary War* (New York: Oxford University Press, 1994).
23. Chernus, *General Eisenhower*, 172.
24. Martin J. Medhurst, "Reconceptualizing Rhetorical History: Eisenhower's Farewell Address," *Quarterly Journal of Speech* 80 (1994): 205.
25. Dwight D. Eisenhower, Speech before the American Bar Association, September 5, 1949, quoted in Martin J. Medhurst, "Dwight D. Eisenhower," in *U.S. Presidents as Orators: A Bio-Critical Sourcebook*, ed. Halford Ryan (Westport, CT: Greenwood Press, 1995), 193–194.
26. Steven Wagner, *Eisenhower Republicanism: Pursuing the Middle Way* (DeKalb: Northern Illinois University Press, 2006), 5.
27. Dwight D. Eisenhower, *Crusade in Europe* (Baltimore: Johns Hopkins University Press, 1948), 4.
28. Eisenhower, *Crusade in Europe*, 3.
29. Eisenhower, *Crusade in Europe*, 4.
30. Simon Williams, *Wagner and the Romantic Hero* (New York: Cambridge University Press, 2004), 12.
31. Williams, *Wagner and the Romantic Hero*, 12.
32. Ivie, "Eisenhower's 'Chance for Peace,'" 228.
33. Gaddis, *Strategies of Containment*, 173.
34. Ivie, "Eisenhower as Cold Warrior," 9.

35. Medhurst, "Eisenhower's Rhetorical Leadership," 295.
36. Medhurst, "Eisenhower's Rhetorical Leadership," 294–295.
37. Bowie and Immerman, *Waging Peace*, 47.
38. Berlin, *The Roots of Romanticism*, 93.
39. Jean-Jacques Rousseau, "Discourse on the Origin and Foundation of Inequality among Men *or* Second Discourse," in *Rousseau: The Discourses and Other Early Political Writings*, ed. Victor Gourevitch (New York: Cambridge University Press, 1997), 141.
40. Dupré, *Enlightenment*, 221, 225–226.
41. Berlin, *The Roots of Romanticism*, 95.
42. Peter Paret, *Clausewitz and the State: The Man, His Theories, and His Times* (Princeton, NJ: Princeton University Press, 1985), 149. On Eisenhower's engagement with Clausewitz, see Stephen E. Ambrose, *Eisenhower: Soldier and President* (New York: Simon and Schuster, 1990), 39–40, and Gaddis, *Strategies of Containment*, 133.
43. See Clausewitz, *On War*.
44. Ira Chernus, *Eisenhower's Atoms for Peace* (College Station: Texas A&M University Press, 2002), 9; and Chernus, *Apocalypse Management*, 2.
45. Chernus, *Apocalypse Management*, 2.
46. Dwight D. Eisenhower, "Annual Message to the Congress on the State of the Union," *PPP*, document 6, February 2, 1953, http://www.presidency.ucsb.edu/ws/?pid=9829.
47. Eisenhower, *The Eisenhower Diaries*, ed. Robert H. Ferrell (New York: W. W. Norton, 1981), 168.
48. Medhurst, "Dwight D. Eisenhower," 192; see also Martin J. Medhurst, *Dwight D. Eisenhower: Strategic Communicator* (Westport, CT: Greenwood Press, 1993); Medhurst, "Eisenhower's Rhetorical Leadership," especially 287–289; and Medhurst, "Reconceptualizing Rhetorical History."
49. Medhurst, *Dwight D. Eisenhower*, 18.
50. Ivie, "Eisenhower as Cold Warrior," 8.
51. Chernus, *General Eisenhower*, 301.
52. Dwight D. Eisenhower, *Mandate for Change* (Garden City, NJ: Doubleday, 1963), 11.
53. Burke, *A Rhetoric of Motives*, xiii.
54. See Bowie and Immerman, *Waging Peace*, chapter 2; and Gaddis, *Strategies of Containment*, 143–159.

55. Osgood, *Total Cold War*, 47.
56. The economic impetus behind Eisenhower's "New Look" has received a great deal of attention. Three especially helpful discussions of the New Look can be found in Bowie and Immerman, *Waging Peace*; Gaddis, *Strategies of Containment*; and Hogan, *Cross of Iron*.
57. Dwight D. Eisenhower to Dulles, June 20, 1952, Dulles Papers, Box 60.
58. Osgood, *Total Cold War*, 154. Osgood's book includes a thorough discussion of the efforts by the Eisenhower administration to publicize the "peaceful" use of the atom.
59. Hogan, *Cross of Iron*, 209–210, 220–264.
60. Records of Thomas E. Stephens, "Miscellaneous (2) 1956 Campaign," Dwight D. Eisenhower Presidential Library, Box 30.
61. Eric Wilson, *Emerson's Sublime Science* (New York: St. Martin's Press, 1999), 6.
62. Dwight D. Eisenhower, Address at the Tenth Anniversary Meeting of the United Nations, San Francisco," *PPP*, document 126, June 20, 1955, http://www.presidency.ucsb.edu/ws/?pid=10261.
63. Oakes, *The Imaginary War*, 48–59, 66–71.
64. NSC 126, Report to the National Security Council by the Psychological Strategy Board, Subenclosure: "Memorandum on Public Statements with Respect to Certain American Weapons," February 28, 1952, *FRUS*, 1952–1954, vol. 2, National Security Affairs, 871–872. For background material on NSC 126, including Truman's December 5, 1950, directive "Public Discussion of Foreign and Military Policy" quoted above, see White House Office, National Security Council Staff: Papers, 1948–1961, Disaster File, Eisenhower Presidential Library, Box 6.
65. Richard G. Hewlett and Jack M. Holl, *Atoms for Peace and War, 1953–1961: Eisenhower and the Atomic Energy Commission*, (Berkeley: University of California Press, 1989), xxi. The chart is included in "Fact Sheet: Increasing Transparency in the U.S. Nuclear Weapons Stockpile," released by the U. S. Department of Defense, May 3, 2010, accessed at www.defense.gov/npr/docs/10-05-03_fact_sheet_us_nuclear_transparency__final_w_date.pdf on January 19, 2011.
66. Records of Thomas E. Stephens, "Miscellaneous (2) 1956 Campaign," Eisenhower Presidential Library, Box 30.
67. Burke, *Permanence and Change*, 134; see also Burke's frequent discussion of "transcendence upwards" in *Attitudes toward History*. Dave Tell's essay on Burke's "Four Master Tropes" is helpful for understanding Burke's perspective on metonymy and synecdoche; see Tell, "Burke's Encounter with Ransom: Rhetoric and Epistemology

in 'Four Master Tropes,'" *Rhetoric Society Quarterly* 34.4 (2004): 33–54.
68. White, *Metahistory*, 8–9.
69. Seneca, *Letters from a Stoic*, 52.
70. Ralph Waldo Emerson, "Abraham Lincoln," in *The Essential Writings of Ralph Waldo Emerson* (New York: Modern Library, 2000), 833.
71. Walter J. Ong, *Rhetoric, Romance, and Technology: Studies in the Interaction of Expression and Culture* (Ithaca, NY: Cornell University Press, 1971), 279. Hans-Georg Gadamer succinctly captures the relationship of the Enlightenment and romanticism, writing of romanticism, "It shares the presupposition of the Enlightenment and only reverses its values," valuing the old, mythic, and magical not as an expression of fundamental belief but as a response to the disenchantment of the world wrought by the Enlightenment. Romanticism thus "actually perpetuates the abstract contrast between myth and reason" engendered by the Enlightenment (*Truth and Method*, 273).
72. Philip F. Gura, *The Wisdom of Words: Language, Theology, and Literature in the New England Renaissance* (Middletown, CT: Wesleyan University Press, 1981), 18.
73. Philip F. Gura, *American Transcendentalism* (New York: Hill and Wang, 2007), 43–44.
74. Gura, *American Transcendentalism*, 44.
75. Gura, *The Wisdom of Words*, 18.
76. Ralph Waldo Emerson, "The American Scholar," in *Essential Writings*, 43–44.
77. Burke, "Four Master Tropes," 506, 509.
78. Walt Whitman, "The Death of Abraham Lincoln," in *The Complete Poetry and Prose of Walt Whitman: As Prepared by Him for the Deathbed Edition* (New York: Pellegrini and Cudahy, 1948), 322.
79. Whitman, "The Death of Abraham Lincoln," 323.
80. James P. McDaniel, "Fantasm: The Triumph of Form (an Essay on the Democratic Sublime)," *Quarterly Journal of Speech* 86.1 (2000): 55.
81. Woodrow Wilson's breakdown in the League of Nations campaign is chronicled in PBS's *American Experience: Woodrow Wilson*, part 2, "The Redemption of the World," directed by Carl Byker and Mitch Wilson, 2001. Transcript available at http://www.pbs.org/wgbh/amex/wilson/filmmore/fm_trans2.html; Herbert Hoover, "Speech given in New York City, October 22, 1928," also known as the "Rugged Individualism" speech, in *The New Day: Campaign Speeches of Herbert Hoover* (Stanford, CA: Stanford University Press, 1928), 149–176.
82. On the religion of Eisenhower's parents, see Chernus, *General Eisenhower*. In

emphasizing mystical univocity, Emerson was most faithful to the synechdochal form of the *Naturphilosophie* of German romantics like Schelling and Schlegel. Arguing that all Being was an organic unity, German romantics drew upon Kant's description of a living organism in the *Critique of Judgement* (§ 65) as conforming to two general characteristics, which Frederick Beiser summarizes as "the idea of the whole precedes its parts; and the parts are mutually the cause and effect of one another." German romantics were thus able to claim for their philosophy an exhaustive account of nature that was neither materialistic nor mechanistic by transforming "the paradigm of explanation: to understand an event is not to explain it as the result of prior events in time but to see it as a necessary part of a whole." This romantic paradigm of explanation, as I will show, foreshadows Eisenhower's with respect to deterrence through nuclear stockpiling. Frederick Beiser, "The Enlightenment and Idealism," in *The Cambridge Companion to German Idealism*, ed. Karl Ameriks (New York: Cambridge University Press, 2000), 33, 35.
83. Emerson, "The American Scholar," 57.
84. Emerson, "The American Scholar," 57.
85. Emerson, "Abraham Lincoln," 833.
86. Harold Bloom, "Emerson and Whitman: The American Sublime," in *Sticky Sublime*, ed. Bill Beckley (New York: Allworth Press, 2001), 17.
87. A similar thesis to mine can be found in Stephen John Hartnett, *Democratic Dissent and the Cultural Fictions of Antebellum America* (Urbana: University of Illinois Press, 2002). American democracy emerged in tandem with modernity, and thus, as Hartnett has written, has had to address "two driving questions," namely: "how does modernity affect the status of and relationships among selves and society, and how does modern capitalism affect the promises of democracy?" (135). Hartnett argues that Whitman's poetry is a paradoxical attempt at answering these two questions, as it "claims repeatedly to embody the spirit of presence, immediacy, and physicality while simultaneously claiming an oceanic and all-knowing position that illustrates absence, mediation, and totality" (161). In the language of my essay, Whitman tried simultaneously to metonymically embody the American sublime and synecdochally mediate it.
88. John Foster Dulles, "Toward World Order," March 5, 1942, Dulles Papers, Box 290.
89. Osgood, *Total Cold War*, 4.
90. Osgood, *Total Cold War*, 5.
91. See Greenstein, *Hidden-Hand Presidency*. The connection between the notion of a "hidden-hand" presidency and Adam Smith's "hidden-hand" economics is not

incidental or insignificant. Eisenhower's ideological commitment to free-market economics, as I will suggest, meant a resistance to FDR-type "statist" leadership.

92. Very helpful cased studies of Eisenhower's rhetorical approach to each of these crises can be found in Medhurst, *Eisenhower's War of Words*.
93. Emmet John Hughes, *The Ordeal of Power: A Political Memoir of the Eisenhower Years* (New York: Atheneum, 1963), 152.
94. Eisenhower, *The Eisenhower Diaries*, 78.
95. C. D. Jackson, in "Eisenhower, Dwight D.—Correspondence, 1954," CDJ Papers, Box 50.
96. Stephen E. Ambrose, *Ike: Abilene to Berlin* (New York: Harper and Row, 1973), xii–xiii.
97. Eisenhower, *The Eisenhower Diaries*, 84.
98. Chernus, *General Eisenhower*, 293.
99. Eisenhower, "Address before the American Alumni Council on Presentation of the Council's Award of Merit, Amherst, Massachusetts, July 11, 1946," in *Eisenhower Speaks*, 120.
100. Eisenhower, "Address at Veterans' Day, Nebraska State Fair, Lincoln, Nebraska, September 1, 1946," in *Eisenhower Speaks*, 121.
101. Eisenhower, "Address before Convention of Veterans of Foreign Wars, Boston, Massachusetts, September 3, 1946," in *Eisenhower Speaks*, 130–131.
102. Eisenhower, *Eisenhower Diaries*, 168.
103. Eisenhower, *Eisenhower Diaries*, 374.
104. Hughes, *The Ordeal of Power*, 346–347. See also chapter 2 of William E. Leuchtenburg, *In the Shadow of FDR: From Harry Truman to Ronald Reagan* (Ithaca, NY: Cornell University Press, 1989).
105. Ira Chernus, *Eisenhower's Atoms for Peace: Eisenhower and the Discourse of National Insecurity* (Stanford, CA: Stanford University Press, 2008), 27.
106. Robert J. Art, "The Four Functions of Force," in *International Politics: Enduring Concepts and Contemporary Issues*, ed. Robert J. Art and Robert Jervis, 7th ed. (New York: Pearson Longman, 2005), 142. I should note that because deterrence is designed to prevent actions of an adversary, it does not necessarily do so. For example, Richard Ned Lebow and Janice Gross Stein have suggested, "Strategic buildups are more likely to provoke than to restrain adversaries because of their impact on the domestic balance of political power in the target state." See Lebow and Stein, "Deterrence and the Cold War," *Political Science Quarterly* 110.2 (1995): 178.

107. Lawrence Freedman, *The Evolution of Nuclear Strategy*, 3rd ed. (New York: Palgrave Macmillan, 2003), 82.
108. Steve Fetter, "Ballistic Missiles and Weapons of Mass Destruction: What Is the Threat? What Should Be Done?" *International Security* 16 (Summer 1991): 36, emphasis added.
109. Deterrence can also be sought through denial. See Lawrence Freedman, *Deterrence* (Malden, MA: Polity Press, 2004), 36–40.
110. Lebow and Stein argue for the instability of the effects of nuclear deterrence in "Deterrence and the Cold War."
111. Ong, *Rhetoric, Romance, and Technology*, 279.
112. Oliver O'Donovan, *Peace and Certainty: A Theological Essay on Deterrence* (Oxford: Clarendon Press Oxford, 1989), 23.
113. O'Donovan, *Peace and Certainty*, 20.
114. In the review of an ad hoc committee of the Oppenheimer Report, May 8, 1953, a key set of assumptions (really arguments) was presented regarding "candor" with the public about atomic energy. The committee stressed that it should be claimed publicly, "No physical phenomenon is inherently good or bad in itself. Atomic weapons must be considered a part of our total weapons system, so that the question of morality will relate only to the way in which this or any other weapon is used. This will give us greater freedom of action with respect to all elements of our military strength" (1153). Furthermore, the committee said it should be stressed that "Atomic energy is *not* something unique and apart from other new developments in technology" (1153). "Morality" here was explicitly confined to the application of technology rather than to technologies themselves. See *FRUS*, 1952–1954, vol. 2, National Security Affairs.
115. NSC 162/2 stressed that a militant image risked not only war with the Soviets, but a significant weakening of the confidence of allies: "Many consider U.S. attitudes toward the Soviets as too rigid and unyielding and, at the same time, as unstable, holding risks ranging from preventative war and 'liberation' to withdrawal into isolation. Many consider that these policies fail to reflect the perspective and confidence expected in the leadership of a great nation, and reflect too great a preoccupation with anti-communism" (12, NSC 162/2).
116. Eisenhower, "Address—Art in Peace and War—After Being Made Honorary Fellow by the Metropolitan Museum of art, New York, N.Y., April 2, 1946," in *Eisenhower Speaks*, 81.
117. The liberal-developmentalist ideology is discussed by Emily S. Rosenberg in

Spreading the American Dream: American Economic and Cultural Expansion, 1890–1945 (New York: Hill and Wang, 1982).

118. Eisenhower, "Address at Fourth of July Observance, Warren County Courthouse, Vicksburg, Mississippi, July 4, 1947," in *Eisenhower Speaks*, 243.
119. Eisenhower, "Address on Receiving an Honorary Doctorate from Toronto University, Toronto, Canada, January 12, 1946," in *Eisenhower Speaks*, 71.
120. Barnett Newman, "The Sublime Is Now," in *Theories of Modern Art: A Source Book by Artists and Critics*, ed. Herschel B. Chipp (Berkeley: University of California Press, 1968), 552.
121. Newman, "The Sublime Is Now," 553.
122. Lawrence Alloway, "The American Sublime," *Living Arts* 2 (1963): 14.
123. Max Weber, *Sociology of Religion*, trans. Ephriam Fischoff (Boston: Beacon Press, 1993), especially 1–46.
124. See Weber, *Sociology of Religion*, 30. On the priestly function of the presidency, in addition to the scholarship on civil religion cited above see James David Fairbanks, "The Priestly Functions of the Presidency: A Discussion of the Literature on Civil Religion and Its Implications for the Study of Presidential Leadership," *Presidential Studies Quarterly* 11 (1981): 214–232.
125. Stephen J. Whitfield, *The Culture of the Cold War* (Baltimore: Johns Hopkins University Press, 1991), 54.
126. All quotations of and references to Eisenhower's first inaugural address are taken from Dwight D. Eisenhower, "Inaugural Address," *PPP*, document 1, January 20, 1953, http://www.presidency.ucsb.edu/ws/index.php?pid=9600&st=&st1=.
127. Franklin D. Roosevelt, "Inaugural Address," *PPP*, doc. 7, January 20, 1945, http://www.presidency.ucsb.edu/ws/?pid=16607.
128. Eisenhower was directly and actively involved in the composition of his speeches. For a window into his approach, see Medhurst, *Dwight D. Eisenhower*, 75–77.
129. Eisenhower, *Mandate for Change*, 100.
130. Editors, "The President's Prayer," *The Nation*, January 31, 1953, 91.
131. James Reston, "Inaugural Is Held to Extend U.S. Commitments to the World," *New York Times*, January 21, 1953, 17.
132. Eisenhower, "'The Chance for Peace' Delivered Before the American Society of Newspaper Editors," *PPP*, doc. 50, April 16, 1953, http://www.presidency.ucsb.edu/ws/index.php?pid=9819&st=&st1=.
133. Eisenhower, "Opening Statement at the Geneva Conference," *PPP*, document 164, July 18, 1955, http://www.presidency.ucsb.edu/ws/index.php?pid=10304&st=Surpri

se&st1=destruction.

134. Ivie, "Eisenhower as Cold Warrior," 9–11; Chernus, *Apocalypse Management*, 10–14.
135. For the tragic portrayal of Eisenhower, see Hewlett and. Holl, *Atoms for Peace and War*; and for the ironic rendering, see Chernus, *Apocalypse Management*, 197–239 and Ivie, "Eisenhower as Cold Warrior."
136. In rhetorical studies, this tension is revealed in via incongruent interpretations of Eisenhower's rhetoric. Wander claims that the Eisenhower-Dulles administration was characterized by a "prophetic dualism" that insists on "America's moral or spiritual superiority" and "divides the world into two camps." Wander casts this as highly ideological discourse, funded by the "Protestant Establishment." Martin Medhurst, on the other hand, has argued that Eisenhower's discourse is pragmatically motivated and based on "realist assumptions." Still, even Medhurst describes Eisenhower as having a "'fanatical' devotion to democracy" that was expressed in a "religious sentiment." Explaining a third approach, Robert Ivie argues that Eisenhower was a "realist" who nevertheless "left a rhetorical legacy of fear that perpetuated the age of peril." See Wander, "The Rhetoric of American Foreign Policy,"156–57; Medhurst, "Atoms for Peace Speech," 204; Medhurst, *Dwight D. Eisenhower*, 13; Ivie, "Eisenhower as Cold Warrior," 21.
137. Wander, "Rhetoric of American Foreign Policy" in *Quarterly Journal of Speech*.
138. Hariman, *Political Style*, 17.
139. Weber, *Sociology of Religion*, 4, 32ff.
140. Eisenhower, "Annual Message to the Congress on the State of the Union," January 10, 1957.
141. Eisenhower, "Special Message to the Congress on the Situation in the Middle East," also known as the "Eisenhower Doctrine Speech," *PPP*, document 6, January 5, 1957, http://www.presidency.ucsb.edu/ws/index.php?pid=11007&st=&st1=.
142. Quoted in Bowie and Immerman, *Waging Peace*, 44.
143. Eisenhower, "Address at Annual Dinner of Wings Club, New York, N.Y., May 5, 1947," in *Eisenhower Speaks*, 185.
144. See Eisenhower, "Address at Meeting of United Jewish Appeal, Washington D.C., February 23, 1947," in *Eisenhower Speaks*, 176, and "Address on Receiving the Churchman Award for the Promotion of Good Will and Better Understanding Among All Peoples, New York, N.Y., December 3, 1946," in *Eisenhower Speaks*, 168.
145. Eisenhower, "Radio and Television Address to the American People on the State of the Nation," *PPP*, document 72, April 5, 1954, http://www.presidency.ucsb.edu/ws/?pid=10201._

146. Weber, *Sociology of Religion*, 33.
147. Patrick J. Deneen, *Democratic Faith* (Princeton, NJ: Princeton University Press, 2005), 4–5, emphasis original.
148. Quoted in William S. White, "'Internationalist' Inaugural Acclaimed in Both Parties," *New York Times*, January 21, 1953, 1.
149. Anonymous, "Nation Off to a Fresh Start as Eisenhower Takes the Helm," *Newsweek*, January 26, 1953, 25.
150. Editors, "The Inaugural Address," *New York Herald Tribune*, January 21, 1953, 22.
151. Anonymous, "Excerpts from Editorial Comment," *New York Times*, January 21, 1953, 20.
152. Anonymous, "Eisenhower Talk Praised by Many in Both Parties," *St. Louis Post Dispatch*, January 20, 1953, 2A.
153. Chernus, *Apocalypse Management*, 8. See also his *General Eisenhower*, 58–62.
154. Chernus, *Apocalypse Management*, 162.
155. Perhaps it is time to stop adopting Reinhold Niebuhr's "Augustinianism," with Niebuhr, as a helpful label for the latter's thought. Niebuhr offered neither a wholehearted endorsement of Augustine's theology, nor a particularly rich reading of Augustine. In fact, Niebuhr repeatedly qualified his endorsement of Augustine, and for good reasons with respect to his own purposes: for Niebuhr would have little of Augustine's "metaphysics" other than the latter's invocation of the doctrine of original sin and a theory of human finitude. The result was the equivalent of a Marxism without materialism or a concept of class. Indeed, Niebuhr sought an Augustine without the vestiges of Neoplatonism, the doctrine of the goodness of creation, belief in the resurrection, or the eschatological promise—the result being an "Augustine" that is hardly recognizable as such, and indeed one that looks far more like the stoic worldview than an Augustinian one. See Reinhold Niebuhr, "Augustine's Political Realism," in *The Essential Reinhold Niebuhr: Selected Essays and Addresses* (New Haven: Yale University Press, 1986), 123–141. See also John Milbank, "The Poverty of Niebuhrianism," in *The World Made Strange: Theology, Language, and Culture* (Cambridge, MA: Blackwell, 1997), 233–254.
156. Chernus, *Apocalypse Management*, 162, emphasis added.
157. Quoted in Chernus, *Apocalypse Management*, 162, emphasis added.
158. Chernus, *General Eisenhower*, 293.
159. Hogan, *Cross of Iron*, 209.
160. Qtd. in Whitfield, *Culture of the Cold War*, 91.
161. Chernus thus finds in the Cold War a "synthesis of the 'realist' and apocalyptic

traditions," which he associates with Eisenhower. See *General Eisenhower*, 12.

162. Robert Wuthnow, *The Restructuring of American Religion: Society and Faith since World War II* (Princeton, NJ: Princeton University Press, 1988), 241–242. It is worth noting here that in 1954 Congress voted to insert "under God" into the Pledge of Allegiance, after "one nation"—indicating both a strong religious turn in American ideals of citizenship and a new emphasis on unity. Obviously, the action was motivated by a desire to distinguish the United States from its atheistic enemy, the Soviet Union. But it also came on the heels of *Brown v. Board of Education*, and thus could not but be a response to impending crises over civil rights in America (see Danielle Allen, *Talking to Strangers* [Chicago: University of Chicago Press, 2004], 13–14). Indeed, America was clearly not "one" during the era. Religious rhetorics of transcendent unity served to mitigate this and other crises during the period (e.g., nuclear weaponry, as I have argued here).

163. Hogan, *Cross of Iron*, 414.
164. Medhurst, *Dwight D. Eisenhower*, 12.
165. Robert Jervis, *The Illogic of American Nuclear Strategy* (Ithaca, NY: Cornell University Press, 1984), 12.
166. Consistent with this Ira Chernus notes, "The 'Atoms for Peace' speech made the bomb, not the Soviets, the primary enemy. It identified both the United States and the Soviets as partners in endangering the world. So it stated clearly that the superpowers would have to become partners in eliminating the danger." See Chernus, *Eisenhower's Atoms for Peace*, 12.
167. O'Donovan, *Peace and Certainty*, 27.

Conclusion

1. Ninkovich, *Modernity and Power*, xiv–xv.
2. Ninkovich, *Modernity and Power*, 317.
3. Charles Taylor, *Modern Social Imaginaries* (Durham, NC: Duke University Press, 2004), 23.
4. Taylor, *Modern Social Imaginaries*, 109–141, 143.
5. Ninkovich, *Modernity and Power*, 318.
6. Medhurst, *Dwight D. Eisenhower*, 10–11; Medhurst, "Eisenhower's Rhetorical Leadership," 291–293.
7. Medhurst, "Eisenhower's Rhetorical Leadership," 291.
8. Quoted in Medhurst, "Eisenhower's Rhetorical Leadership," 291.

9. Quoted in Medhurst, "Eisenhower's Rhetorical Leadership," 291. Eisenhower's leadership style is discussed by Medhurst in this essay, 291–293. See also Greenstein, *Hidden-Hand Presidency*.
10. Chernus, *Apocalypse Management*, 40.
11. Hinds and Windt, *Cold War as Rhetoric*, 153.
12. Nixon and Kissinger's détente, of course, entailed an embrace of *Realpolitik* that was positioned against an ideologically driven foreign policy platform. That such a program might be a foreign policy adventure, which Robert Dallek has shown it to be, was possible only as ideology itself became the limit which détente sought to spectacularly negate. See Dallek, *Nixon and Kissinger: Partners in Power* (New York: HarperCollins, 2007).
13. Campbell Craig and Fredrik Logevall, *America's Cold War: The Politics of Security* (Cambridge: Harvard University Press, 2009), 290–291.
14. Ronald Reagan, "Address to the Nation on the Explosion of the Space Shuttle Challenger," January 28, 1986, *PPP*, http://www.presidency.ucsb.edu/ws/?pid=37646.
15. Millikan, preface to *The American Style*, vii.
16. See, for a few examples, Charles A. Beard and Mary R. Beard, *The American Spirit: A Study of the Idea of Civilization in the United States* (New York: Macmillan, 1942); Morison, *The American Style*; W. W. Rostow, *The United States in the World Arena: An Essay in Recent History* (New York: Harper and Brothers, 1960); Robert Dallek, *The American Style of Foreign Policy: Cultural Politics and Foreign Affairs* (New York: Alfred A. Knopf, 1983); Walter McDougal, *Promised Land, Crusader State: The American Encounter with the World since 1776* (New York: Mariner Books, 1998); and Mead, *Special Providence*.
17. Niebuhr, *Irony of American History*, 130.
18. Niebuhr, *Irony of American History*, 133.
19. Niebuhr, *Irony of American History*, 141.
20. Niebuhr, *Irony of American History*, 140.
21. Niebuhr, *Irony of American History*, 143.
22. See Arthur M. Schlesinger, Jr., *The Cycles of American History* (Boston: Houghton Mifflin, 1986),
23. White, *Metahistory*, 1, 7.
24. White, *Metahistory*, 6.
25. Niebuhr, *Irony of American History*, 9.
26. Niebuhr, *Irony of American History*, 9.
27. Weber, *Economy and Society*, 10.

28. Jean-François Lyotard, *The Postmodern Condition: A Report on Knowledge*, trans. Goeff Bennington and Brian Massumi (Minneapolis: University of Minnesota Press, 1984), 40.
29. Hariman, *Political Style*, 184.
30. Weber, *Protestant Ethic*, 65.
31. Hans Morgenthau, *Politics Among Nations* (New York: McGraw-Hill, 1993), 6.
32. Kennedy, "Grand Strategy," 5.
33. See Ned O'Gorman, "Aristotle's *Phantasia* in the *Rhetoric*: *Lexis*, Appearance, and the Epideictic Function of Discourse," *Philosophy and Rhetoric* 38 (2005): 16–40.
34. Alasdair MacIntyre, *After Virtue*, 2nd ed. (Notre Dame, IN: University of Notre Dame Press, 1984) and *Whose Justice? Which Rationality?* (Notre Dame, IN: University of Notre Dame Press, 1988); Robert Neelly Bellah, Richard Madsen, William M. Sullivan, Ann Swidler, and Steven M. Tipton, *Habits of the Heart* (Berkeley: University of California Press, 1985).

Bibliography

SOURCES IN COLLECTIONS

Declassified Documents Reference System (abbreviated as DDRS), Farmington Hills, MI: Gale.
Papers at the Dwight D. Eisenhower Presidential Library, including those of C. D. Jackson.
Foreign Relations of the United States (abbreviated as *FRUS*).
George F. Kennan Papers, Princeton University.
Harry S. Truman Papers, Harry S. Truman Library.
John Foster Dulles Papers, Princeton University.
The National Security Archive's "The Nuclear Vault," http://www2.gwu.edu/~nsarchiv/nukevault/index.htm.
Public Papers of the Presidents of the United States (abbreviated as *PPP*), available from John Woolley and Gerhard Peters, *The American Presidency Project*, www.presidency.ucsb.edu.

Published Sources

Aldrich, Richard. "Liberation: Rolling Back the Frontiers of Clandestine Cold War History?" *Cold War History* 1 (2001): 127–138.

Allen, Danielle. *Talking to Strangers*. Chicago: University of Chicago Press, 2004.

Alloway, Lawrence. "The American Sublime." *Living Arts* 2 (1963): 11–22.

Ambrose, Stephen E. *Eisenhower: Soldier and President*. New York: Simon and Schuster, 1990.

———. *Ike: Abilene to Berlin*. New York: Harper and Row, 1973.

Anonymous. "Eisenhower Talk Praised by Many in Both Parties." *St. Louis Post Dispatch*, January 20, 1953, 2A.

Anonymous, "Excerpts from Editorial Comment." *New York Times*, January 21, 1953, 20.

Anonymous. "Nation Off to a Fresh Start as Eisenhower Takes the Helm." *Newsweek*, January 26, 1953, 25.

Arendt, Hannah. *The Human Condition*. Chicago: University of Chicago Press, 1998.

Aristotle. *On Rhetoric*. Translated by George Kennedy. New York: Oxford University Press, 1991.

Aron, Raymond. *Main Currents in Sociological Thought*. Vol. 2. New Brunswick, NJ: Transaction Publishers, 1999.

Art, Robert J. "The Four Functions of Force." In *International Politics: Enduring Concepts and Contemporary Issues*, 7th edition, edited by Robert J. Art and Robert Jervis, 141–148. New York: Pearson Longman, 2005.

Aurelius, Marcus. *Meditations*. Translated by A. S. L. Farquharson. New York: Oxford University Press, 1989.

Barnard, F. M. "Accounting for Actions: Causality and Teleology," *History and Theory* 20 (1981): 291–312.

———. *Herder on Nationality, Humanity, and History*. Montreal: McGill University Press, 2003.

Beard, Charles A., and Mary R. Beard. *The American Spirit: A Study of the Idea of Civilization in the United States*. New York: Macmillan, 1942.

Beer, Francis A., and Robert Hariman. "Realism and Rhetoric in International Relations." In *Post-Realism: The Rhetorical Turn in International Relations*, edited by Francis A. Beer and Robert Hariman, 1–30. East Lansing, MI: Michigan State University Press, 1996.

Beiser, Frederick. "The Enlightenment and Idealism." In *The Cambridge Companion to German Idealism*, edited by Karl Ameriks, 18–36. New York: Cambridge University Press, 2000.

Bellah, Robert Neelly, Richard Madsen, William M. Sullivan, Ann Swidler, and Steven M. Tipton. *Habits of the Heart.* Berkeley: University of California Press, 1985.

Bercovitch, Sacvan. *The American Jeremiad.* Madison: University of Wisconsin Press, 1978.

Bergson, Henri. *The Two Sources of Morality and Religion.* Translated by R. Ashley Audra and Cloudesley Brereton. Garden City, NY: Doubleday, [1935] 1956.

Berlin, Isaiah. *The Roots of Romanticism.* Princeton, NJ: Princeton University Press, 1999.

Bizzell, Patricia, and Bruce Herzberg. "Introduction to Baldesar Catiglione's *The Book of the Courtier.*" In *The Rhetorical Tradition: Readings from Classical Times to the Present*, 2nd edition, edited by Patricia Bizzell and Bruce Herzberg, 651–660. New York: Bedford / St. Martins, 2001.

Bloom, Harold. "Emerson and Whitman: The American Sublime." In *Sticky Sublime*, edited by Bill Beckley, 16–39. New York: Allworth Press, 2001.

Bowie, Robert, and Richard Immerman. *Waging Peace: How Eisenhower Shaped an Enduring Cold War Strategy.* New York: Oxford University Press, 1998.

Bradford, William. *The History of Plymouth Colony.* New York: Walter J. Black, 1948.

Brands, H. W. "The Age of Vulnerability: Eisenhower and the National Insecurity State." *American Historical Review* 94 (1989): 963–989.

———. *Cold Warriors.* New York: Columbia University Press, 1988.

Brockriede, Wayne. "John Foster Dulles: A New Rhetoric Justifies an Old Policy." In *Rhetoric and Communication*, edited by Jane Blankenship and Hermann G. Stelzner, 183–204. Urbana: University of Illinois Press, 1976.

Burke, Kenneth. *Attitudes toward History.* 3rd edition. Berkeley: University of California Press, 1984.

———. *A Grammar of Motives.* Berkeley: University of California Press, 1969.

———. *Permanence and Change: An Anatomy of Purpose.* 3rd edition. Berkeley: University of California Press, 1984.

———. *A Rhetoric of Motives.* Berkeley: University of California Press, 1969.

Burnham, James. *Containment or Liberation?* New York: John Day, 1953.

———. *The Machiavellians.* New York: John Day, 1943.

———. *The Managerial Revolution.* New York: John Day, 1941.

Campbell, David. *Writing Security: United States Foreign Policy and the Politics of Identity.* Revised edition. Minneapolis: University of Minnesota Press, 1998.

Campbell, Karlyn Kohrs. "Agency: Promiscuous and Protean." *Communication and Critical/Cultural Studies* 2 (2005): 1–19.

Carlyle, Thomas. *On Heroes, Hero-Worship, and the Heroic in History.* Edited by John

Chester Adams. New York: Houghton Mifflin, 1907.
Castiglione, Baldesar. *The Book of the Courtier.* Translated by Charles S. Singleton. In *The Rhetorical Tradition: Readings from Classical Times to the Present,* 2nd edition, edited by Patricia Bizzell and Bruce Herzberg, 661–673. New York: Bedford / St. Martins, 2001.
Chernus, Ira. *Apocalypse Management: Eisenhower and the Discourse of National Insecurity.* Stanford, CA: Stanford University Press, 2008.
———. *Eisenhower's Atoms for Peace.* College Station: Texas A&M University Press, 2002.
———. *General Eisenhower: Ideology and Discourse.* East Lansing: Michigan State University Press, 2002.
Clausewitz, Carl von. *On War.* Translated by Michael Howard and Peter Paret. Princeton, NJ: Princeton University Press, 1984.
Commission on a Just and Durable Peace of the Federal Council of the Churches of Christ in America. *Six Pillars of Peace: A Study Guide based on "A Statement of Political Propositions."* New York: Federal Council of the Churches of Christ in America, 1943.
Cook, Blanche Wiesen. *The Declassified Eisenhower: A Divided Legacy.* Garden City, NY: Doubleday, 1981.
Cooper, John M. "Justus Lipsius and the Revival of Stoicism in Late Sixteenth-Century Europe." In *New Essays on the History of Autonomy,* edited by Natalie Brender and Larry Krasnoff, 7–29. New York: Cambridge University Press, 2004.
Costigliola, Frank. "'Unceasing Pressure for Penetration': Gender, Pathology, and Emotion in George Kennan's Formation of the Cold War." *Journal of American History* 83 (1997): 1309–1339.
Craig, Campbell, and Fredrik Logevall. *America's Cold War: The Politics of Security.* Cambridge: Harvard University Press, 2009.
Dallek, Robert. *The American Style of Foreign Policy: Cultural Politics and Foreign Affairs.* New York: Alfred A. Knopf, 1983.
———. *Nixon and Kissinger: Partners in Power.* New York: HarperCollins, 2007.
Darsey, James. *The Prophetic Tradition and Radical Rhetoric in America.* New York: New York University Press, 1997.
DeBrabander, Firmin. "Psychotherapy and Moral Perfection: Spinoza and the Stoics on the Prospect of Happiness." In *Stoicism: Traditions and Transformations,* edited by Steven K. Strange and Jack Zupko, 198–213. New York: Cambridge University Press, 2004.
Deneen, Patrick J. *Democratic Faith.* Princeton, NJ: Princeton University Press, 2005.

Department of Defense. "Fact Sheet: Increasing Transparency in the U.S. Nuclear Weapons Stockpile." Released by the U. S. Department of Defense, May 3, 2010. Accessed at www.defense.gov/npr/docs/10-05-03_fact_sheet_us_nuclear_transparency__final_w_date.pdf on January 19, 2011.

Der Derian, James. *Antidiplomacy: Spies, Terror, Speed, and War.* Malden, MA: Blackwell, 1992.

Dilthey, Wilhelm. *The Formation of the Historical World in the Human Sciences.* Translated by Rudolf A. Makkreel and John Scanlon, edited by Rudolf A. Makkreel and Frithjof Rodi. Vol. 3, *Dilthey: Selected Works.* Princeton: Princeton University Press, 2002.

Divine, Robert A. *Foreign Policy and U.S. Presidential Elections, 1952–1960.* New York: New Viewpoints, 1974.

Douglas, Stephen A., and Abraham Lincoln. *Lincoln-Douglas Debates of 1858.* Edited by Robert Johannsen. New York: Oxford University Press, 2008.

Dulles, John Foster. "Policy for Security and Peace." *Foreign Affairs* 32 (1954): 353–364.

———. "A Policy of Boldness." *Life,* May 19, 1952, 146–160.

———. "Thoughts on Soviet Foreign Policy and What to Do About It." *Life,* June 10, 1946, 112–126.

Dupré, Louis. *The Enlightenment and the Intellectual Foundations of Modern Culture.* New Haven: Yale University Press, 2004.

Eisenhower, Dwight D. *Crusade in Europe.* Baltimore: Johns Hopkins University Press, 1948.

———. *The Eisenhower Diaries.* Edited by Robert H. Ferrell. New York: W. W. Norton, 1981.

———. *Eisenhower Speaks.* Edited by Rudolph L. Treuenfels. New York: Farrar, Straus, 1948.

———. *Mandate for Change.* Garden City, NJ: Doubleday, 1963.

———. "Text of Gen. Eisenhower's Foreign Policy Speech in San Francisco," October 8, 1952. *New York Times,* October 9, 1952, 24.

Emerson, Ralph Waldo. "Abraham Lincoln." In *The Essential Writings of Ralph Waldo Emerson,* 829–833. New York: Modern Library, 2000.

———. "The American Scholar." In *The Essential Writings of Ralph Waldo Emerson,* 43–59. New York: Modern Library, 2000.

———. "The Poet." In *The Heath Anthology of American Literature,* 2nd edition, vol. 1, edited by Paul Laute, 1566–1581. Lexington, MA: D.C. Heath, 1994.

Epictetus. *Discourses.* Excerpted in *Hellenistic Philosophy,* 2nd edition, translated by Brad

Inwood and L. P. Gerson. Indianapolis: Hackett, 1997.
Etzold, Thomas H., and John Lewis Gaddis, editors. *Containment: Documents on American Policy and Strategy, 1945–1950*. New York: New York University Press, 1978.
Fairbanks, David. "The Priestly Functions of the Presidency: A Discussion of the Literature on Civil Religion and its Implications for the Study of Presidential Leadership." *Presidential Studies Quarterly* 11 (1981): 214–232.
Fetter, Steve. "Ballistic Missiles and Weapons of Mass Destruction: What Is the Threat? What Should Be Done?" *International Security* 16 (Summer 1991): 5–41.
Field, John. *A View of Popishe Abuses Yet Remaining in the Englishe Church, for the which Godly Ministers have Refused to Subcribe* (1571). In *Puritan Manifestoes: A Study of the Origin of the Puritan Revolt*, edited by W. H. Frere and C. E. Douglas, 20–34. London: SPCK, 1907.
Foucault, Michel. *Discipline and Punish*. Translated by Alan Sheridan. New York: Vintage, 1977.
Freedman, Lawrence. *Deterrence*. Malden, MA: Polity Press, 2004.
———. *The Evolution of Nuclear Strategy*. 3rd edition. New York: Palgrave Macmillan, 2003.
Freud, Sigmund. *Civilization and Its Discontents*. Translated by James Strachey. New York: W. W. Norton, 1961.
Fukuyama, Francis. "The End of History?" *National Interest* 16 (Summer 1989): 3–18.
Gadamer, Hans-Georg. *Truth and Method*, 2nd edition, translation revised by Joel Weinsheimer and Donald G. Marshall. New York: Continuum, 1989.
Gaddis, John Lewis. "Containment: A Reassessment." *Foreign Affairs* 55 (July 1977): 873–887.
———. *Strategies of Containment: A Critical Appraisal of American National Security Policy During the Cold War*. Revised edition. New York: Oxford University Press, 2005.
Garver, Margaret R. *Stoicism and Emotion*. Chicago: University of Chicago Press, 2007.
Gati, Charles. "What Containment Meant." *Foreign Policy* 7 (Summer 1972): 22–40.
Gibbon, Edward. *The Decline and Fall of the Roman Empire*. 3 vols. New York: Heritage Press, 1946.
Gilbert, Felix. *To the Farewell Address*. Princeton, NJ: Princeton University Press, 1961.
Greenstein, Fred I. *The Hidden-Hand Presidency: Eisenhower as Leader*. New York: Basic Books, 1982.
Gura, Philip F. *American Transcendentalism*. New York: Hill and Wang, 2007.
———. *The Wisdom of Words: Language, Theology, and Literature in the New England Renaissance*. Middletown, CT: Wesleyan University Press, 1981.

Hamilton, Alexander, James Madison, and John Jay. *The Federalist Papers*. Whitefish, MT: Kessinger, 2004.
Hariman, Robert. *Political Style: The Artistry of Power*. Chicago: University of Chicago Press, 1995.
Harper, John Lamberton. *American Visions of Europe: Franklin D. Roosevelt, George F. Kennan, and Dean G. Acheson*. New York: Cambridge University Press, 1994.
Hart, Hornell. "Social Science and the Atomic Crisis." *Journal of Social Issues*, Supplement Series, 2 (1949): 4–29.
Hartnett, Stephen John. *Democratic Dissent and the Cultural Fictions of Antebellum America*. Urbana: University of Illinois Press, 2002.
Hewlett, Richard G., and Jack M. Holl. *Atoms for Peace and War, 1953–1961: Eisenhower and the Atomic Energy Commission*. Berkeley: University of California Press, 1989.
Hill, Christopher. *The Collected Essays of Christopher Hill*. Vol. 3, *People and Ideas in 17th Century England*. Amherst: University of Massachusetts Press, 1986.
Hinds, Lynn Boyd, and Theodore Otto Windt, Jr. *The Cold War as Rhetoric: The Beginnings, 1945–1950*. New York: Praeger, 1991.
Hixson, Walter L. *George F. Kennan: Cold War Iconoclast*. New York: Columbia University Press, 1989.
Hobbes, Thomas. *De Homine*. In *Man and Citizen*. Edited by Bernard Gert, translated by Charles T. Wood. Indianapolis: Hackett, 1991.
———. *Leviathan, or the Matter, Forme, and Power of a Commonwealth Ecclesiastical and Civil*. New York: Macmillan, 1962.
Hogan, Michael J. *A Cross of Iron: Harry S. Truman and the Origins of the National Security State, 1945–1954*. New York: Cambridge University Press, 1998.
———. "Eisenhower and Open Skies: A Case Study in Psychological Warfare." In *Eisenhower's War of Words*, edited Martin J. Medhurst, 137–55. East Lansing: Michigan State University Press, 1995.
———. "The Science of Cold War Strategy: Propaganda and Public Opinion in the Eisenhower Administration's 'War of Words.'" In *Critical Reflections on the Cold War: Linking Rhetoric and History*, edited by Martin J. Medhurst and H. W. Brands, 134–168. College Station: Texas A&M University Press, 2000.
Hoover, Herbert. "Speech Given in New York City, October 22, 1928." In *The New Day: Campaign Speeches of Herbert Hoover*, 149–176. Stanford, CA: Stanford University Press, 1928.
Hughes, Emmet John. *The Ordeal of Power: A Political Memoir of the Eisenhower Years*. New York: Atheneum, 1963.

"The Inaugural Address." *New York Herald Tribune*, January 21, 1953, 22.
Ivie, Robert L. "Cold War Motives and the Rhetorical Metaphor: A Framework of Criticism." In *Cold War Rhetoric: Strategy, Metaphor, Ideology*, edited by Martin J. Medhurst, Robert L. Ivie, Philip Wander, and Robert L. Scott, 71–79. New York: Greenwood Press, 1990.
———. "Dwight D. Eisenhower's 'Chance for Peace': Quest or Crusade?" *Rhetoric & Public Affairs* 1 (1998): 227–243.
———. "Eisenhower as Cold Warrior." In *Eisenhower's War of Words: Rhetoric and Leadership*, edited by Martin J. Medhurst, 7–25. East Lansing: Michigan State University Press, 1994.
———. "Fire, Flood, and Red Fever: Motivating Metaphors of Global Emergency in the Truman Doctrine Speech." *Presidential Studies Quarterly* 29 (1999): 570–591.
———. "Realism Masking Fear: George F. Kennan's Political Rhetoric." In *Post-Realism: The Rhetorical Turn in International Relations*, edited by Francis A. Beer and Robert Hariman, 55–74. East Lansing: Michigan State University Press, 1996.
Janis, Irving L. "Problems of Theory in the Analysis of Stress Behavior." *Journal of Social Issues* 10 (1954): 12–23.
———. *Victims of Groupthink: A Psychological Study of Foreign Policy Decisions and Fiascos*. Boston: Houghton, Mifflin, 1972.
Jasinski, James. "The Status of Theory and Method in Rhetorical Criticism." *Western Journal of Communication* 65 (2001): 249–270.
Jervis, Robert. *The Illogic of American Nuclear Strategy*. Ithaca, NY: Cornell University Press, 1984.
John of Salisbury. *Policraticus*. Edited and translated by Cary J. Nederman. New York: Cambridge University Press, 1990.
Kagan, Robert. *Dangerous Nation*. New York: Alfred A. Knopf, 2006.
Kant, Immanuel. *Critique of Judgment*. Translated by J. H. Bernard. New York: Hafner Press, 1951.
———. "To Perpetual Peace: A Philosophical Sketch." In *Perpetual Peace and Other Essays*, translated by Ted Humphrey, 107–144. Indianapolis: Hackett, 1983.
Kaye, Howard L. "Rationalization as Sublimation: On the Cultural Analyses of Weber and Freud." *Theory, Culture, & Society* 9 (1992): 45–74.
Kennan, George F. *American Diplomacy, 1900–1950*. New York: New American Library, 1951.
———. "Containment Then and Now." *Foreign Affairs* 65 (1987): 885–890.
———. "In the American Mirror." In *At a Century's Ending*, 209–218. New York: W. W.

Norton, 1996.

———. *Memoirs 1925–1950*. New York: Pantheon, 1967.

———. "Morality and Foreign Policy." In *At a Century's Ending*, 269–272. New York: W. W. Norton, 1996.

———. ("X"). "The Sources of Soviet Conduct." *Foreign Affairs* 25 (1947): 566–582.

Kennedy, Paul. "Grand Strategy in War and Peace: Toward a Broader Definition." In *Grand Strategy in War and Peace*, edited by Paul Kennedy, 1–7. New Haven: Yale University Press, 1991.

Kuklick, Bruce. *Blind Oracles: Intellectuals and War from Kennan to Kissinger*. Princeton, NJ: Princeton University Press, 2006.

Lagrée, Jacqueline. "Constancy and Coherence." In *Stoicism: Traditions and Transformations*, edited by Steven K. Strange and Jack Zupko, 148–176. New York: Cambridge University Press, 2004.

Lancaster, Carol. *Foreign Aid: Diplomacy, Development, and Domestic Politics*. Chicago: University of Chicago Press, 2007.

Lasch, Christopher. *The World of Nations: Reflections on American History, Politics, and Culture*. New York: Vintage, 1972.

Layne, Christopher. *The Peace of Illusions: American Grand Strategy from 1940 to the Present*. Ithaca, NY: Cornell University Press, 2006.

Lebow, Richard Ned, and Janice Gross Stein. "Deterrence and the Cold War." *Political Science Quarterly* 110 (1995): 157–181.

Leuchtenburg, William E. *In the Shadow of FDR: From Harry Truman to Ronald Reagan*. Ithaca, NY: Cornell University Press, 1989.

Lévi-Strauss, Claude. *The Savage Mind*. Chicago: University of Chicago Press, 1966.

Lewis, C. S. Preface to *George MacDonald*, edited by C. S. Lewis, xxiii–xxxix. New York: Macmillan, 1947.

Lincoln, Abraham. "Address to the Washington Temperance Society of Springfield, Illinois, February 22, 1842." In *Lincoln: Speeches and Writings, 1832–1858*, edited by Don E. Fehrenbacher, 81–90. New York: Library of America, 1989.

Lippmann, Walter. *The Cold War: A Study in U.S. Foreign Policy*. New York: Harper, 1947.

———. *The Phantom Public*. New Brunswick, NJ: Transaction Publishers, 2004.

Lipsius, Justus. *Politica: Six Books of Politics or Political Instruction*. Edited and translated by Jan Waszink. Assen: Koninklijke Van Gorcum, 2004.

Locke, John. *Two Treatises of Government*. New York: Cambridge University Press, 1960.

Long, A. A. "The Socratic Imprint on Epictetus' Philosophy." In *Stoicism: Traditions and Transformations*, edited by Steven K. Strange and Jack Zupko, 10–29. New York:

Cambridge University Press, 2004.
Lucas, Scott. *Freedom's War: The American Crusade against the Soviet Union*. New York: New York University Press, 1999.
Lukacs, John. *George Kennan: A Study of Character*. New Haven: Yale University Press, 2007.
Lyon, Janet. *Manifestos: Portents of the Modern*. Ithaca, NY: Cornell University Press, 1999.
Lyotard, Jean-François. *The Postmodern Condition: A Report on Knowledge*. Translated by Goeff Bennington and Brian Massumi. Minneapolis: University of Minnesota Press, 1984.
Machiavelli, Niccolò. *The Prince and the Discourses*. Translated by Luigi Ricci and E. R. P. Vincent. New York: Modern Library, 1950.
MacIntyre, Alasdair. *After Virtue*. 2nd edition. Notre Dame, IN: University of Notre Dame Press, 1984.
———. *Whose Justice? Which Rationality?* Notre Dame, IN: University of Notre Dame Press, 1988.
Mannheim, Karl. *Ideology and Utopia*. Vol. 1 in the *Collected Works of Karl Mannheim*, translated by Louis Wirth and Edward A. Shils. New York: Routledge, 1997.
Marx, Karl. *The Eighteenth Brumaire of Louis Bonaparte*. Translated by Daniel De Leon. Chicago: Charles H. Kerr, 1907.
McDaniel, James P. "Fantasm: The Triumph of Form (an Essay on the Democratic Sublime)." *Quarterly Journal of Speech* 86 (2000): 48–66.
———. "Figures for New Frontiers, from Davy Crockett to Cyberspace Gurus." *Quarterly Journal of Speech* 88 (2002): 91–111.
McDougal, Walter. *Promised Land, Crusader State: The American Encounter with the World Since 1776*. New York: Mariner Books, 1998.
Mead, Walter Russell. *Special Providence: American Foreign Policy and How It Changed the World*. New York: Routledge, 2002.
Medhurst, Martin J. "Dwight D. Eisenhower." In *U.S. Presidents as Orators: A Bio-Critical Sourcebook*, edited by Halford Ryan, 190–209. Westport, CT: Greenwood Press, 1995.
———. *Dwight D. Eisenhower: Strategic Communicator*. Westport, CT: Greenwood Press, 1993.
———. "Eisenhower's 'Atoms for Peace' Speech: A Case Study in the Strategic Use of Language." *Communication Monographs* 54 (1987): 204–220.
———. "Eisenhower's Rhetorical Leadership: An Interpretation." In *Eisenhower's War*

of Words, edited by Martin J. Medhurst, 287–297. East Lansing: Michigan State University Press, 1994.

———, editor. *Eisenhower's War of Words*. East Lansing: Michigan State University Press, 1994.

———. "Reconceptualizing Rhetorical History: Eisenhower's Farewell Address." *Quarterly Journal of Speech* 80 (1994): 195–218.

———. "Rhetoric and Cold War: A Strategic Approach." In *Cold War as Rhetoric: Strategy, Metaphor, and Ideology*, edited by Martin J. Medhurst, Robert L. Ivie, Philip Wander, and Robert L. Scott, 19–50. New York: Greenwood Press, 1990.

Milbank, John. "The Poverty of Niebuhrianism." In *The World Made Strange: Theology, Language, and Culture*, 233–254. Cambridge, MA: Blackwell, 1997.

Millikan, Max F. Preface to *The American Style: Essays in Value and Performance*, edited by Elting E. Morison, vii–ix. New York: Harper and Brothers, 1958.

Miscamble, Wilson D. *George F. Kennan and the Making of American Foreign Policy, 1947–1950*. Princeton, NJ: Princeton University Press, 1992.

Mitchell, Gordon. *Strategic Deception: Rhetoric, Science, and Politics in Missile Defense Advocacy*. East Lansing: Michigan State University Press, 2000.

Morgenthau, Hans. *Politics among Nations*. New York: McGraw-Hill, 1993.

Morison, Elting E., editor. *The American Style: Essays in Value and Performance*. New York: Harper and Brothers, 1958.

Newman, Barnett. "The Sublime Is Now." In *Theories of Modern Art: A Source Book by Artists and Critics*, edited by Herschel B. Chipp, 552–553. Berkeley: University of California Press, 1968.

Niebuhr, Reinhold. "Augustine's Political Realism." In *The Essential Reinhold Niebuhr: Selected Essays and Addresses*, edited by Robert McAfee Brown, 123–141. New Haven: Yale University Press, 1986.

———. *The Irony of American History*. New York: Charles Scribner's Sons, 1952.

Ninkovich, Frank. *Modernity and Power: A History of the Domino Theory in the Twentieth Century*. Chicago: University of Chicago Press, 1994.

Nussbaum, Martha. "Kant and Stoic Cosmopolitanism." *Journal of Political Philosophy* 5 (1997): 1–25.

———. *The Therapy of Desire: Theory and Practice in Hellenistic Ethics*. Princeton, NJ: Princeton University Press, 1994.

O'Donovan, Oliver. *Peace and Certainty: A Theological Essay on Deterrence*. Oxford: Clarendon Press Oxford, 1989.

O'Gorman, Ned. "Aristotle's *Phantasia* in the *Rhetoric: Lexis*, Appearance, and the

Epideictic Function of Discourse." *Philosophy and Rhetoric* 38 (2005): 16–40.
Oakes, Guy. *The Imaginary War.* New York: Oxford University Press, 1994.
Oestreich, Gerhard. *Neostoicism and the Early Modern State.* New York: Cambridge University Press, 2008.
Ong, Walter J. *Rhetoric, Romance, and Technology: Studies in the Interaction of Expression and Culture.* Ithaca, NY: Cornell University Press, 1971.
Osgood, Kenneth. *Total Cold War: Eisenhower's Secret Propaganda Battle at Home and Abroad.* Lawrence: University Press of Kansas, 2006.
Paret, Peter. *Clausewitz and the State: The Man, His Theories, and His Times.* Princeton, NJ: Princeton University Press, 1985.
Parry-Giles, Shawn J. *The Rhetorical Presidency, Propaganda, and the Cold War, 1945–1955.* Westport, CT: Praeger, 2002.
Pearce, Kimber Charles. *Rostow, Kennedy, and the Rhetoric of Foreign Aid.* East Lansing: Michigan State University Press, 2001.
Peirce, Charles Sanders. *The Essential Peirce: Selected Philosophical Writings, 1893–1913.* Bloomington: Indiana University Press, 1998.
Peters, John Durham. *Courting the Abyss: Free Speech and the Liberal Tradition.* Chicago: University of Chicago Press, 2005.
Peterson, Val. "Panic: The Ultimate Weapon?" *Collier's,* August 21, 1953, 99–107.
Philpott, Daniel. *Revolutions in Sovereignty: How Ideas Shaped Modern International Relations.* Princeton, NJ: Princeton University Press, 2001.
Plato. *The Dialogues of Plato: Republic, Timaeus, and Critias.* Translated by Benjamin Jowett. London: Macmillan, 1892.
———. *Gorgias.* The Loeb Classical Library Vol. 3. Edited by Jeffery Henderson. Translated by W. R. M. Lamb. Cambridge: Harvard University Press, 2001.
Pocock, J. G. A. *The Machiavellian Moment: Florentine Political Thought and the Atlantic Republican Tradition.* Princeton, NJ: Princeton University Press, 1975.
Popper, Karl. *The Poverty of Historicism.* New York: Routledge, 2002.
"The President's Prayer," *The Nation,* January 31, 1953, 91.
Public Broadcasting System (PBS). *American Experience: Woodrow Wilson.* Part 2, "The Redemption of the World." Directed by Carl Byker and Mitch Wilson, 2001. Transcript available at http://www.pbs.org/wgbh/amex/wilson/filmmore/fm_trans2.html.
Rebhorn, Wayne. *Courtly Performances: Masking and Festivity in Castiglione's "Book of the Courtier."* Detroit: Wayne State University Press, 1978.
Reston, James. "Inaugural Is Held to Extend U.S. Commitments to the World." *New York Times,* January 21, 1953, 17.

———. "Washington: 'Massive Atomic Retaliation' and the Constitution." *New York Times*, January 17, 1954, E8.

———. "Washington: 'Massive Retaliation' is '2X' Now." *New York Times*, January 9, 1955, E8.

Riesman, David, Reuel Denney, and Nathan Glazer. *The Lonely Crowd: A Study of the Changing American Character*. New Haven: Yale University Press, 1952.

Rodgers, Daniel T. "Republicanism: The Career of a Concept." *Journal of American History* 79 (June 1992): 11–38.

Rosenberg, Emily S. *Spreading the American Dream: American Economic and Cultural Expansion, 1890–1945*. New York: Hill and Wang, 1982.

Rostow, W. W. *Concept and Controversy: Sixty Years of Taking Ideas to Market*. Austin: University of Texas Press, 2003.

———. "The National Style." In *The American Style: Essays in Value and Performance*, edited by Elting E. Morison, 246–313. New York: Harper and Brothers, 1958.

———. *The United States in the World Arena: An Essay in Recent History*. New York: Harper and Brothers, 1960.

Rostow, W. W., and Max Millikan. *A Proposal: Key to an Effective Foreign Policy*. New York: Harper and Brothers, 1957.

Rousseau, Jean-Jacques. "Discourse on the Origin and Foundation of Inequality among Men *or* Second Discourse." In *Rousseau: The Discourses and Other Early Political Writings*, edited by Victor Gourevitch, 111–188. New York: Cambridge University Press, 1997.

Schlesinger, Arthur M., Jr. *The Cycles of American History*. Boston: Houghton Mifflin, 1986.

Scott, Robert L. "Cold War and Rhetoric: Conceptually and Critically." In *Cold War Rhetoric: Strategy, Metaphor, Ideology*, edited by Martin J. Medhurst, Robert L. Ivie, Philip Wander, and Robert L. Scott, 1–16. New York: Greenwood Press, 1990.

Seneca. *Letters from a Stoic*. Translated by Robin Campbell. New York: Penguin, 1969.

Shapiro, Michael J. *Language and Political Understanding: The Politics of Discursive Practice*. New Haven: Yale University Press, 1981.

Sherman, Nancy. *Stoic Warriors: The Ancient Philosophy Behind the Military Mind*. New York: Oxford University Press, 2005.

Simmel, Georg. *On Individuality and Social Forms*. Edited by Donald N. Levine. Chicago: University of Chicago Press, 1971.

Simpson, Christopher. *Science of Coercion: Communication Research and Psychological Warfare*. New York: Oxford University Press, 1994.

Skinner, Quentin. *Foundations of Modern Political Thought.* Vol. 1. New York: Cambridge University Press, 1978.

———. *Reason and Rhetoric in the Philosophy of Hobbes.* New York: Cambridge University Press, 1996.

Smith, M. Brewster. Preface. *Journal of Social Issues* 10 (1954): 1.

Soulez, Philippe, and Frédérick Worms. *Bergson: Biographie.* Paris: Flammarion, 1997.

Sproule, J. Michael. *Propaganda and Democracy: The American Experience of Media and Mass Persuasion.* New York: Cambridge University Press, 1997.

Stephanson, Anders. *Kennan and the Art of Foreign Policy.* Cambridge: Harvard University Press, 1989.

Stevenson, Adlai. "The Contest of Freedom and Tyranny." September 9, 1952. In *Documents on American Foreign Relations,* edited by Clarence W. Baier and Richard P. Stebbins, 94–99. New York: Harper and Brothers / Council on Foreign Relations, 1953.

Stillman, Edmund, and William Pfaff. *The Politics of Hysteria: The Sources of Twentieth-Century Conflict.* New York: Harper and Row, 1964.

Stivachtis, Yannis S. "U.S. Foreign Policy and International Order." In *International Order in a Globalizing World,* edited by Yannis S. Stivachtis, 39–66. London: Ashgate, 2007.

Stoff, Michael B., Jonathan F. Fanton, and R. Hal Williams, editors. *The Manhattan Project: A Documentary Introduction to the Atomic Age.* New York: McGraw-Hill, 1991.

Strange, Steven K. "The Stoics on the Voluntariness of the Passions." In *Stoicism: Traditions and Transformations,* edited by Steven K. Strange and Jack Zupko, 32–51. New York: Cambridge University Press, 2004.

Tacitus. *The Annals of Imperial Rome.* Translated by Alfred John Church and William Jackson Brodribb. New York: Barnes and Noble, 2007.

Taubman, William. *Khrushchev: The Man and His Era.* New York: W. W. Norton, 2003.

Taylor, Charles. *Modern Social Imaginaries.* Durham, NC: Duke University Press, 2004.

Tell, Dave. "Burke's Encounter with Ransom: Rhetoric and Epistemology in 'Four Master Tropes.'" *Rhetoric Society Quarterly* 34 (Fall 2004): 33–54.

Thompson, Kenneth W. *Ethics, Functionalism, and Power in International Politics: The Crisis in Values.* Baton Rouge: Louisiana State University Press, 1979.

———. Foreword to Richard L. Russell, *George F. Kennan's Strategic Thought.* Westport, CT: Praeger, 1999.

Thorpe, Charles. *Oppenheimer: The Tragic Intellect.* Chicago: University of Chicago Press, 2006.

Time-Life International, editors. "So We Went Abroad." Unpublished manuscript available in the library of the University of Illinois, Urbana-Champaign.

Tocqueville, Alexis de. *Democracy in America*. Translated by Gerald Bevan. New York: Penguin, 2003.

Toulouse, Mark G. *The Transformation of John Foster Dulles: From Prophet of Realism to Priest of Nationalism*. Macon, GA: Mercer University Press, 1985.

Toye, John, and Richard Toye. *The UN and Global Political Economy: Trade, Finance, and Development*. Bloomington: Indiana University Press, 2004.

Toye, Richard. "The Churchill Syndrome: Reputational Entrepreneurship and the Rhetoric of Foreign Policy since 1945." *British Journal of Politics and International Relations* 10 (2008): 364–378.

Trilling, Lionel. *Sincerity and Authenticity*. Cambridge: Harvard University Press, 1972.

Tuck, Richard. *Philosophy and Government, 1572–1651*. New York: Cambridge University Press, 1993.

Tudda, Chris. *The Truth Is Our Weapon: The Rhetorical Diplomacy of Dwight D. Eisenhower and John Foster Dulles*. Baton Rouge: Louisiana State University Press, 2006.

Vico, Giambattista. *On the Study Methods of Our Time*. Translated by Elio Gianturco. Ithaca, NY: Cornell University Press, 1990.

Wagner, Steven. *Eisenhower Republicanism: Pursuing the Middle Way*. DeKalb: Northern Illinois University Press, 2006.

Walzer, Michael. *Revolution of the Saints*. Cambridge: Harvard University Press, 1965.

Wander, Philip. "The Rhetoric of American Foreign Policy." In *Cold War Rhetoric: Strategy, Metaphor, Ideology*, edited by Martin J. Medhurst, Robert L. Ivie, Philip Wander, and Robert L. Scott, 153–183. New York: Greenwood Press, 1990.

Washington, George. "Final Manuscript of the Farewell Address." September 19, 1796. In Felix Gilbert, *To the Farewell Address: Ideas of Early American Foreign Policy*, 144–147. Princeton, NJ: Princeton University Press, 1961.

Weber, Max. *Economy and Society*. Translated by Ephraim Fischoff et al., edited by Guether Roth and Claus Wittich. Vol. 1. Berkeley: University of California Press, 1978.

———. *The Protestant Ethic and the Spirit of Capitalism*. Translated by Talcott Parsons. New York: Dover, 2003.

———. *Sociology of Religion*. Translated by Ephriam Fischoff. Boston: Beacon Press, 1993.

White, Hayden. *Metahistory: The Historical Imagination in Nineteenth-Century Europe*. Baltimore: Johns Hopkins University Press, 1973.

White, William S. "'Internationalist' Inaugural Acclaimed in Both Parties." *New York Times,* January 21, 1953, 1.
Whitehead, Alfred North. *Adventures in Ideas.* New York: The Free Press, 1933.
Whitfield, Stephen J. *The Culture of the Cold War.* Baltimore: Johns Hopkins University Press, 1991.
Whitman, Walt. "The Death of Abraham Lincoln." In *The Complete Poetry and Prose of Walt Whitman: As Prepared by Him for the Deathbed Edition,* 321–324. New York: Pellegrini and Cudahy, 1948.
Williams, Simon. *Wagner and the Romantic Hero.* New York: Cambridge University Press, 2004.
Williams, William Appleman. *The Tragedy of American Diplomacy.* New York: Delta, 1962.
Wilson, Eric. *Emerson's Sublime Science.* New York: St. Martin's Press, 1999.
Witte, John. *The Reformation of Rights: Law, Religion, and Human Rights in Early Modern Calvinism.* New York: Cambridge University Press, 2008.
Wright, C. Ben. "Mr. 'X' and Containment." *Slavic Review* 35 (March 1976): 1–31.
Wright, N. T. "Gospel and Theology in Galatians." In *Gospel in Paul: Studies on Corinthians, Galatians and Romans for Richard N. Longenecker,* edited by L. Ann Jervis and Peter Richardson, 222–239. London: Sheffield Academic Press, 1994.
———. *What Saint Paul Really Said.* Cincinnati: Forward Movement Publications, 1997.
Wuthnow, Robert. *The Restructuring of American Religion: Society and Faith since World War II.* Princeton, NJ: Princeton University Press, 1988.

Index

A

abduction, xiv
Adams, Sherman, 149
Adenauer, Konrad, 119
adventurism, 129–135, 155, 163, 235; and the courtier, 131–132, 147, 154–155, 161; and glory, 130, 133–134, 165; and irony, 18–19, 134–135, 165; and opportunism, 129, 131, 132, 163; sense of "limits," 237; similarities with evangelicalism, 132–133; similarities with stoicism, 163
Allen, George, 155
Alloway, Lawrence, 211
Ambrose, Stephen, 202
Arendt, Hannah, 13
Aristotle, xiv, xviii, 130–131, 244, 246, 248
Armstrong, Hamilton Fish, 106
Art, Robert J., 206
Aurelius, Marcus, 33, 34, 38, 41

B

Beer, Francis, 9
Bellah, Robert, 249
Bercovitch, Sacvan, 94
Bergson, Henri, 82–84, 88–89, 91
Berlin, Isaiah, 53, 179
Bernays, Edward, 66
Bloom, Harold, 198

Bohlen, Charles, 58, 144
Bowie, Robert, 178–179, 217–218
Bradford, William, 84–85, 132
Brands, H. W., 126
Brockriede, Wayne, 115–116
Burke, Kenneth, xviii, 14, 19, 183, 191, 195–196
Burnham, James, 125, 134–135, 147
Bury, J. B., 37
Byrnes, James, 107

C

Calvinists, 80–83, 84–85, 88, 93
Campbell, Karlyn Kohrs, 14
Carlyle, Thomas, 173
Carter, Jimmy, 241
Castiglione, Baldassare, 131
Chernus, Ira, 175, 180, 183, 206, 218, 226–227, 240
Churchill, Winston, 56, 107–108
Cicero, Marcus Tullius, 36, 37
Clausewitz, Carl von, 11, 12, 178, 179–180
Cold War consensus, 240
Coleridge, Samuel Taylor, 193
Commission on the Organization of the Executive Branch of Government (Hoover Commission), 27
communication sciences, 136–137
Conolly, Richard L. "R. L.," 3, 4
containment, 22–25, 27, 28–32, 56–64, 65–66, 68–69, 71–74
Cook, Blanche Wiesen, 175
Cooper, John M., 35
Costigliola, Frank, 23–24
covenants, 81–82, 84–87, 92, 93–97, 101, 102, 109, 114
Critchfield, Charles, 173

D

Darsey, James, 94
DeBrabander, Firmin, 40
Dedham Conference, 123–124, 242
Deneen, Patrick, 225
deterrence, 206–207. *See also* nuclear deterrence
Dewey, Thomas, 102
Dilthey, Wilhelm, 251 (n. 3)
Dulles, Allen, 144, 148
Dulles, John Foster: and Henri Bergson, 82–84, 88–89, 91; and Christianity, 82, 86, 99, 106–107; and containment, 139; differences with Eisenhower, 78–79, 168–169, 229–230; differences with Kennan, 77–79, 88, 90, 101, 103; and Federal Council of Churches of Christ in America, 96–99; jeremiads of, 97–102, 106–107; and League of Nations, 86; and liberation, 141; "massive retaliation" speech, 104–106, 110–115, 116; and moral equivocation, 117, 119, 137; 1937 Oxford church conference, 86, 97; and 1945 United Nations San Francisco Conference, 97; and Project Solarium, 2; "Six Pillars of Peace," 98–99; and Harry S. Truman, 97, 100, 107, 110; and U.S. constitution, 86–87, 102; *War, Peace, and Change,* 86–92, 102, 103–104, 112; and Woodrow Wilson, 85, 108–109,

117; and world federalism, 86, 90, 102; and "world opinion," 108, 117
Dupré, Louis, 172, 179

E

economic development, 139, 151

Eisenhower, Dwight D.: and "absolute war," 178; American exceptionalism, 209–210; "Atoms for Peace" address, 168, 171–172, 186–187, 200, 217; and "balance," 175–176, 178, 180, 181, 184; "Chance for Peace" address, 216–217, 157 (n. 102); *Crusade in Europe*, 176–177; dislike of partisan politics, 201–203, 205; and dualism, 137,172, 209, 211, 218; and economy, 169–170; "Eisenhower Doctrine" address, 220–221; election of, 2; Farewell Address, 171; first inaugural address, 211, 213–216, 225–226; and heroism, 176–177; and historicism, 178–179, 217–218, 238; and human transformation, 223–225; and isolationism, 205; and leadership, 176, 178, 203–205, 227; and liberality, 181–182, 191; and liberation, 141; *Mandate for Change*, 183; Metropolitan Museum of Art address, 209–210, 225; New Look of, 6, 104, 110–111, 185; 1953 State of the Union Address, 181, 183; 1955 United Nations speech, 187–188; 1957 State of the Union Address, 169, 219–220, 221–222; and nuclear deterrence, 167–169, 184–185, 189–190, 191, 192, 229–230; political philosophy of, 223–224; and "psychological warfare," 136, 141–142, 143, 149, 184–185; and romanticism, 172–173, 228; and Franklin Roosevelt, 205; scholarly attention to, 175, 182; and the "spiritual," 170–171, 201, 211, 212, 213–216, 217–218; and surprise nuclear attack, 216–217; and synecdoche, 197–198, 200, 209, 212, 230–231; and synthesis of strategies, 238–239; and technology, 174; and "total war," 142; and wholeness, 183–184

Emerson, Ralph Waldo, 173, 193–194, 195, 198

Epictetus, 31

evangelicalism, 18, 79–80, 84–85, 117–118, 119, 234–235; and adventurism, 132–133; and romanticism, 199; and sense of "limits," 237; and stoicism, 79–80, 85, 87, 117–118

F

Fetter, Steve, 206
Forrestal, James, 70
Freedman, Lawrence, 206
Freud, Sigmund, 39–40, 42, 53, 65, 66
Fukuyama, Francis, 167

G

Gaddis, John Lewis, 21, 56, 118–119, 177–178, 184, 230
Gati, Charles, 23
Gibbon, Edward, 37, 46–47, 65
Gilbert, Felix, 132

Gura, Philip, 194–195

H
Halle, Louis, 118
Hamilton, Alexander, 38
Hariman, Robert, 9, 154–155, 219, 247
Harriman, William Averell, 139
Hart, Hornell, 66
Herberg, Will, 227
Herder, Johann Gottfried, xii, 10, 179
Hinds, Lynn, 58, 73, 240
Hixson, Walter, 42
Hobbes, Thomas, 33–34, 35, 37, 40, 81–82, 87
Hogan, J. Michael, 136–137, 147
Hogan, Michael J., 227, 229
Hoover Commission, 27
Hoover, Herbert, 2, 27, 197
Hughes, Emmet, 201

I
Immerman, Richard, 178–179, 217–218
Ivie, Robert L., 10, 24, 42, 58, 62, 73, 142, 151, 177, 182, 218

J
Jackson Committee, 142, 145, 149, 153
Jackson, Charles Douglas "C. D.," 126, 128, 202; and artistry, 149, 155; and "Atoms for Peace," 147, 149, 153, 156–157; and "Chance for Peace" address, 147, 151, 153, 157, 158; and historicism, 152; and irony, 137–138; and Kennedy administration, 128–129, 164; and liberation, 146–147, 148, 154; and Henry Luce, 147, 150, 152; and 1952 Princeton meeting, 143–145; and 1954 Princeton meeting, 158–159, 162; and "Open Skies" address, 147, 153; and opportunism, 152–153, 154, 161; and "orchestration," 149; and "political warfare," 147; role in Eisenhower administration, 141; and the role of ideology, 148–149; as speechwriter for Eisenhower, 126, 128, 153; and strategic deception, 153, 161
James, William, 82
Janis, Irving L., 67
Jasinski, James, xiv
jeremiads, 92, 93–94
Jervis, Robert, 229
John of Salisbury, 34
Johnson, Lyndon, 225
Joyce, Robert, 144, 145

K
Kant, Immanuel, 33, 49, 49 (n. 90)
Kateb, George, 54
Kaye, Howard L., 40
Kennan, George: *American Diplomacy,* 46–53; analysis of Soviet personality, 58–61, 64; and behaviorism, 61; and James Burnham, 135; clinical posture of, 57–58; and conservatism of, 44; "Containment Then and Now," 28; differences with John Foster Dulles, 77–79, 88, 90, 101, 103; dislike for technocrats, 41; and Edward Gibbon, 37 (n. 57); and "interests," 51, 59; and leadership, 76–77; and "legalism," 49,

51–52; as a "literalist," 135; "Long Telegram," 23, 26, 56–64; and metaphor, 25, 29; and "moralism," 49–50, 51–52; 1949 Dartmouth College address, 27–28; and Project Solarium, 2–3; "public philosophy" of, 42–46; and republicanism, 49; and rhetorical style, 24, 26; and romantic nationalism, 44, 45–46, 45 (n. 83); "The Sources of Soviet Conduct", 22–23, 26, 38, 50, 56–64; and subjectivity, 42–43, 47, 51
Kennedy, John F., 126, 127
Kennedy, Paul, 21–22, 248

L

Lasch, Christopher, 46
Laswell, Harold, 136
Lévi-Strauss, Claude, 19
liberation, 138–141, 143, 144–146, 148, 154; as Cold War ideology, 164; and containment, 138–139, 140, 141; and liberal economic policies, 139–140, 151, 157, 165; as military intervention, 138–139, 140, 141; and "peaceful liberation," 140, 141, 143, 144
Lincoln, Abraham, 38, 38 (n. 60), 38 (n. 61), 174–175, 194, 196, 248
Lippman, Walter, 23 (n. 5), 57, 101 (n. 61), 101, 154 (n. 92)
Lipsius, Justus, 33, 34, 37
Locke, John, 36
Luce, Henry, 101, 132–133, 147, 150, 210
Lukacs, John, 28, 71
Lyon, Janet, 95

Lyotard, Jean-François, 246

M

Machiavelli, Niccolò, 129–130, 132, 133, 147
MacIntyre, Alasdair, 249
Madison, James, 38
manifestos, 92, 94–96
Mannheim, Karl, 88
Marlowe, Christopher, 131
Marx, Karl, 10, 12, 159
McCormack, James, Jr., 3, 4
McDaniel, James, 196
Medhurst, Martin, 9, 147, 175, 178, 182, 217–218, 229, 239, 218 (n. 136)
metonymy, 18–19, 195–199
Millikan, Max, 124
Miscamble, Wilson D., 27
Morgenthau, Hans, 65, 248

N

"necessity," 26, 34, 85
neostoicism, 25–26, 29, 34–38, 39
Newman, Barnett, 210–211
Niebuhr, Reinhold, 35, 65, 96, 242–245, 227 (n. 155)
Ninkovich, Frank, 108, 236, 238
Nixon, Richard, 240–241
National Security Council documents: NSC 68, 148, 172, 148 (n. 70), 172 (n. 13); NSC 126, 188; NSC 162/2, 104, 145, 209 (n. 115)
nuclear deterrence, 168–169, 208; as a rhetoric, 169. See also deterrence
nuclear legitimacy, 207–209
Nussbaum, Martha, 31–32

O

Oakes, Guy, 187
O'Donovan, Oliver, 207, 207–208, 230
Ong, Walter, 194, 207
Oppenheimer, Robert, 173
Oppenheimer Report, 106 (n. 78), 208 (n. 114)
Osgood, Kenneth, 136, 185, 199

P

Paret, Peter, 179
Parry-Giles, Shawn, 10, 12, 149
Paul (St. Paul), 35
Peirce, Charles Sanders, xiv
Peters, John Durham, 41
Peterson, Val, 68r
Plato, 29–31, 248
Pocock, J. G. A., 93, 130
political warfare, 136, 141–143, 155, 162
Politics of Hysteria (Stillman and Pfaff), 39
Popper, Karl, 30
President's Committee on International Information Activities, 142, 145, 149, 153
Project Solarium, 2–6, 104, 239, 241–142
psychological warfare, 136, 141–143, 155, 162
Puritans, 84–85, 93, 95, 109–110, 132

Q

Quarles, Donald, 115

R

Reagan, Ronald, 240, 241
realism, xiii, 9, 25, 29, 35–36, 65, 67–68, 242–243
republicanism, 26 (n. 14)
Reston, James, 105, 106, 216
Riesman, David, 123, 125
romanticism, 172–173, 192–201, 208, 235; and evangelicalism, 199; and heroism, 173; and history, 179; and human transformation, 224–225; and interpretation, 173, 194–195; as prevailing American worldview, 238–241; and the self, 179, 195; and sense of "limits," 237–238; and stoicism, 193; and the sublime, 195–199
Roosevelt, Franklin, 85, 196–197, 213
Roosevelt, Theodore, 197
Rostow, Walt Whitman "W. W.", 72, 123, 124–125, 126, 128, 129, 144, 148, 152; and the "take off" model of development, 151
Rousseau, Jean-Jacques, 179

S

Schlesinger, Arthur, 43
Scott, Robert L., 10
Seneca, 41, 193
Stettinius, Edward, 57
Simmel, Georg, 133
Skinner, Quentin, xiii (n. 4), 81
Smith, Adam, 159
Smith, M. Brewster, 67
"social imaginary," 237
"Sources of Soviet Conduct, The " (X; George Kennan), 22–23, 26, 38, 50, 56–64

Spencer, Herbert, 82
spirit (*Geist*), xiii, xii (n. 3), xiii (n. 4), 12, 123, 166
Sproule, J. Michael, 136
Steele, John, 127–128, 129
Stephanson, Anders, 44
Stevenson, Adlai, 54, 140–141
Stimson, Henry, 107
stoicism, 18, 25–26, 31–41, 42, 37 (n. 57), 234; and constancy, 24–25, 33; and cosmopolitanism, 70; and disaster research, 66–68; and evangelicalism, 79–80, 85, 87, 117–118; and realism, 65; and sense of "limits," 237; and society as a self, 18–19, 35, 32 (n. 35)
strategy, 8–9, 21–22, 29, 247–248; and adventurism, 165–166; "classical age" of, xi–xii, 8; as "grand strategy," 21–22, 27, 72, 116, 119–120, 248; as ideology, 163–164; and language, 8–10, 13, 116; "political strategy," 143; and value rationality (*Wertrationalität*), xiii, 9, 11–12
sublime, 195–199
synecdoche, 18–19, 195–199

T

Tacitus, 34, 36
Taft, Robert, 140
Taylor, Charles, 237
Tocqueville, Alexis de, 109, 131, 134
Toulouse, Mark, 102
Toye, John, 140
Toye, Richard, 140
Toynbee, Arnold, 52

transcendentalism, 194–195, 219
Trilling, Lionel, 131
trope, 18–19
Truman, Harry S., 138, 141, 213
Tuck, Richard, 25, 85
typology, xiv, xviii, 8, 17, 17 (n. 31), 18

U

United Nations, 97, 157–158

V

Vico, Giambattista, 10, 73–74, 248–249
Vollmer, Cyrus, 54

W

Wagner, Steven, 176
Walzer, Michael, 80–81, 119, 130
Wander, Philip, 10, 218 (n. 136)
Washburn, Abbot, 143, 144
Washington, George, 25–26
Weber, Max, 8, 9, 10–11, 17, 131, 211, 219, 224, 245–246
White, Hayden, 19, 193, 244
Whitehead, Alfred North, 166
Whitman, Walt, 196
Williams, Simon, 177
Wilson, Eric, 186
Wilson, Woodrow, 82, 85, 139, 197, 238
Windt, Theodore, 58, 73, 240
Wisner, Frank, 153
World Economic Plan, 156–163
worldview, xii–xiii, 6, 7–8, 15, 17–18, 234, 236–237
Wright, C. Ben, 23, 72
Wuthnow, Robert, 228–229